Shojo Beat

Komomo Confiserie

Volume 5

Story & Art by Maki Minami

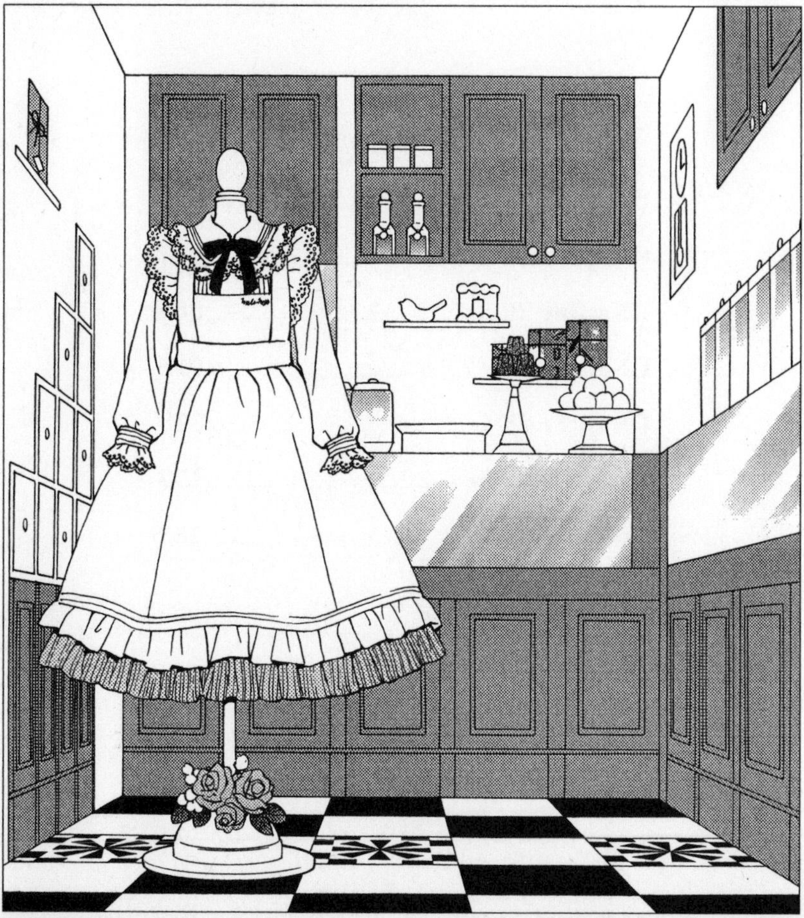

Komomo Confiserie

CONTENTS

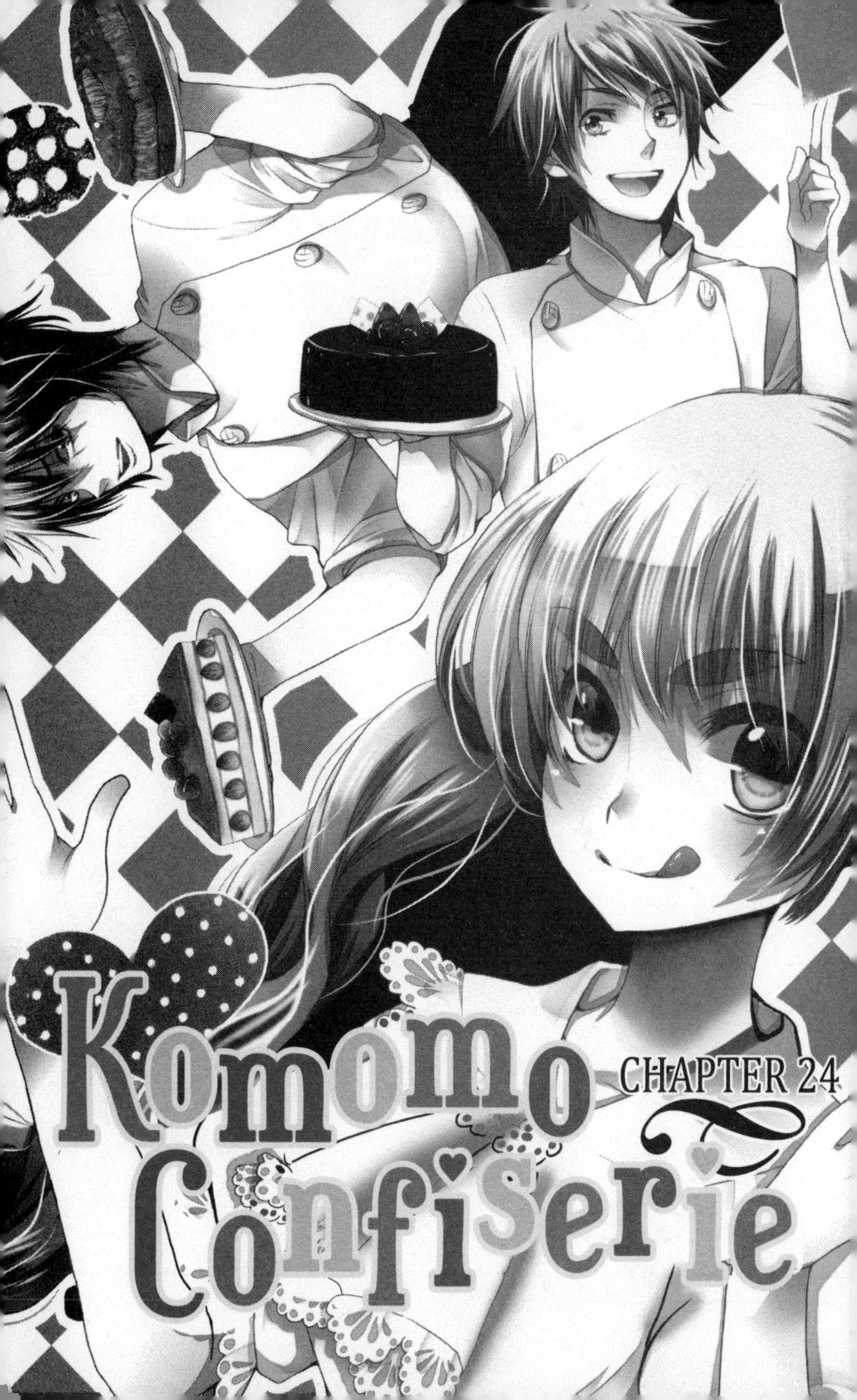
Komomo Confiserie
CHAPTER 24

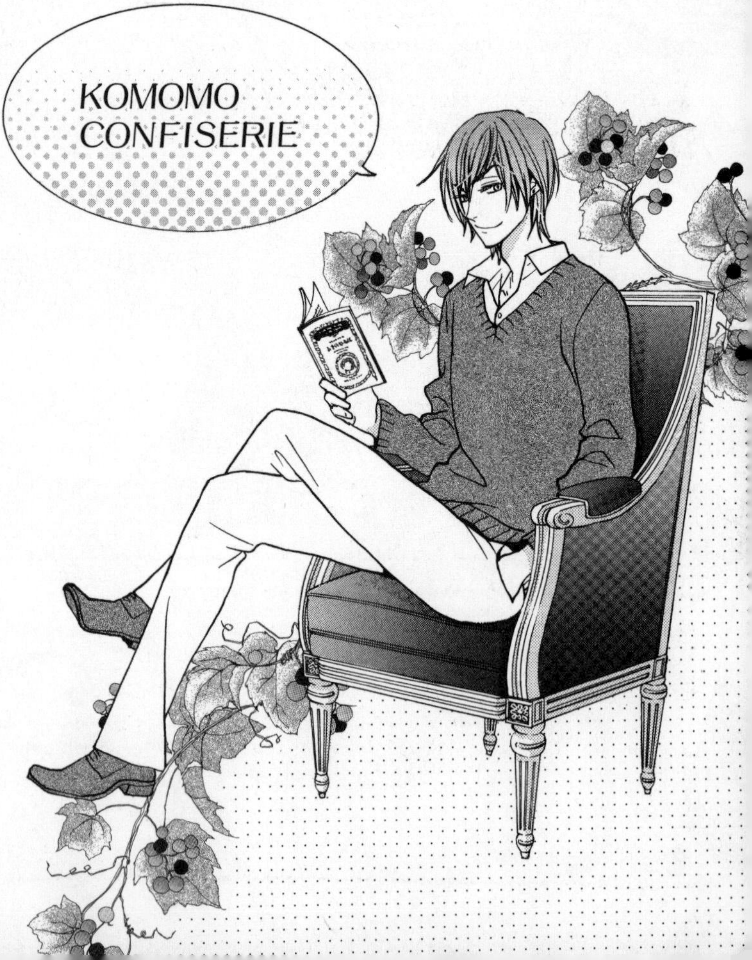
KOMOMO CONFISERIE

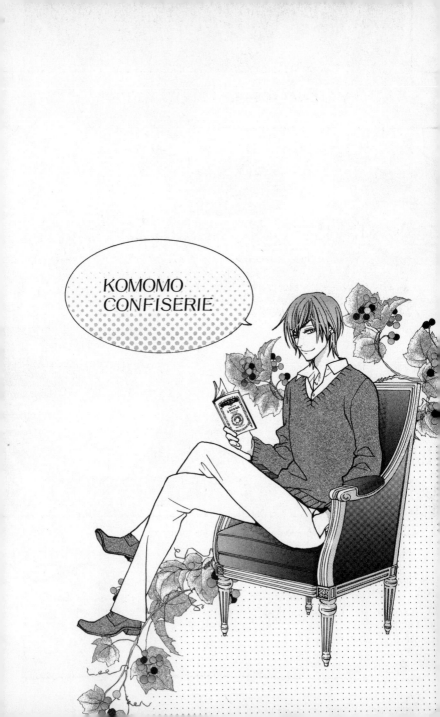

NATSU CAN'T POSSIBLY BE IN LOVE WITH ME.
MIKAMO BUS
SO.
DID YOU ENJOY YOUR DATE TODAY...
...KOMOMO-SAMA?

1

• Front Cover •

In honor of this being the last volume, I made it a Komomo and Natsu couple shot. In the back, I drew Komomo's rose caramels that grant one love. I enjoyed myself!! I also had a fun time painting in the pink flowers in the background. Painting and painting and painting!!

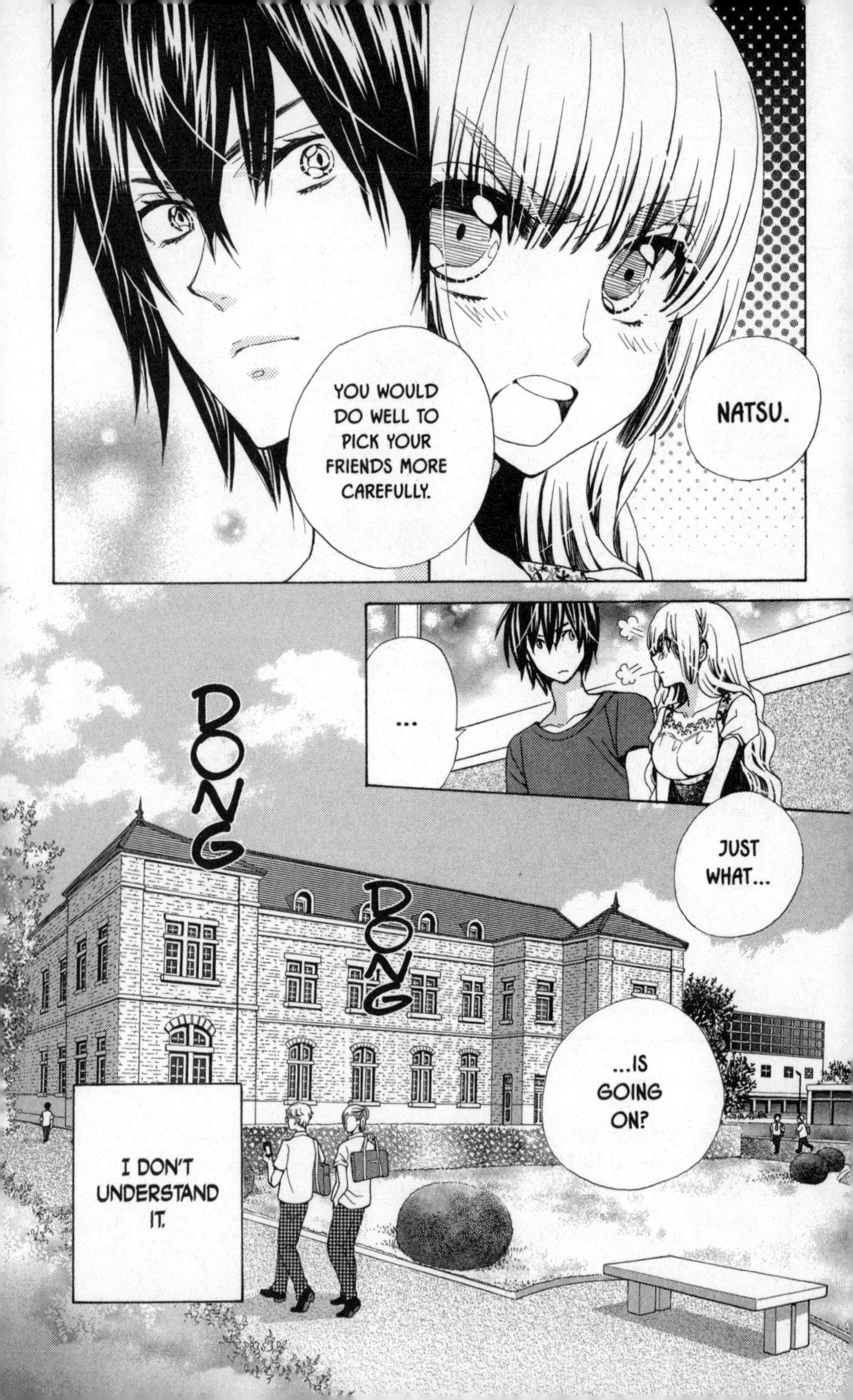
NATSU.
YOU WOULD DO WELL TO PICK YOUR FRIENDS MORE CAREFULLY.
...
JUST WHAT...
DONG
DONG
...IS GOING ON?
I DON'T UNDERSTAND IT.

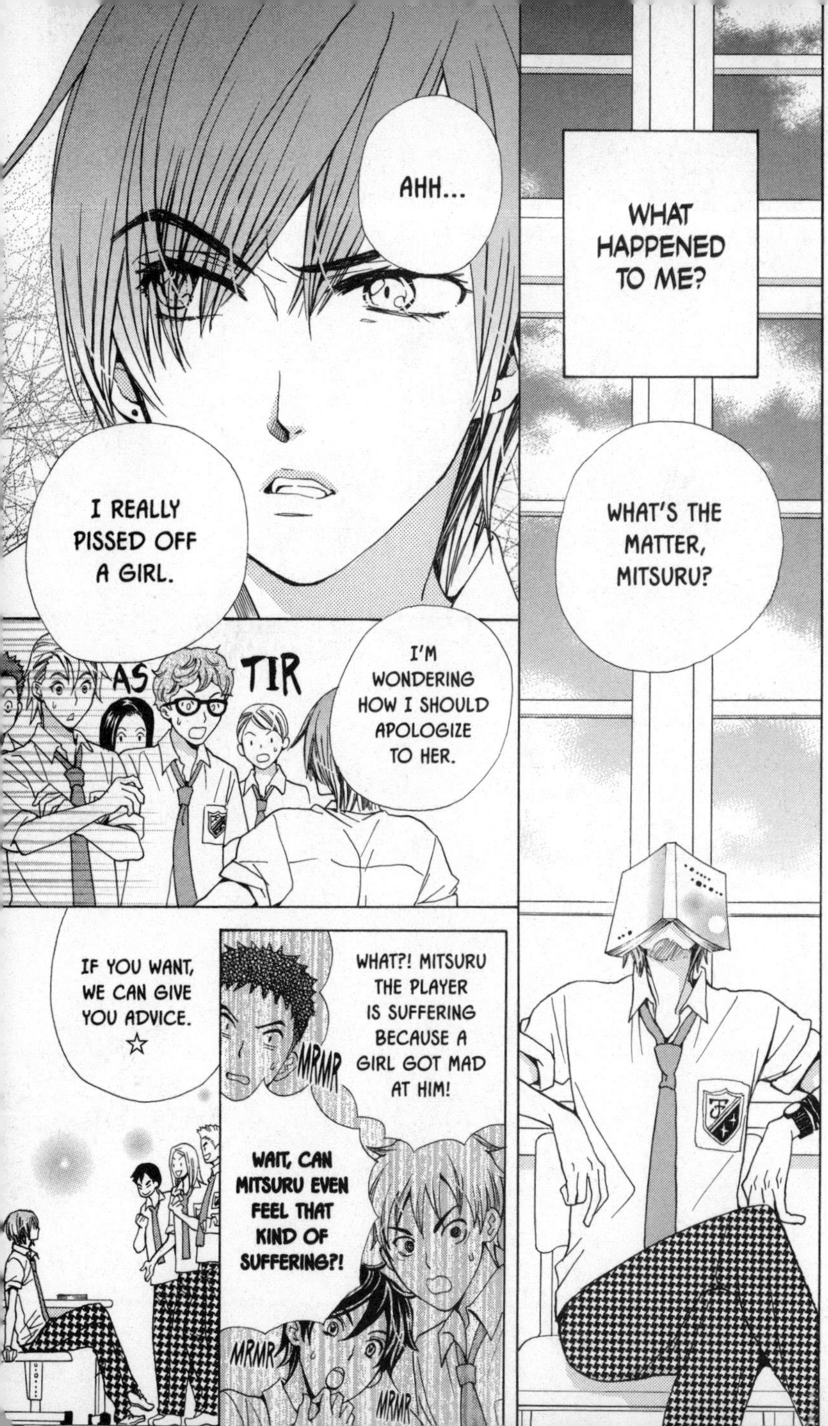
WHAT HAPPENED TO ME?
WHAT'S THE MATTER, MITSURU?
AHH...
I REALLY PISSED OFF A GIRL.
AS
TIR
I'M WONDERING HOW I SHOULD APOLOGIZE TO HER.
WHAT?! MITSURU THE PLAYER IS SUFFERING BECAUSE A GIRL GOT MAD AT HIM!
MRMR
WAIT, CAN MITSURU EVEN FEEL THAT KIND OF SUFFERING?!
MRMR
MRMR
IF YOU WANT, WE CAN GIVE YOU ADVICE. ☆

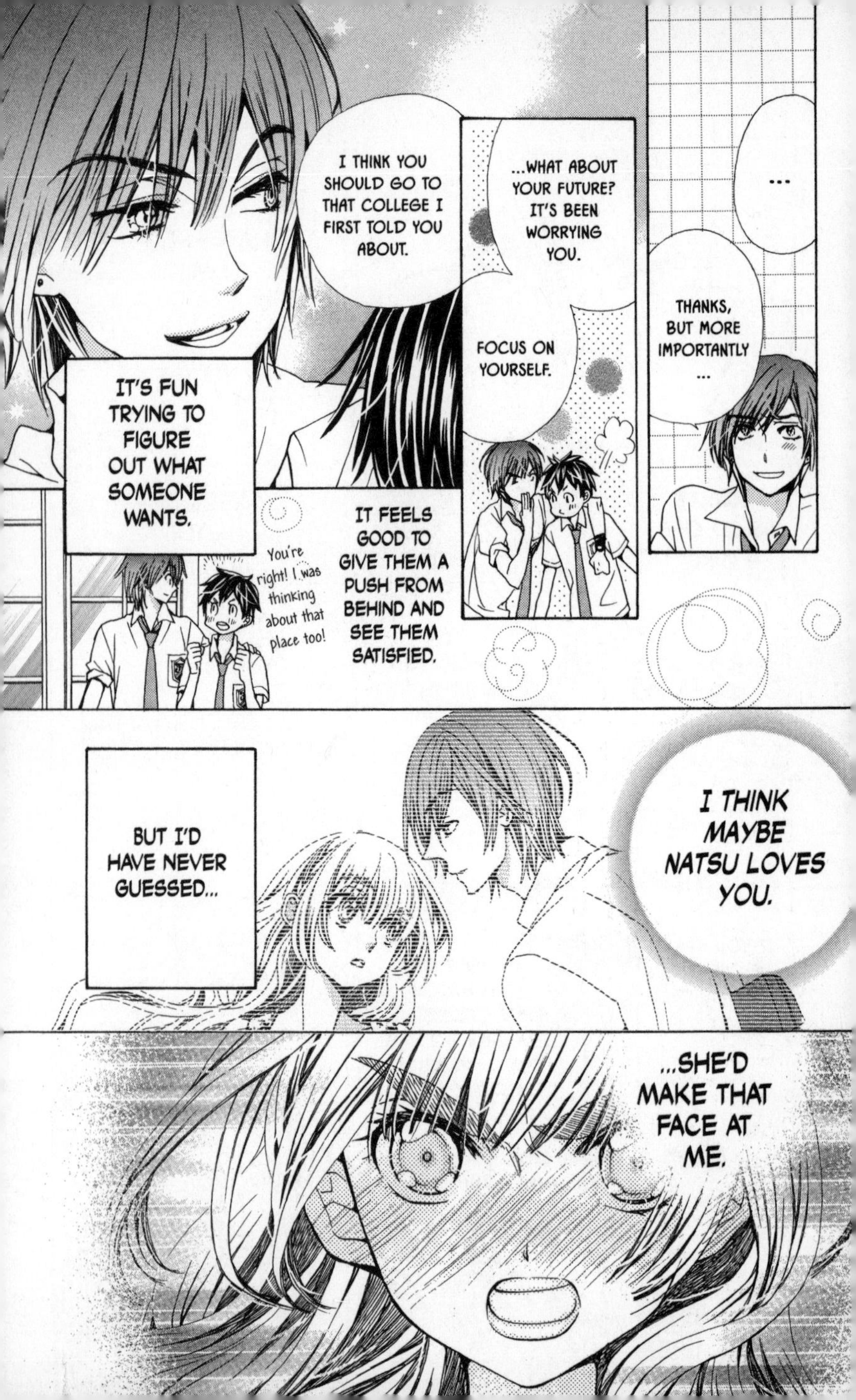
...
THANKS, BUT MORE IMPORTANTLY ...
...WHAT ABOUT YOUR FUTURE? IT'S BEEN WORRYING YOU.
FOCUS ON YOURSELF.
I THINK YOU SHOULD GO TO THAT COLLEGE I FIRST TOLD YOU ABOUT.
IT'S FUN TRYING TO FIGURE OUT WHAT SOMEONE WANTS.
IT FEELS GOOD TO GIVE THEM A PUSH FROM BEHIND AND SEE THEM SATISFIED.
You're right! I was thinking about that place too!
I THINK MAYBE NATSU LOVES YOU.
BUT I'D HAVE NEVER GUESSED...
...SHE'D MAKE THAT FACE AT ME.

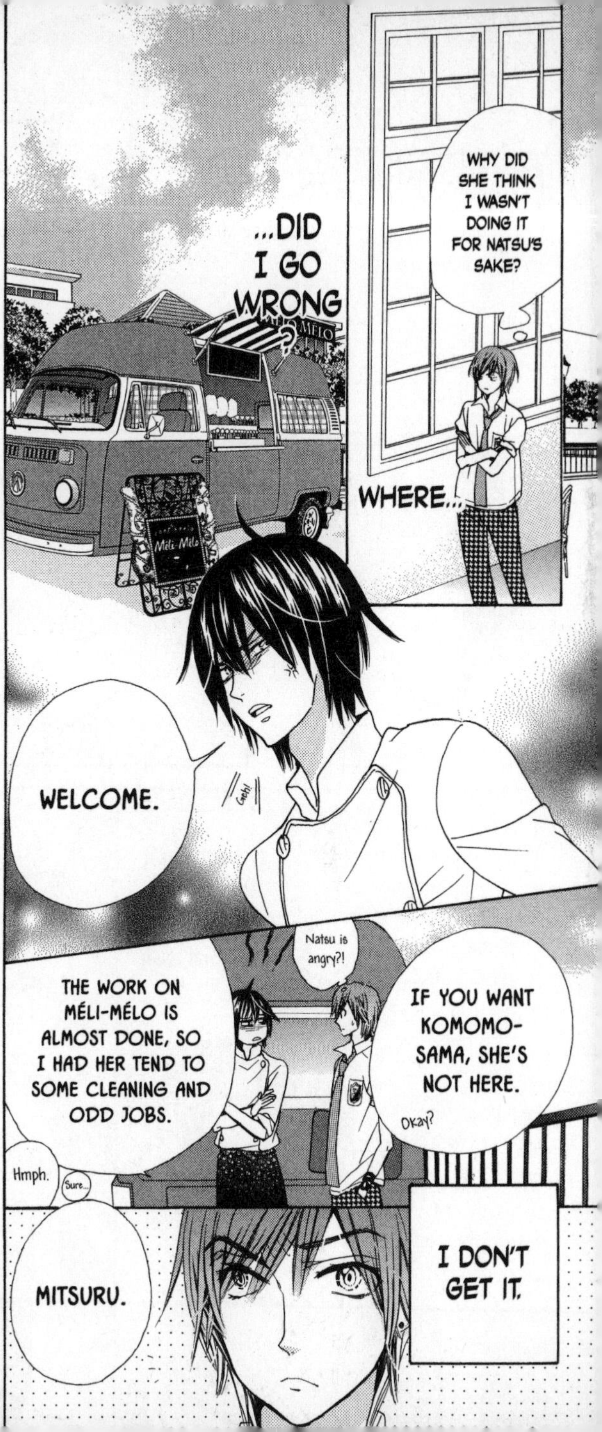
WHY DID SHE THINK I WASN'T DOING IT FOR NATSU'S SAKE?
WHERE...
...DID I GO WRONG?
MÉLO
Méli-Mélo
WELCOME.
Geh!
IF YOU WANT KOMOMO-SAMA, SHE'S NOT HERE.
Okay?
Natsu is angry?!
THE WORK ON MÉLI-MÉLO IS ALMOST DONE, SO I HAD HER TEND TO SOME CLEANING AND ODD JOBS.
Hmph.
Sure...
I DON'T GET IT.
MITSURU.

• Greetings •

Hello and nice to meet you! It's me, Maki Minami, and this is volume 5 of *Komomo Confiserie*. We've arrived at the final volume! Thank you very much for reading all the way to the end!

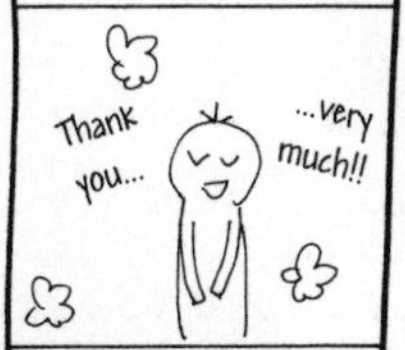
Thank you...
...very much!!

On the day I completed the bonus material for the last volume, my assistants and I went out to light fireworks. It was still December.

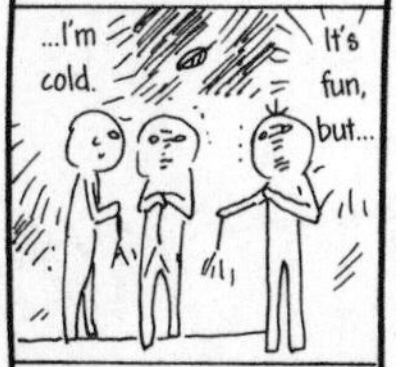
...I'm cold.
It's fun, but...

It seems it's not something you do in the middle of winter.

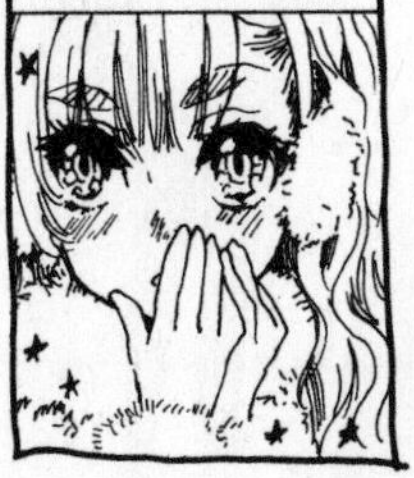

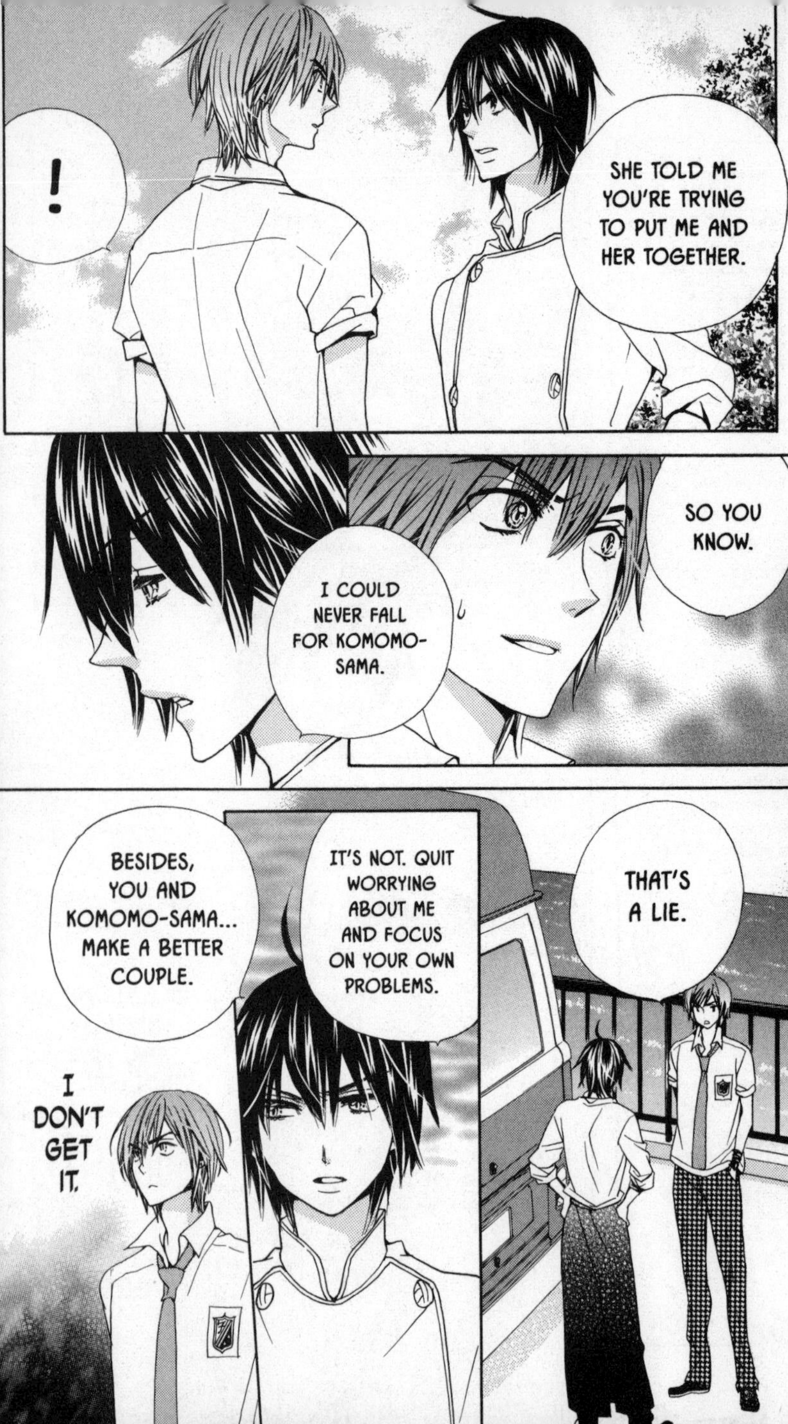
SHE TOLD ME YOU'RE TRYING TO PUT ME AND HER TOGETHER.
!
SO YOU KNOW.
I COULD NEVER FALL FOR KOMOMO-SAMA.
THAT'S A LIE.
IT'S NOT. QUIT WORRYING ABOUT ME AND FOCUS ON YOUR OWN PROBLEMS.
BESIDES, YOU AND KOMOMO-SAMA... MAKE A BETTER COUPLE.
I DON'T GET IT.

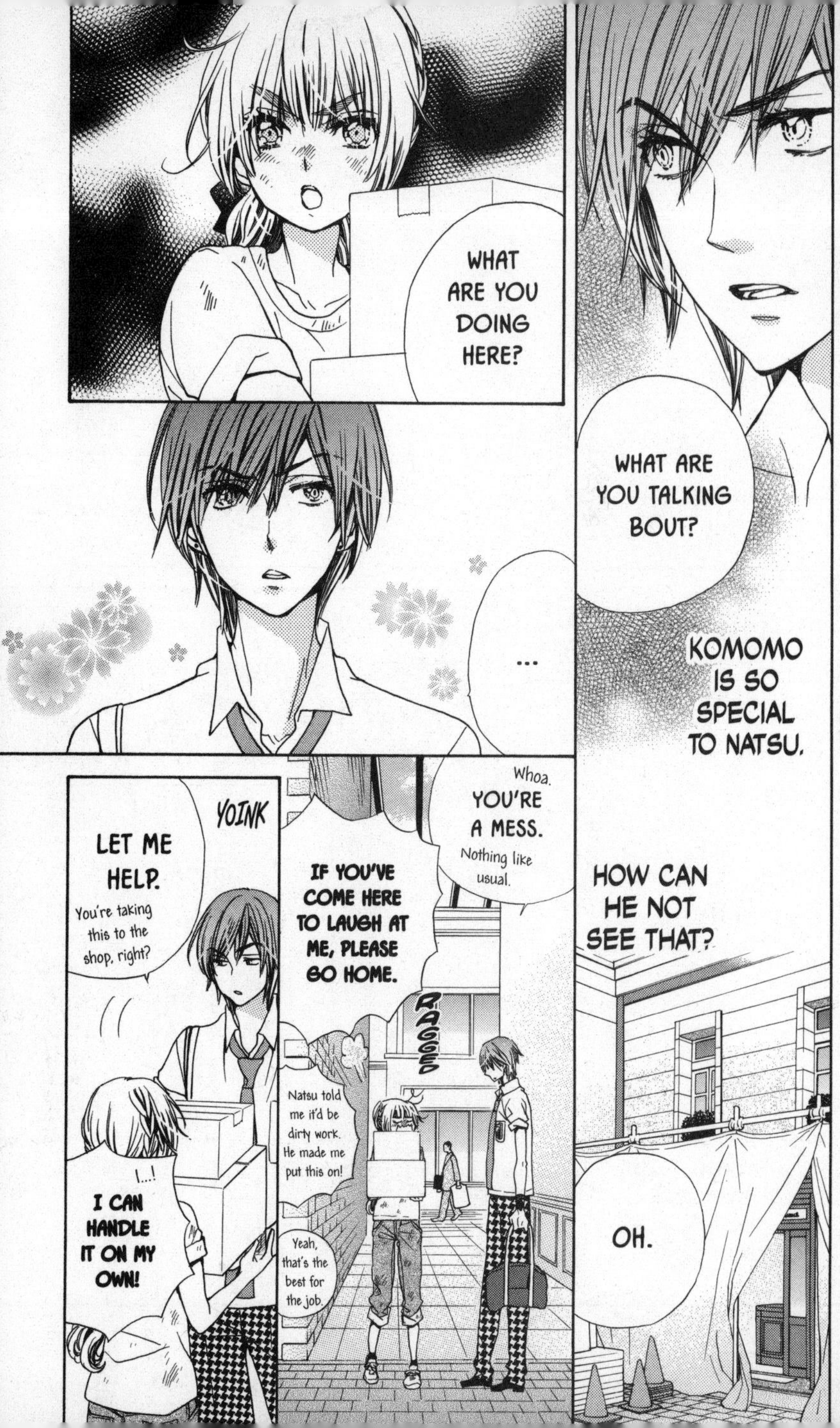
WHAT ARE YOU TALKING BOUT?
KOMOMO IS SO SPECIAL TO NATSU.
WHAT ARE YOU DOING HERE?
...
HOW CAN HE NOT SEE THAT?
OH.
Whoa. YOU'RE A MESS. Nothing like usual.
IF YOU'VE COME HERE TO LAUGH AT ME, PLEASE GO HOME.
RAGGED
Natsu told me it'd be dirty work. He made me put this on!
Yeah, that's the best for the job.
YOINK
LET ME HELP. You're taking this to the shop, right?
I...!
I CAN HANDLE IT ON MY OWN!

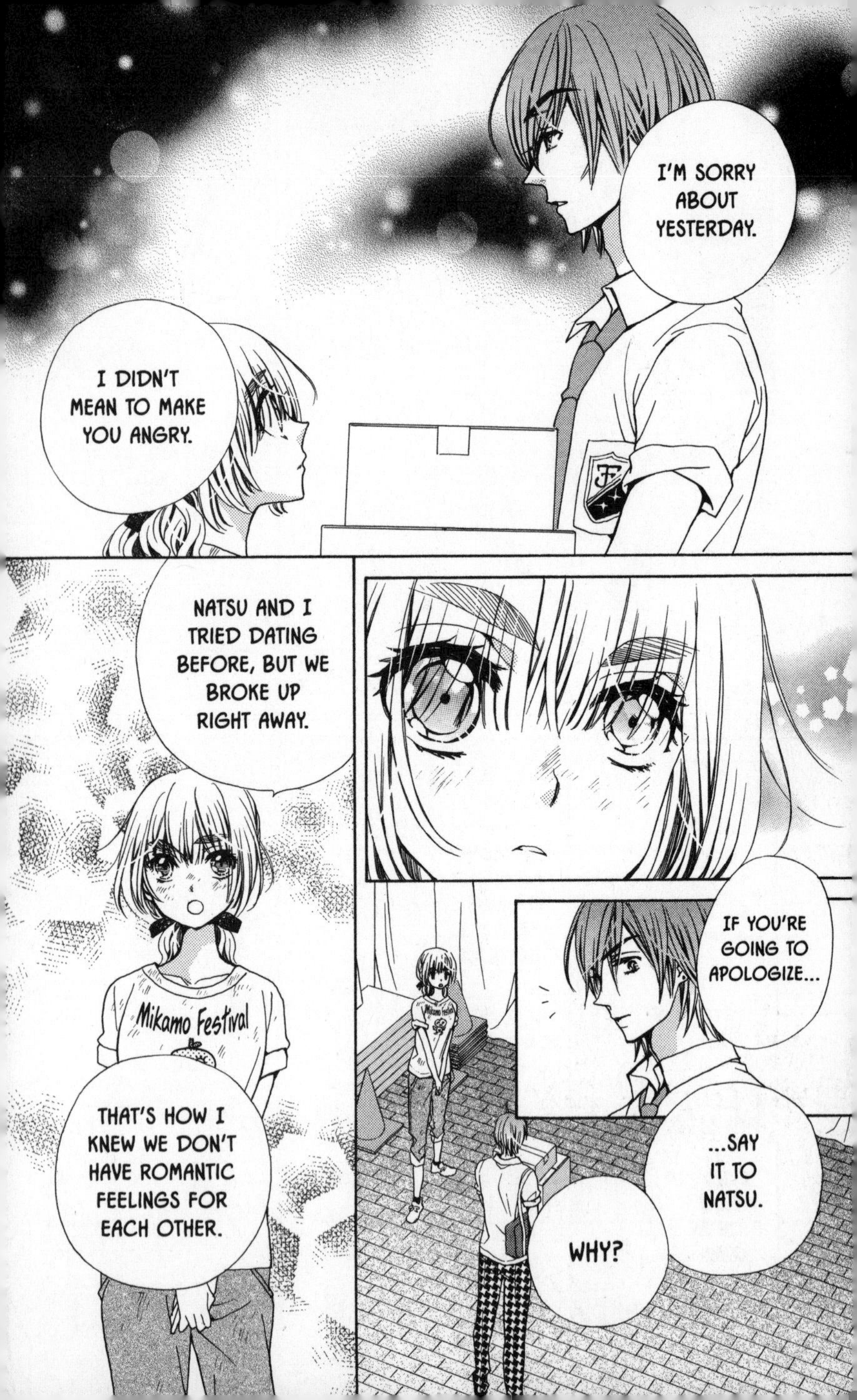
I'M SORRY ABOUT YESTERDAY.
I DIDN'T MEAN TO MAKE YOU ANGRY.
IF YOU'RE GOING TO APOLOGIZE...
...SAY IT TO NATSU.
WHY?
NATSU AND I TRIED DATING BEFORE, BUT WE BROKE UP RIGHT AWAY.
Mikamo Festival
THAT'S HOW I KNEW WE DON'T HAVE ROMANTIC FEELINGS FOR EACH OTHER.

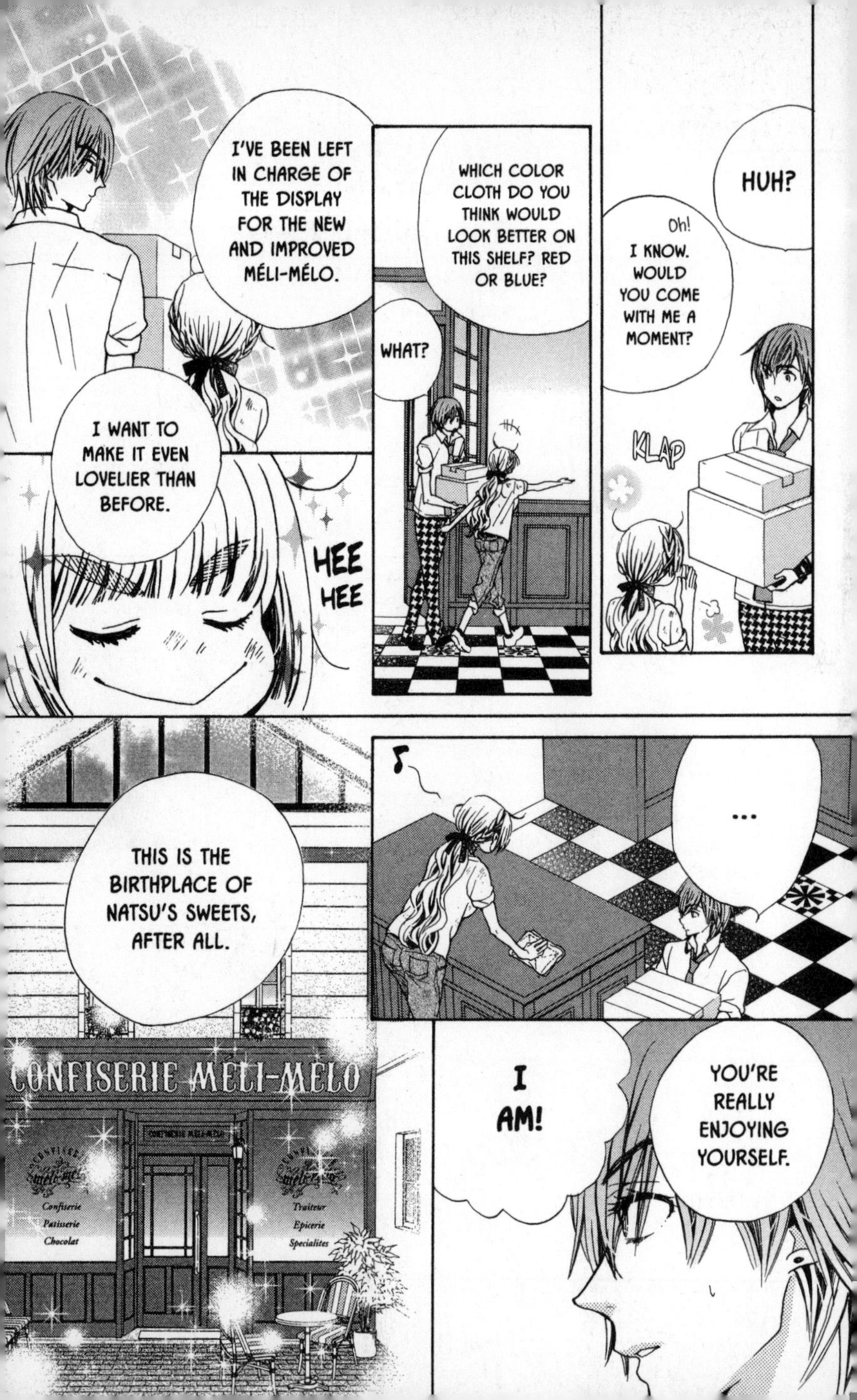
HUH?
Oh!
I KNOW. WOULD YOU COME WITH ME A MOMENT?
KLAP
WHICH COLOR CLOTH DO YOU THINK WOULD LOOK BETTER ON THIS SHELF? RED OR BLUE?
WHAT?
I'VE BEEN LEFT IN CHARGE OF THE DISPLAY FOR THE NEW AND IMPROVED MÉLI-MÉLO.
I WANT TO MAKE IT EVEN LOVELIER THAN BEFORE.
HEE HEE
...
YOU'RE REALLY ENJOYING YOURSELF.
I AM!
THIS IS THE BIRTHPLACE OF NATSU'S SWEETS, AFTER ALL.
CONFISERIE MELI-MELO
Confiserie
Patisserie
Chocolat
Traiteur
Epicerie
Specialites

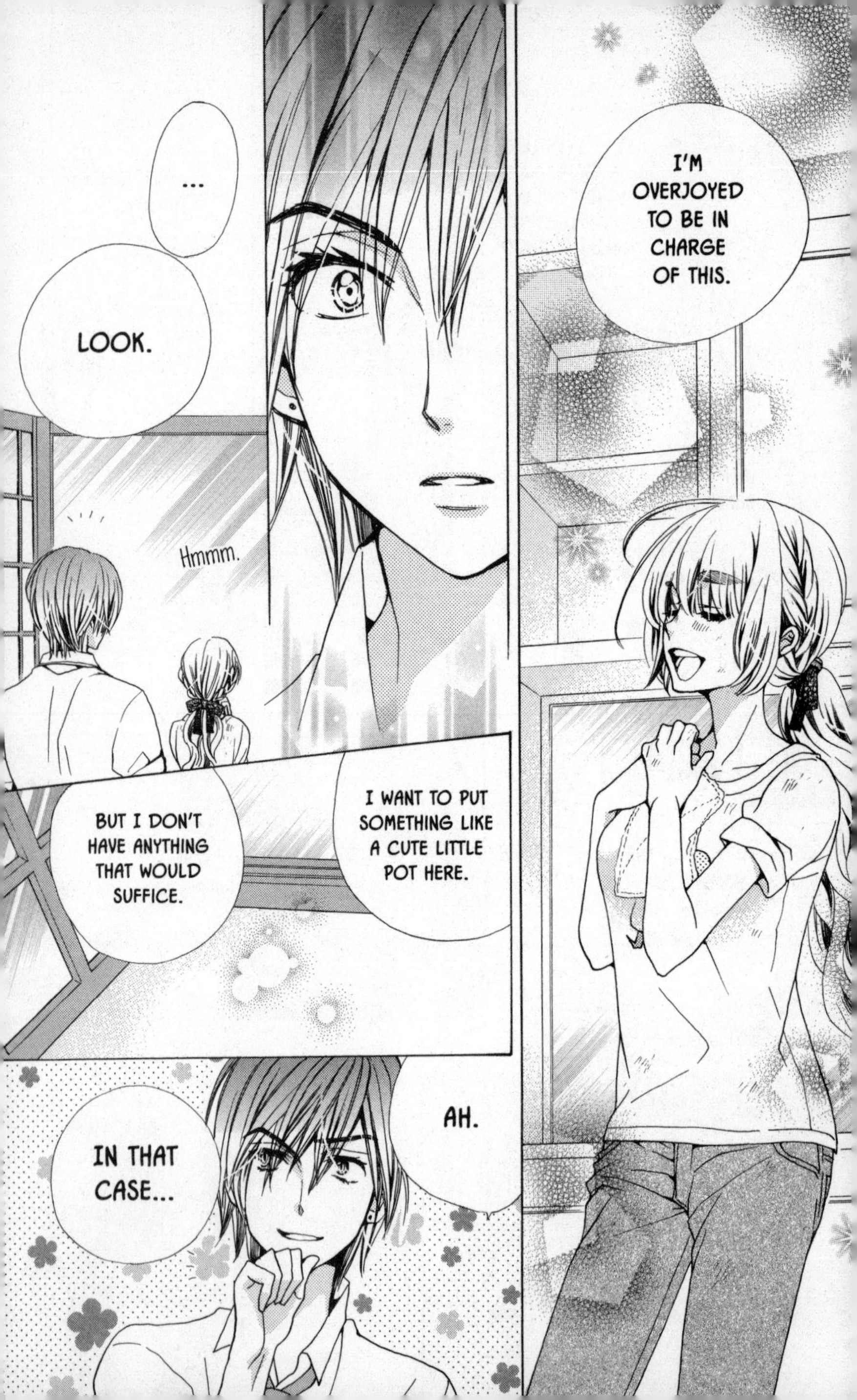
I'M OVERJOYED TO BE IN CHARGE OF THIS.
...
LOOK.
Hmmm.
I WANT TO PUT SOMETHING LIKE A CUTE LITTLE POT HERE.
BUT I DON'T HAVE ANYTHING THAT WOULD SUFFICE.
AH.
IN THAT CASE...

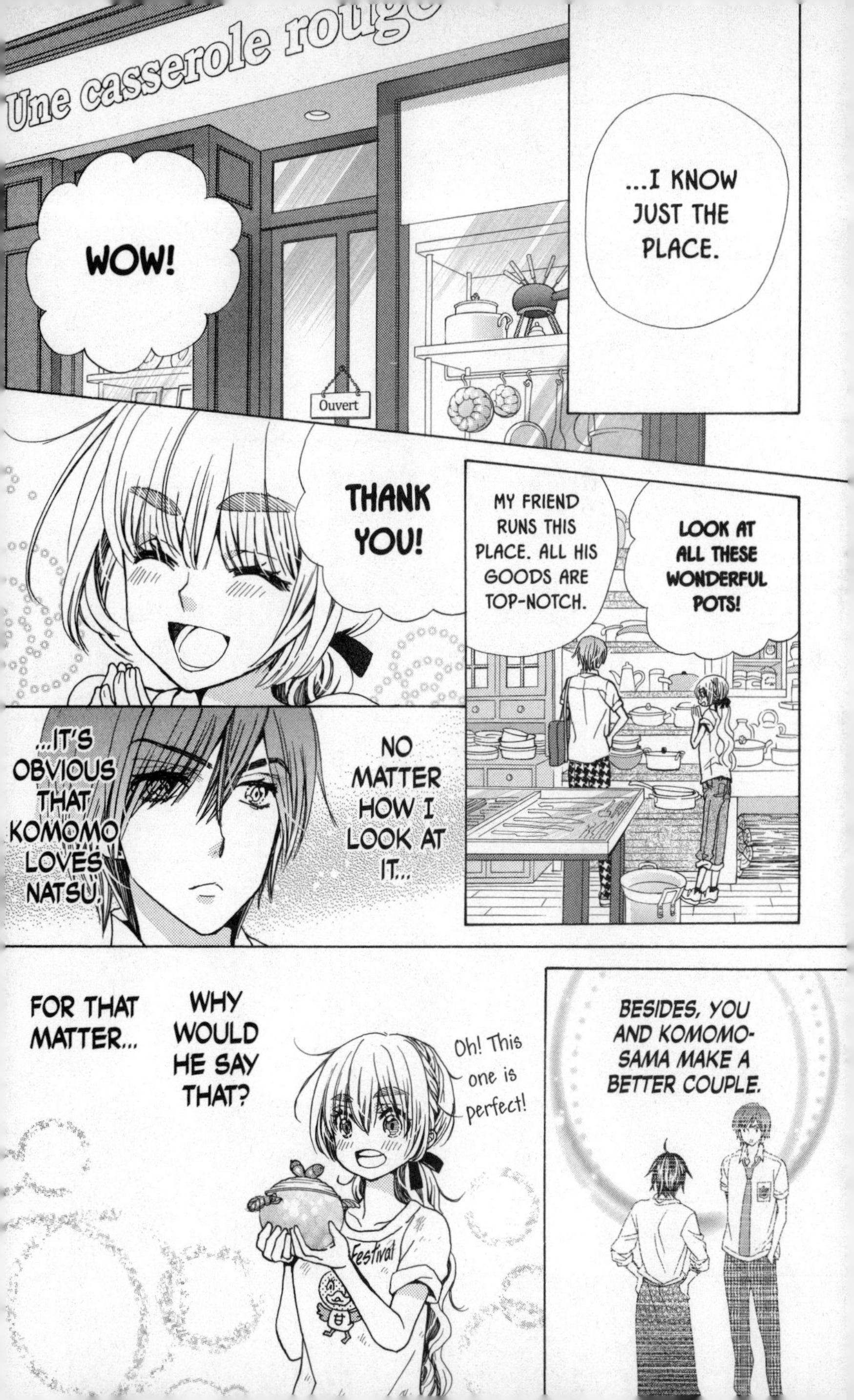
...I KNOW JUST THE PLACE.
Une casserole roug
Ouvert
WOW!
LOOK AT ALL THESE WONDERFUL POTS!
MY FRIEND RUNS THIS PLACE. ALL HIS GOODS ARE TOP-NOTCH.
THANK YOU!
NO MATTER HOW I LOOK AT IT...
...IT'S OBVIOUS THAT KOMOMO LOVES NATSU.
BESIDES, YOU AND KOMOMO-SAMA MAKE A BETTER COUPLE.
Oh! This one is perfect!
Festival
WHY WOULD HE SAY THAT?
FOR THAT MATTER...

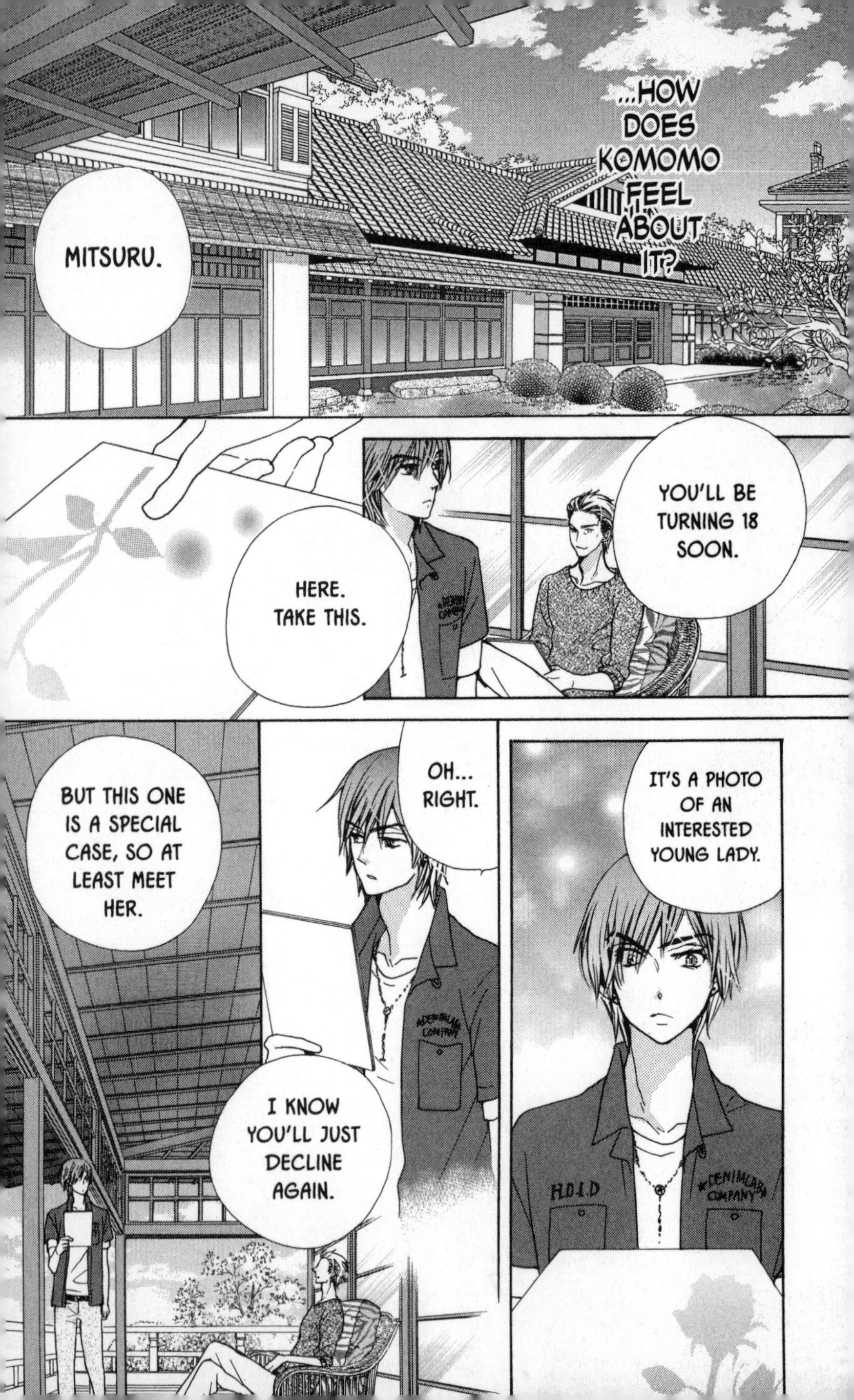
...HOW DOES KOMOMO FEEL ABOUT IT?
MITSURU.
YOU'LL BE TURNING 18 SOON.
HERE. TAKE THIS.
IT'S A PHOTO OF AN INTERESTED YOUNG LADY.
OH... RIGHT.
I KNOW YOU'LL JUST DECLINE AGAIN.
BUT THIS ONE IS A SPECIAL CASE, SO AT LEAST MEET HER.

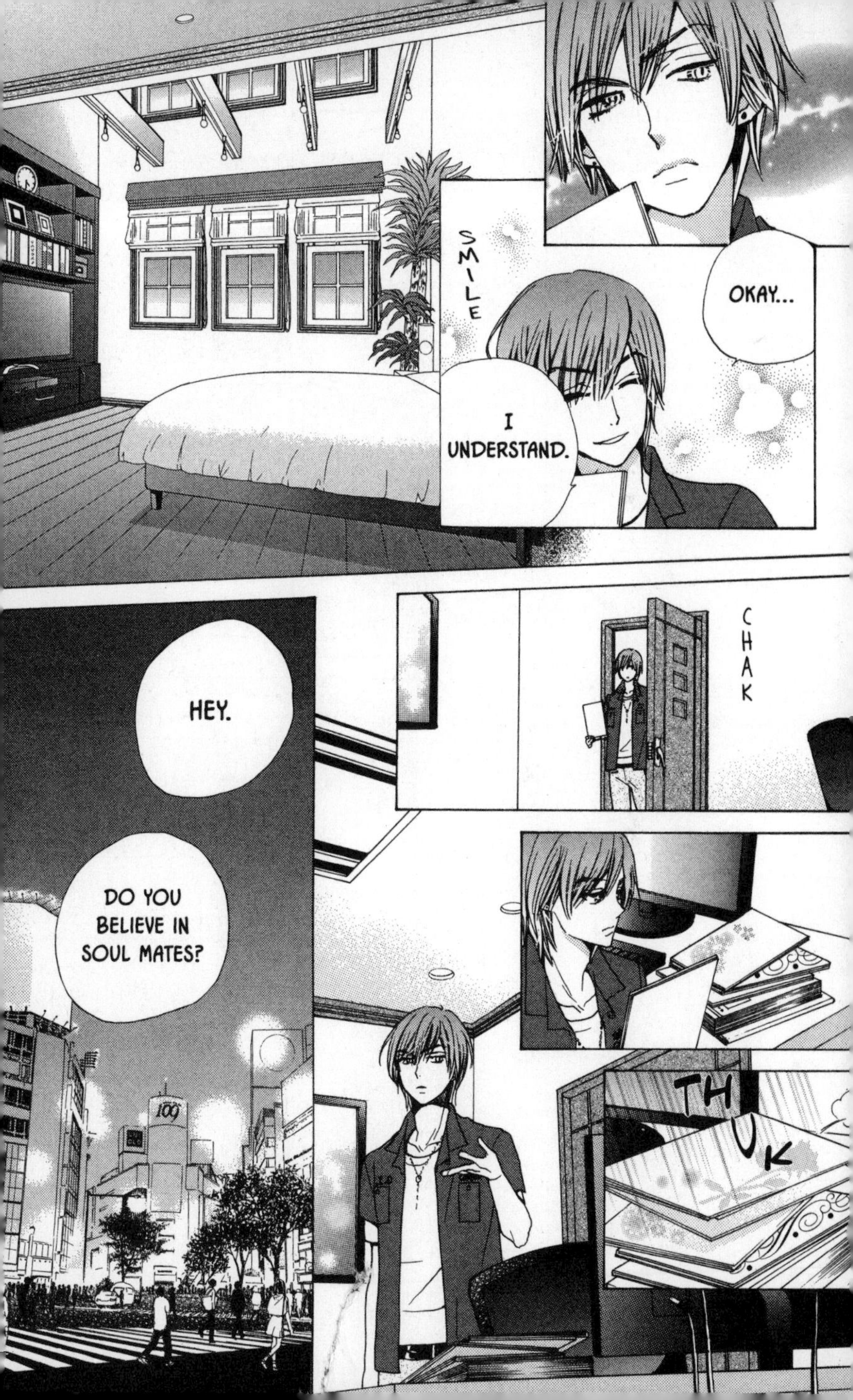
OKAY...
SMILE
I UNDERSTAND.
CHAK
THUK
HEY.
DO YOU BELIEVE IN SOUL MATES?

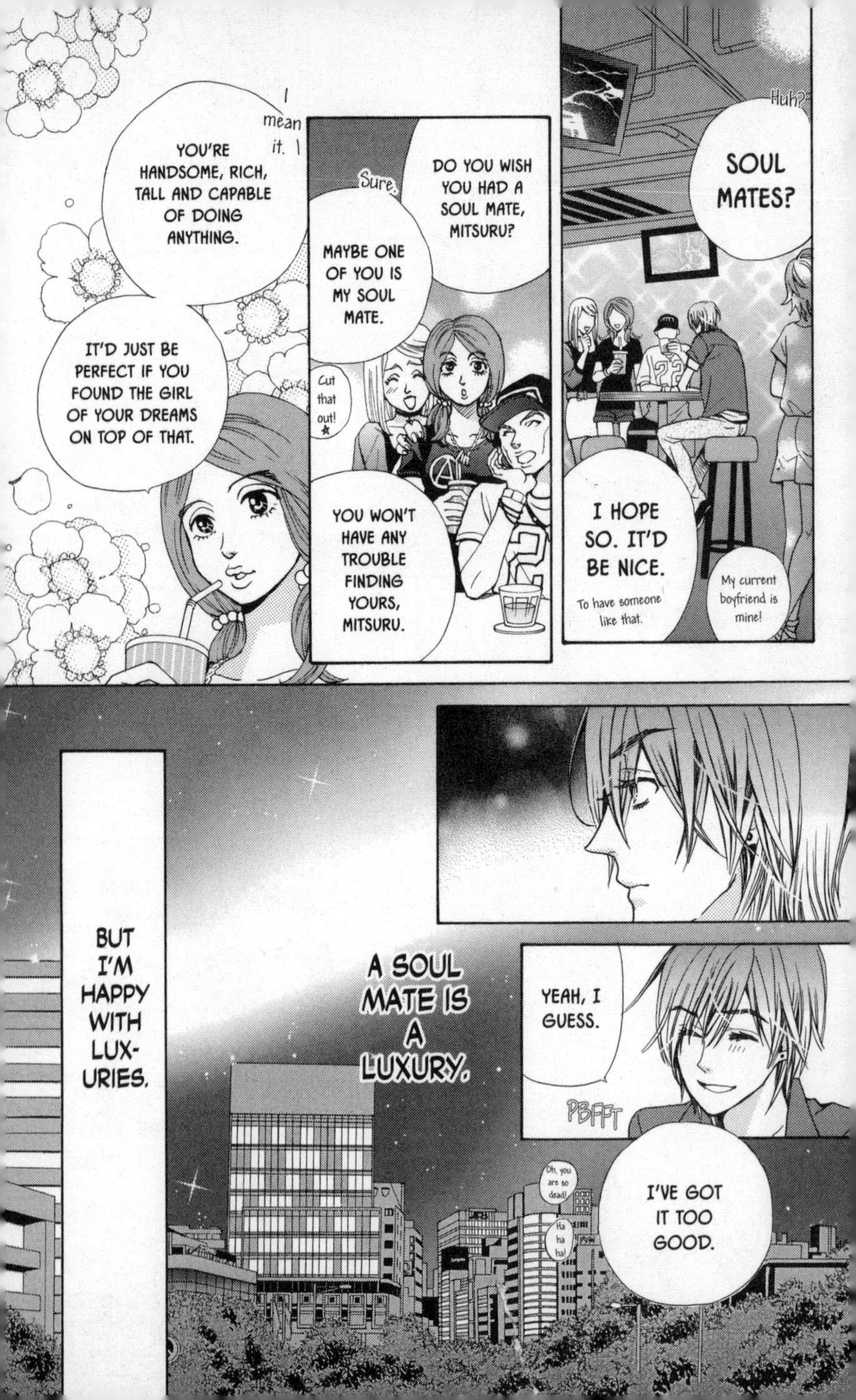
Huh?
SOUL MATES?
My current boyfriend is mine!
I HOPE SO. IT'D BE NICE.
To have someone like that.
DO YOU WISH YOU HAD A SOUL MATE, MITSURU?
Sure.
MAYBE ONE OF YOU IS MY SOUL MATE.
Cut that out! ☆
YOU WON'T HAVE ANY TROUBLE FINDING YOURS, MITSURU.
I mean it.
YOU'RE HANDSOME, RICH, TALL AND CAPABLE OF DOING ANYTHING.
IT'D JUST BE PERFECT IF YOU FOUND THE GIRL OF YOUR DREAMS ON TOP OF THAT.
YEAH, I GUESS.
PBFFT
I'VE GOT IT TOO GOOD.
Oh, you are so dead!
Ha ha ha!
A SOUL MATE IS A LUXURY.
BUT I'M HAPPY WITH LUX-URIES.

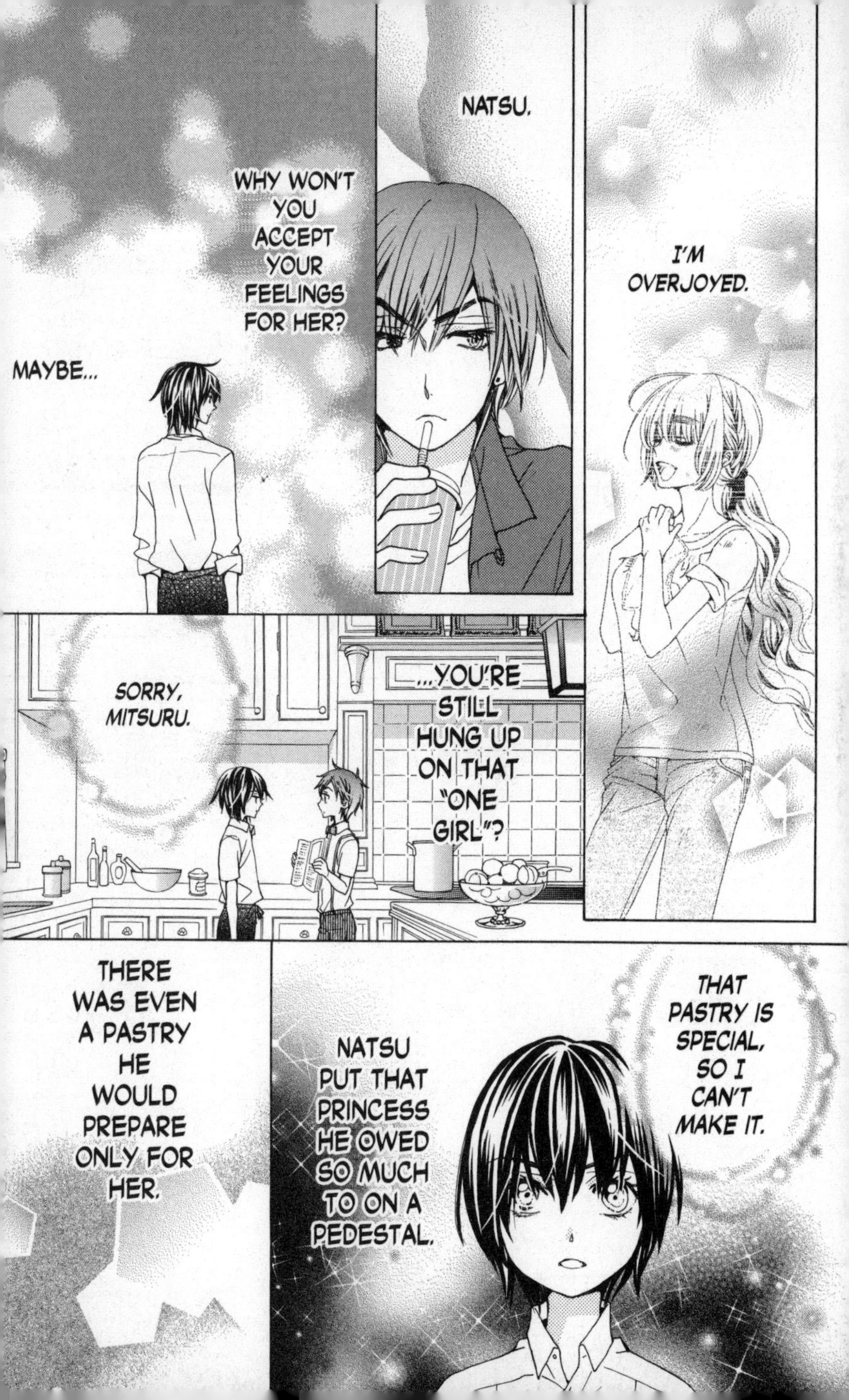
I'M OVERJOYED.
NATSU.
WHY WON'T YOU ACCEPT YOUR FEELINGS FOR HER?
MAYBE...
...YOU'RE STILL HUNG UP ON THAT "ONE GIRL"?
SORRY, MITSURU.
THAT PASTRY IS SPECIAL, SO I CAN'T MAKE IT.
NATSU PUT THAT PRINCESS HE OWED SO MUCH TO ON A PEDESTAL.
THERE WAS EVEN A PASTRY HE WOULD PREPARE ONLY FOR HER.

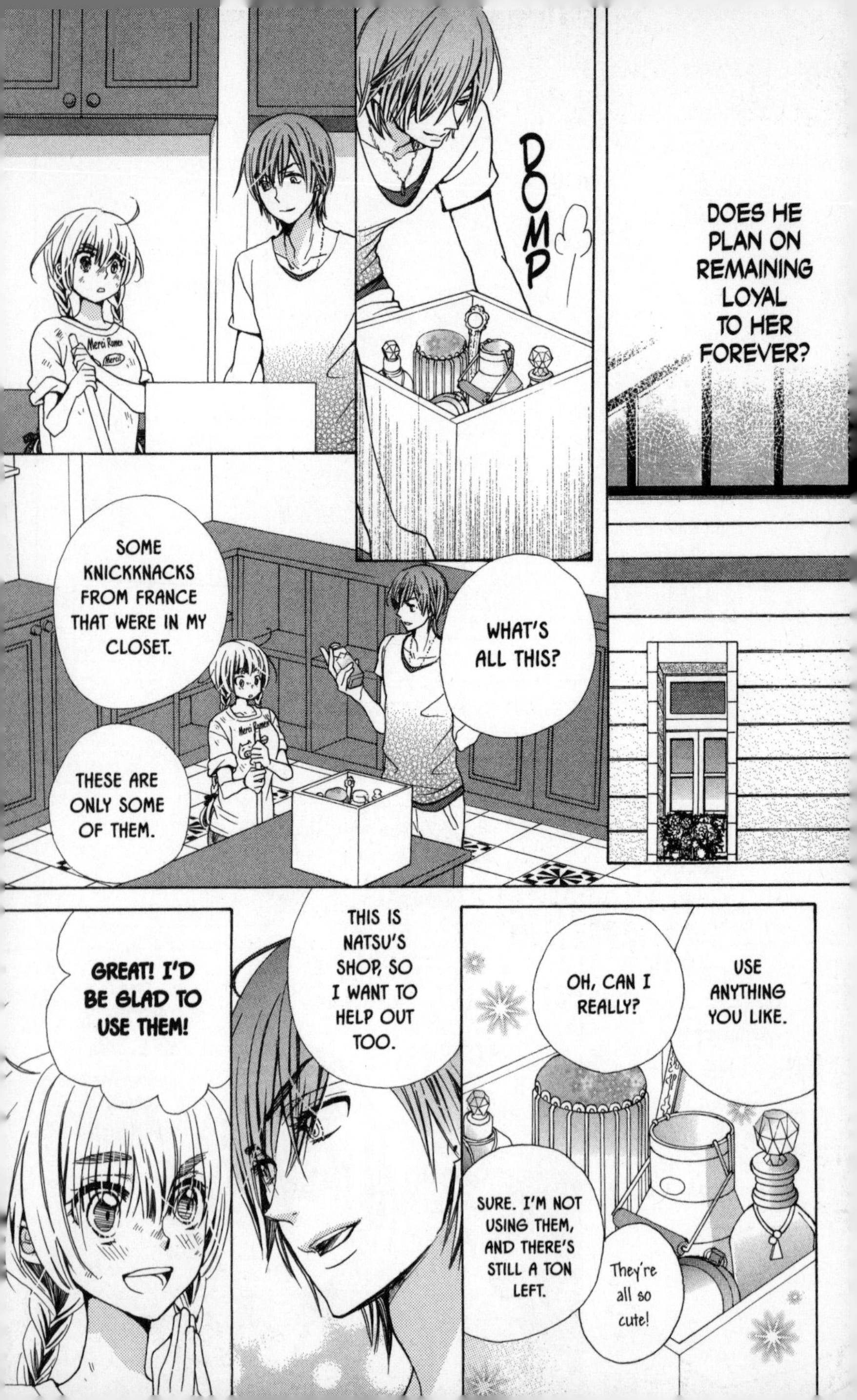
DOES HE PLAN ON REMAINING LOYAL TO HER FOREVER?
DOMP
WHAT'S ALL THIS?
SOME KNICKKNACKS FROM FRANCE THAT WERE IN MY CLOSET.
THESE ARE ONLY SOME OF THEM.
USE ANYTHING YOU LIKE.
OH, CAN I REALLY?
SURE. I'M NOT USING THEM, AND THERE'S STILL A TON LEFT.
They're all so cute!
THIS IS NATSU'S SHOP, SO I WANT TO HELP OUT TOO.
GREAT! I'D BE GLAD TO USE THEM!

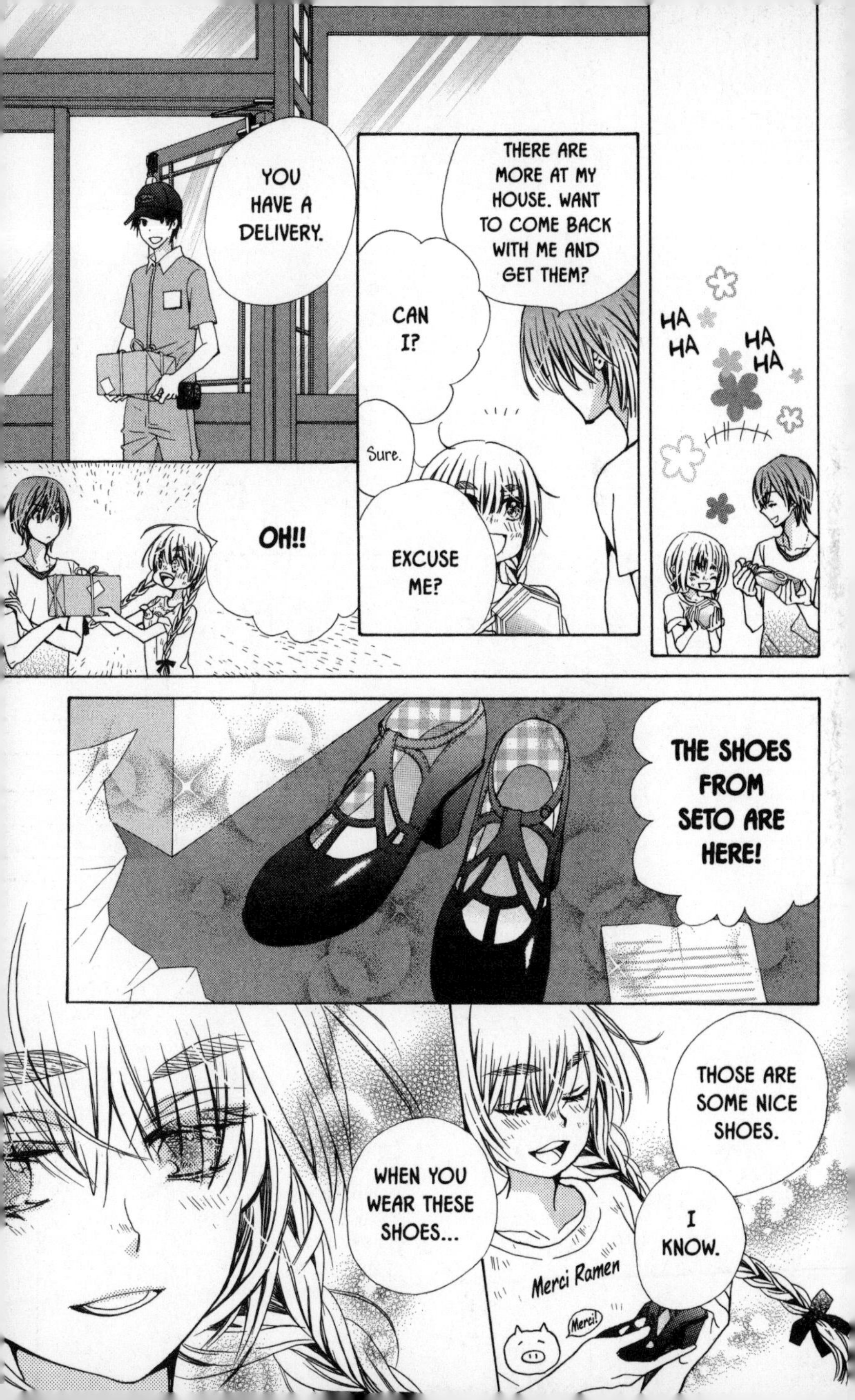
HA HA
HA HA
THERE ARE MORE AT MY HOUSE. WANT TO COME BACK WITH ME AND GET THEM?
CAN I?
Sure.
EXCUSE ME?
YOU HAVE A DELIVERY.
OH!!
THE SHOES FROM SETO ARE HERE!
THOSE ARE SOME NICE SHOES.
I KNOW.
Merci Ramen
Merci!
WHEN YOU WEAR THESE SHOES...

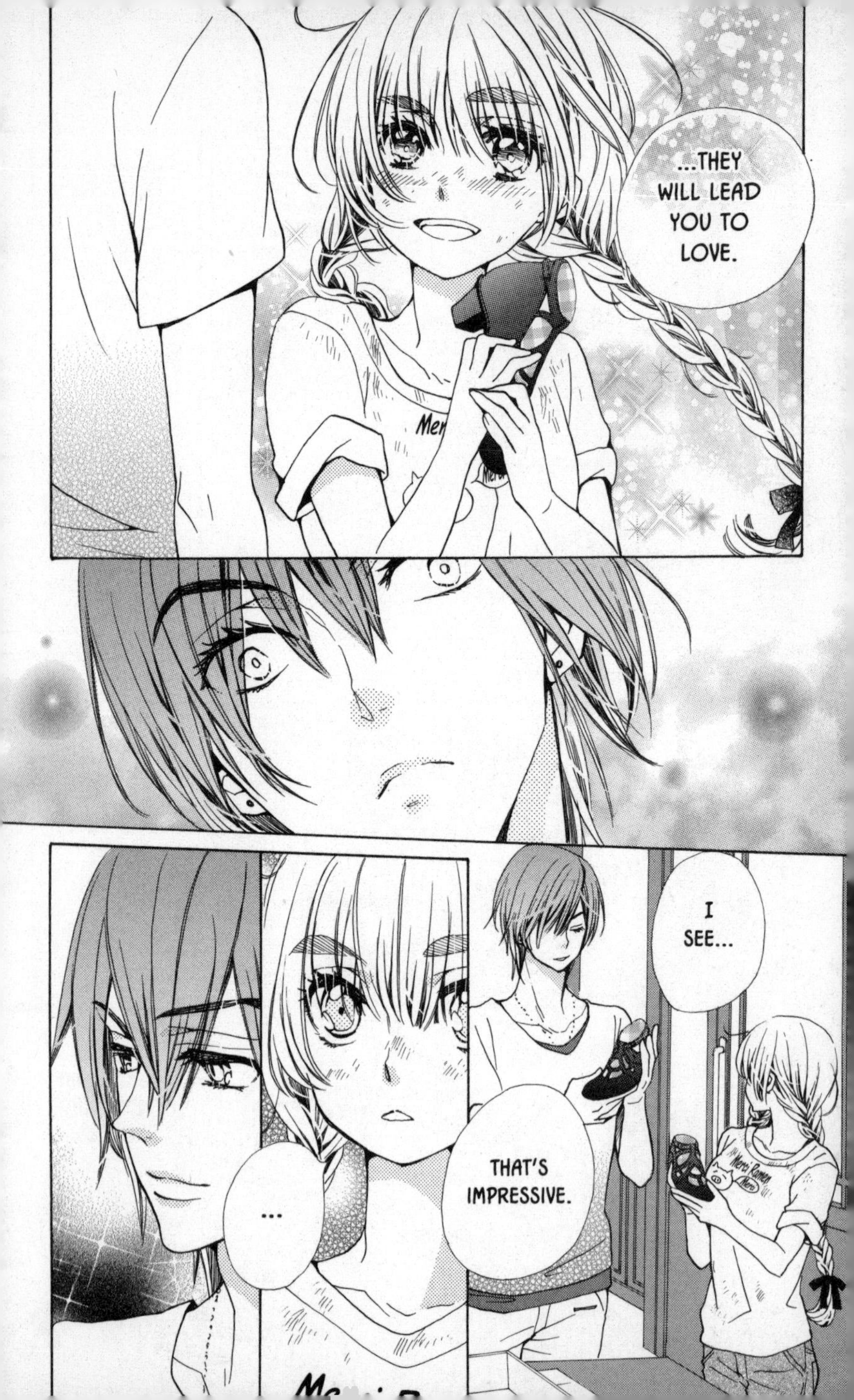
...THEY WILL LEAD YOU TO LOVE.
I SEE...
THAT'S IMPRESSIVE.
...

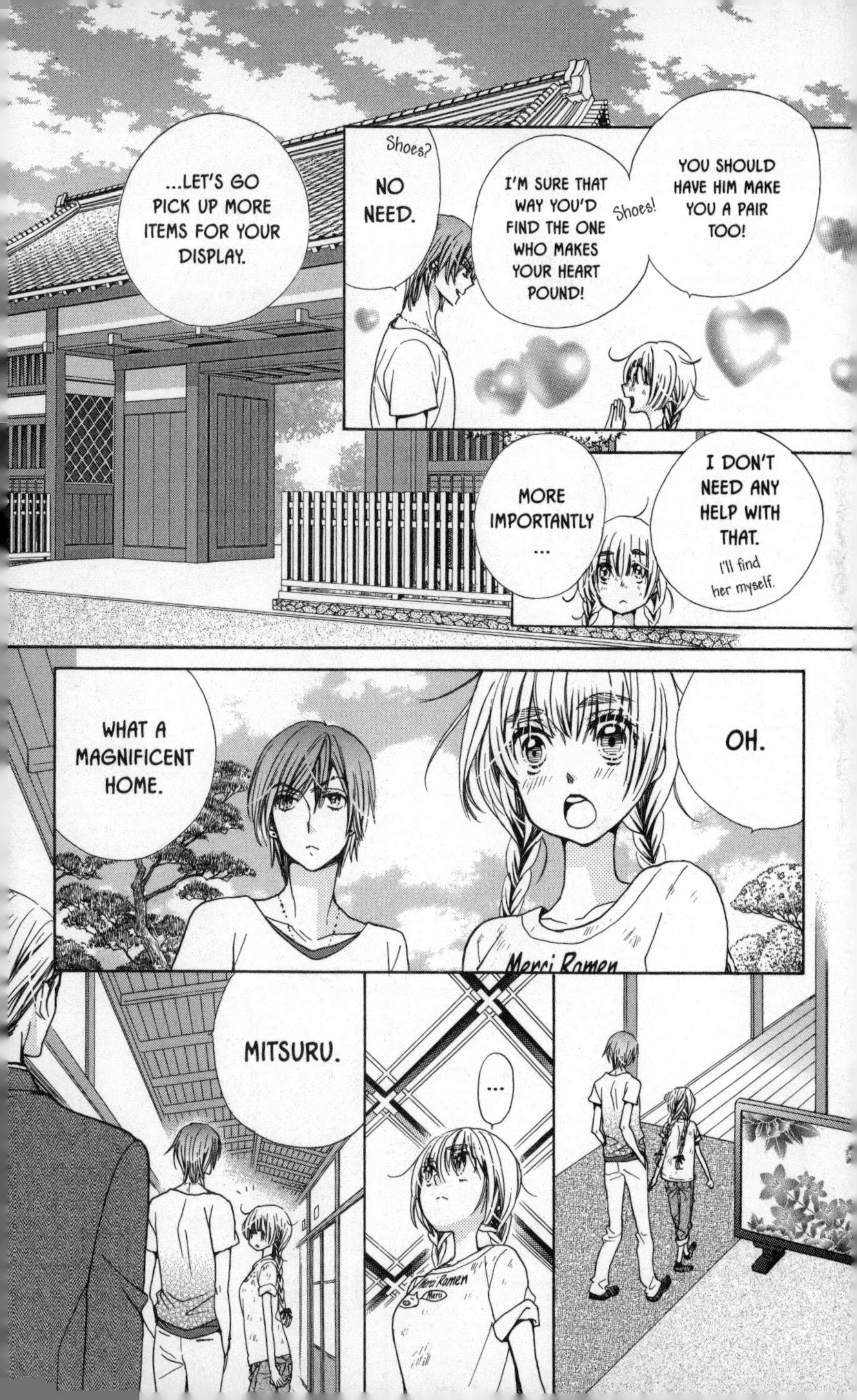
YOU SHOULD HAVE HIM MAKE YOU A PAIR TOO!
Shoes!
I'M SURE THAT WAY YOU'D FIND THE ONE WHO MAKES YOUR HEART POUND!
Shoes?
NO NEED.
I DON'T NEED ANY HELP WITH THAT.
I'll find her myself.
MORE IMPORTANTLY...
...LET'S GO PICK UP MORE ITEMS FOR YOUR DISPLAY.
OH.
WHAT A MAGNIFICENT HOME.
Merci Ramen
Merci Ramen
...
MITSURU.

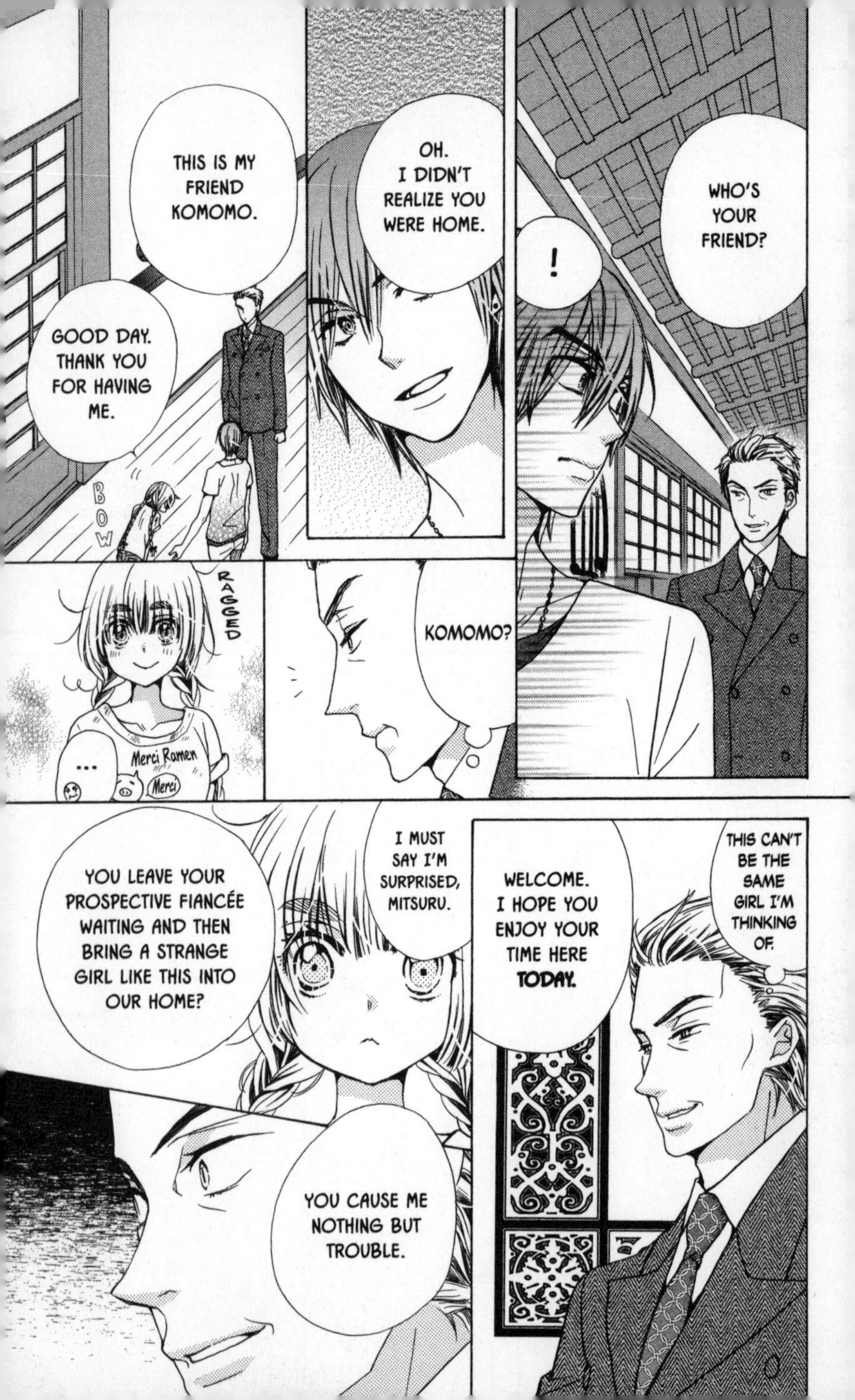
WHO'S YOUR FRIEND?
!
OH. I DIDN'T REALIZE YOU WERE HOME.
THIS IS MY FRIEND KOMOMO.
GOOD DAY. THANK YOU FOR HAVING ME.
BOW
KOMOMO?
RAGGED
...
Merci Ramen
Merci
THIS CAN'T BE THE SAME GIRL I'M THINKING OF.
WELCOME. I HOPE YOU ENJOY YOUR TIME HERE **TODAY.**
I MUST SAY I'M SURPRISED, MITSURU.
YOU LEAVE YOUR PROSPECTIVE FIANCÉE WAITING AND THEN BRING A STRANGE GIRL LIKE THIS INTO OUR HOME?
YOU CAUSE ME NOTHING BUT TROUBLE.

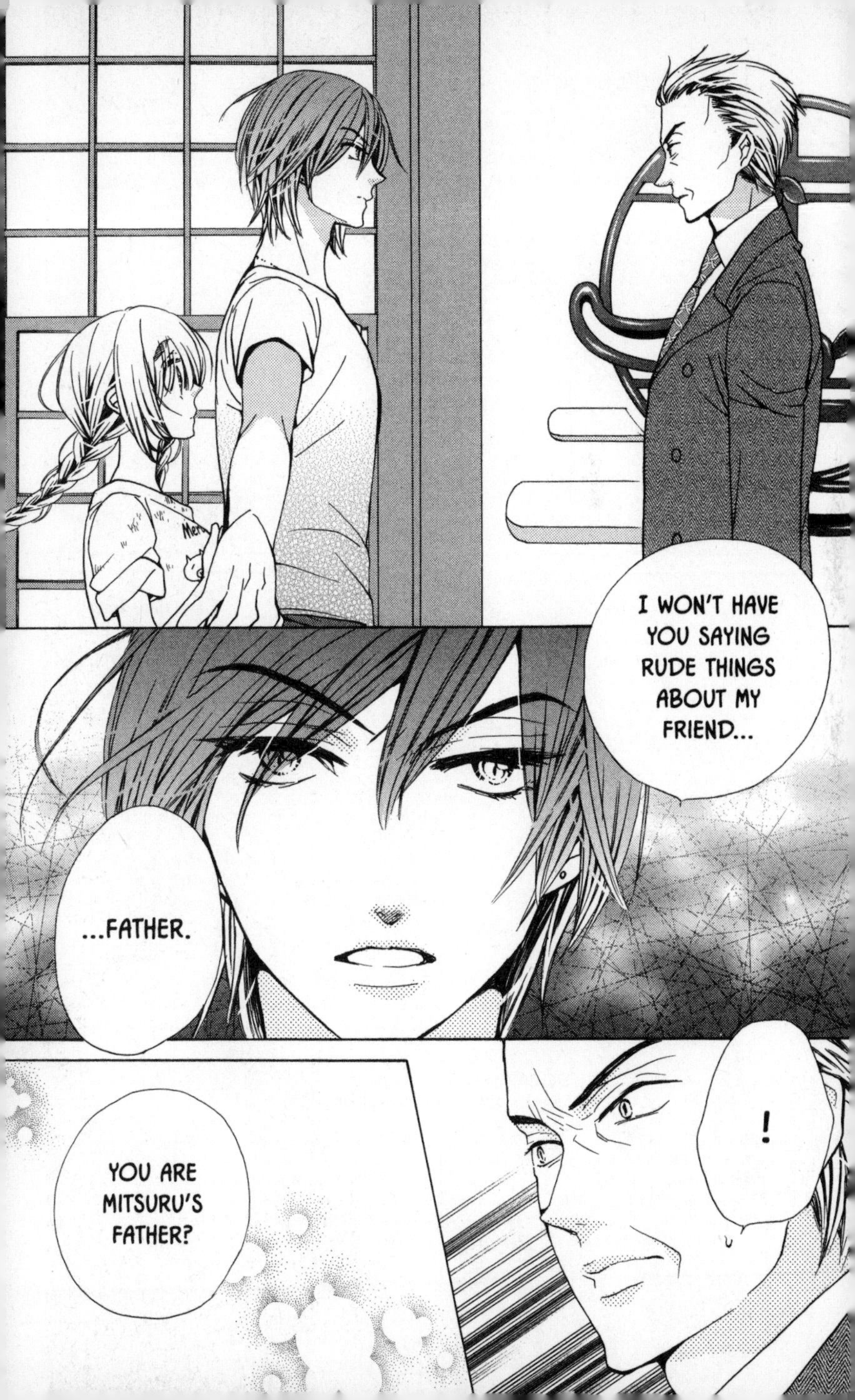
I WON'T HAVE YOU SAYING RUDE THINGS ABOUT MY FRIEND...
...FATHER.
!
YOU ARE MITSURU'S FATHER?

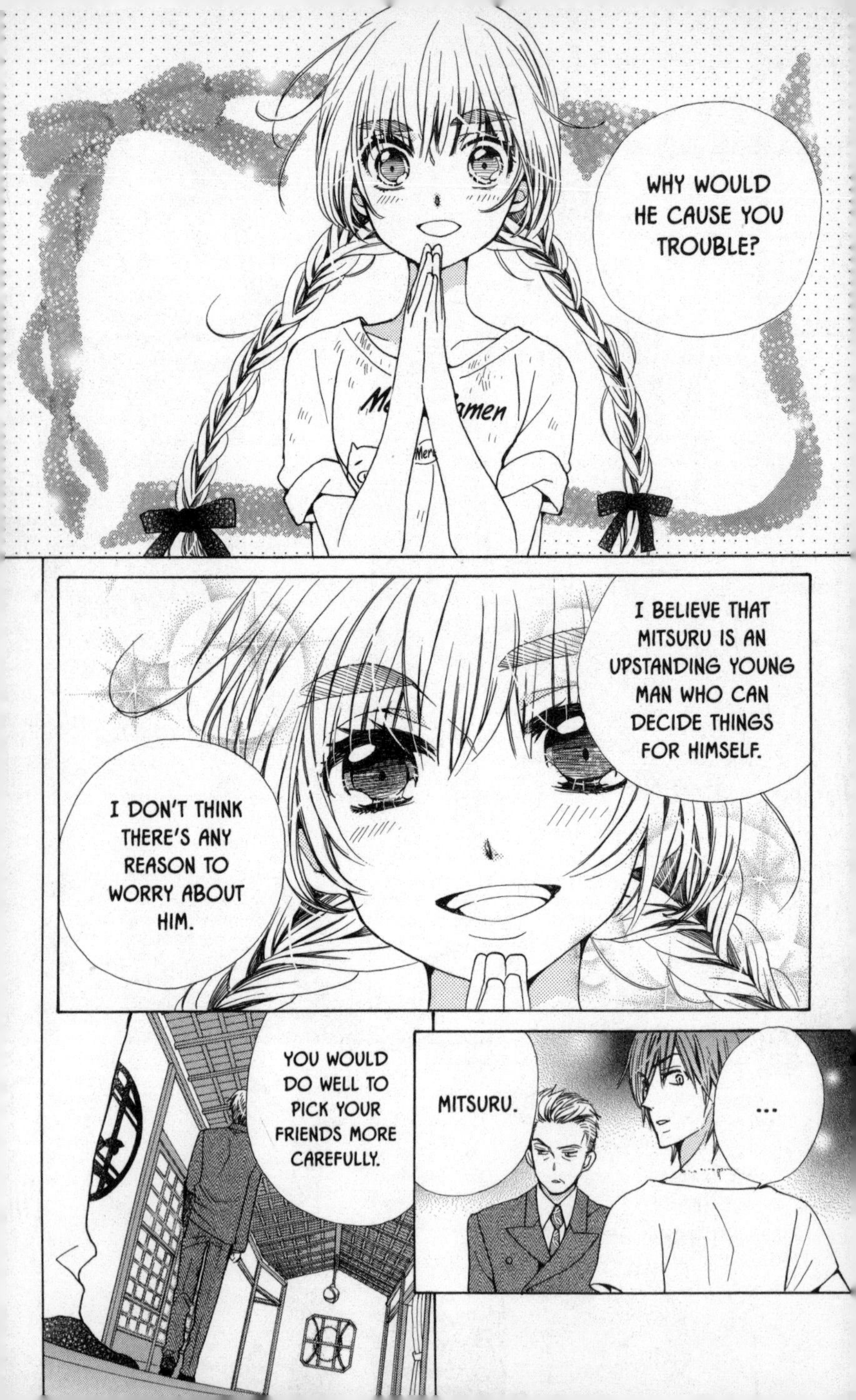
WHY WOULD HE CAUSE YOU TROUBLE?
I BELIEVE THAT MITSURU IS AN UPSTANDING YOUNG MAN WHO CAN DECIDE THINGS FOR HIMSELF.
I DON'T THINK THERE'S ANY REASON TO WORRY ABOUT HIM.
...
MITSURU.
YOU WOULD DO WELL TO PICK YOUR FRIENDS MORE CAREFULLY.

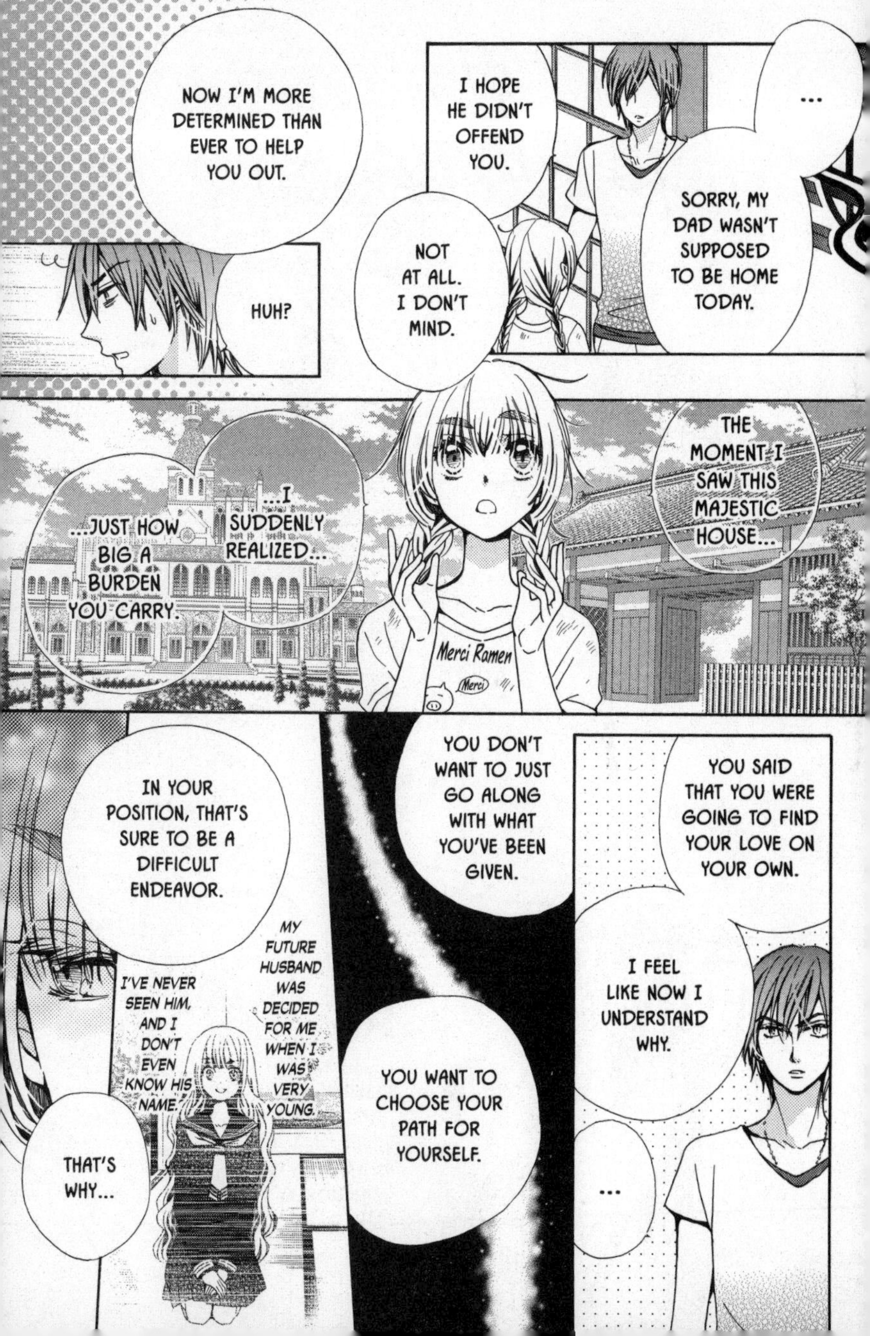
...
SORRY, MY DAD WASN'T SUPPOSED TO BE HOME TODAY.
I HOPE HE DIDN'T OFFEND YOU.
NOT AT ALL. I DON'T MIND.
NOW I'M MORE DETERMINED THAN EVER TO HELP YOU OUT.
HUH?
THE MOMENT I SAW THIS MAJESTIC HOUSE...
...I SUDDENLY REALIZED...
...JUST HOW BIG A BURDEN YOU CARRY.
Merci Ramen
Merci
YOU SAID THAT YOU WERE GOING TO FIND YOUR LOVE ON YOUR OWN.
I FEEL LIKE NOW I UNDERSTAND WHY.
...
YOU DON'T WANT TO JUST GO ALONG WITH WHAT YOU'VE BEEN GIVEN.
YOU WANT TO CHOOSE YOUR PATH FOR YOURSELF.
IN YOUR POSITION, THAT'S SURE TO BE A DIFFICULT ENDEAVOR.
MY FUTURE HUSBAND WAS DECIDED FOR ME WHEN I WAS VERY YOUNG.
I'VE NEVER SEEN HIM, AND I DON'T EVEN KNOW HIS NAME.
THAT'S WHY...

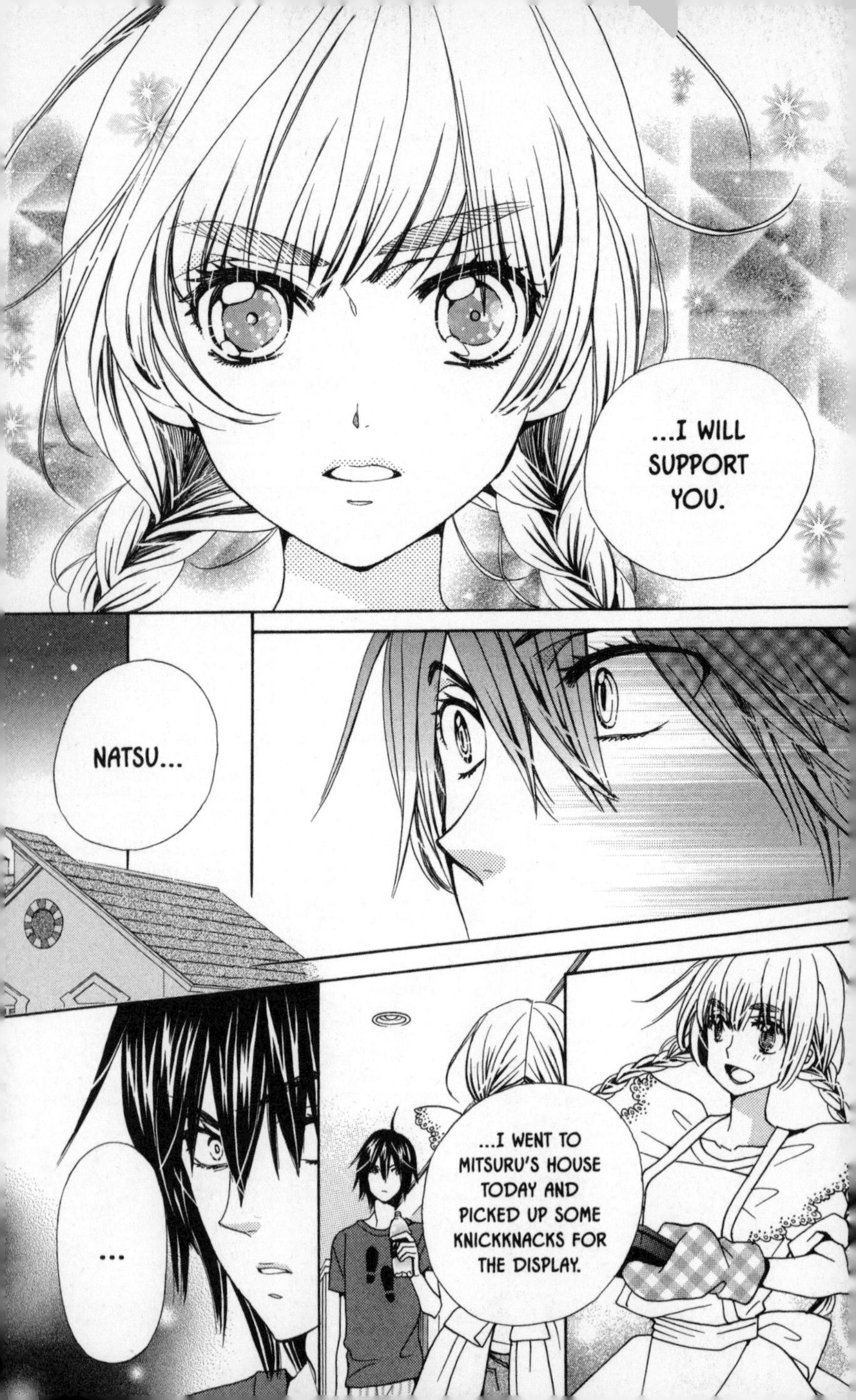
...I WILL SUPPORT YOU.
NATSU...
...I WENT TO MITSURU'S HOUSE TODAY AND PICKED UP SOME KNICKKNACKS FOR THE DISPLAY.
...

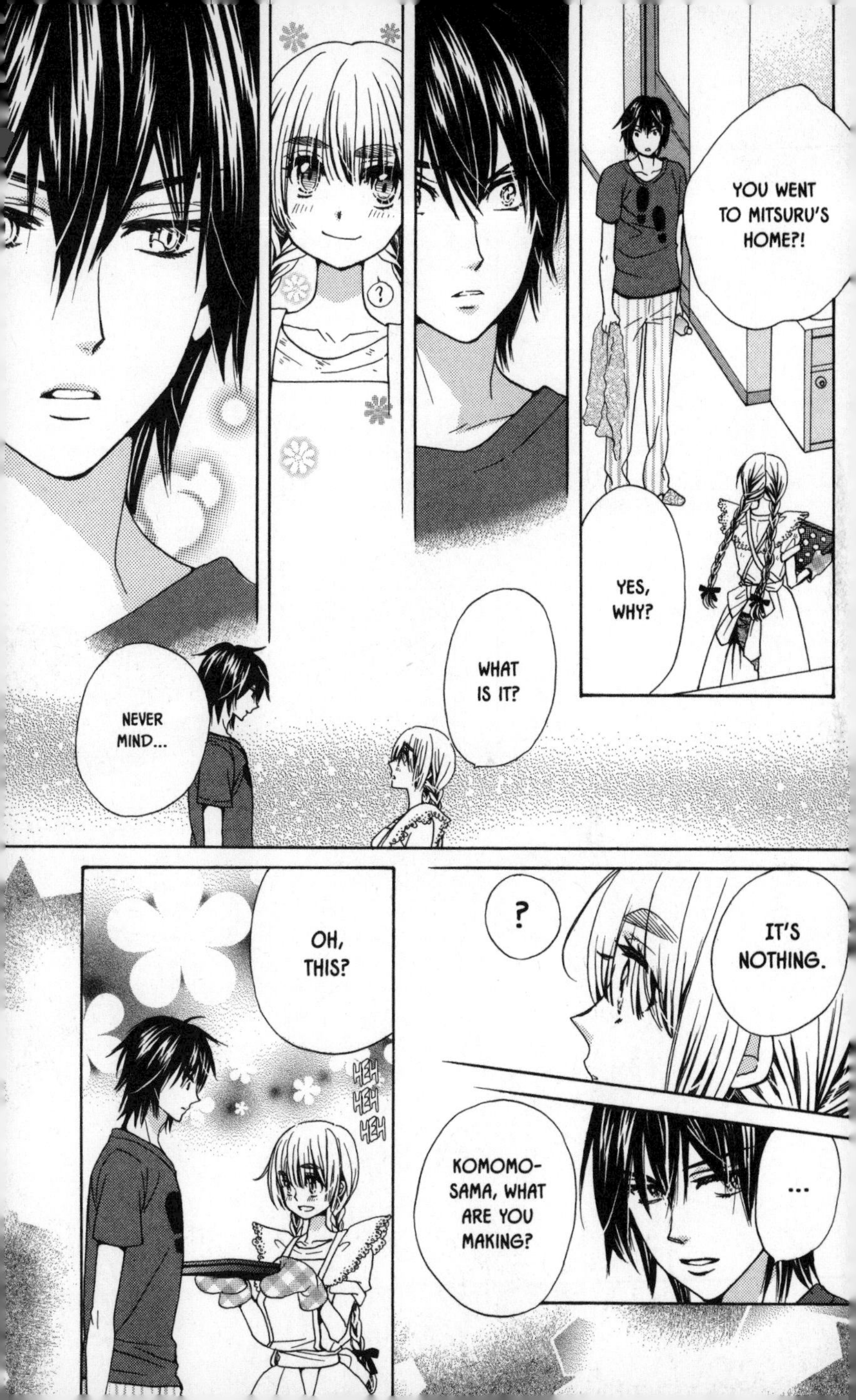
YOU WENT TO MITSURU'S HOME?!
YES, WHY?
?
WHAT IS IT?
NEVER MIND...
IT'S NOTHING.
?
...
KOMOMO-SAMA, WHAT ARE YOU MAKING?
OH, THIS?
HEH HEH HEH

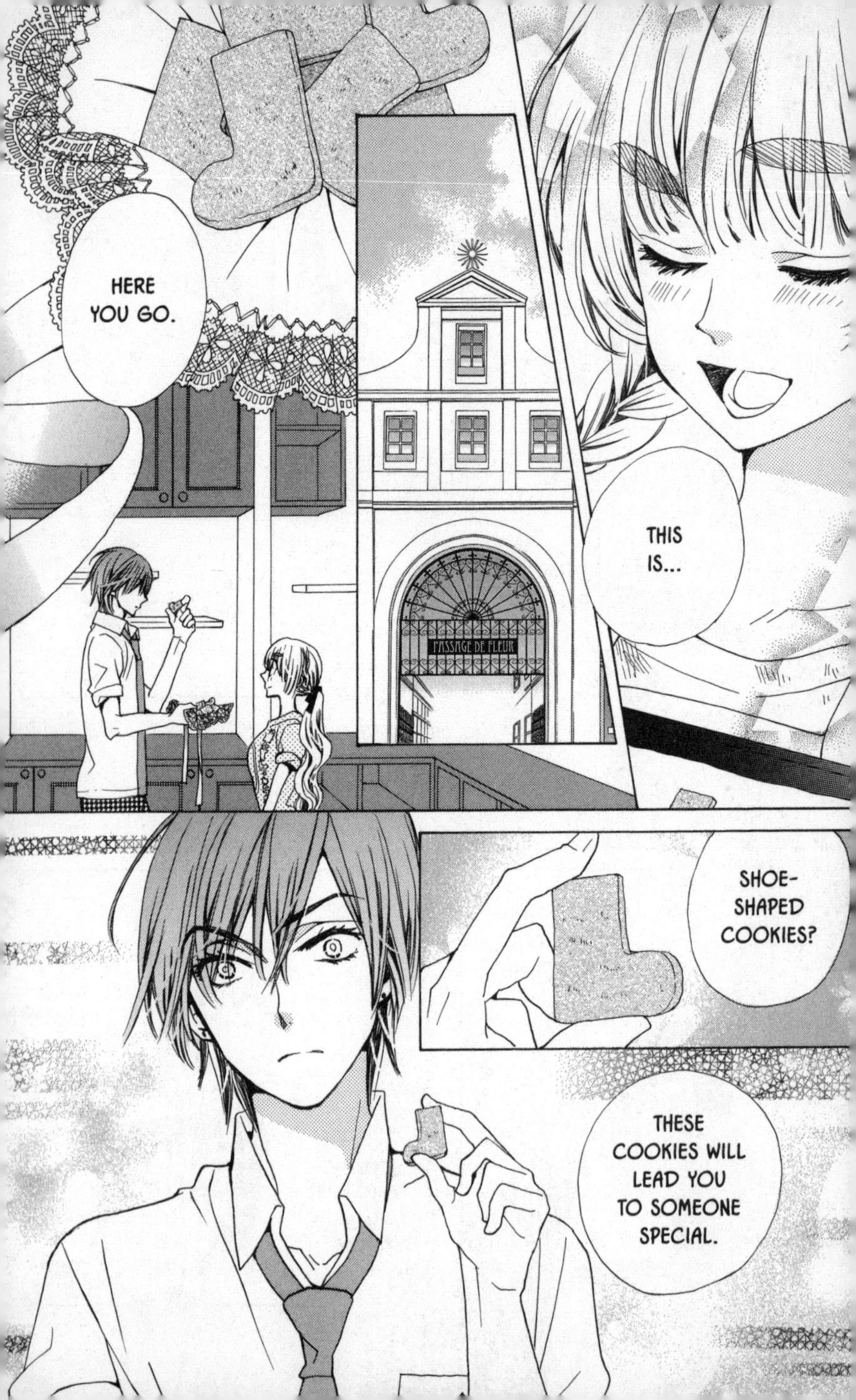
THIS IS...
PASSAGE DE FLEUR
HERE YOU GO.
SHOE-SHAPED COOKIES?
THESE COOKIES WILL LEAD YOU TO SOMEONE SPECIAL.

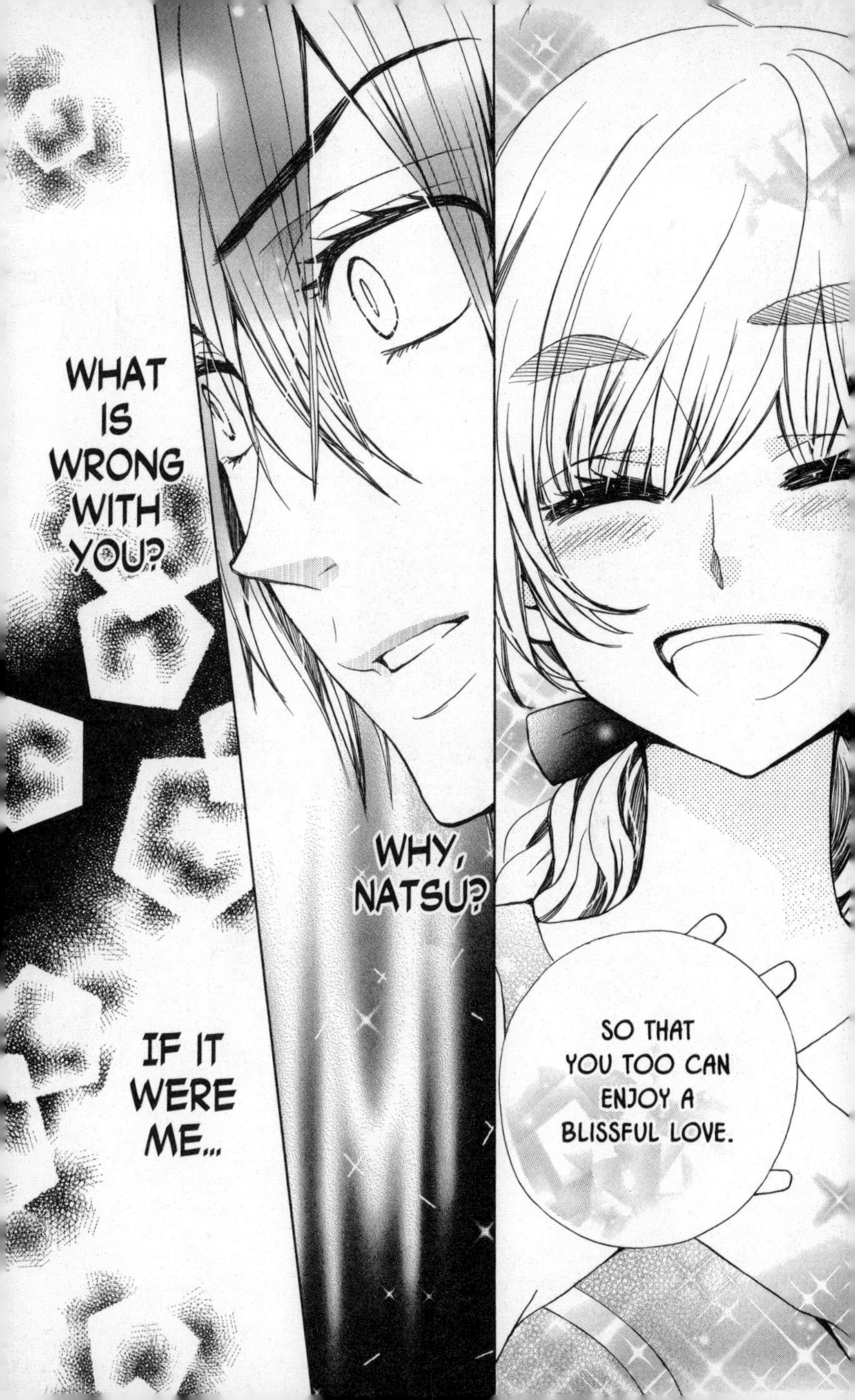
SO THAT YOU TOO CAN ENJOY A BLISSFUL LOVE.
WHY, NATSU?
WHAT IS WRONG WITH YOU?
IF IT WERE ME...

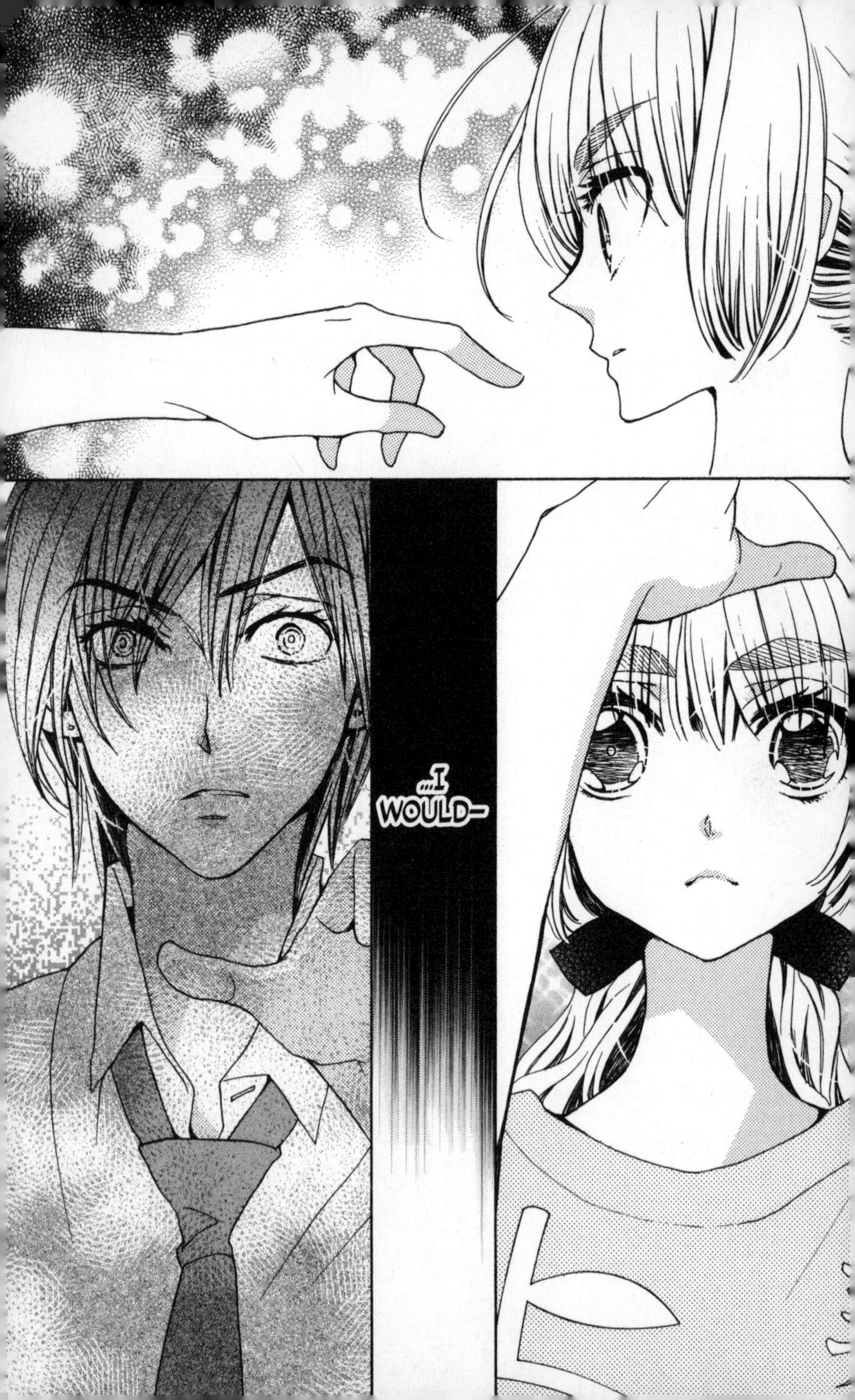
...I WOULD—

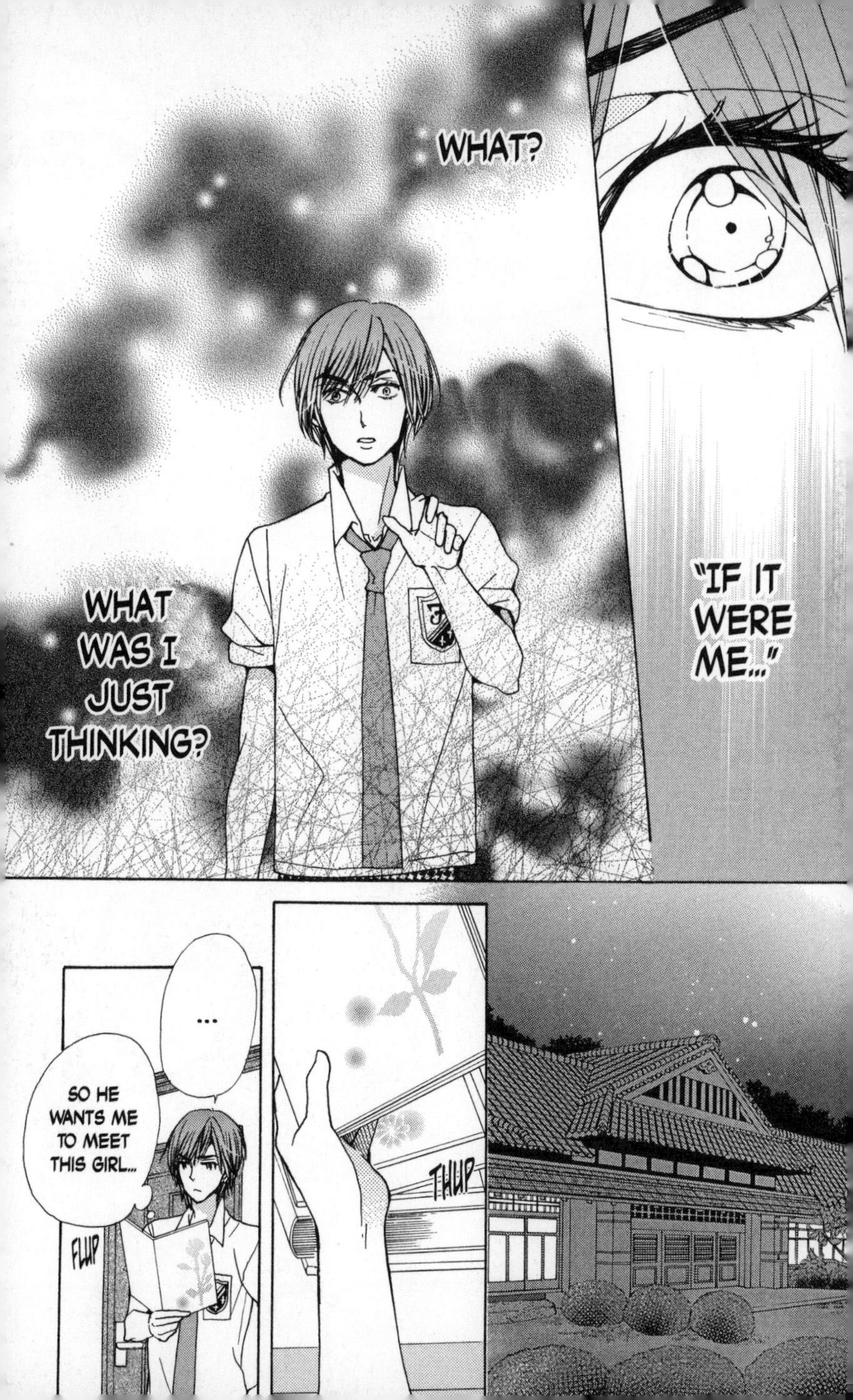
"IF IT WERE ME..."
WHAT?
WHAT WAS I JUST THINKING?
THUP
...
SO HE WANTS ME TO MEET THIS GIRL...
FLIP

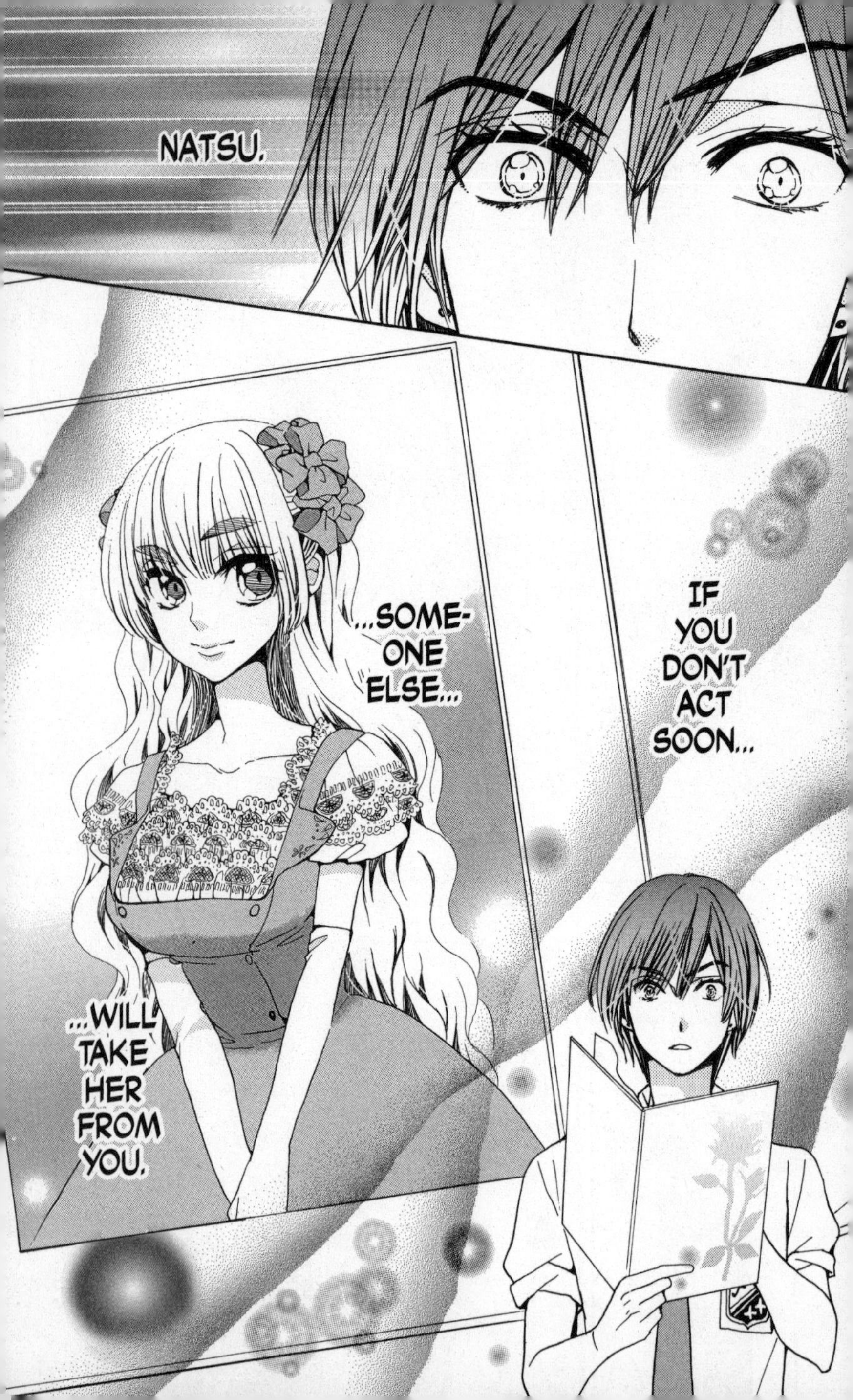
NATSU.
IF YOU DON'T ACT SOON...
...SOME-ONE ELSE...
...WILL TAKE HER FROM YOU.

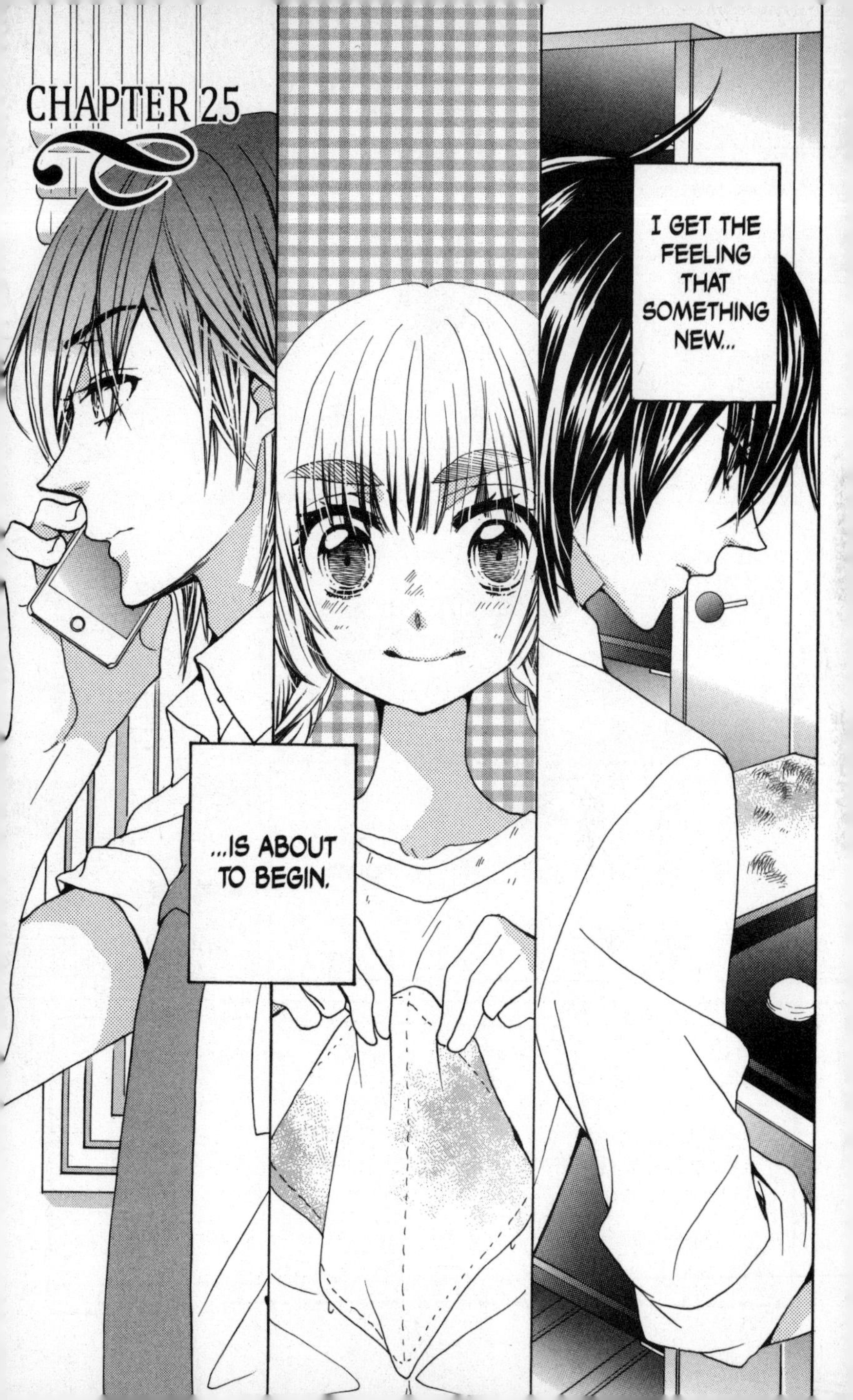
CHAPTER 25
I GET THE FEELING THAT SOMETHING NEW...
...IS ABOUT TO BEGIN.

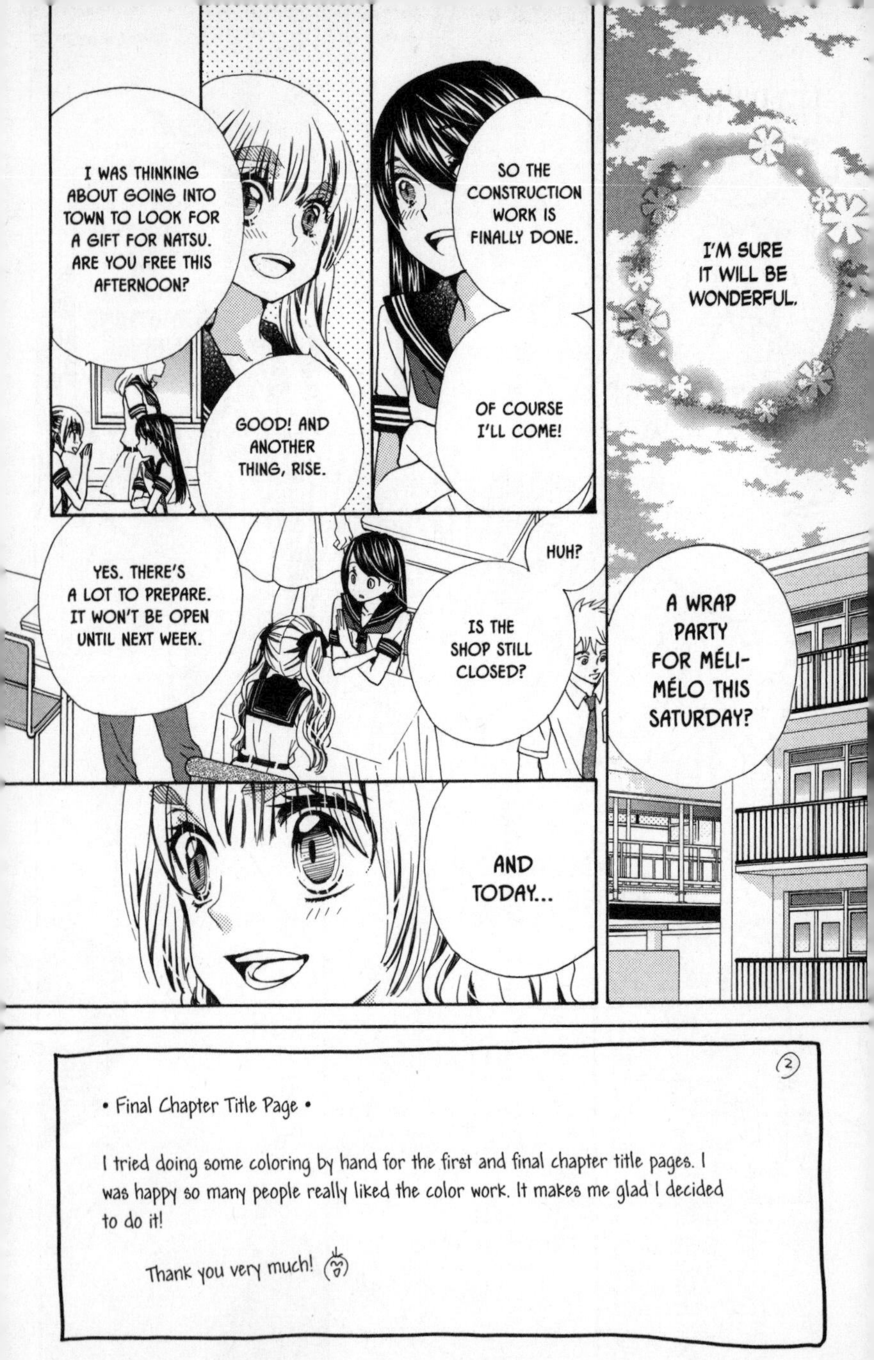
I'M SURE IT WILL BE WONDERFUL.
A WRAP PARTY FOR MÉLI-MÉLO THIS SATURDAY?
SO THE CONSTRUCTION WORK IS FINALLY DONE.
OF COURSE I'LL COME!
I WAS THINKING ABOUT GOING INTO TOWN TO LOOK FOR A GIFT FOR NATSU. ARE YOU FREE THIS AFTERNOON?
GOOD! AND ANOTHER THING, RISE.
HUH?
IS THE SHOP STILL CLOSED?
YES. THERE'S A LOT TO PREPARE. IT WON'T BE OPEN UNTIL NEXT WEEK.
AND TODAY...

(2)

• Final Chapter Title Page •

I tried doing some coloring by hand for the first and final chapter title pages. I was happy so many people really liked the color work. It makes me glad I decided to do it!

Thank you very much!

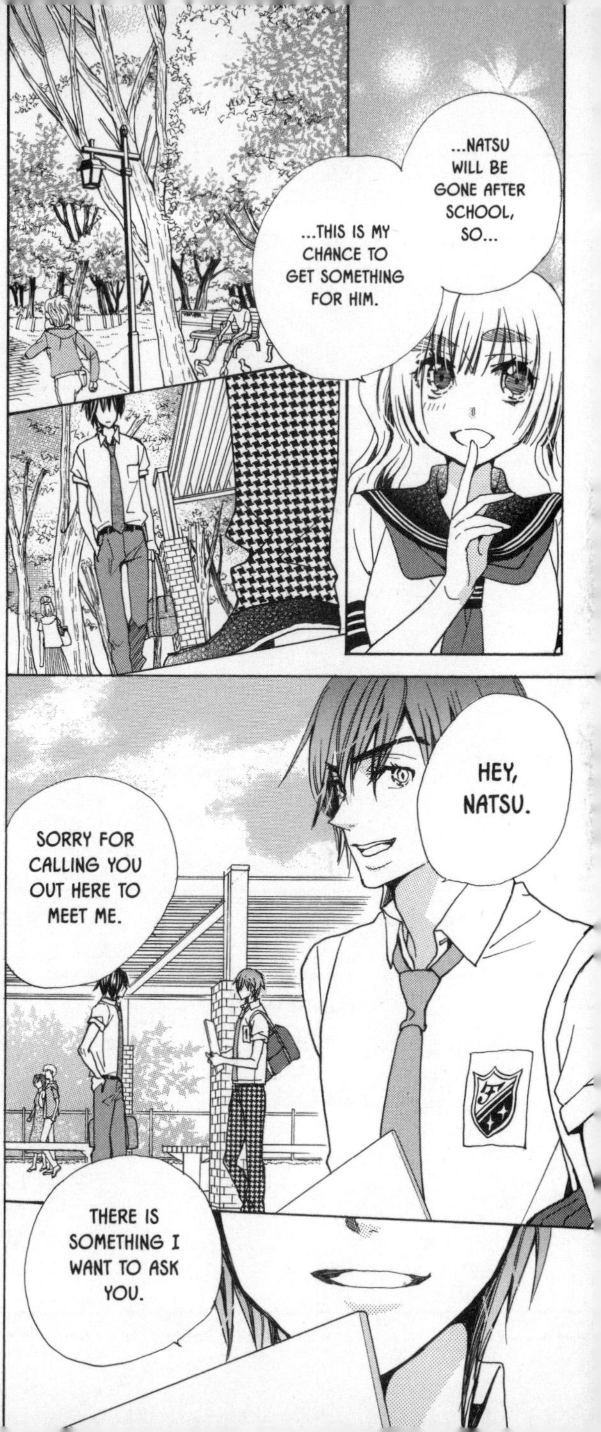
...NATSU WILL BE GONE AFTER SCHOOL, SO...
...THIS IS MY CHANCE TO GET SOMETHING FOR HIM.
HEY, NATSU.
SORRY FOR CALLING YOU OUT HERE TO MEET ME.
THERE IS SOMETHING I WANT TO ASK YOU.

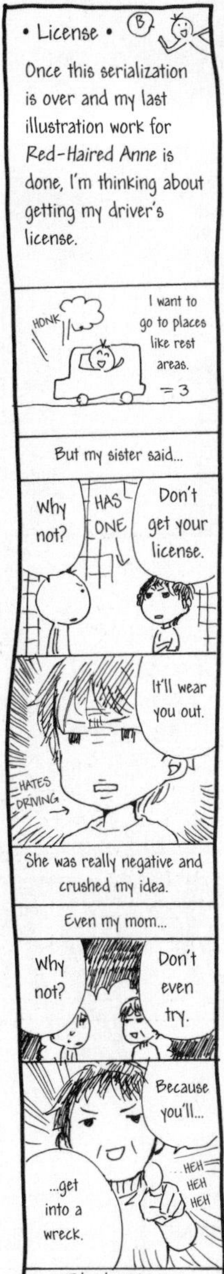
• License • B
Once this serialization is over and my last illustration work for Red-Haired Anne is done, I'm thinking about getting my driver's license.
HONK
I want to go to places like rest areas.
=3
But my sister said...
Don't get your license.
HAS ONE
Why not?
It'll wear you out.
HATES DRIVING
She was really negative and crushed my idea.
Even my mom...
Don't even try.
Why not?
Because you'll...
HEH HEH HEH
...get into a wreck.
Talk about jinxing someone!!!

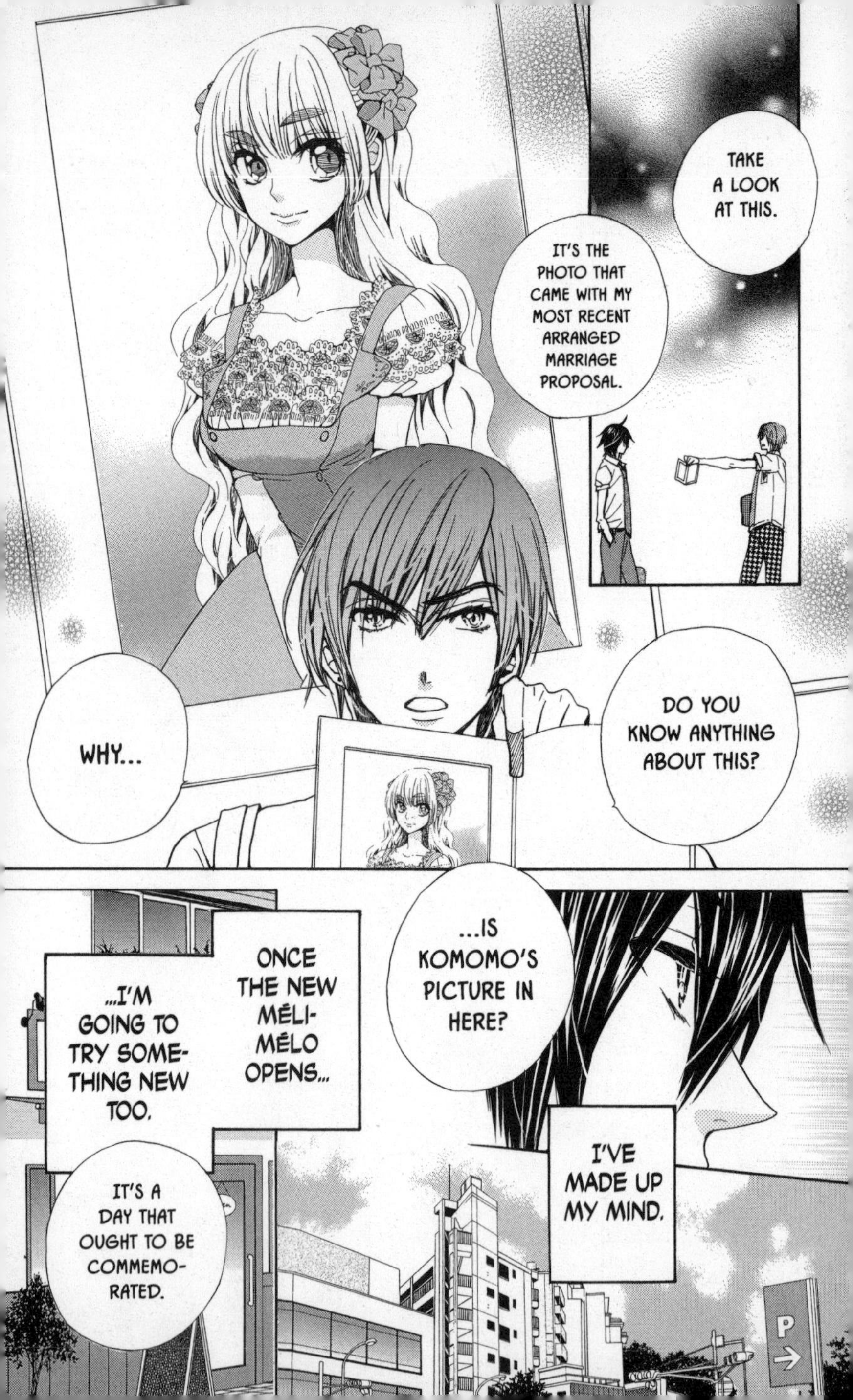
TAKE A LOOK AT THIS.
IT'S THE PHOTO THAT CAME WITH MY MOST RECENT ARRANGED MARRIAGE PROPOSAL.
DO YOU KNOW ANYTHING ABOUT THIS?
WHY...
...IS KOMOMO'S PICTURE IN HERE?
I'VE MADE UP MY MIND.
ONCE THE NEW MÉLI-MÉLO OPENS...
...I'M GOING TO TRY SOME-THING NEW TOO.
IT'S A DAY THAT OUGHT TO BE COMMEMO-RATED.
P

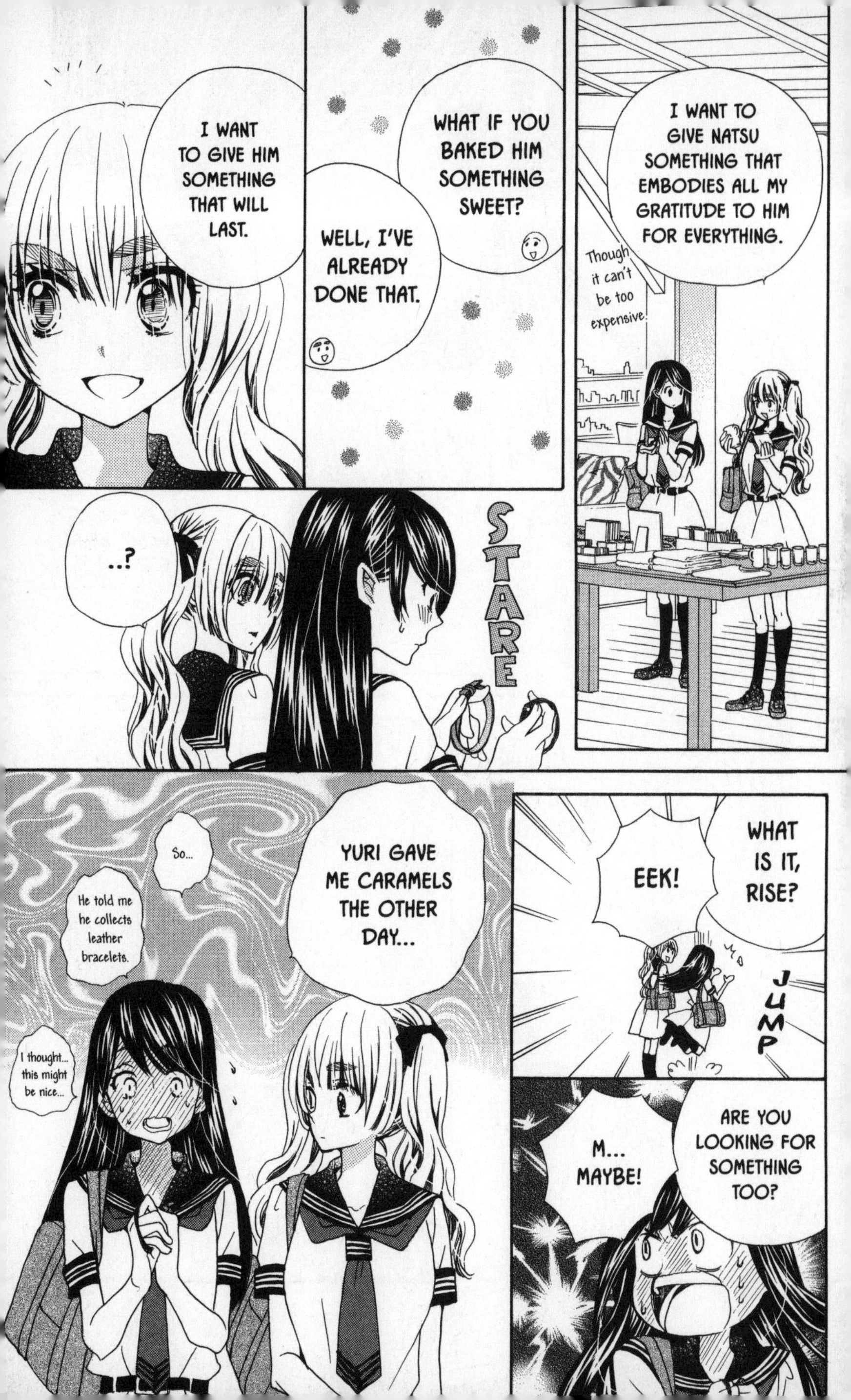
I WANT TO GIVE NATSU SOMETHING THAT EMBODIES ALL MY GRATITUDE TO HIM FOR EVERYTHING.
Though it can't be too expensive.
WHAT IF YOU BAKED HIM SOMETHING SWEET?
WELL, I'VE ALREADY DONE THAT.
I WANT TO GIVE HIM SOMETHING THAT WILL LAST.
STARE
..?
WHAT IS IT, RISE?
EEK!
JUMP
ARE YOU LOOKING FOR SOMETHING TOO?
M... MAYBE!
YURI GAVE ME CARAMELS THE OTHER DAY...
So...
He told me he collects leather bracelets.
I thought... this might be nice...

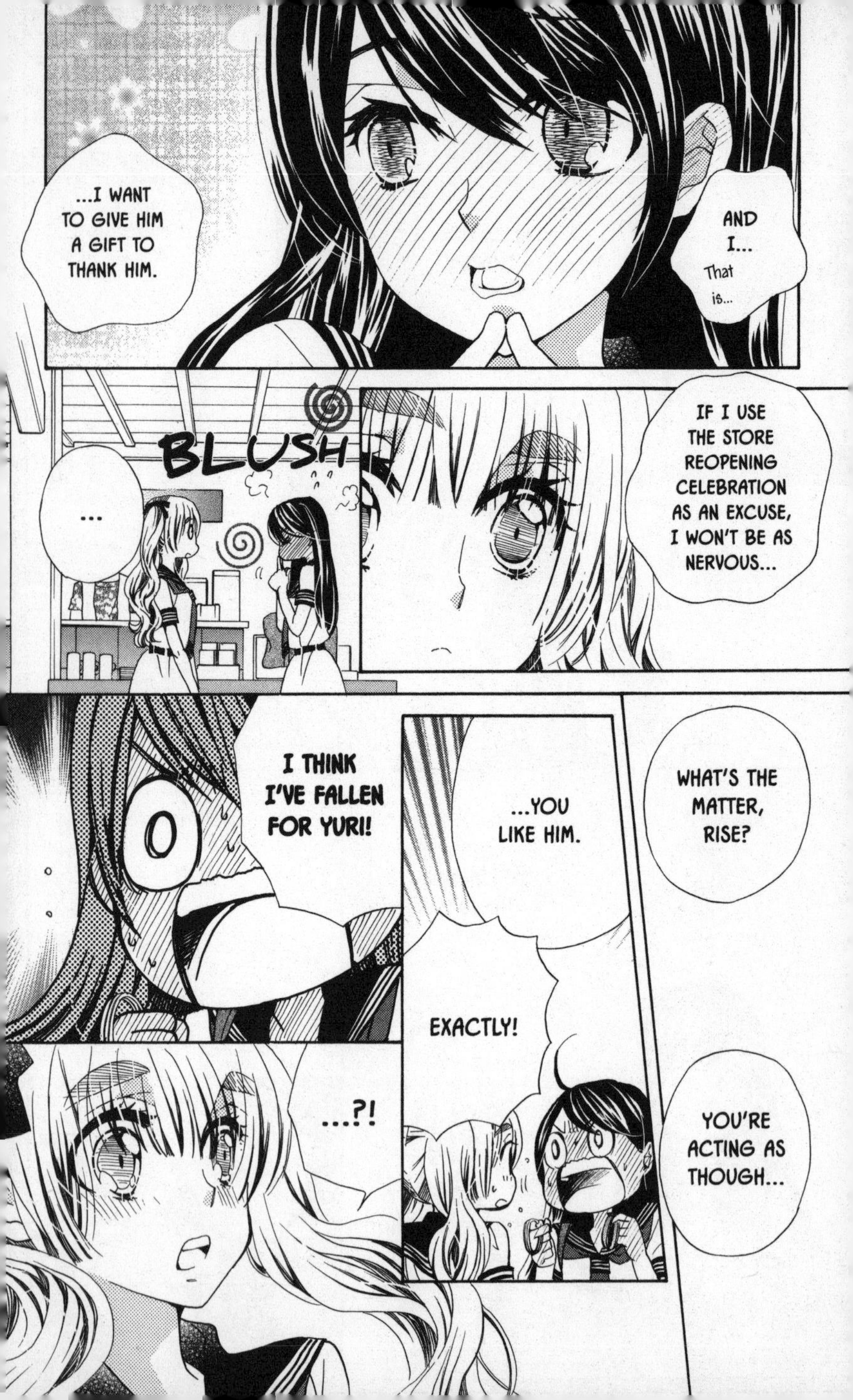
AND I...
That is...
...I WANT TO GIVE HIM A GIFT TO THANK HIM.
IF I USE THE STORE REOPENING CELEBRATION AS AN EXCUSE, I WON'T BE AS NERVOUS...
BLUSH
...
WHAT'S THE MATTER, RISE?
YOU'RE ACTING AS THOUGH...
...YOU LIKE HIM.
EXACTLY!
I THINK I'VE FALLEN FOR YURI!
...?!

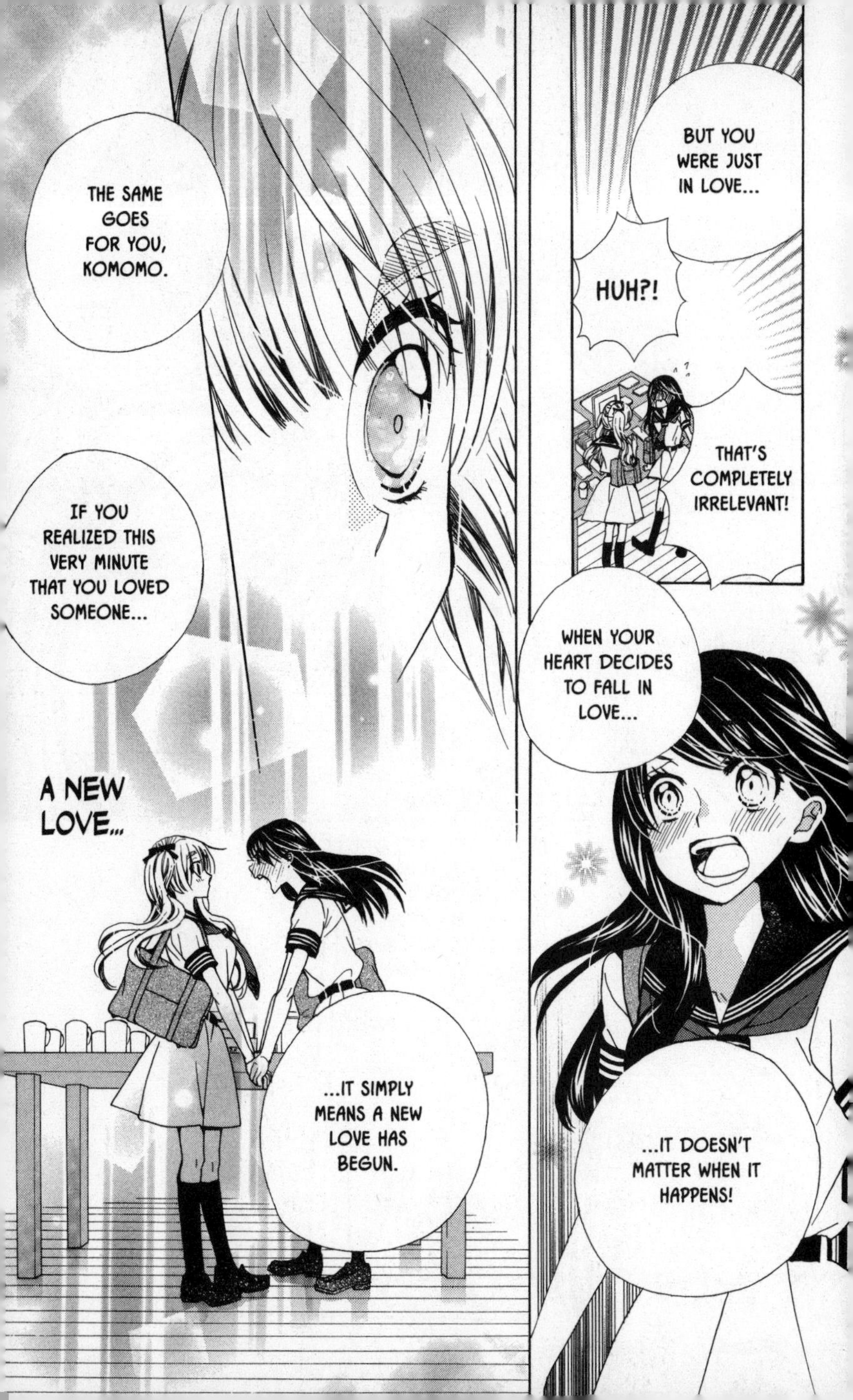
BUT YOU WERE JUST IN LOVE...
HUH?!
THAT'S COMPLETELY IRRELEVANT!
WHEN YOUR HEART DECIDES TO FALL IN LOVE...
...IT DOESN'T MATTER WHEN IT HAPPENS!
THE SAME GOES FOR YOU, KOMOMO.
IF YOU REALIZED THIS VERY MINUTE THAT YOU LOVED SOMEONE...
A NEW LOVE...
...IT SIMPLY MEANS A NEW LOVE HAS BEGUN.

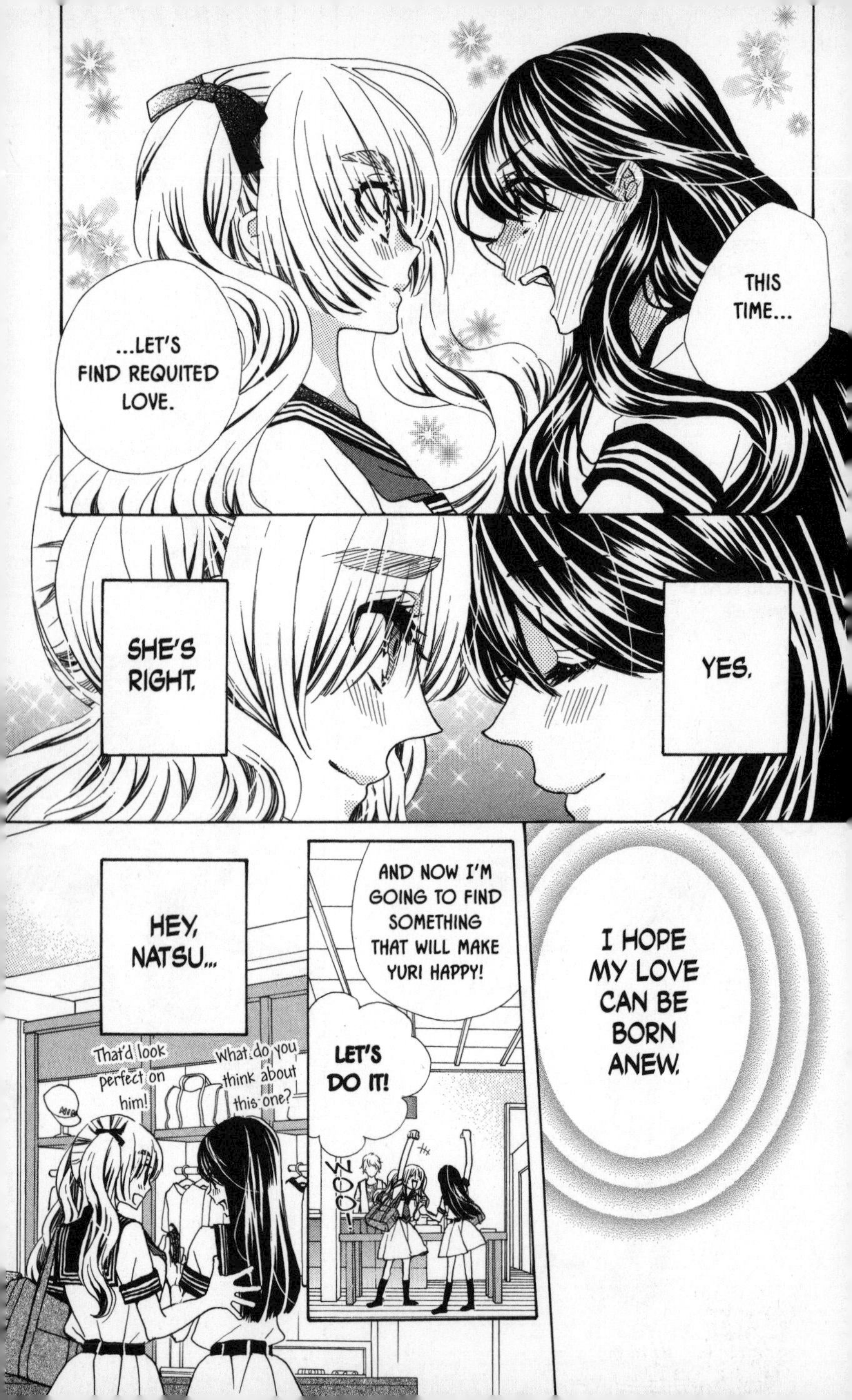
THIS TIME...
...LET'S FIND REQUITED LOVE.
YES.
SHE'S RIGHT.
I HOPE MY LOVE CAN BE BORN ANEW.
AND NOW I'M GOING TO FIND SOMETHING THAT WILL MAKE YURI HAPPY!
LET'S DO IT!
WOO!
HEY, NATSU...
What do you think about this one?
That'd look perfect on him!

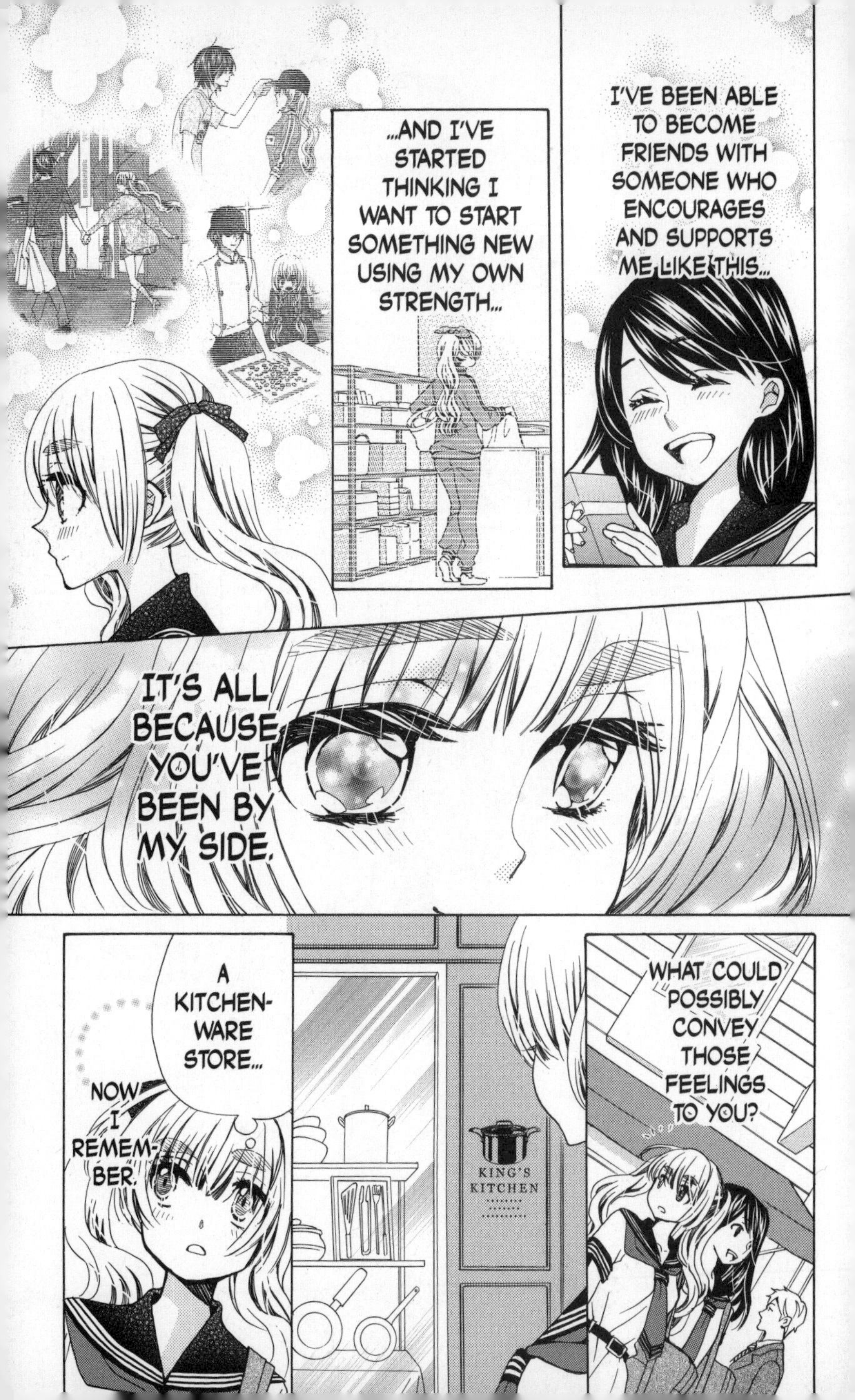
I'VE BEEN ABLE TO BECOME FRIENDS WITH SOMEONE WHO ENCOURAGES AND SUPPORTS ME LIKE THIS...
...AND I'VE STARTED THINKING I WANT TO START SOMETHING NEW USING MY OWN STRENGTH...
IT'S ALL BECAUSE YOU'VE BEEN BY MY SIDE.
WHAT COULD POSSIBLY CONVEY THOSE FEELINGS TO YOU?
KING'S KITCHEN
A KITCHEN-WARE STORE...
NOW I REMEMBER.

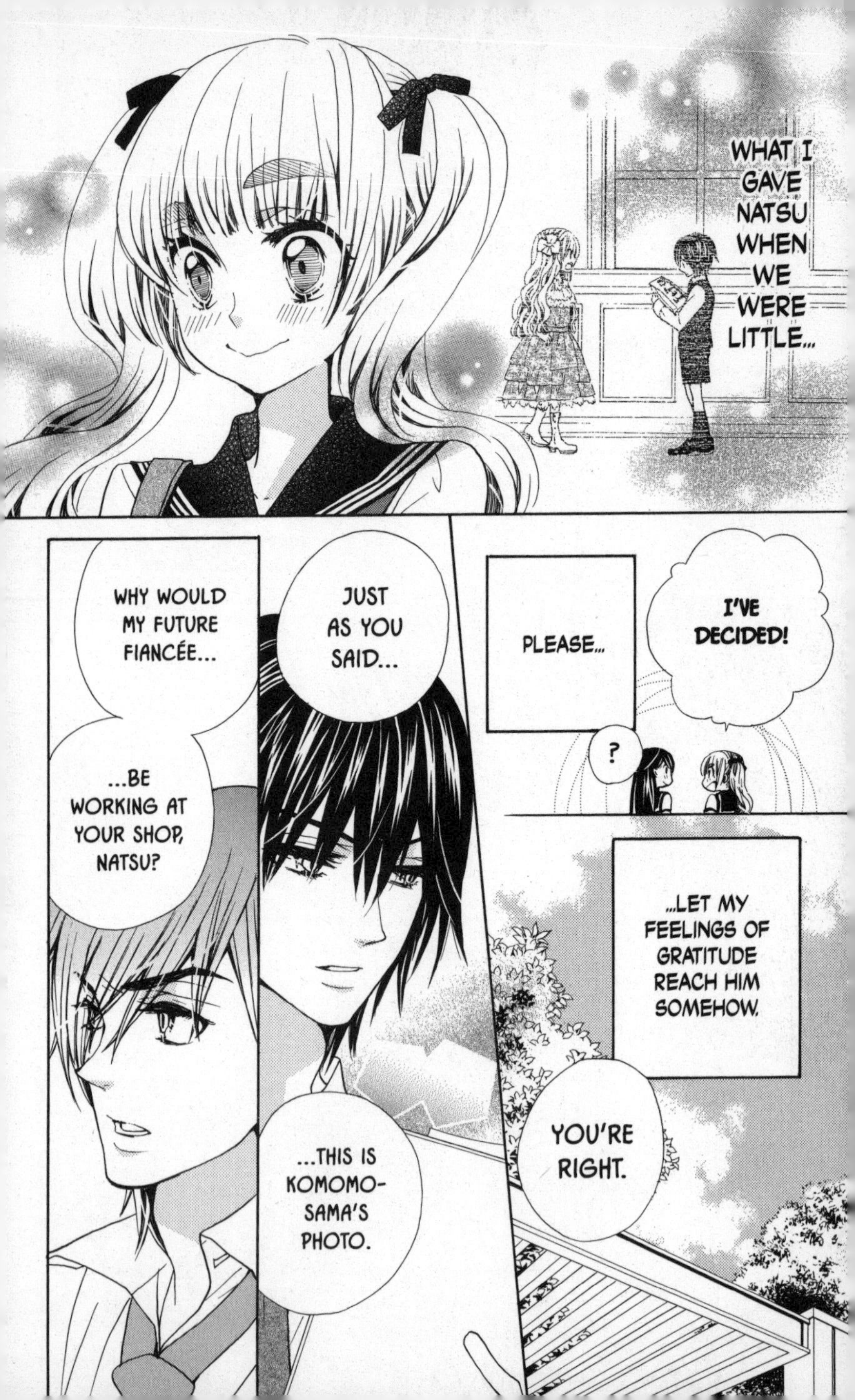
WHAT I GAVE NATSU WHEN WE WERE LITTLE...
I'VE DECIDED!
?
PLEASE...
...LET MY FEELINGS OF GRATITUDE REACH HIM SOMEHOW.
YOU'RE RIGHT.
JUST AS YOU SAID...
...THIS IS KOMOMO-SAMA'S PHOTO.
WHY WOULD MY FUTURE FIANCÉE...
...BE WORKING AT YOUR SHOP, NATSU?

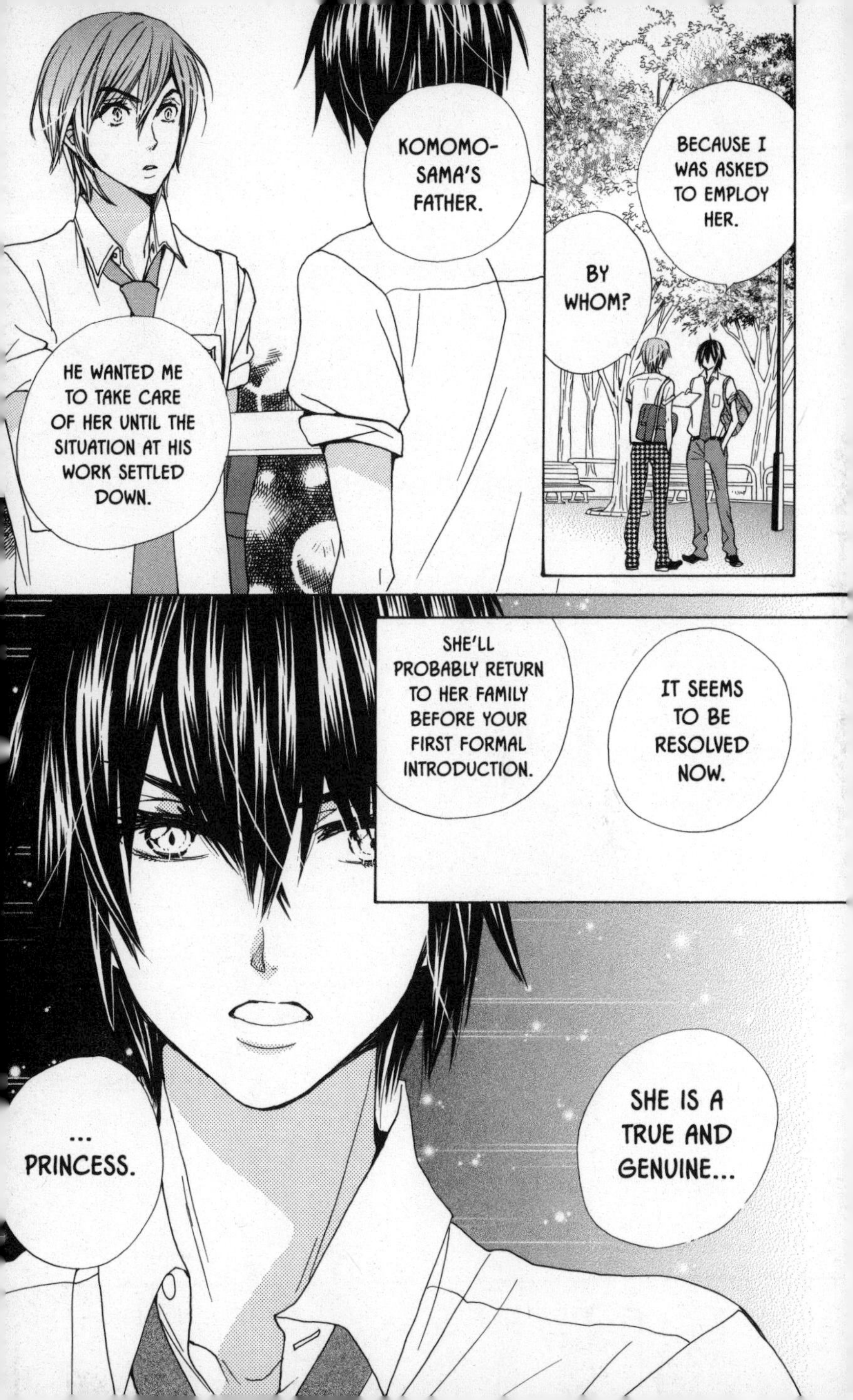
BECAUSE I WAS ASKED TO EMPLOY HER.
BY WHOM?
KOMOMO-SAMA'S FATHER.
HE WANTED ME TO TAKE CARE OF HER UNTIL THE SITUATION AT HIS WORK SETTLED DOWN.
IT SEEMS TO BE RESOLVED NOW.
SHE'LL PROBABLY RETURN TO HER FAMILY BEFORE YOUR FIRST FORMAL INTRODUCTION.
SHE IS A TRUE AND GENUINE...
...PRINCESS.

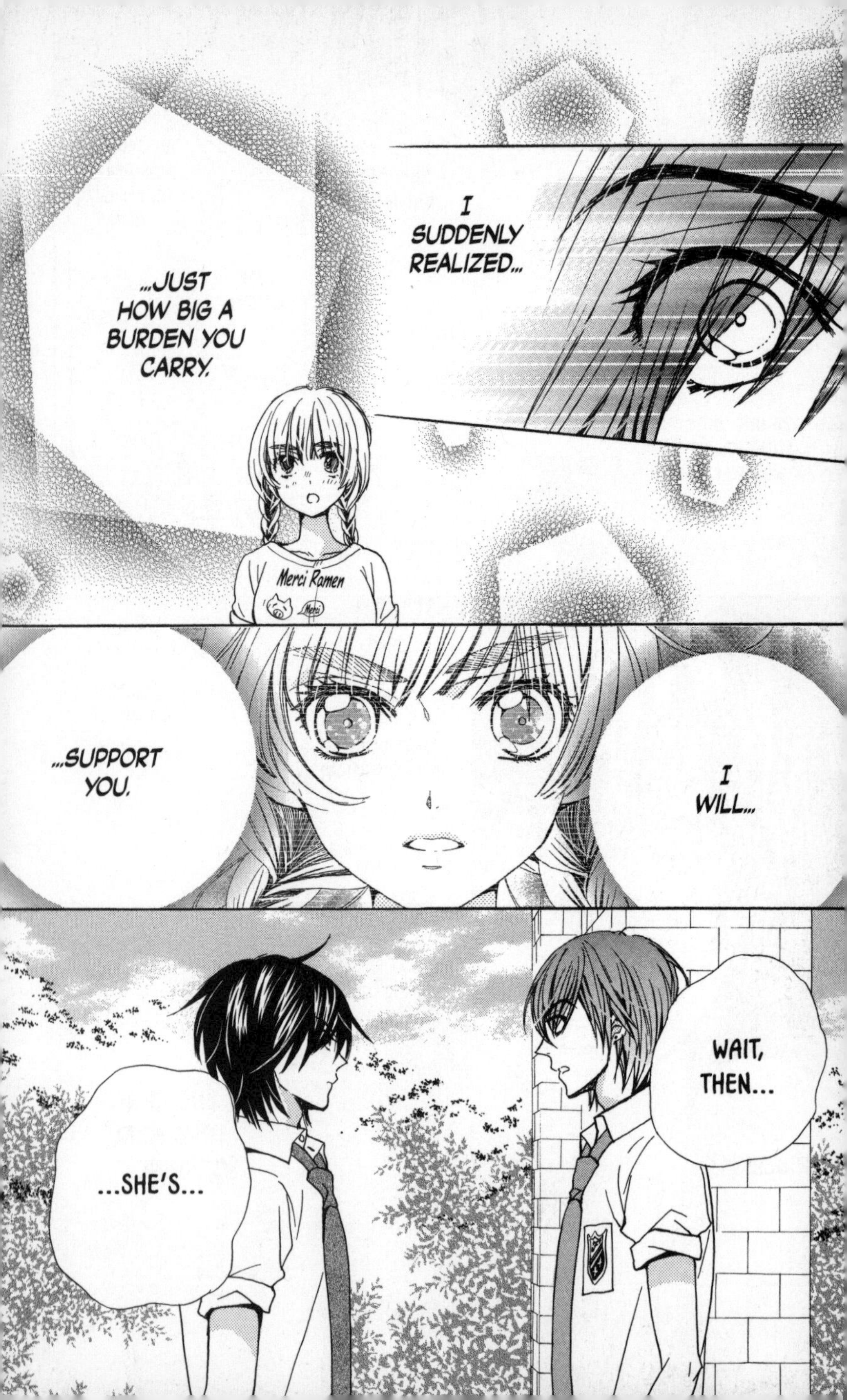
I SUDDENLY REALIZED...
...JUST HOW BIG A BURDEN YOU CARRY.
Merci Ramen
Merci
I WILL...
...SUPPORT YOU.
WAIT, THEN...
...SHE'S...

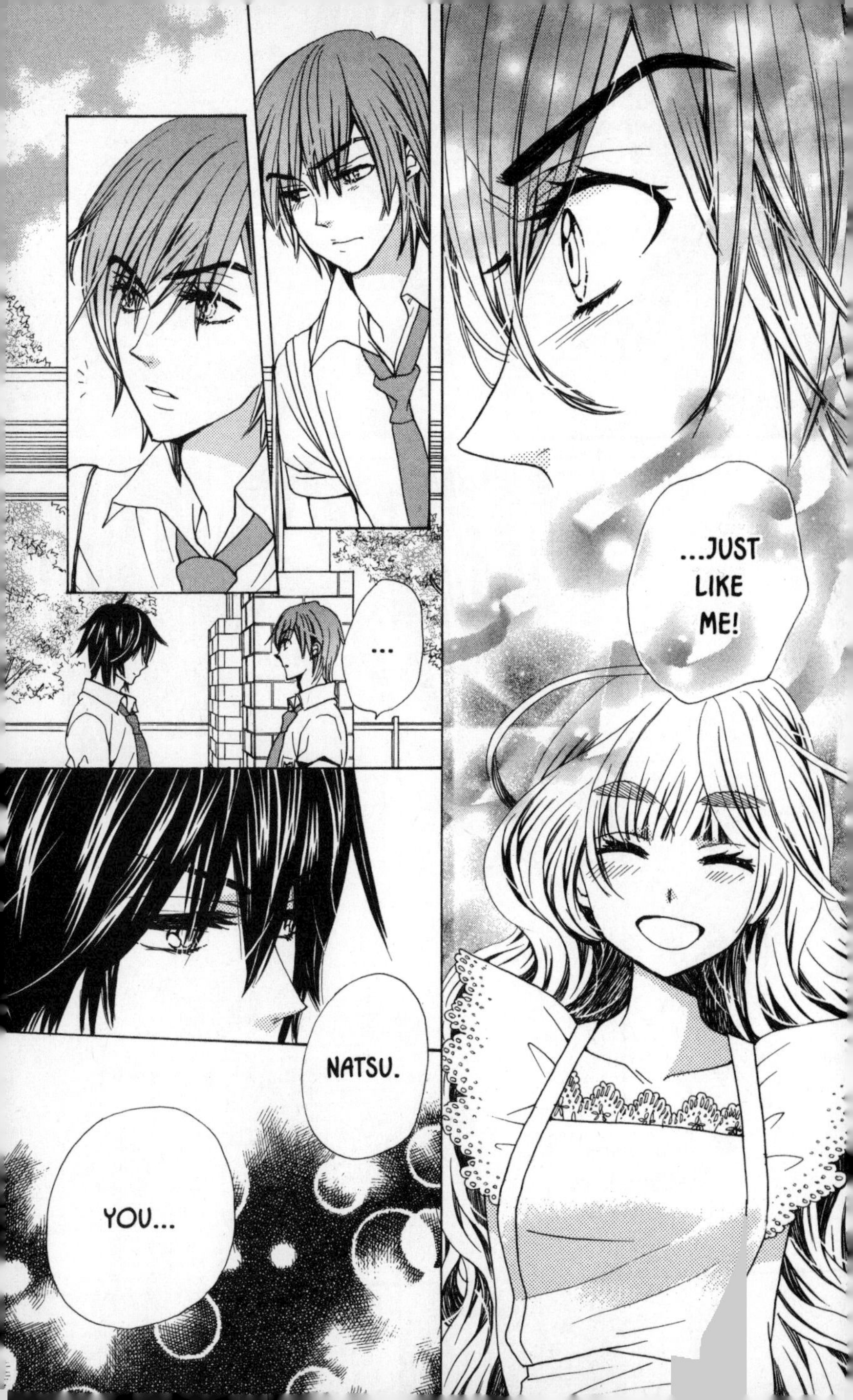
...JUST LIKE ME!
...
NATSU.
YOU...

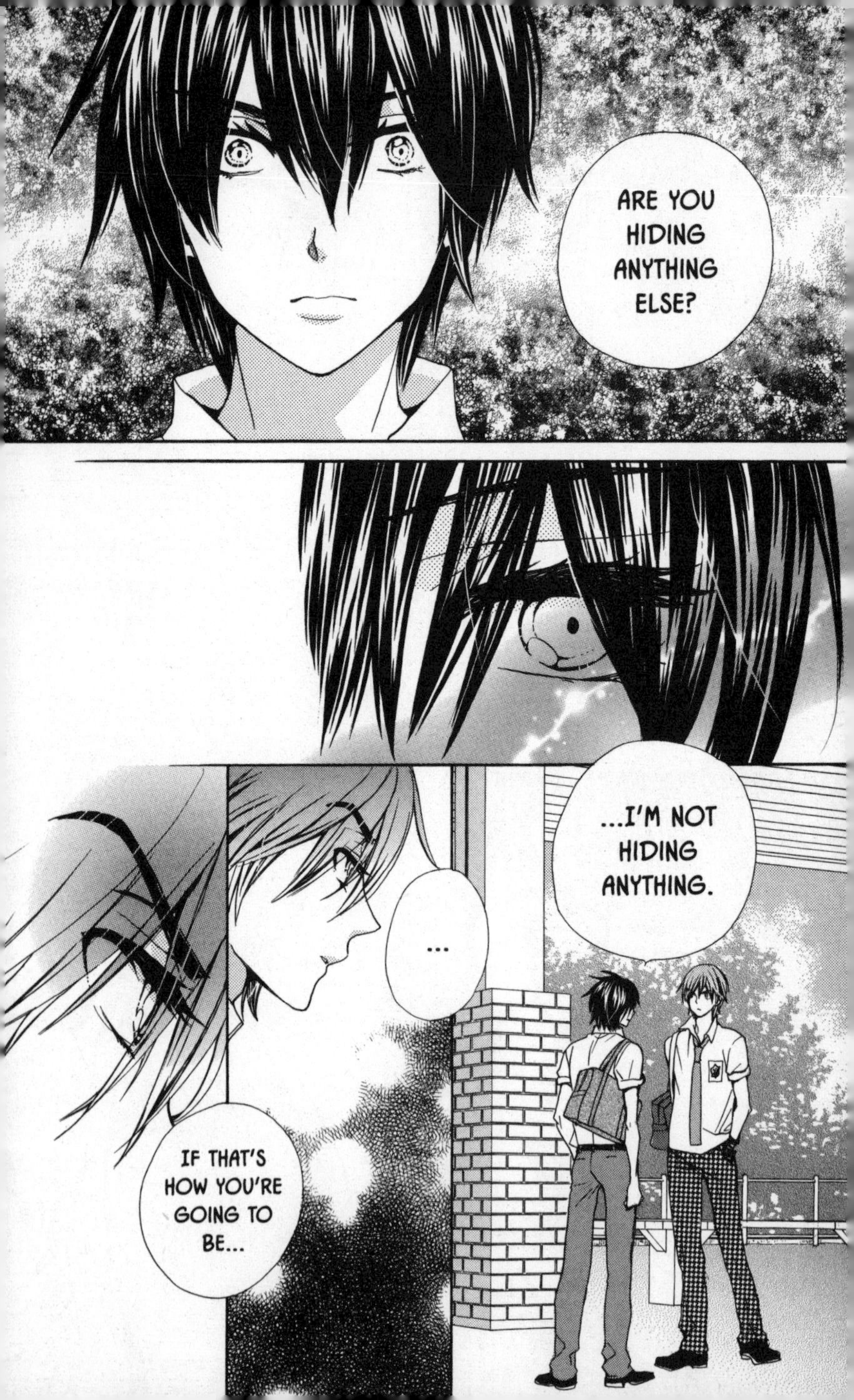
ARE YOU HIDING ANYTHING ELSE?
...I'M NOT HIDING ANYTHING.
...
IF THAT'S HOW YOU'RE GOING TO BE...

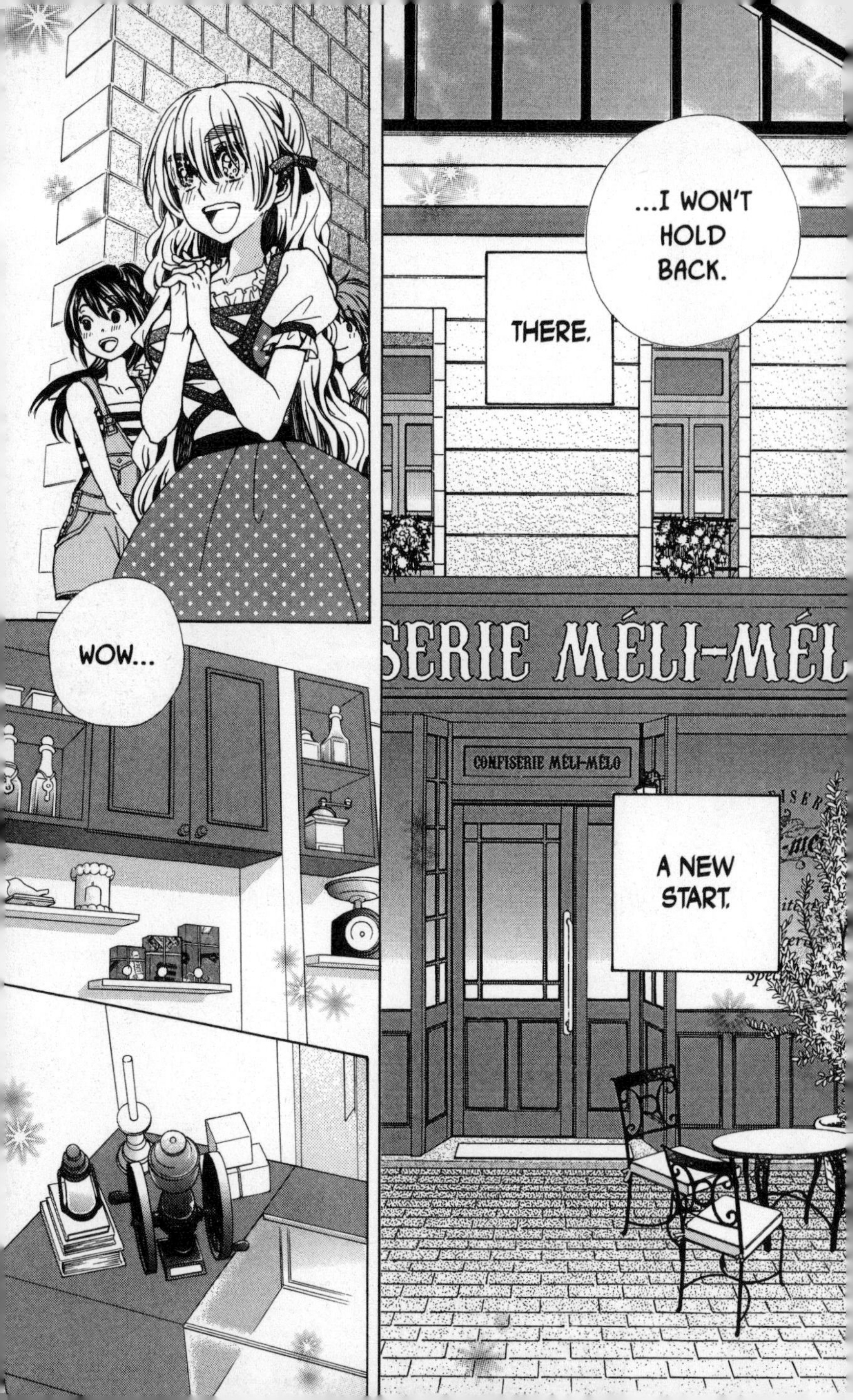
...I WON'T HOLD BACK.
THERE.
SERIE MÉLI-MÉL
CONFISERIE MÉLI-MÉLO
A NEW START.
WOW...

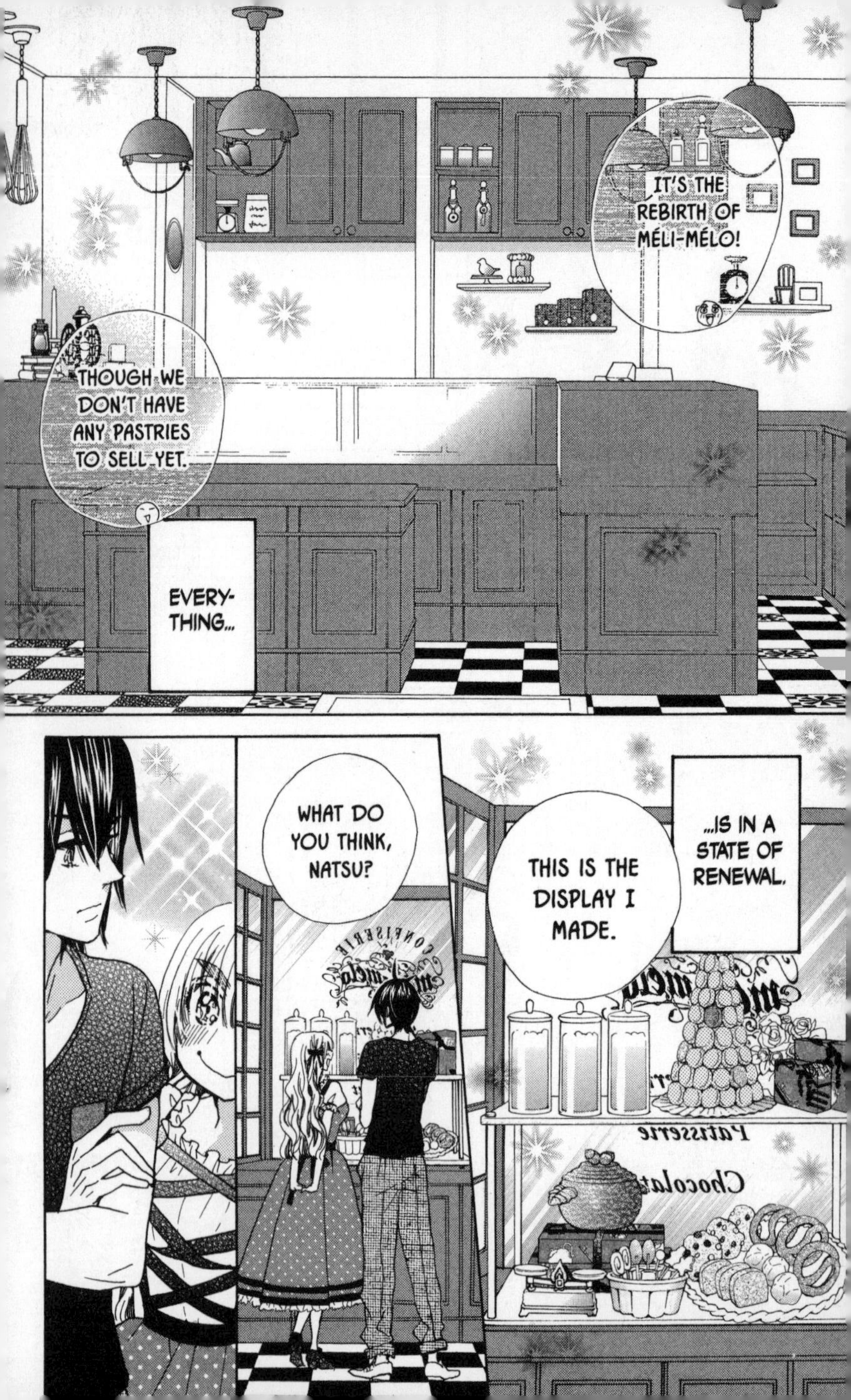
IT'S THE REBIRTH OF MÉLI-MÉLO!
THOUGH WE DON'T HAVE ANY PASTRIES TO SELL YET.
EVERY-THING...
...IS IN A STATE OF RENEWAL.
THIS IS THE DISPLAY I MADE.
WHAT DO YOU THINK, NATSU?

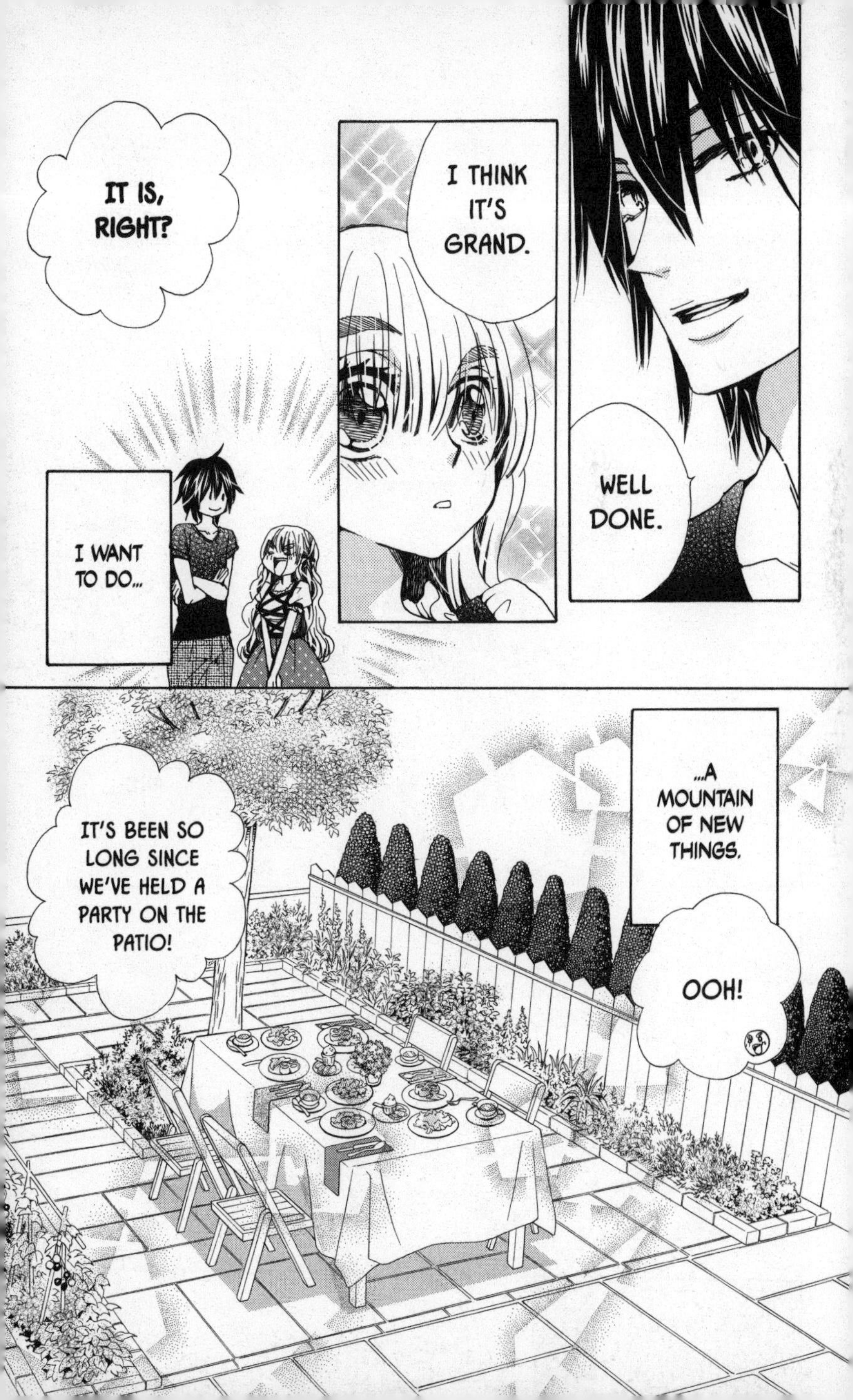
WELL DONE.
I THINK IT'S GRAND.
IT IS, RIGHT?
I WANT TO DO...
...A MOUNTAIN OF NEW THINGS.
OOH!
IT'S BEEN SO LONG SINCE WE'VE HELD A PARTY ON THE PATIO!

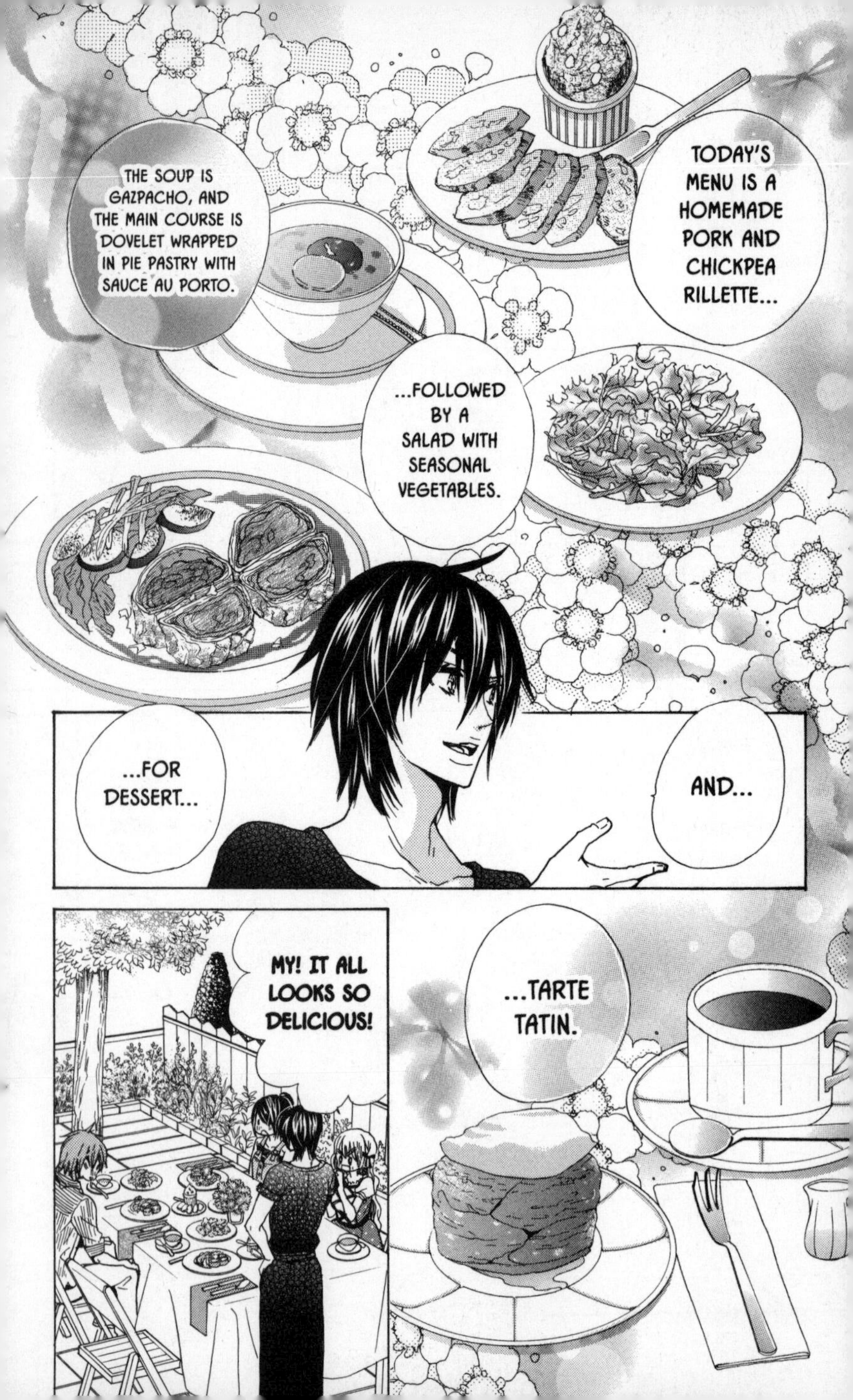
TODAY'S MENU IS A HOMEMADE PORK AND CHICKPEA RILLETTE...
THE SOUP IS GAZPACHO, AND THE MAIN COURSE IS DOVELET WRAPPED IN PIE PASTRY WITH SAUCE AU PORTO.
...FOLLOWED BY A SALAD WITH SEASONAL VEGETABLES.
AND...
...FOR DESSERT...
...TARTE TATIN.
MY! IT ALL LOOKS SO DELICIOUS!

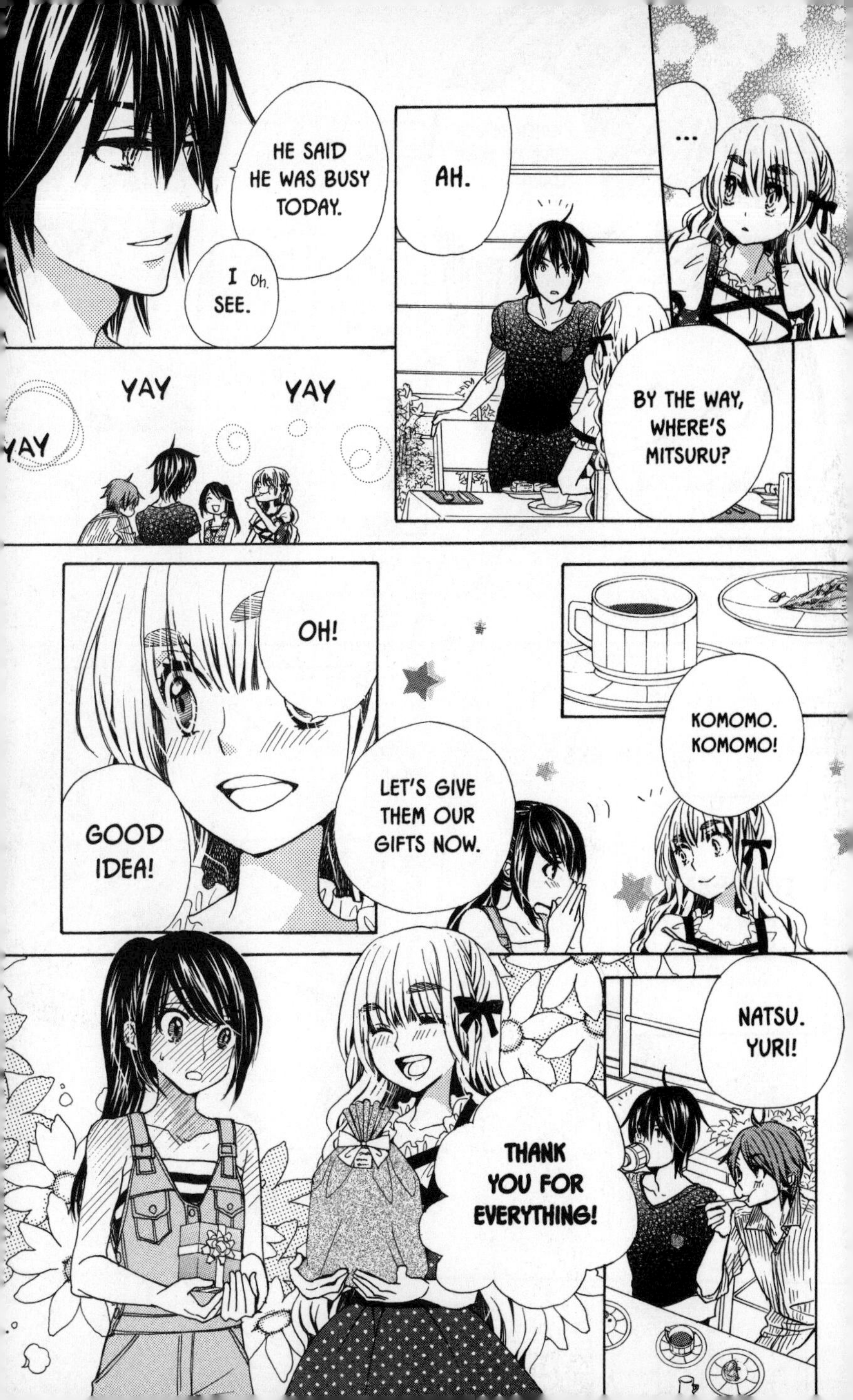
...
AH.
BY THE WAY, WHERE'S MITSURU?
HE SAID HE WAS BUSY TODAY.
I SEE.
Oh.
YAY
YAY
YAY
KOMOMO. KOMOMO!
LET'S GIVE THEM OUR GIFTS NOW.
OH!
GOOD IDEA!
NATSU. YURI!
THANK YOU FOR EVERYTHING!

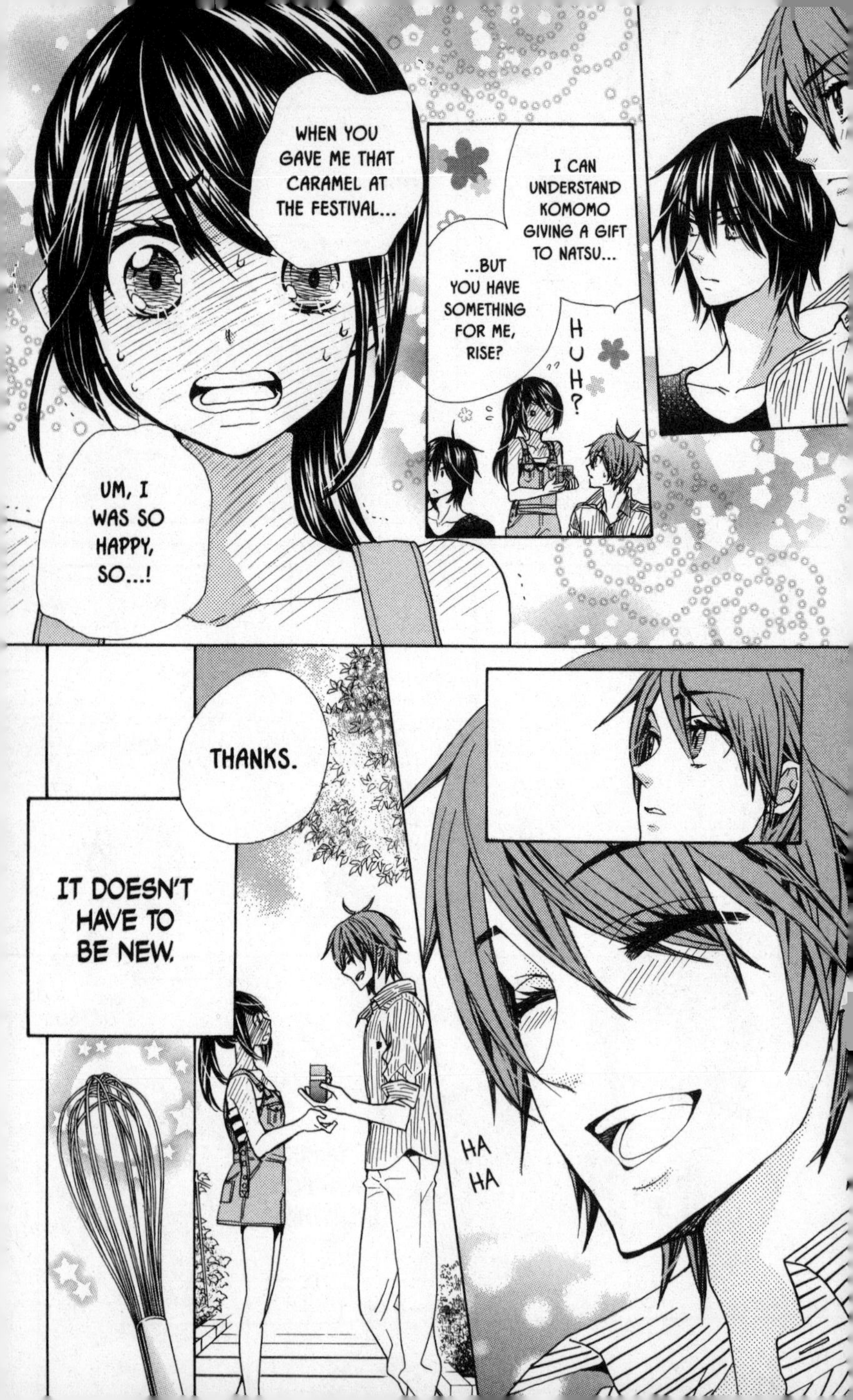
I CAN UNDERSTAND KOMOMO GIVING A GIFT TO NATSU...
...BUT YOU HAVE SOMETHING FOR ME, RISE?
HUH?
WHEN YOU GAVE ME THAT CARAMEL AT THE FESTIVAL...
UM, I WAS SO HAPPY, SO...!
HA HA
THANKS.
IT DOESN'T HAVE TO BE NEW.

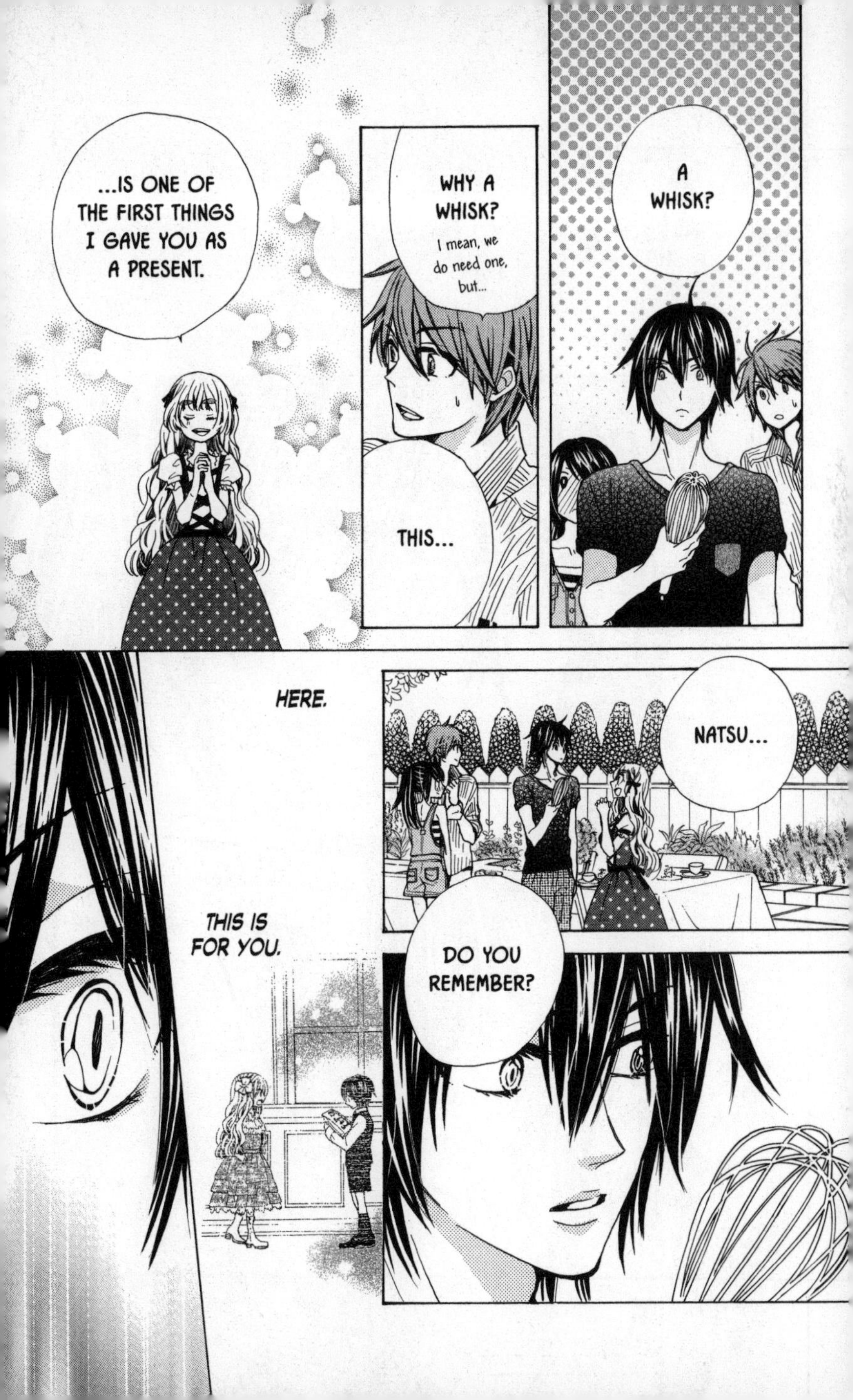
A WHISK?
WHY A WHISK?
I mean, we do need one, but...
THIS...
...IS ONE OF THE FIRST THINGS I GAVE YOU AS A PRESENT.
NATSU...
DO YOU REMEMBER?
HERE.
THIS IS FOR YOU.

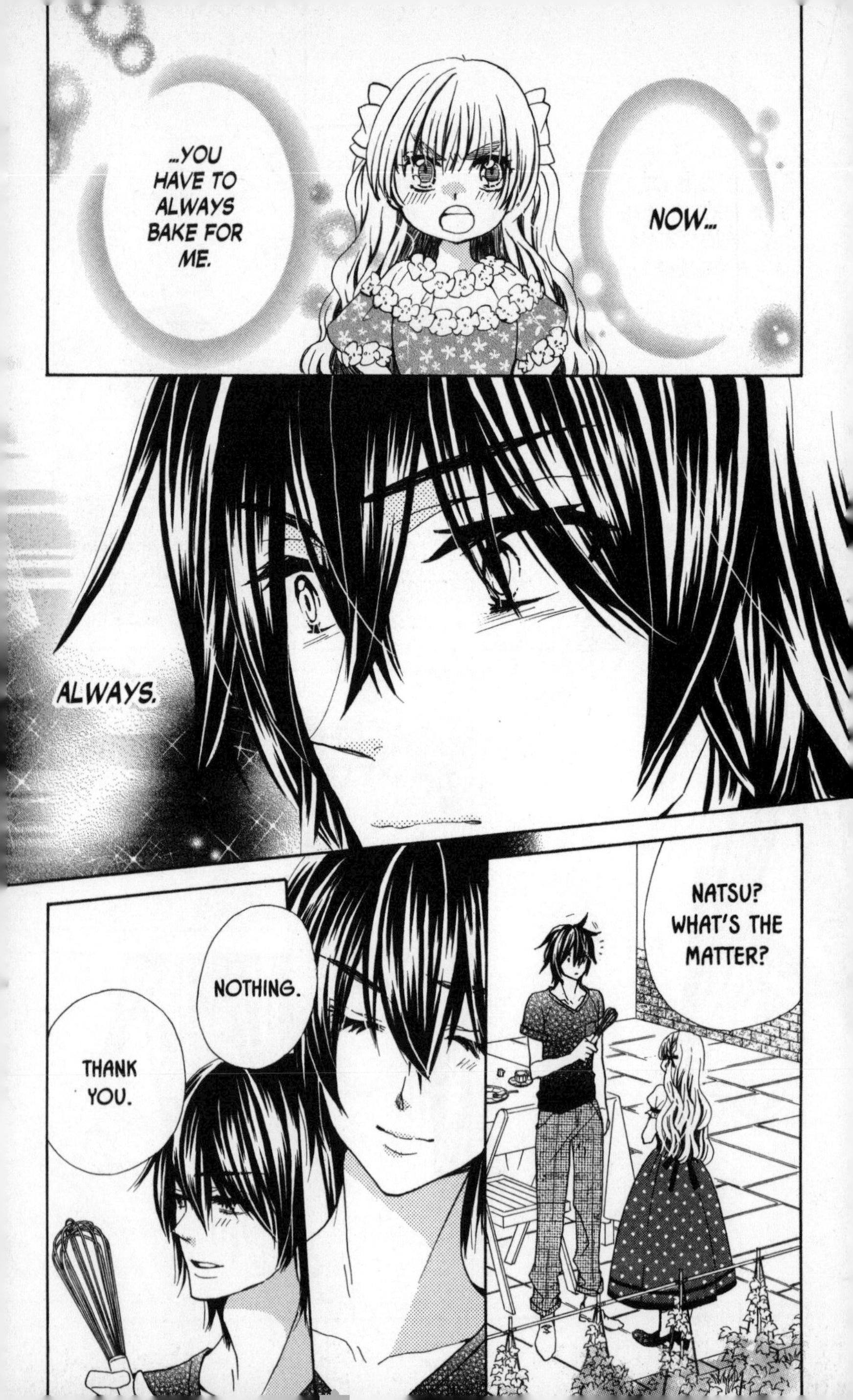
NOW...
...YOU HAVE TO ALWAYS BAKE FOR ME.
ALWAYS.
NATSU? WHAT'S THE MATTER?
NOTHING.
THANK YOU.

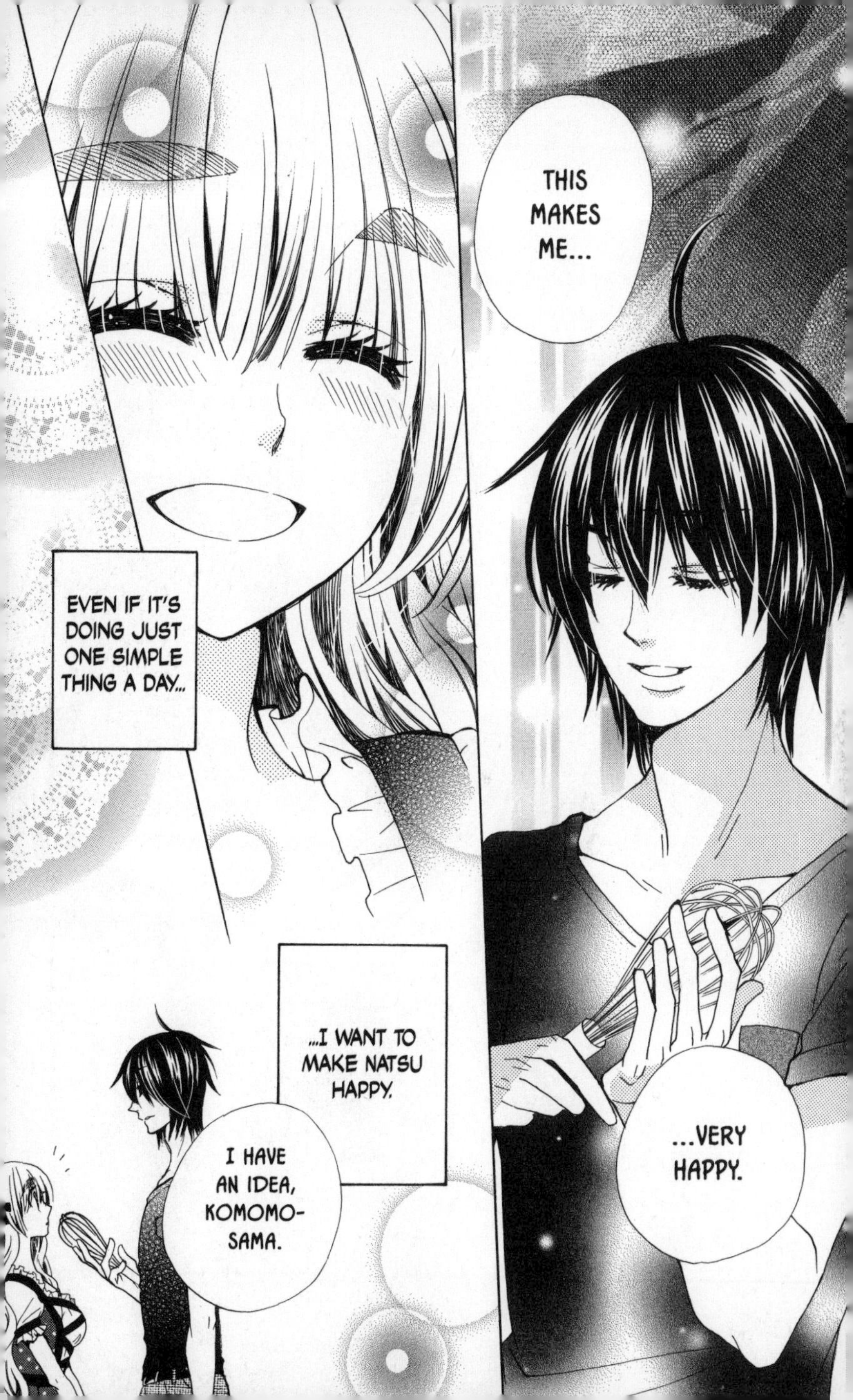
THIS MAKES ME...
...VERY HAPPY.
EVEN IF IT'S DOING JUST ONE SIMPLE THING A DAY...
...I WANT TO MAKE NATSU HAPPY.
I HAVE AN IDEA, KOMOMO-SAMA.

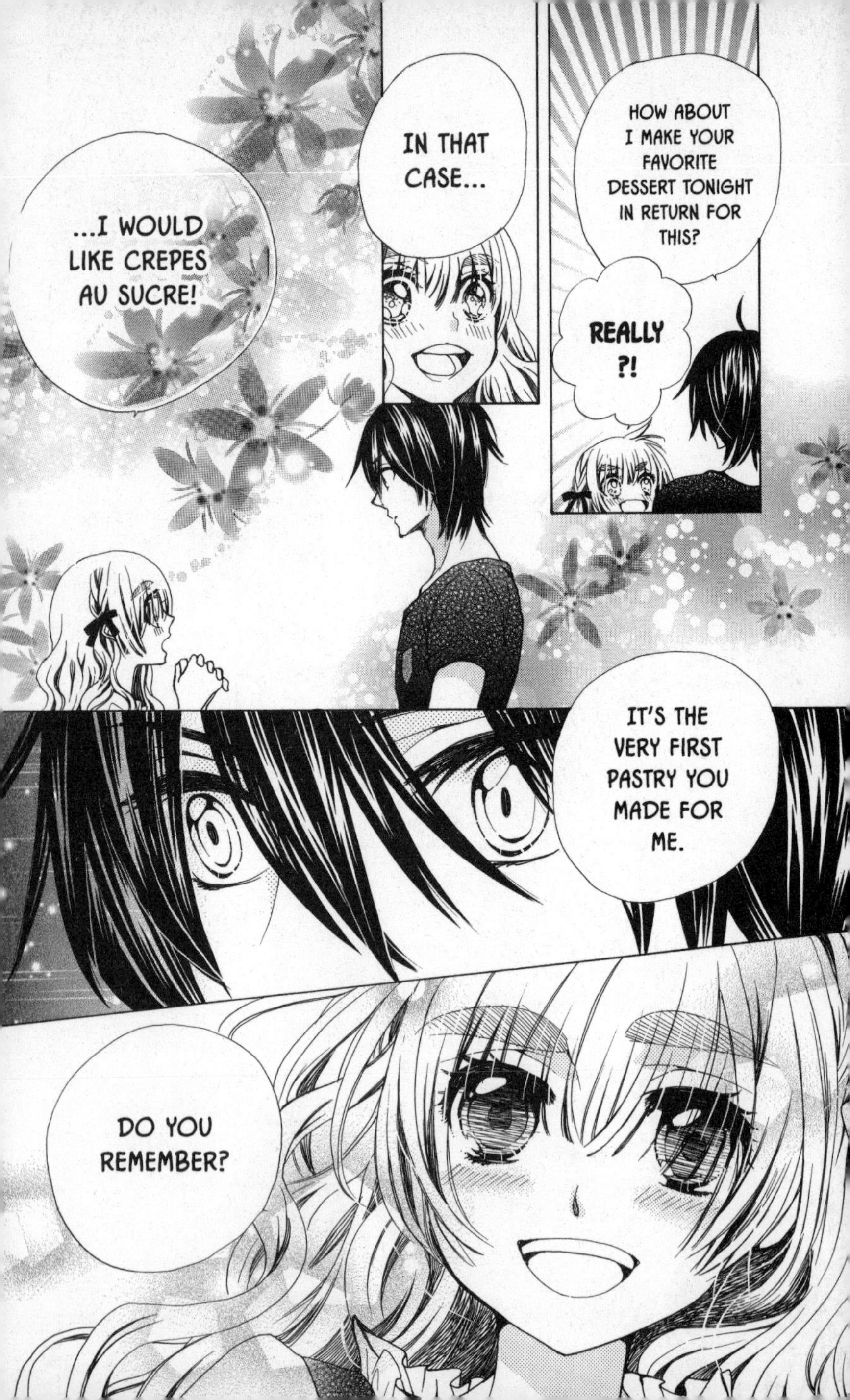
HOW ABOUT I MAKE YOUR FAVORITE DESSERT TONIGHT IN RETURN FOR THIS?
REALLY?!
IN THAT CASE...
...I WOULD LIKE CREPES AU SUCRE!
IT'S THE VERY FIRST PASTRY YOU MADE FOR ME.
DO YOU REMEMBER?

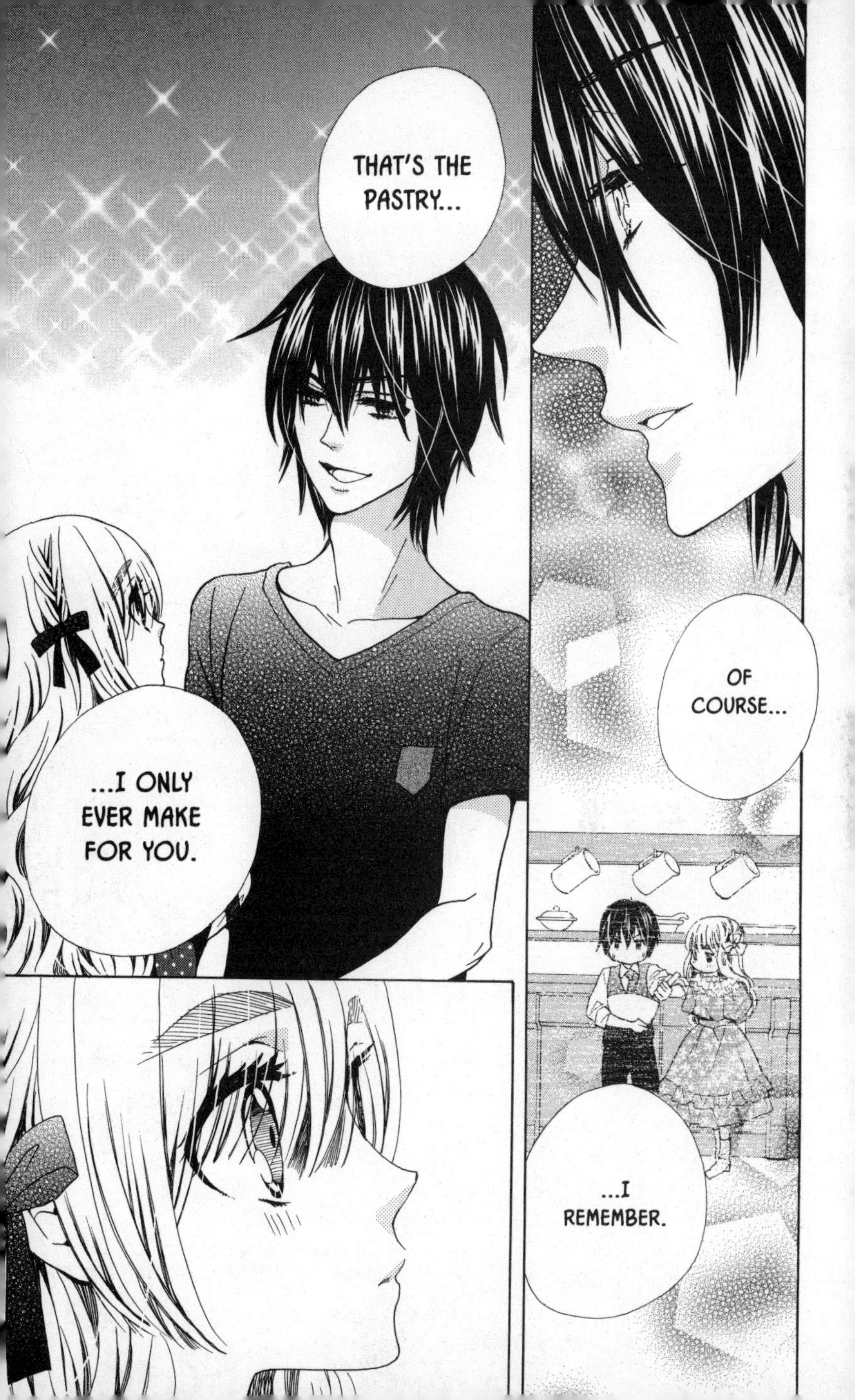
OF COURSE...
...I REMEMBER.
THAT'S THE PASTRY...
...I ONLY EVER MAKE FOR YOU.

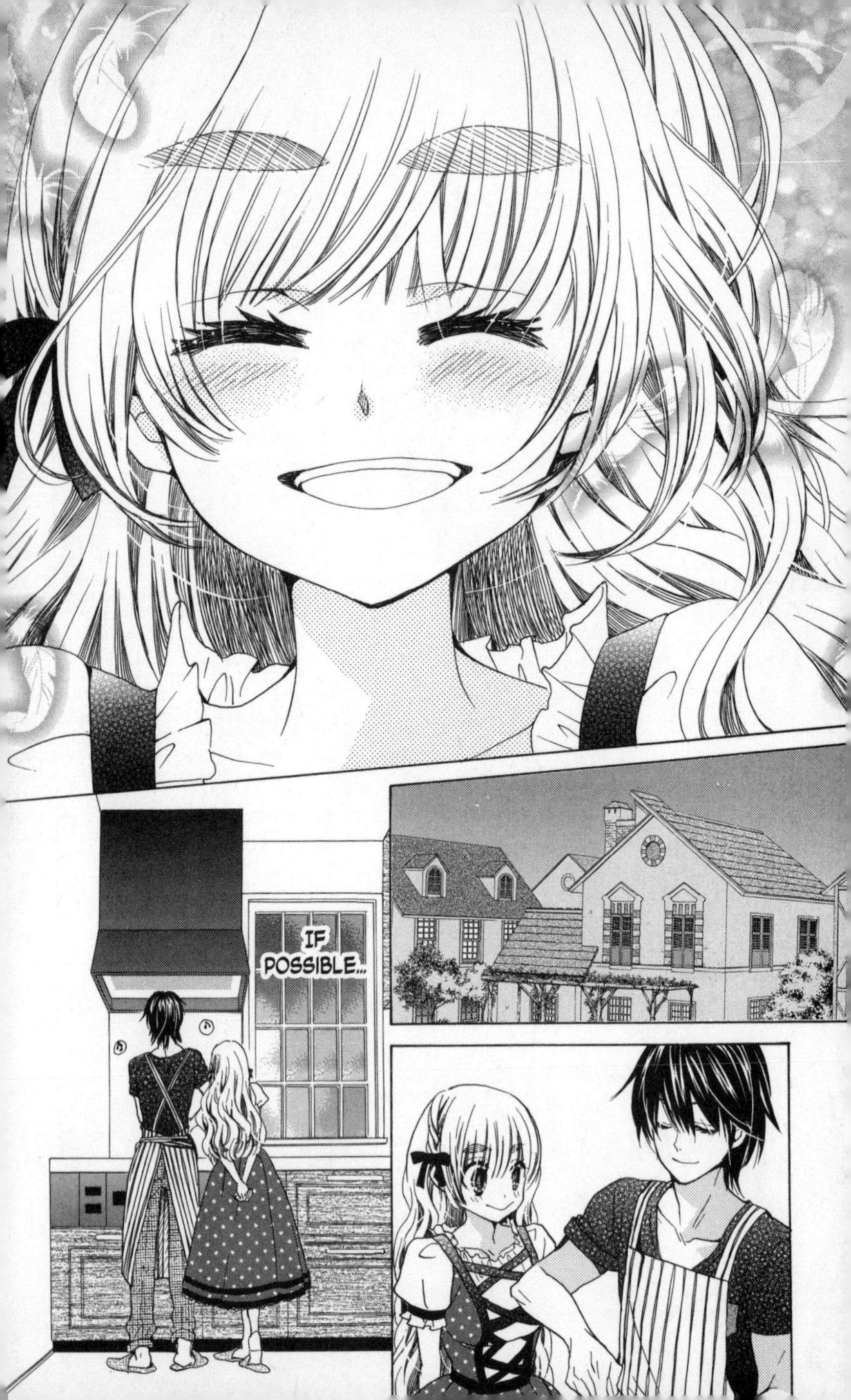
IF POSSIBLE...

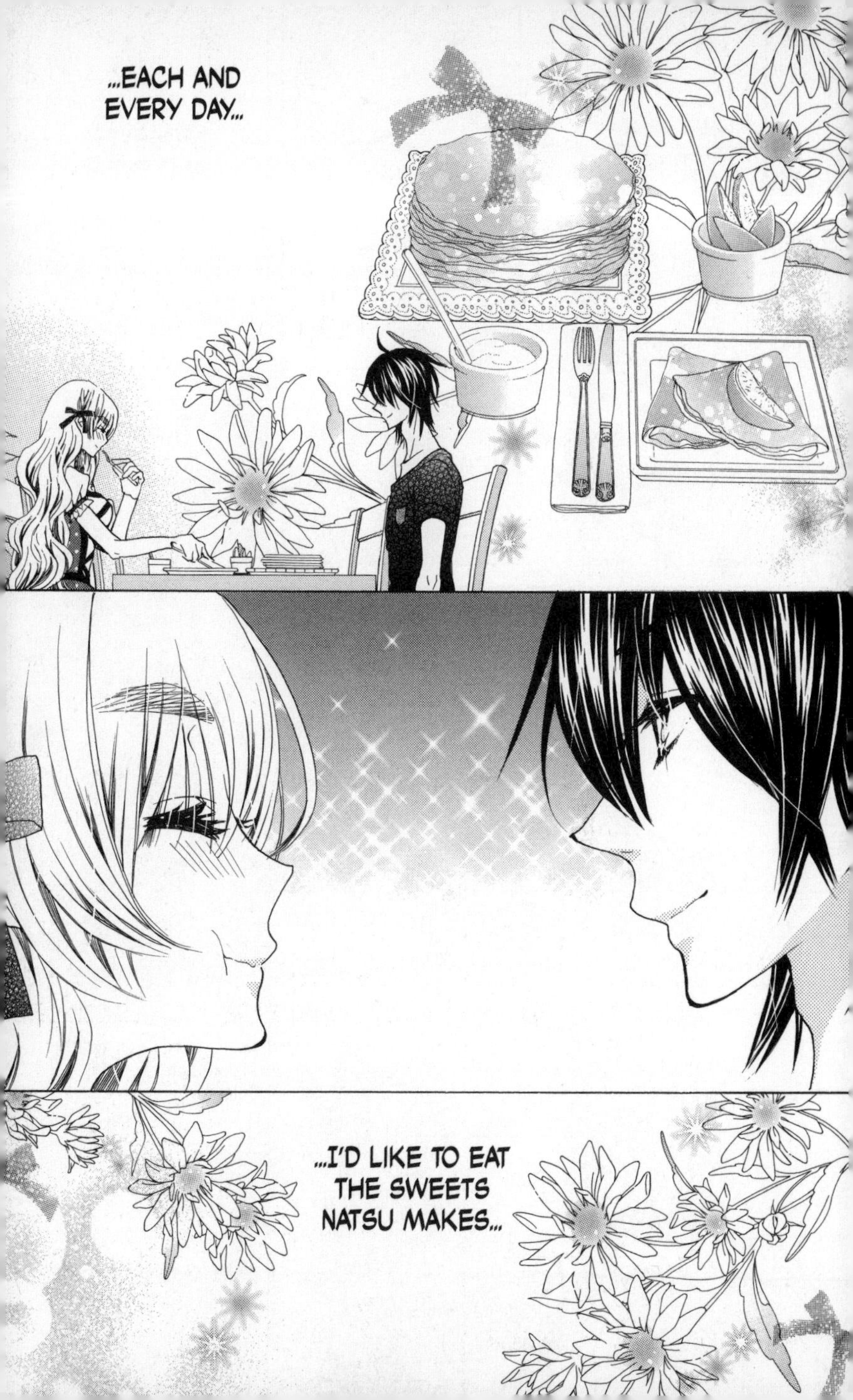
...EACH AND EVERY DAY...
...I'D LIKE TO EAT THE SWEETS NATSU MAKES...

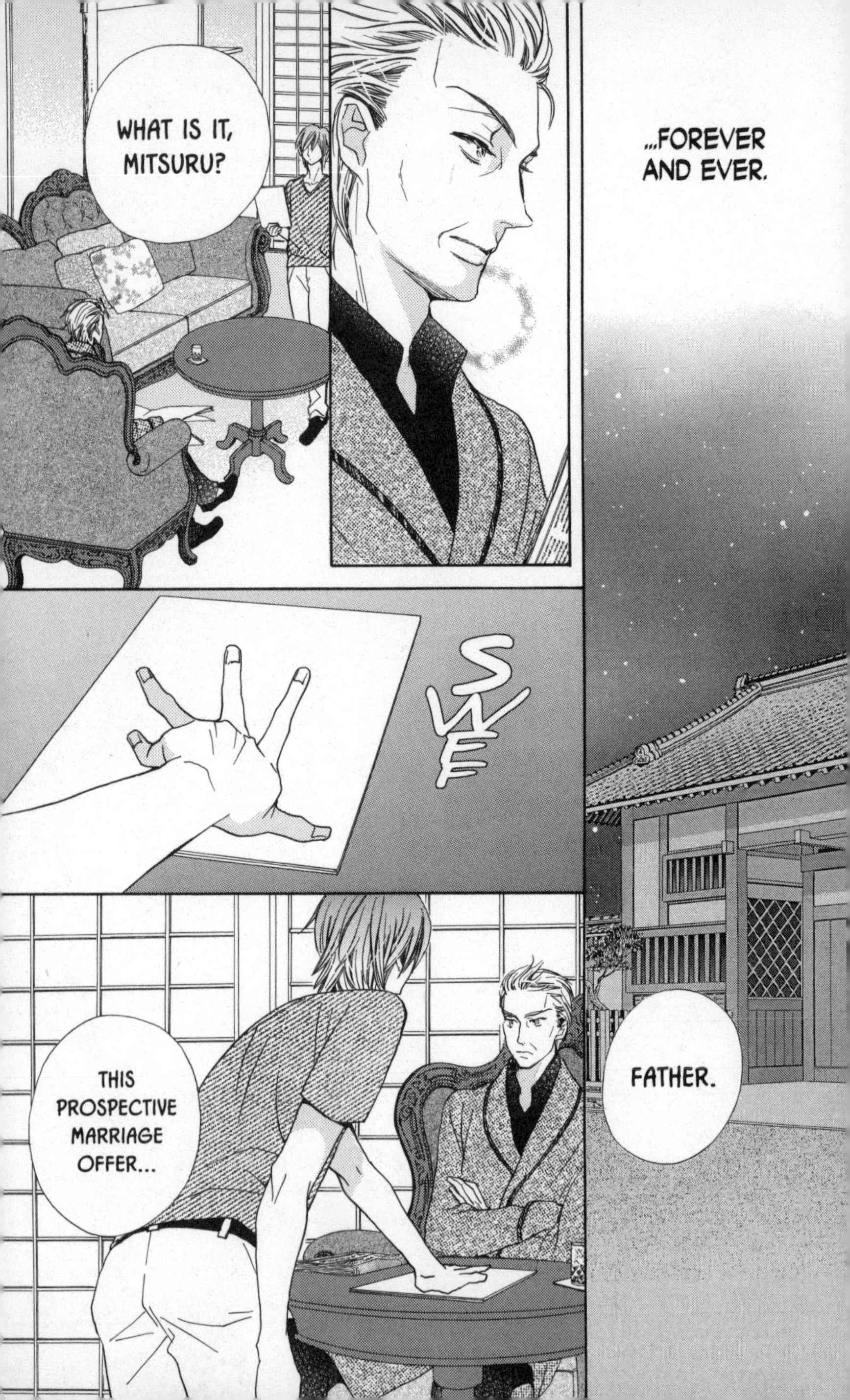
...FOREVER AND EVER.
FATHER.
WHAT IS IT, MITSURU?
SWF
THIS PROSPECTIVE MARRIAGE OFFER...

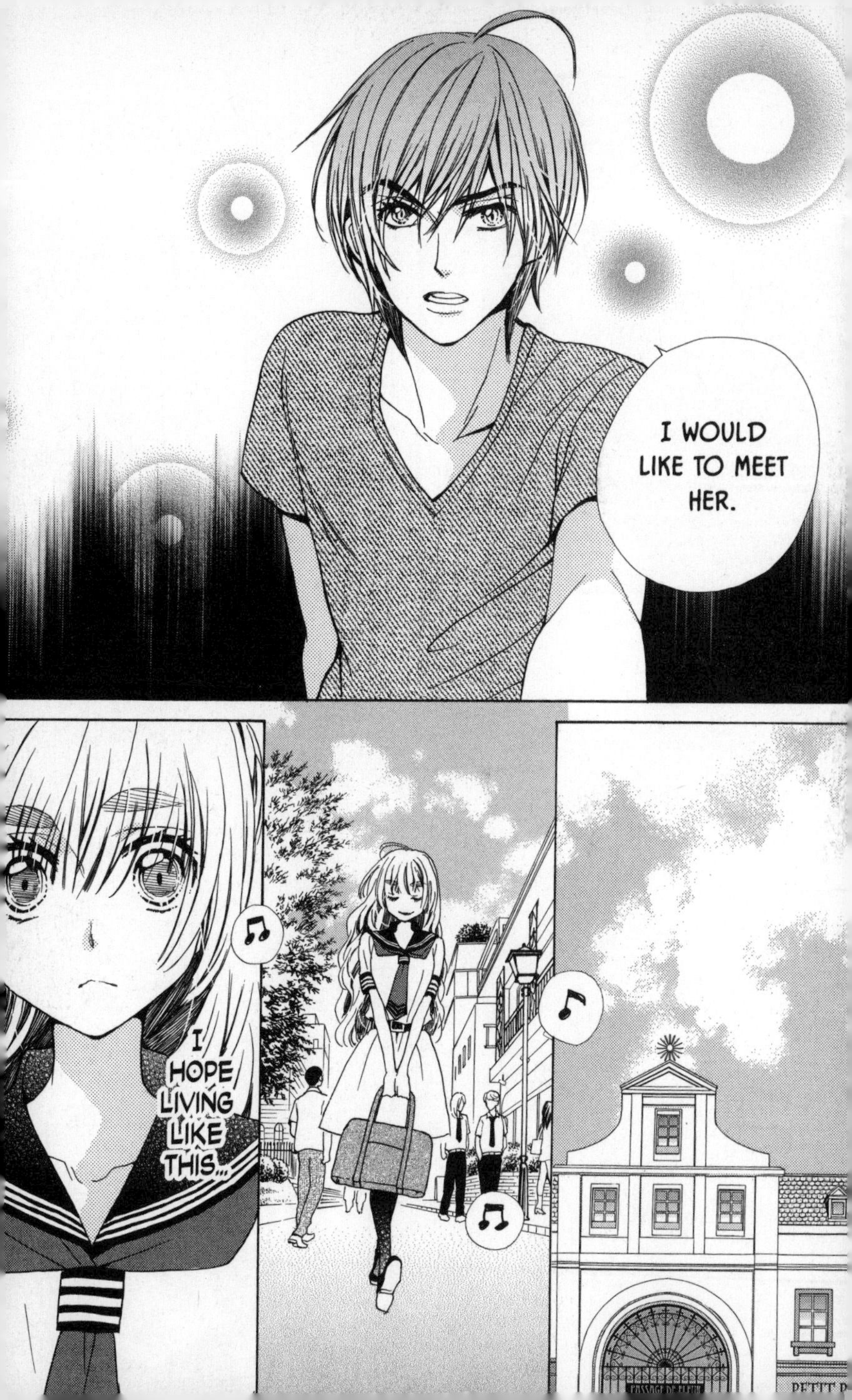
I WOULD LIKE TO MEET HER.
I HOPE LIVING LIKE THIS...

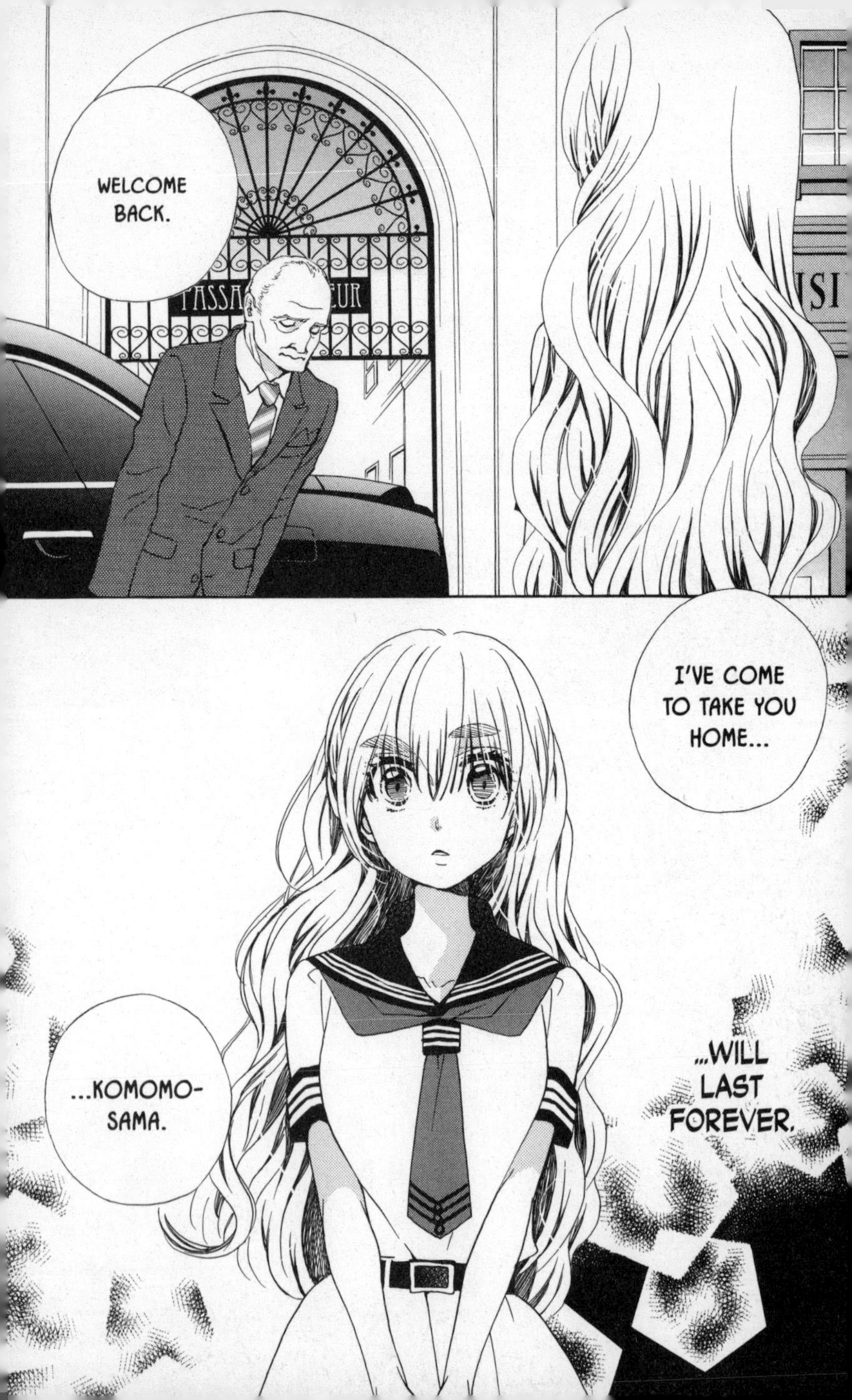
WELCOME BACK.
I'VE COME TO TAKE YOU HOME...
...KOMOMO-SAMA.
...WILL LAST FOREVER.

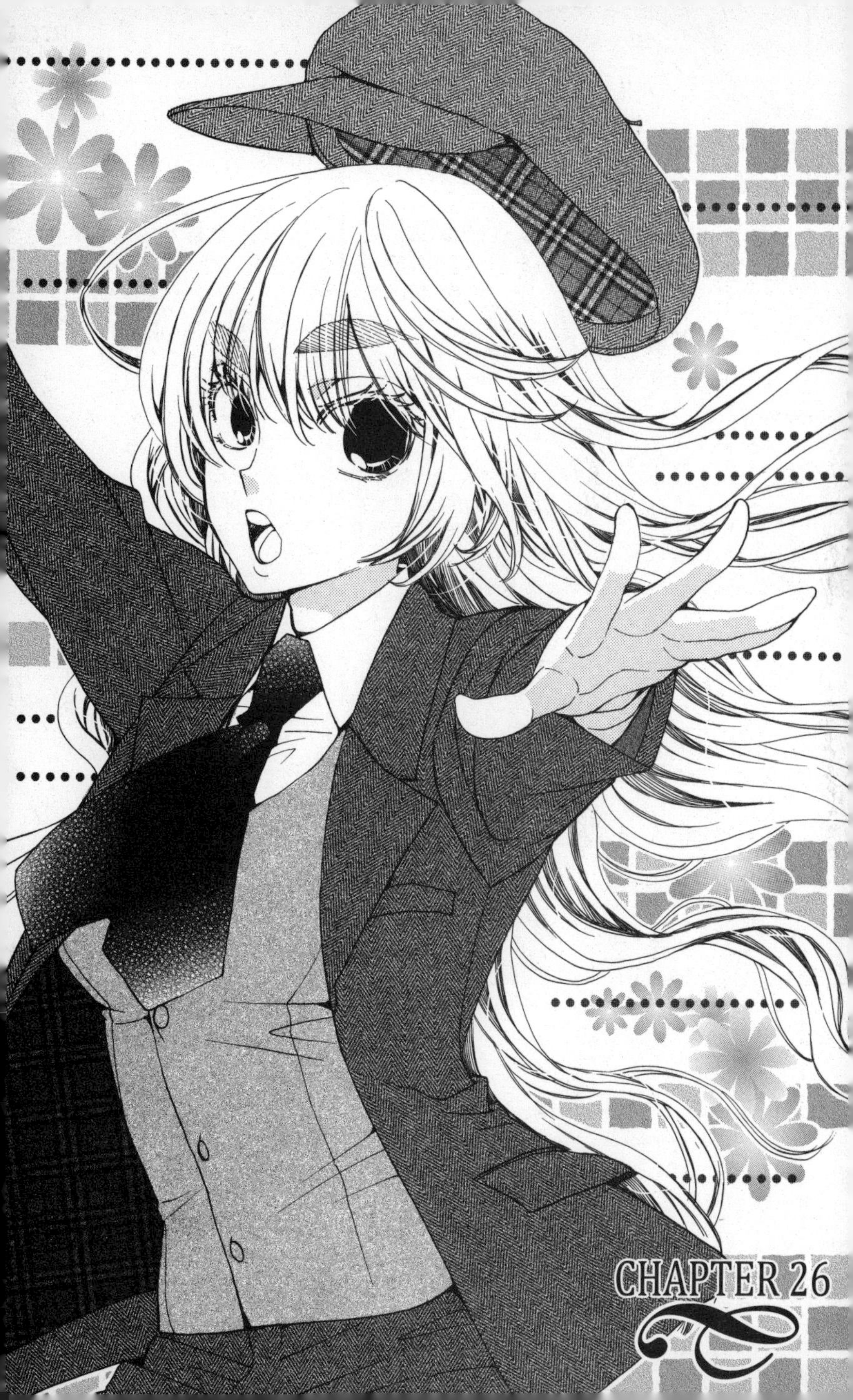
CHAPTER 26

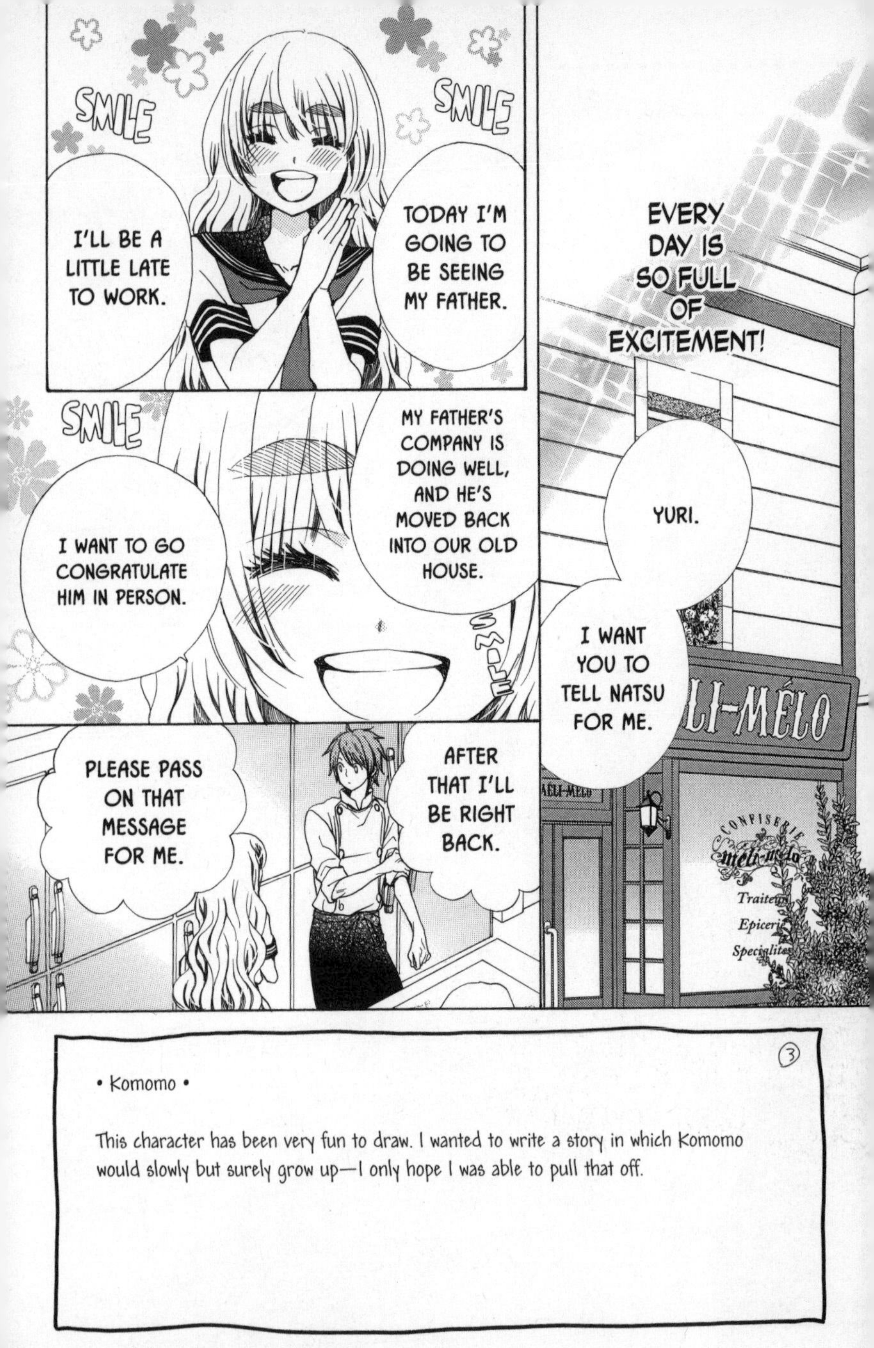
EVERY DAY IS SO FULL OF EXCITEMENT!
YURI.
I WANT YOU TO TELL NATSU FOR ME.
CONFISERIE
SMILE
SMILE
TODAY I'M GOING TO BE SEEING MY FATHER.
I'LL BE A LITTLE LATE TO WORK.
SMILE
MY FATHER'S COMPANY IS DOING WELL, AND HE'S MOVED BACK INTO OUR OLD HOUSE.
I WANT TO GO CONGRATULATE HIM IN PERSON.
SMILE
AFTER THAT I'LL BE RIGHT BACK.
PLEASE PASS ON THAT MESSAGE FOR ME.

(3)

• Komomo •

This character has been very fun to draw. I wanted to write a story in which Komomo would slowly but surely grow up—I only hope I was able to pull that off.

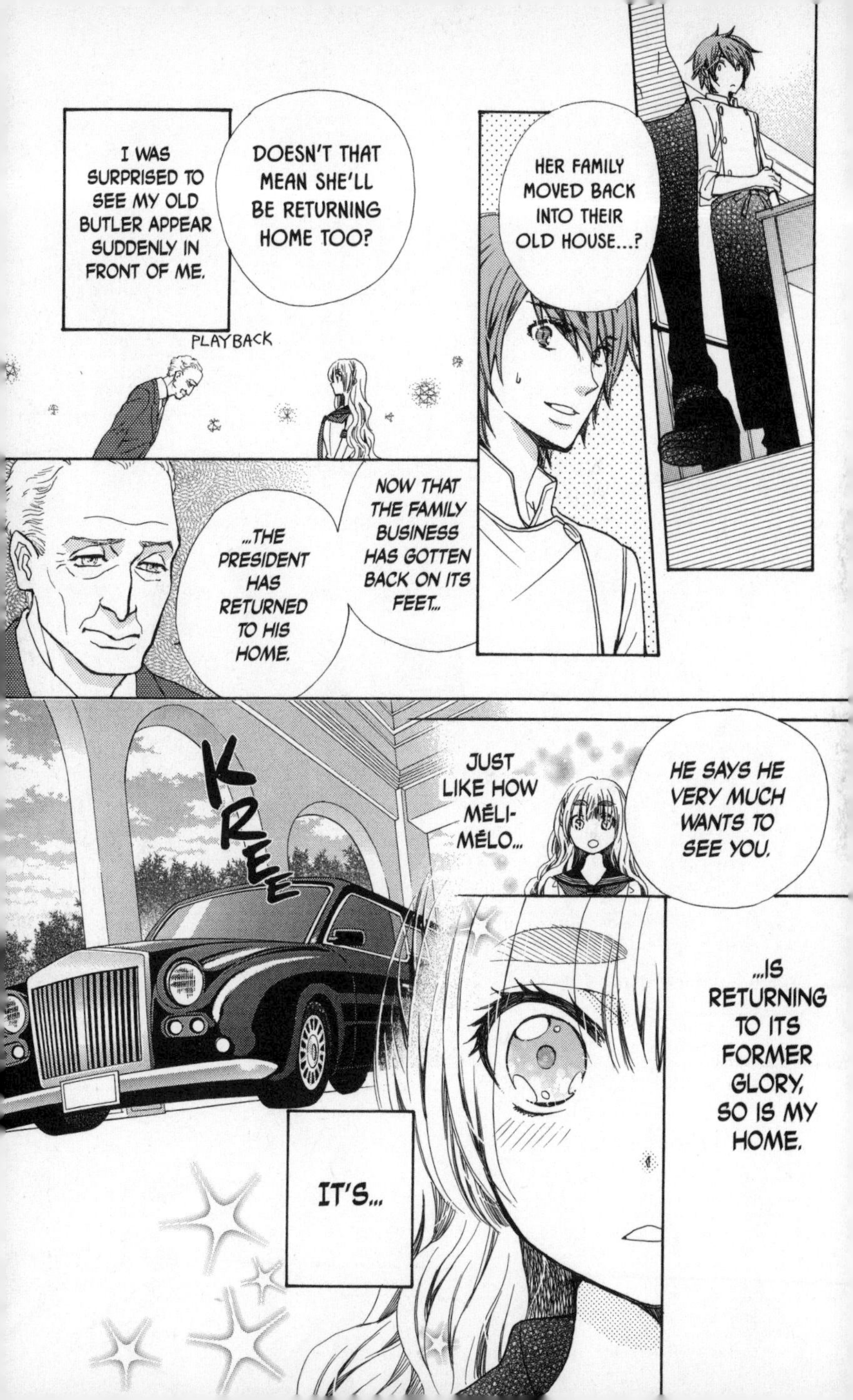
HER FAMILY MOVED BACK INTO THEIR OLD HOUSE...?
DOESN'T THAT MEAN SHE'LL BE RETURNING HOME TOO?
I WAS SURPRISED TO SEE MY OLD BUTLER APPEAR SUDDENLY IN FRONT OF ME.
PLAYBACK
NOW THAT THE FAMILY BUSINESS HAS GOTTEN BACK ON ITS FEET...
...THE PRESIDENT HAS RETURNED TO HIS HOME.
HE SAYS HE VERY MUCH WANTS TO SEE YOU.
JUST LIKE HOW MÉLI-MÉLO...
KREE
...IS RETURNING TO ITS FORMER GLORY, SO IS MY HOME.
IT'S...

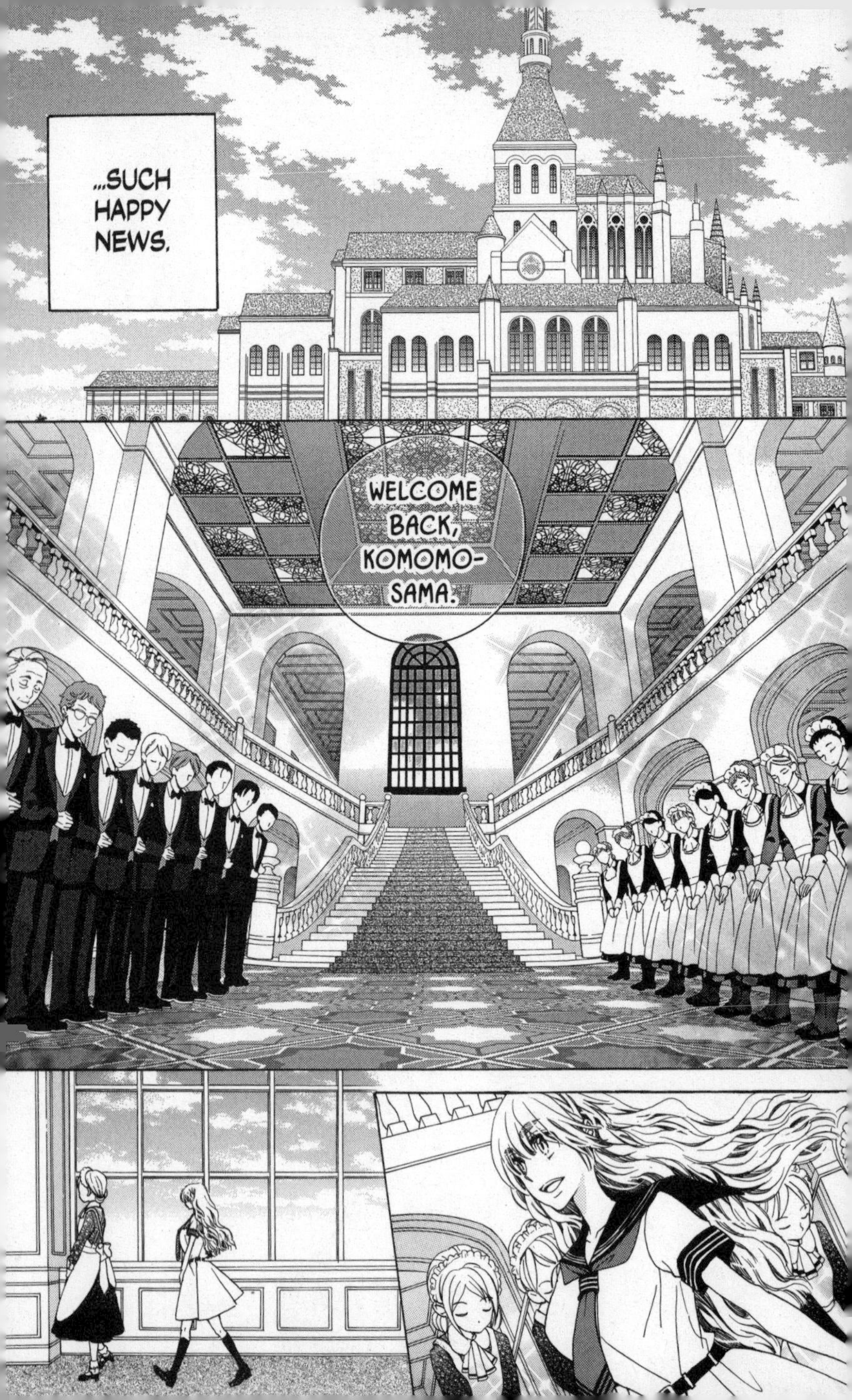
...SUCH HAPPY NEWS.
WELCOME BACK, KOMOMO-SAMA.

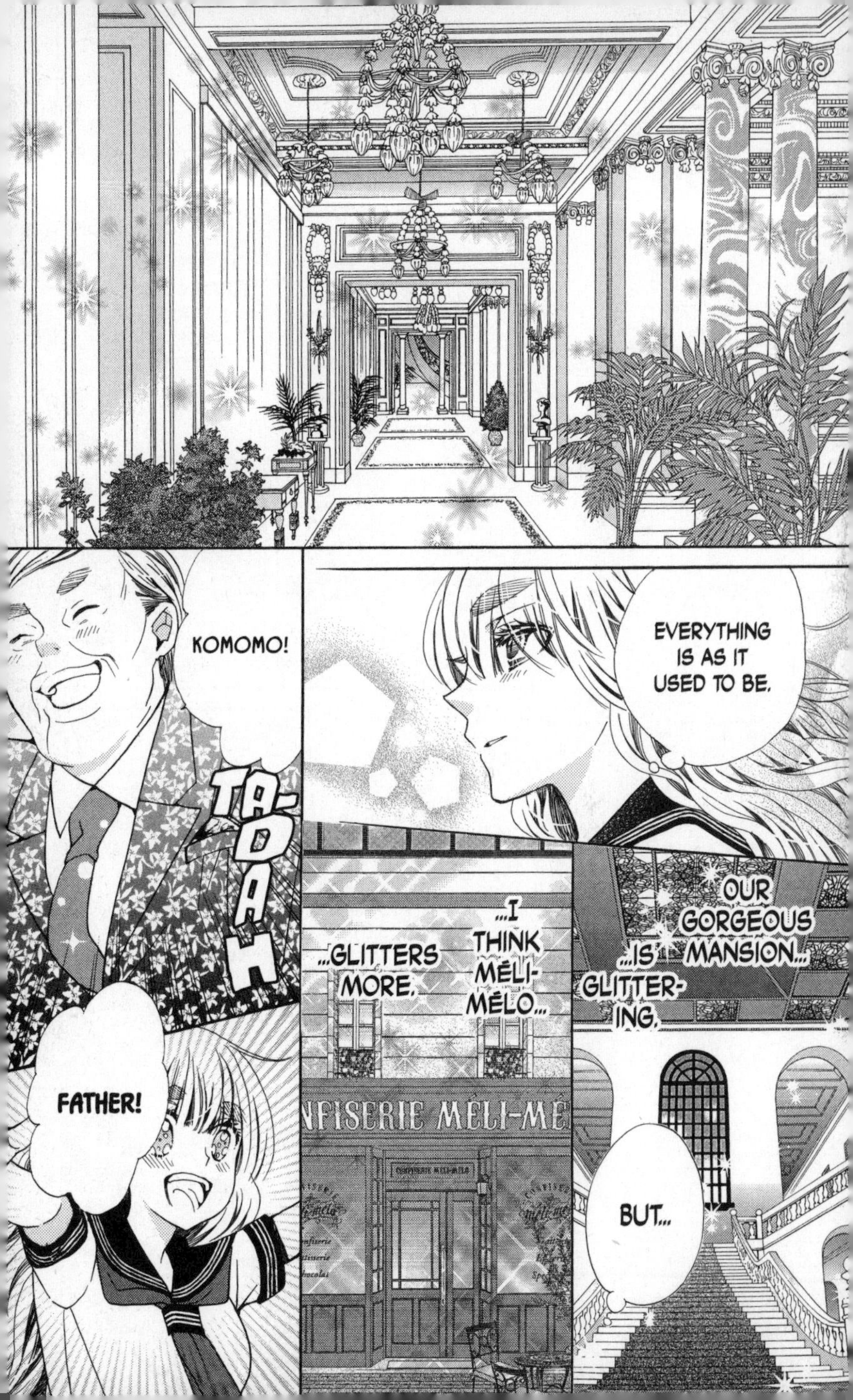

EVERYTHING IS AS IT USED TO BE.
OUR GORGEOUS MANSION...
...IS GLITTERING.
BUT...
...I THINK MÉLI-MÉLO...
...GLITTERS MORE.
NFISERIE MELI-ME
KOMOMO!
TA-DAAAH
FATHER!

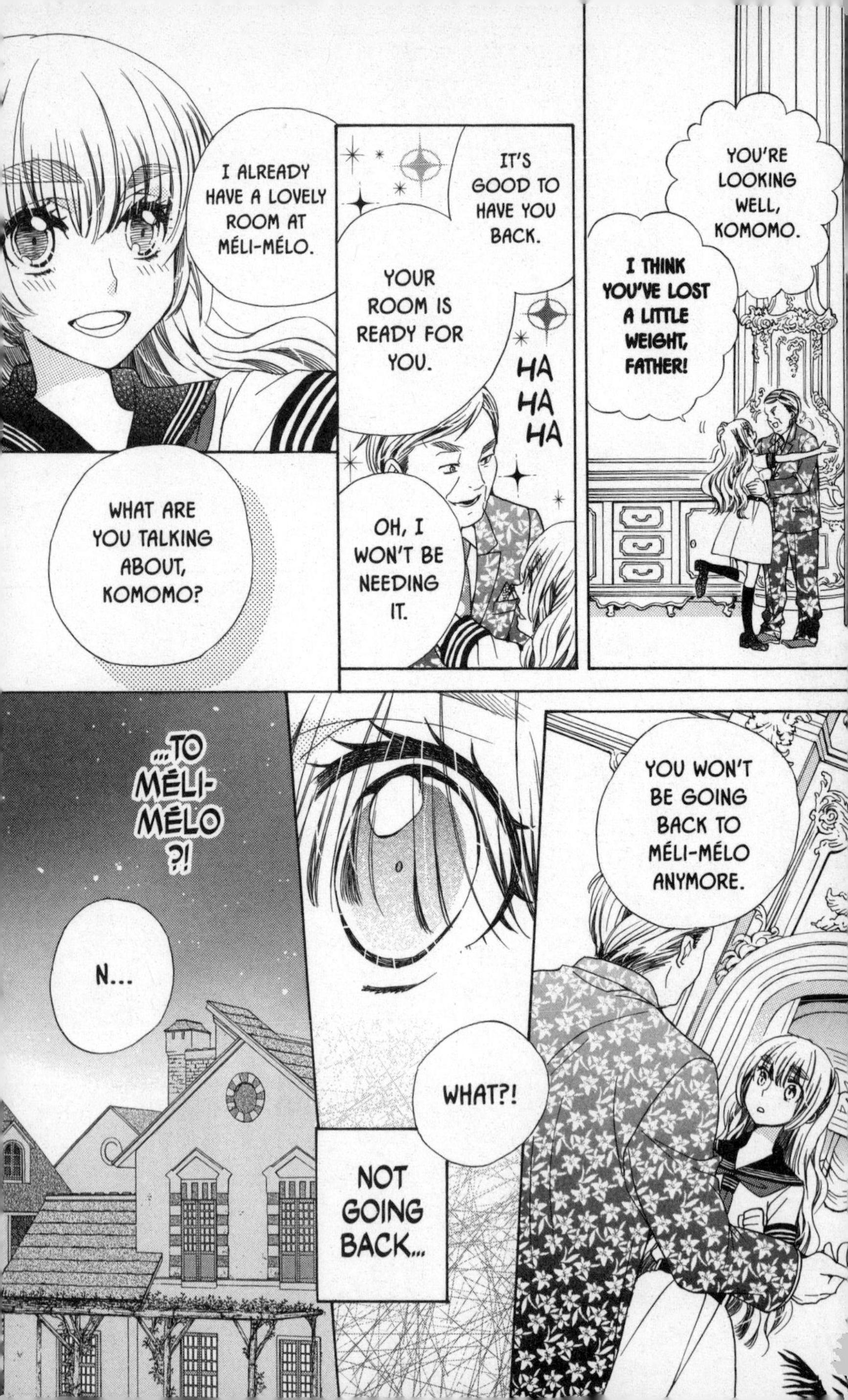
YOU'RE LOOKING WELL, KOMOMO.
I THINK YOU'VE LOST A LITTLE WEIGHT, FATHER!
IT'S GOOD TO HAVE YOU BACK.
YOUR ROOM IS READY FOR YOU.
HA HA HA
OH, I WON'T BE NEEDING IT.
I ALREADY HAVE A LOVELY ROOM AT MÉLI-MÉLO.
WHAT ARE YOU TALKING ABOUT, KOMOMO?
YOU WON'T BE GOING BACK TO MÉLI-MÉLO ANYMORE.
WHAT?!
NOT GOING BACK...
...TO MÉLI-MÉLO?!
N...

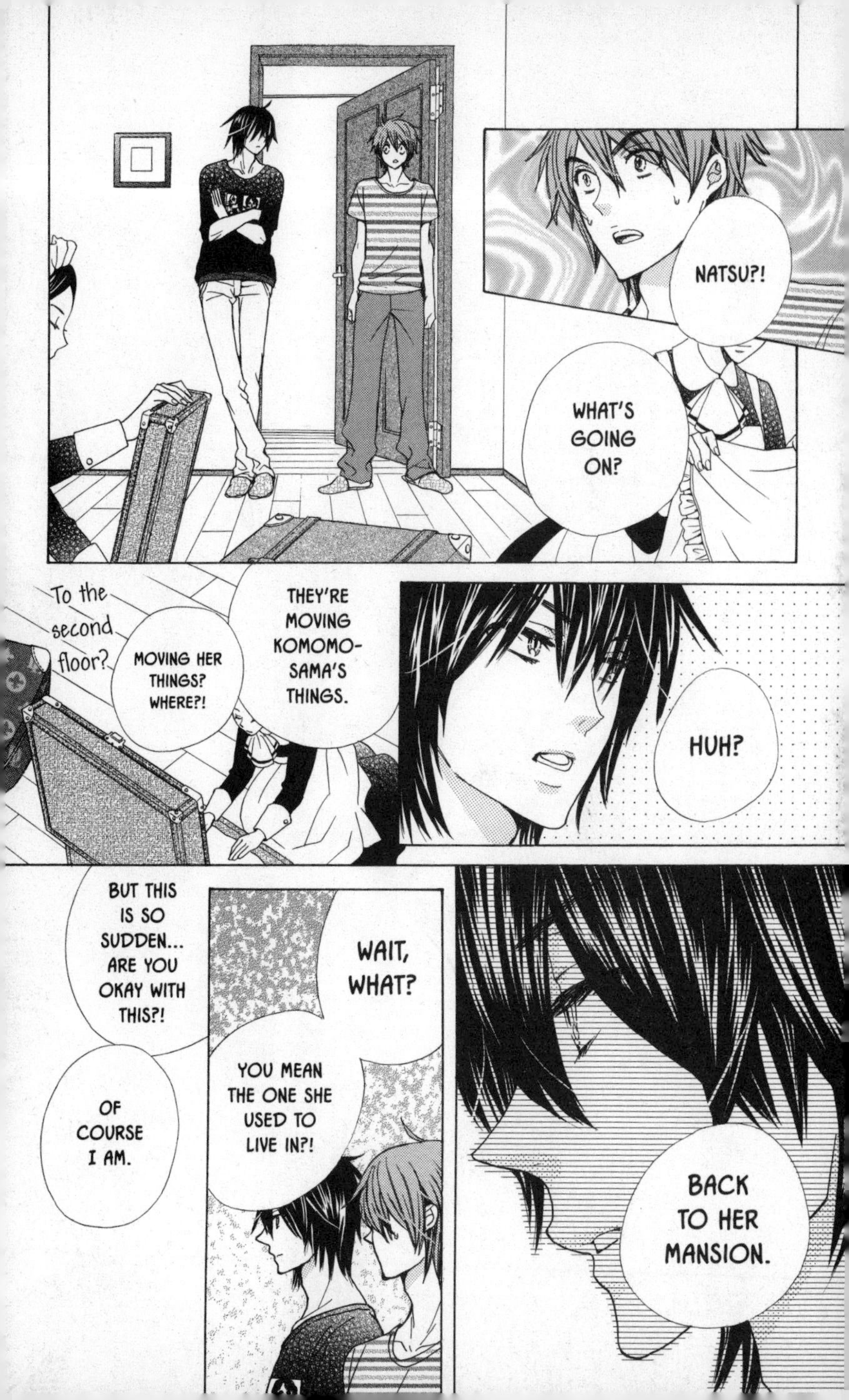
NATSU?!
WHAT'S GOING ON?
HUH?
THEY'RE MOVING KOMOMO-SAMA'S THINGS.
MOVING HER THINGS? WHERE?!
To the second floor?
BACK TO HER MANSION.
WAIT, WHAT?
YOU MEAN THE ONE SHE USED TO LIVE IN?!
BUT THIS IS SO SUDDEN... ARE YOU OKAY WITH THIS?!
OF COURSE I AM.

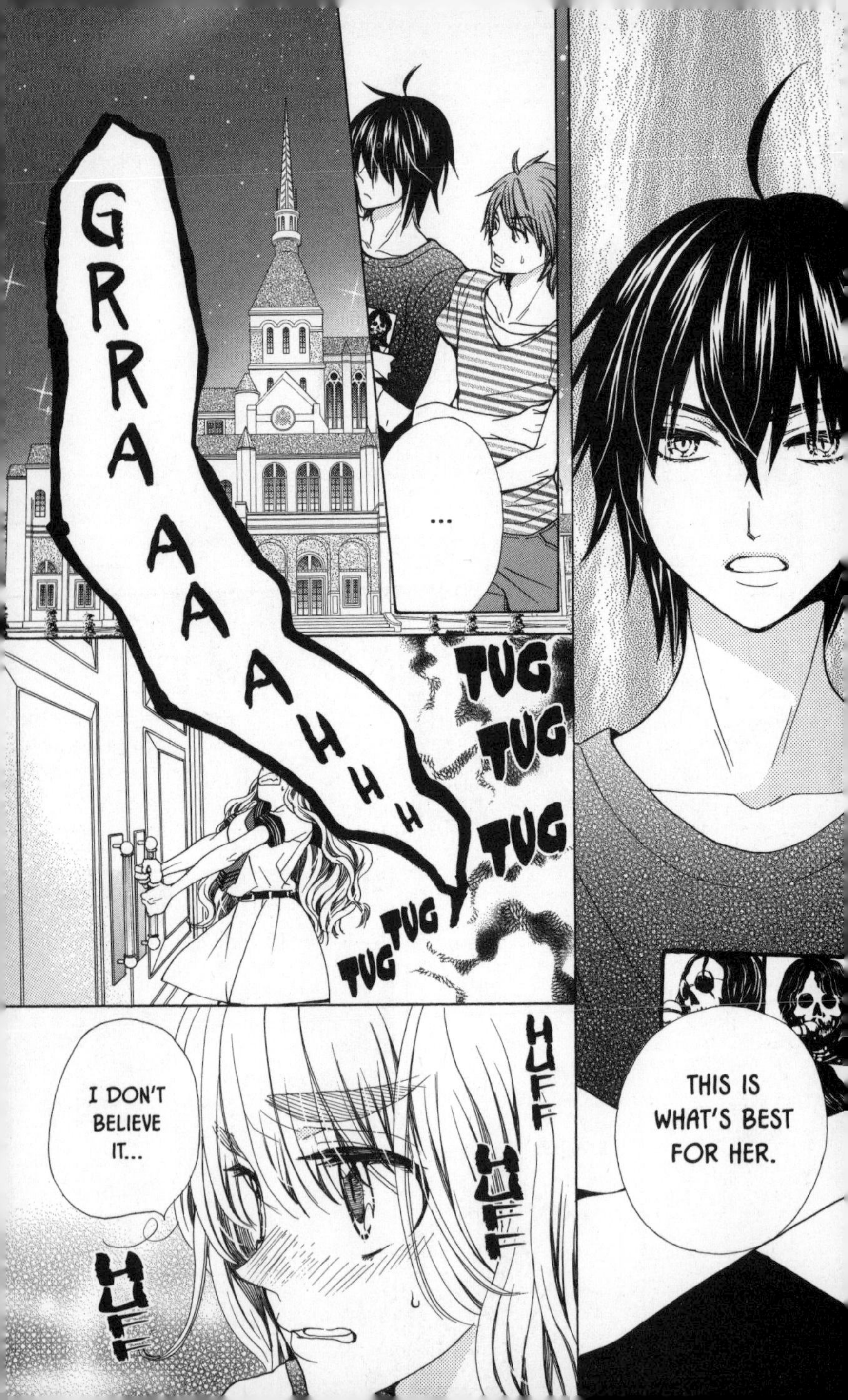
THIS IS WHAT'S BEST FOR HER.
...
GRRAAAAHHH
TUG TUG TUG TUG
TUG TUG
HUFF
HUFF
I DON'T BELIEVE IT...
HUFF

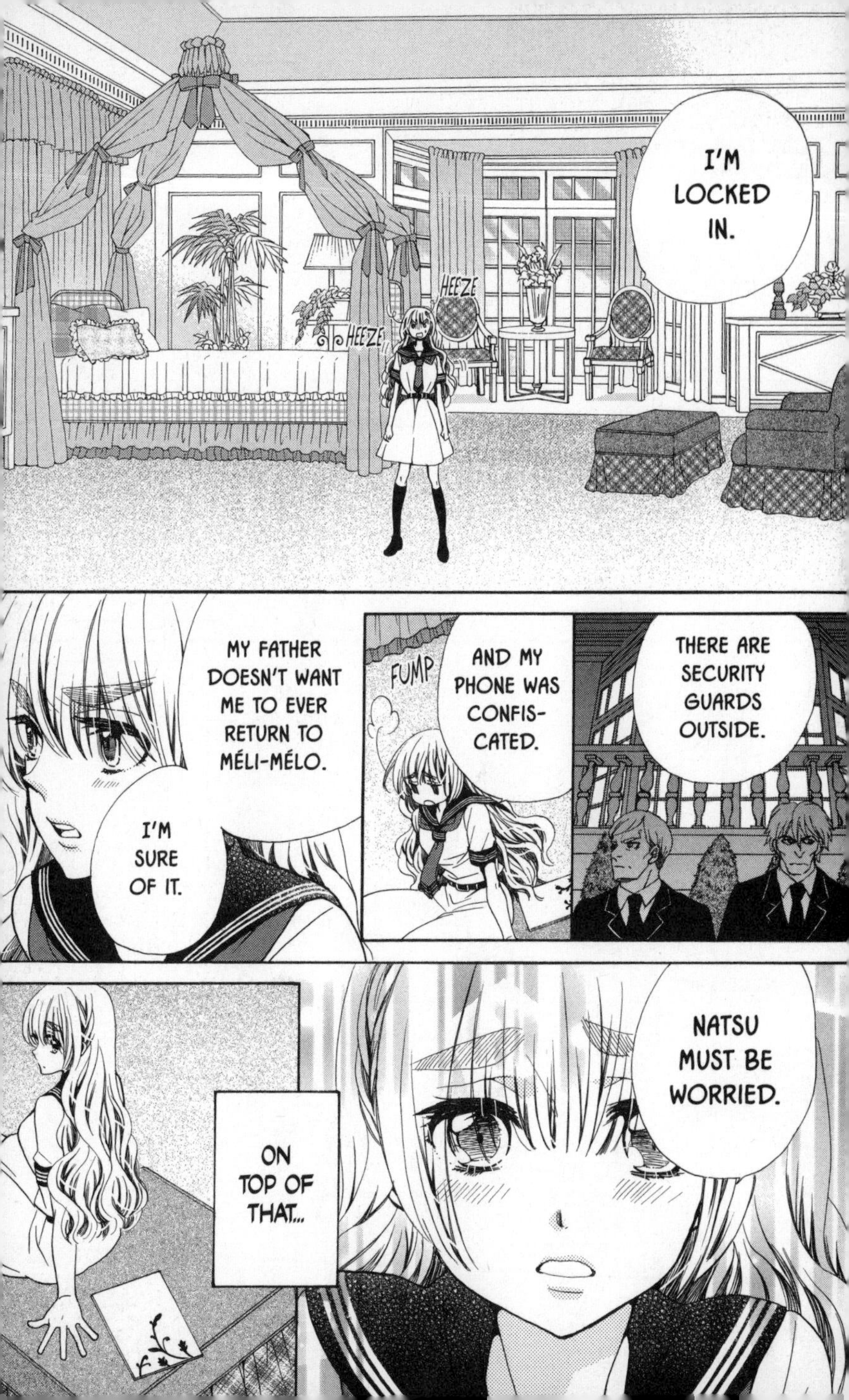
I'M LOCKED IN.
HEEZE
HEEZE
THERE ARE SECURITY GUARDS OUTSIDE.
AND MY PHONE WAS CONFIS-CATED.
FUMP
MY FATHER DOESN'T WANT ME TO EVER RETURN TO MÉLI-MÉLO.
I'M SURE OF IT.
NATSU MUST BE WORRIED.
ON TOP OF THAT...

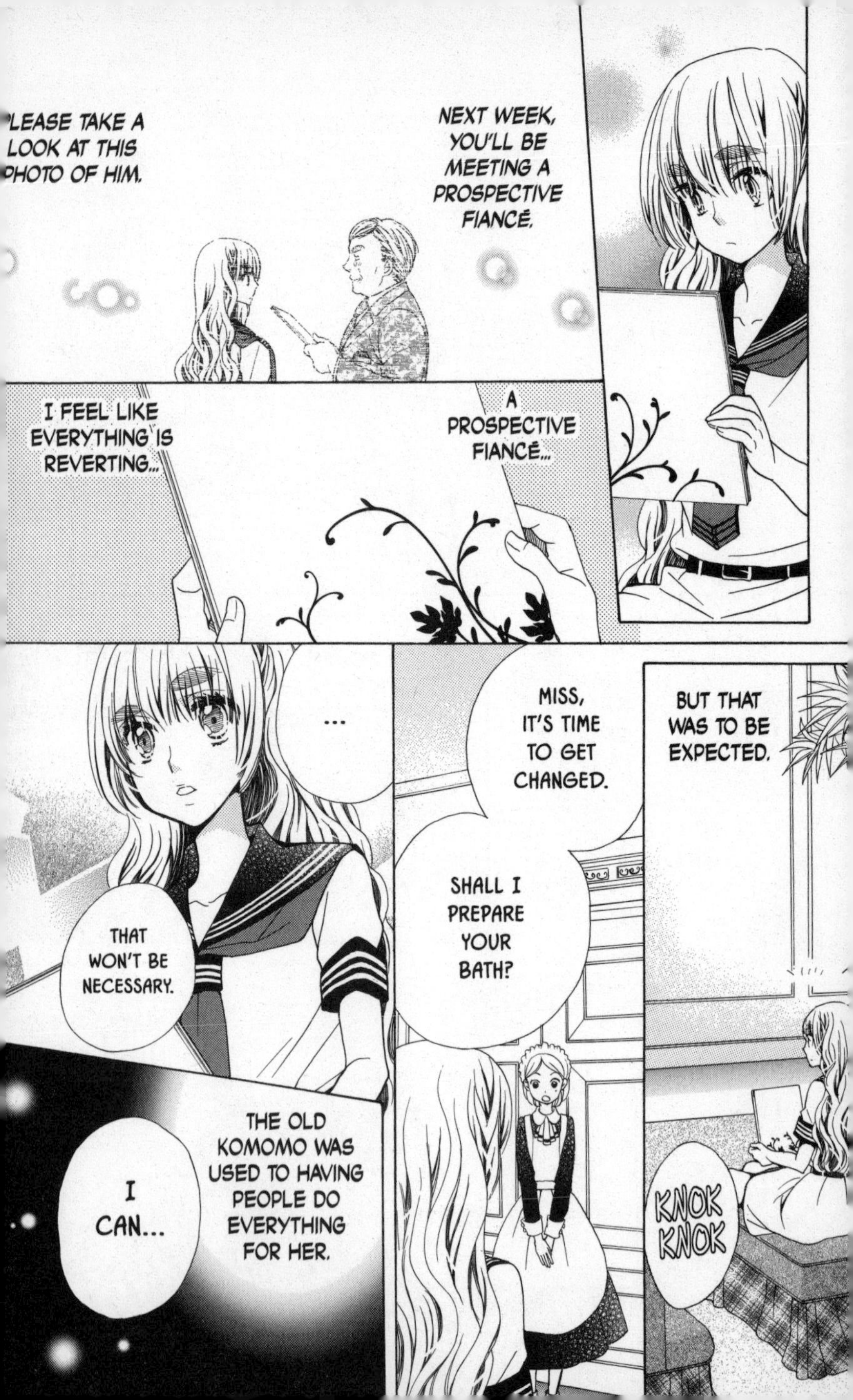
NEXT WEEK, YOU'LL BE MEETING A PROSPECTIVE FIANCÉ.
LEASE TAKE A LOOK AT THIS HOTO OF HIM.
A PROSPECTIVE FIANCÉ...
I FEEL LIKE EVERYTHING IS REVERTING...
BUT THAT WAS TO BE EXPECTED.
KNOK KNOK
MISS, IT'S TIME TO GET CHANGED.
SHALL I PREPARE YOUR BATH?
...
THAT WON'T BE NECESSARY.
THE OLD KOMOMO WAS USED TO HAVING PEOPLE DO EVERYTHING FOR HER.
I CAN...

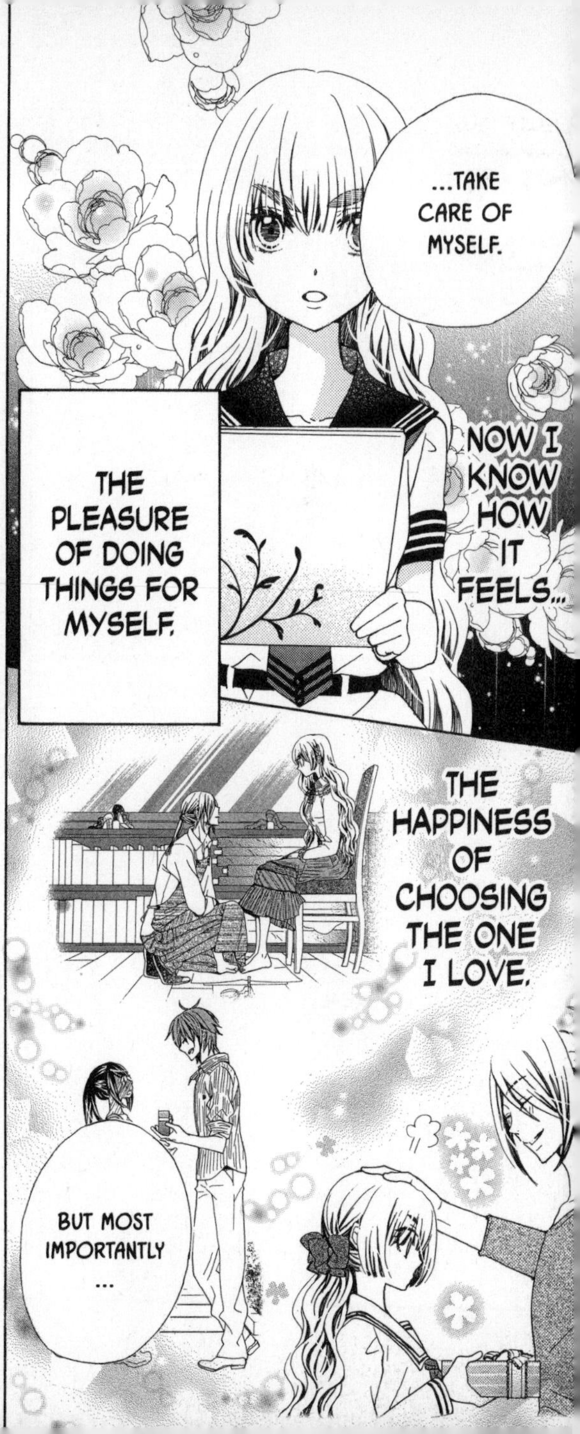
...TAKE CARE OF MYSELF.
NOW I KNOW HOW IT FEELS...
THE PLEASURE OF DOING THINGS FOR MYSELF.
THE HAPPINESS OF CHOOSING THE ONE I LOVE.
BUT MOST IMPORTANTLY ...

• Double Booking •

Ever since I stopped carrying around my notebook, I've been double-booked on so many events. I feel really bad about it... One day, my assistant got really fed up and said...

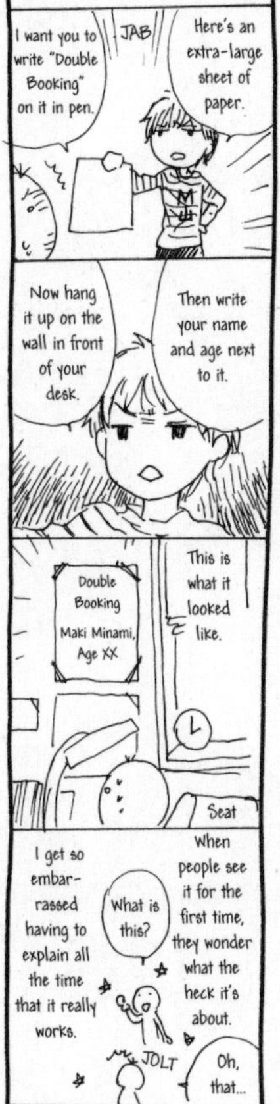
Here's an extra-large sheet of paper.
JAB
I want you to write "Double Booking" on it in pen.
Then write your name and age next to it.
Now hang it up on the wall in front of your desk.
This is what it looked like.
Double Booking Maki Minami, Age XX
Seat
When people see it for the first time, they wonder what the heck it's about.
What is this?
I get so embar-rassed having to explain all the time that it really works.
JOLT
Oh, that...

It's helped me keep my schedule in order. These days I haven't been double-booked in a long time. I'll be careful not to again.

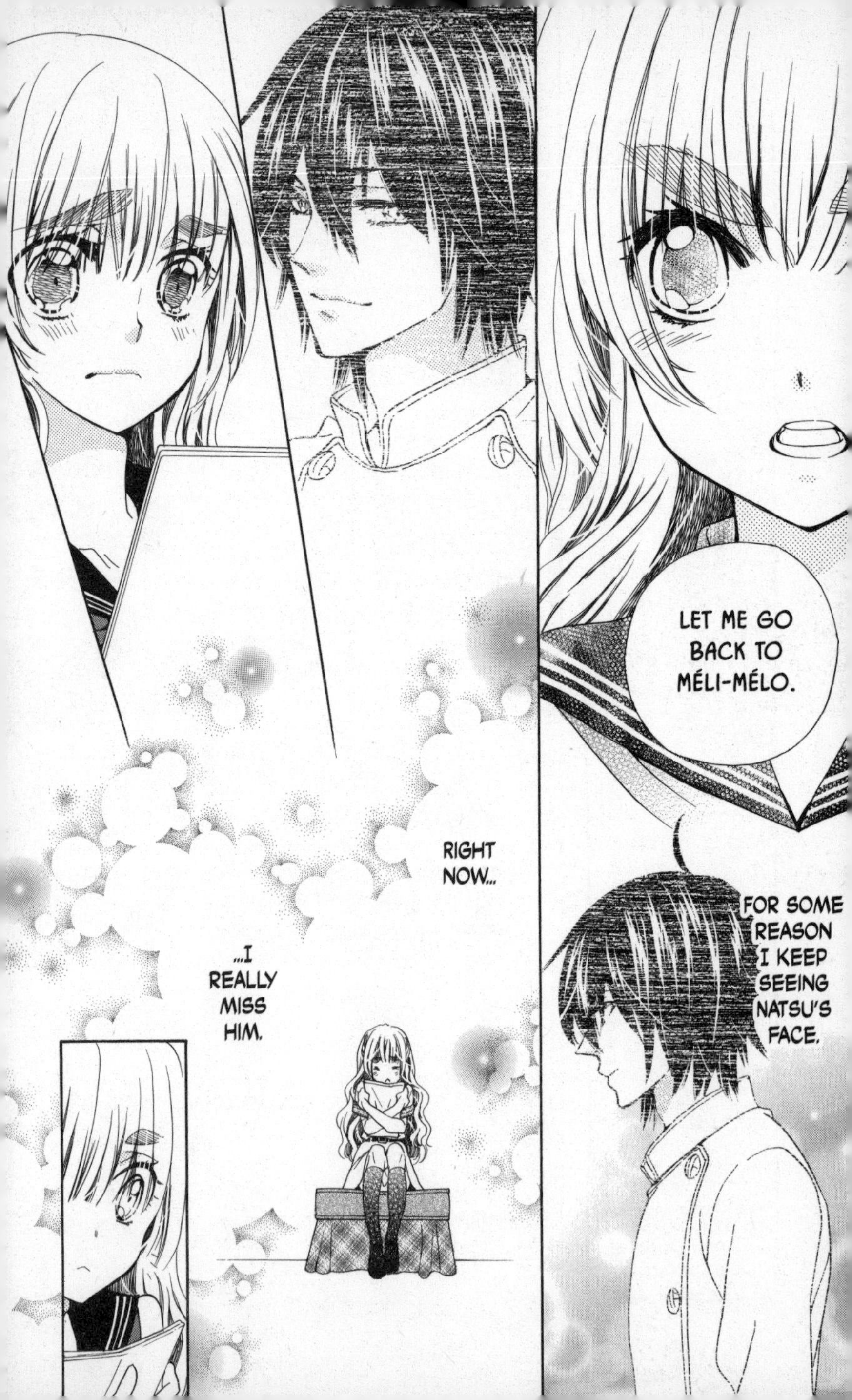
LET ME GO BACK TO MÉLI-MÉLO.
FOR SOME REASON I KEEP SEEING NATSU'S FACE.
RIGHT NOW...
...I REALLY MISS HIM.

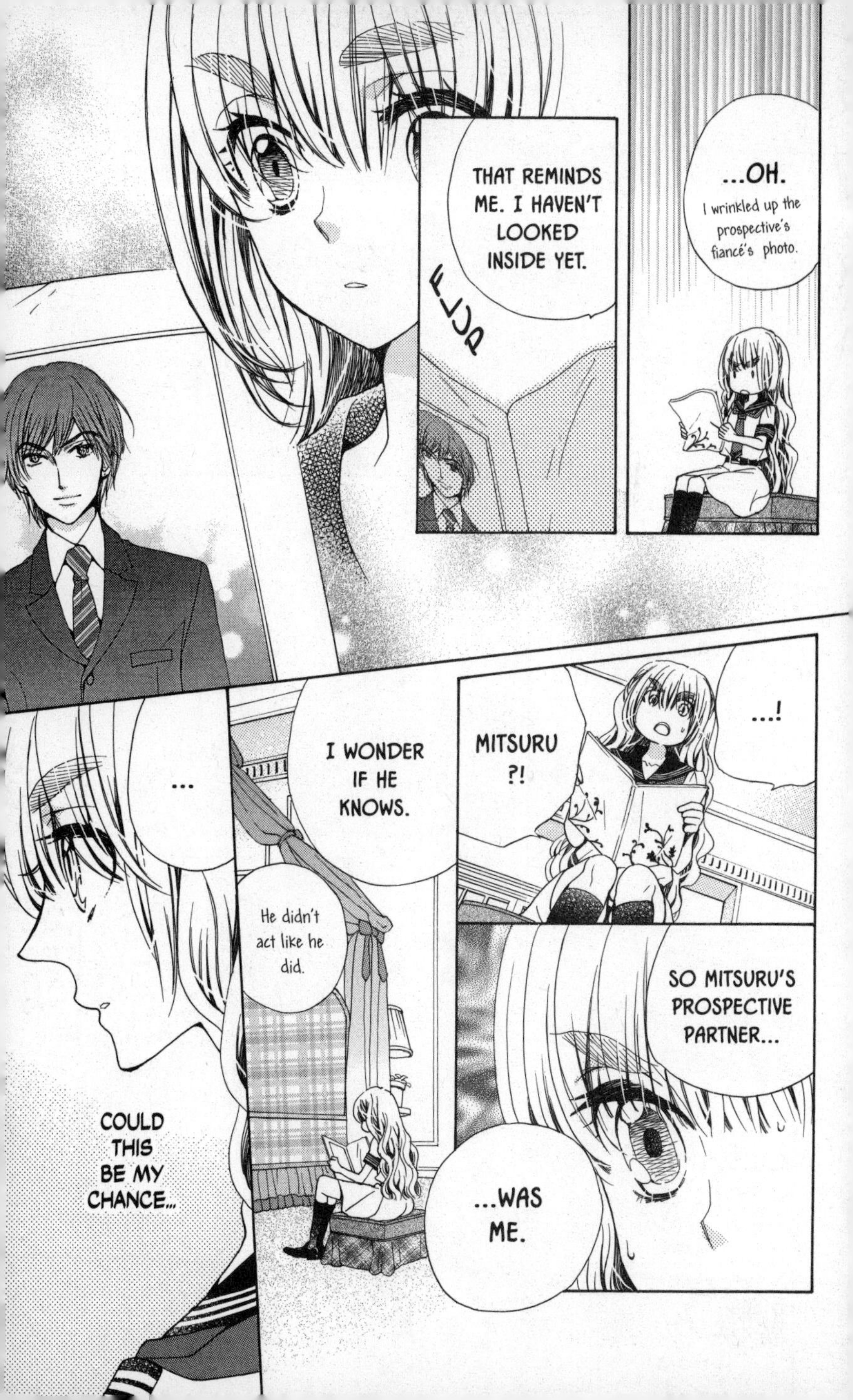
...OH.
I wrinkled up the prospective's fiancé's photo.
THAT REMINDS ME. I HAVEN'T LOOKED INSIDE YET.
...!
MITSURU ?!
SO MITSURU'S PROSPECTIVE PARTNER...
...WAS ME.
I WONDER IF HE KNOWS.
He didn't act like he did.
...
COULD THIS BE MY CHANCE...

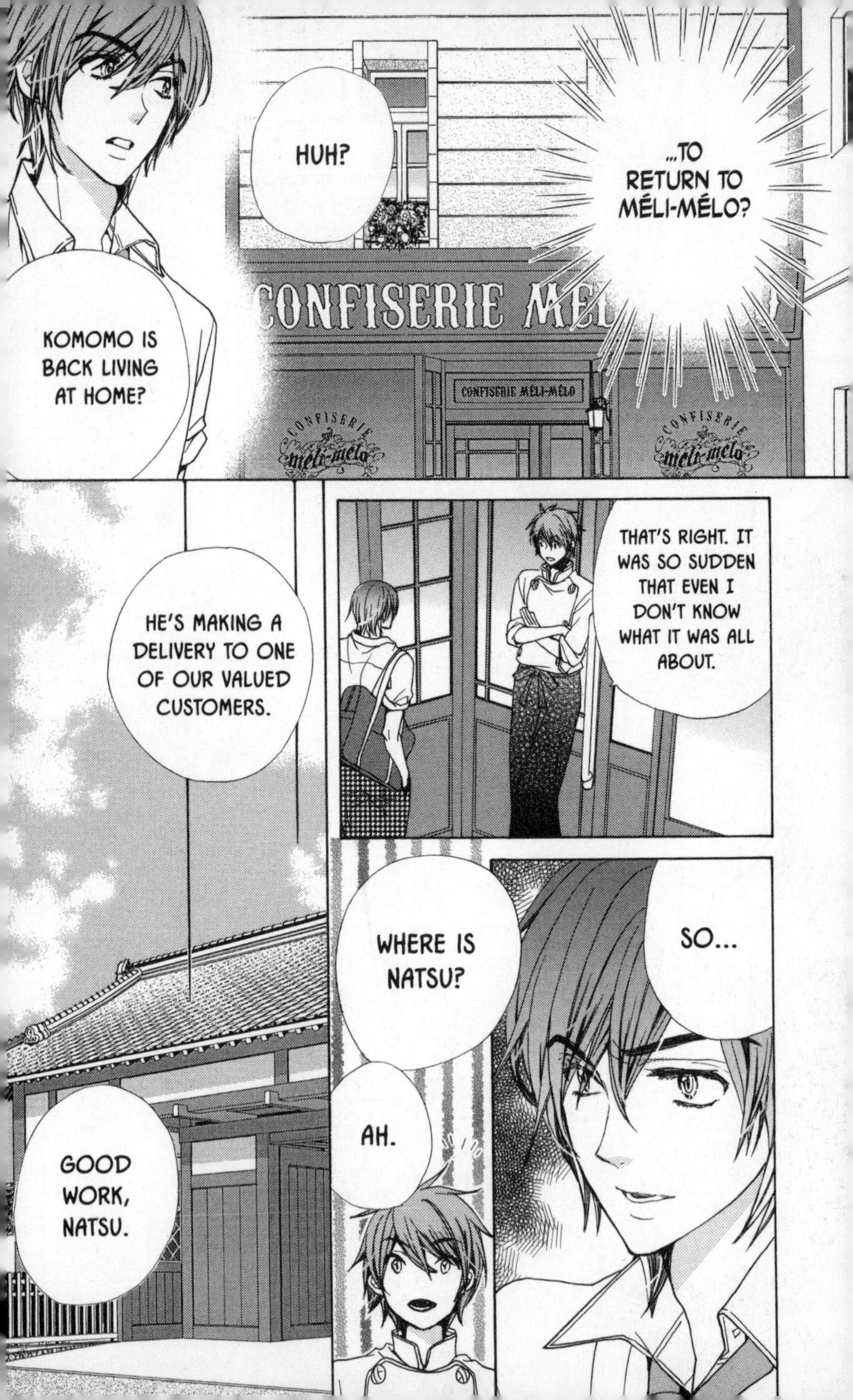
...TO RETURN TO MÉLI-MÉLO?
HUH?
KOMOMO IS BACK LIVING AT HOME?
CONFISERIE MÉLI-MÉLO
THAT'S RIGHT. IT WAS SO SUDDEN THAT EVEN I DON'T KNOW WHAT IT WAS ALL ABOUT.
SO...
WHERE IS NATSU?
AH.
HE'S MAKING A DELIVERY TO ONE OF OUR VALUED CUSTOMERS.
GOOD WORK, NATSU.

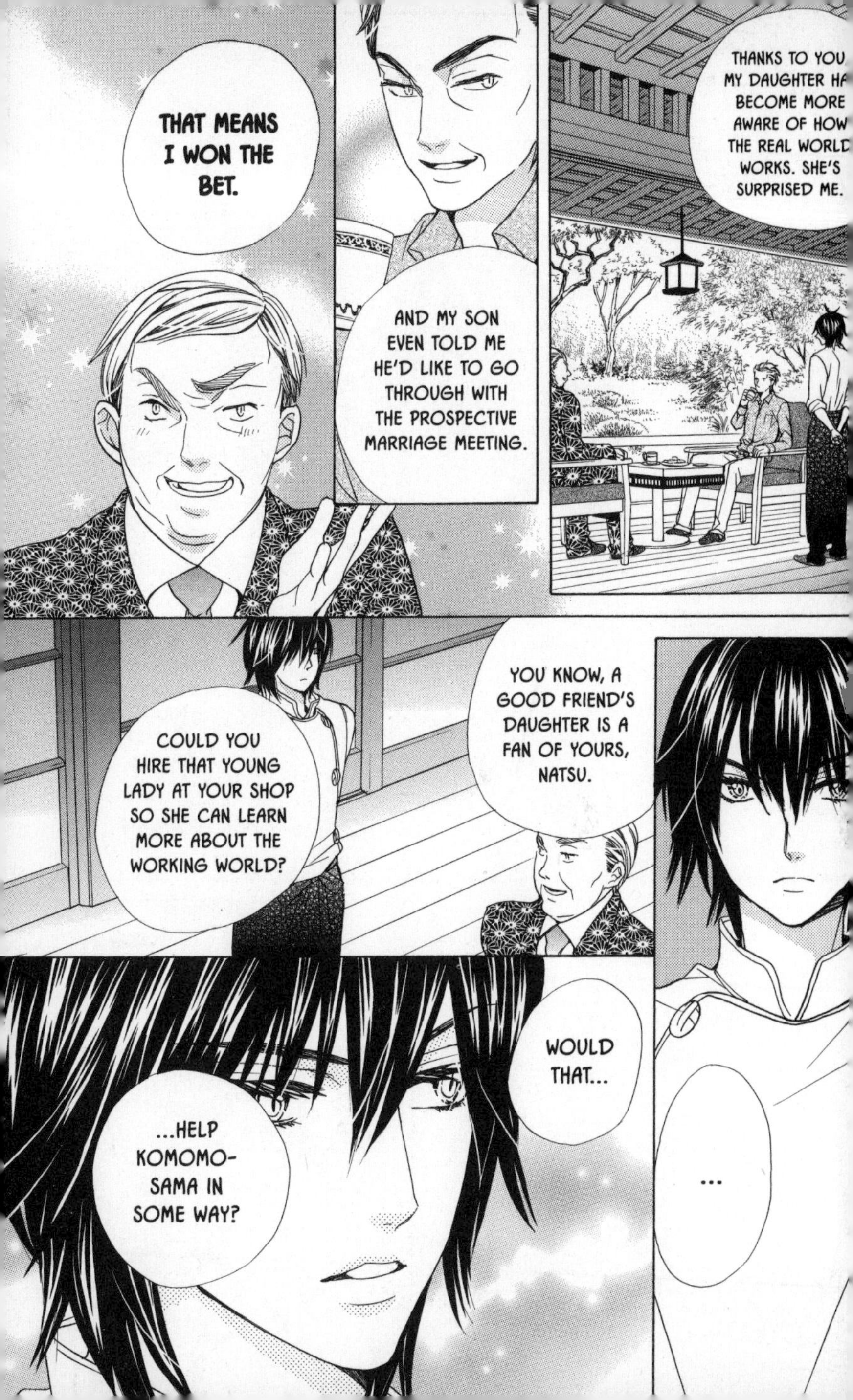
THANKS TO YOU, MY DAUGHTER HA BECOME MORE AWARE OF HOW THE REAL WORLD WORKS. SHE'S SURPRISED ME.
AND MY SON EVEN TOLD ME HE'D LIKE TO GO THROUGH WITH THE PROSPECTIVE MARRIAGE MEETING.
THAT MEANS I WON THE BET.
...
YOU KNOW, A GOOD FRIEND'S DAUGHTER IS A FAN OF YOURS, NATSU.
COULD YOU HIRE THAT YOUNG LADY AT YOUR SHOP SO SHE CAN LEARN MORE ABOUT THE WORKING WORLD?
WOULD THAT...
...HELP KOMOMO-SAMA IN SOME WAY?

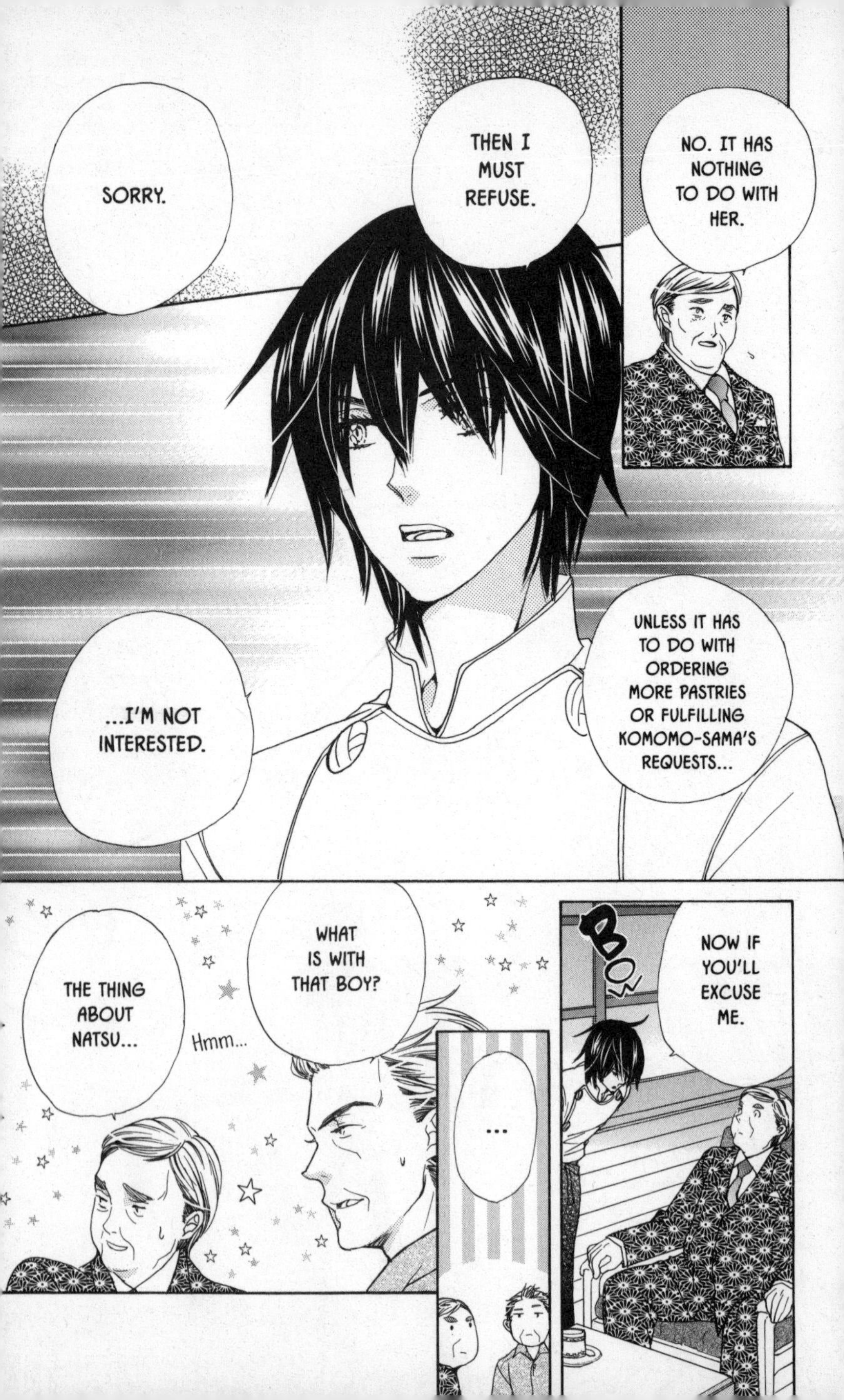
NO. IT HAS NOTHING TO DO WITH HER.
THEN I MUST REFUSE.
SORRY.
UNLESS IT HAS TO DO WITH ORDERING MORE PASTRIES OR FULFILLING KOMOMO-SAMA'S REQUESTS...
...I'M NOT INTERESTED.
BOW
NOW IF YOU'LL EXCUSE ME.
...
WHAT IS WITH THAT BOY?
Hmm...
THE THING ABOUT NATSU...

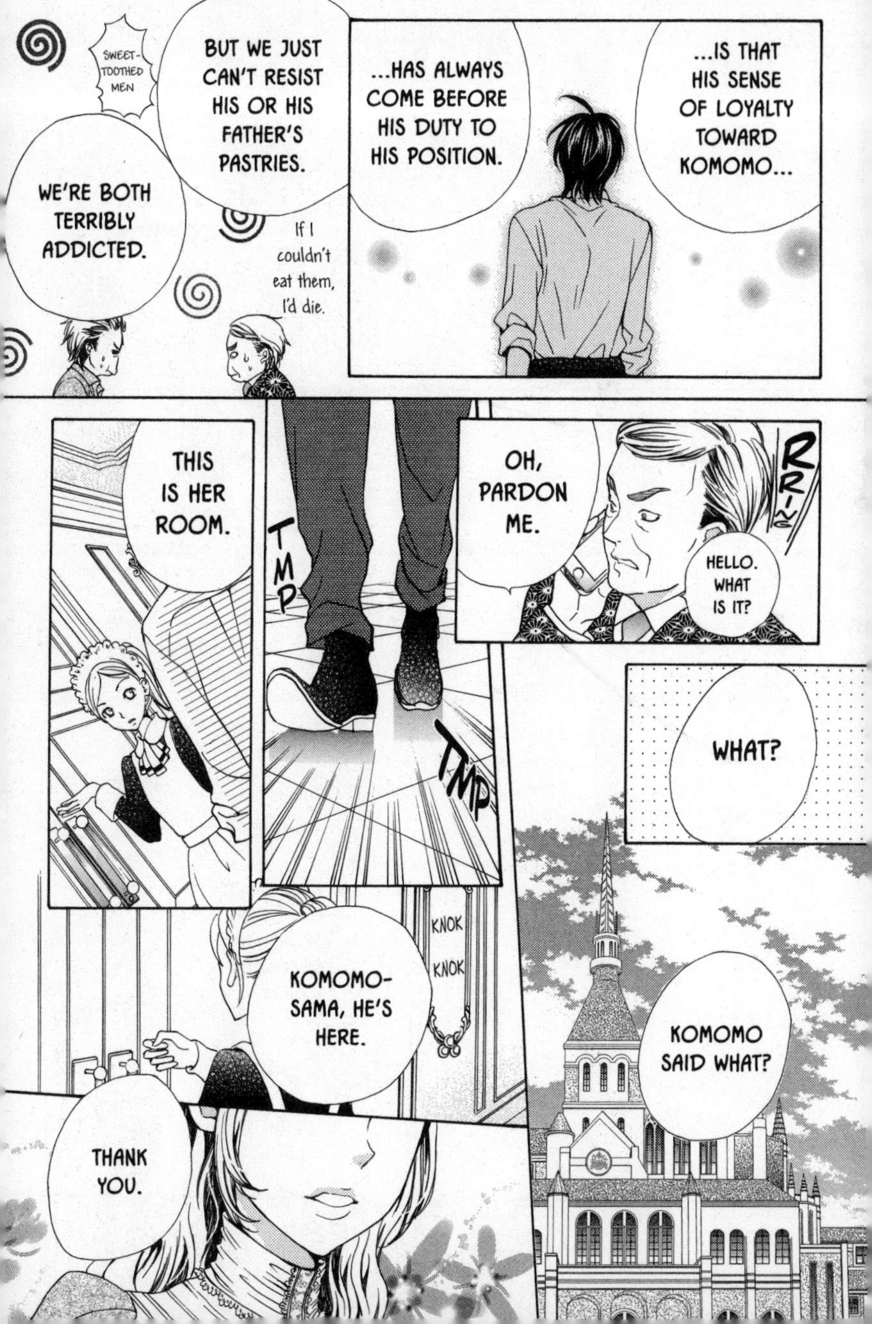
...IS THAT HIS SENSE OF LOYALTY TOWARD KOMOMO...
...HAS ALWAYS COME BEFORE HIS DUTY TO HIS POSITION.
BUT WE JUST CAN'T RESIST HIS OR HIS FATHER'S PASTRIES.
SWEET-TOOTHED MEN
WE'RE BOTH TERRIBLY ADDICTED.
If I couldn't eat them, I'd die.
RRING
OH, PARDON ME.
HELLO. WHAT IS IT?
TMP
TMP
THIS IS HER ROOM.
WHAT?
KOMOMO SAID WHAT?
KNOK KNOK
KOMOMO-SAMA, HE'S HERE.
THANK YOU.

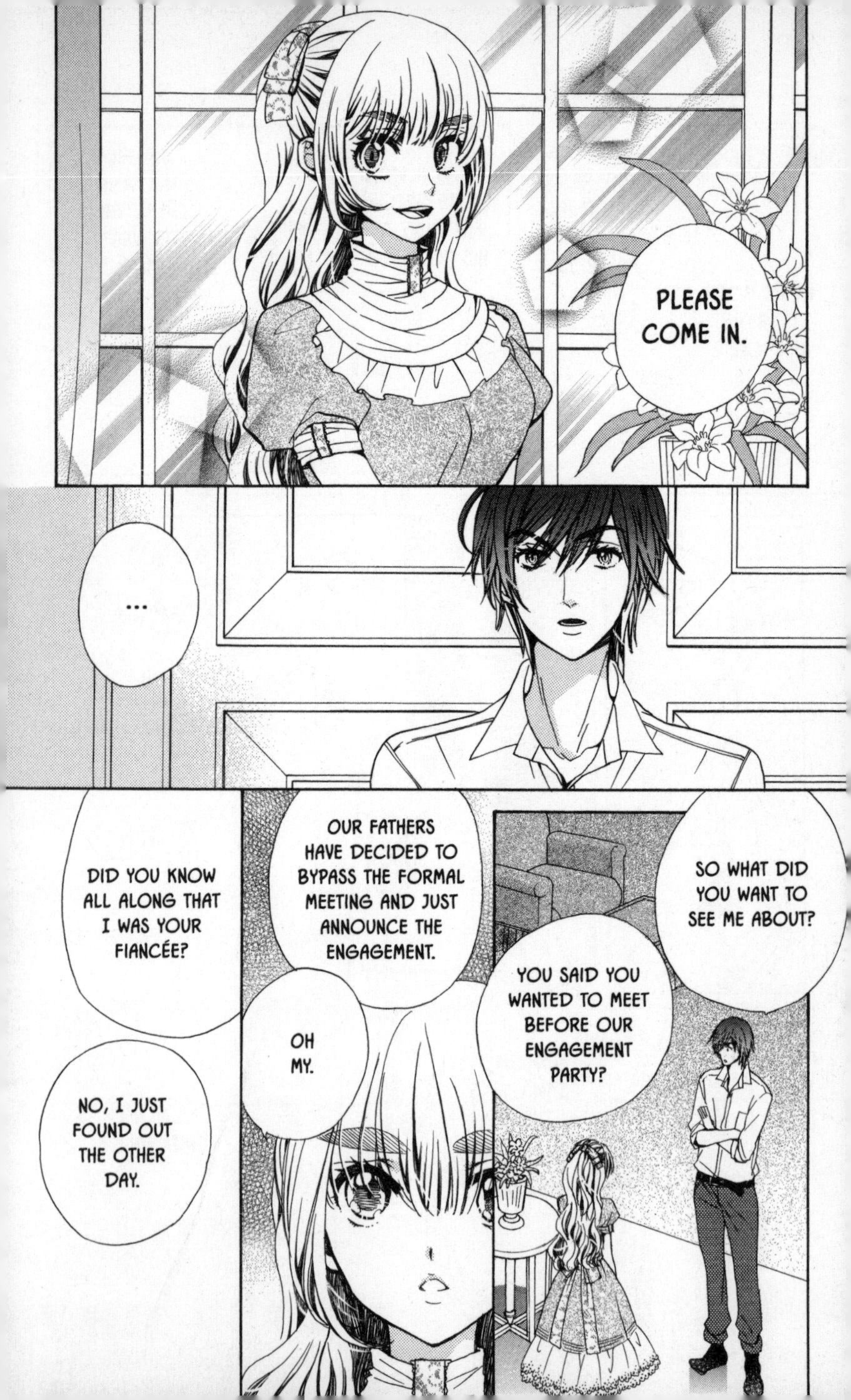
PLEASE COME IN.
...
SO WHAT DID YOU WANT TO SEE ME ABOUT?
YOU SAID YOU WANTED TO MEET BEFORE OUR ENGAGEMENT PARTY?
OUR FATHERS HAVE DECIDED TO BYPASS THE FORMAL MEETING AND JUST ANNOUNCE THE ENGAGEMENT.
OH MY.
DID YOU KNOW ALL ALONG THAT I WAS YOUR FIANCÉE?
NO, I JUST FOUND OUT THE OTHER DAY.

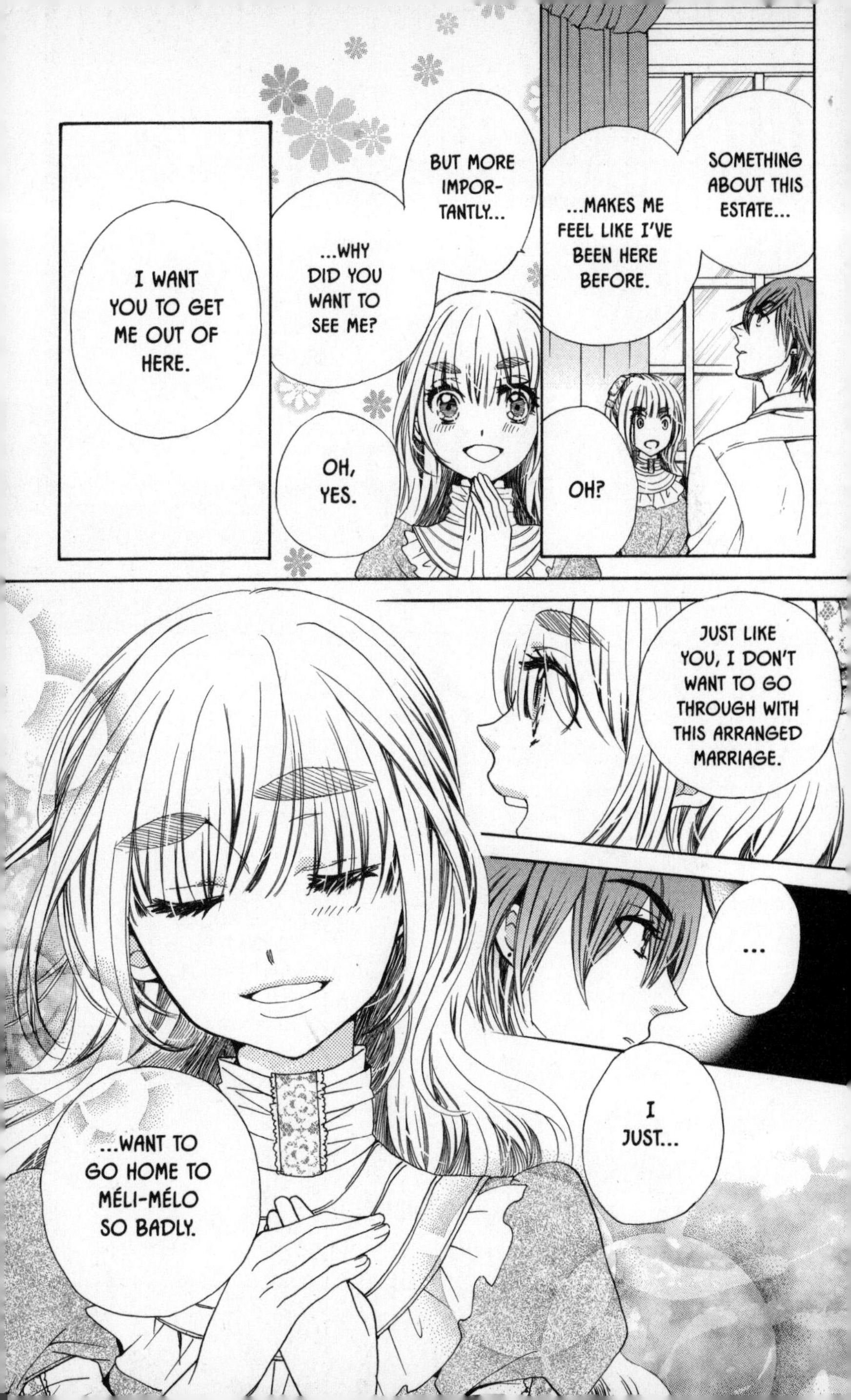
SOMETHING ABOUT THIS ESTATE...
...MAKES ME FEEL LIKE I'VE BEEN HERE BEFORE.
OH?
BUT MORE IMPOR-TANTLY...
...WHY DID YOU WANT TO SEE ME?
OH, YES.
I WANT YOU TO GET ME OUT OF HERE.
JUST LIKE YOU, I DON'T WANT TO GO THROUGH WITH THIS ARRANGED MARRIAGE.
...
I JUST...
...WANT TO GO HOME TO MÉLI-MÉLO SO BADLY.

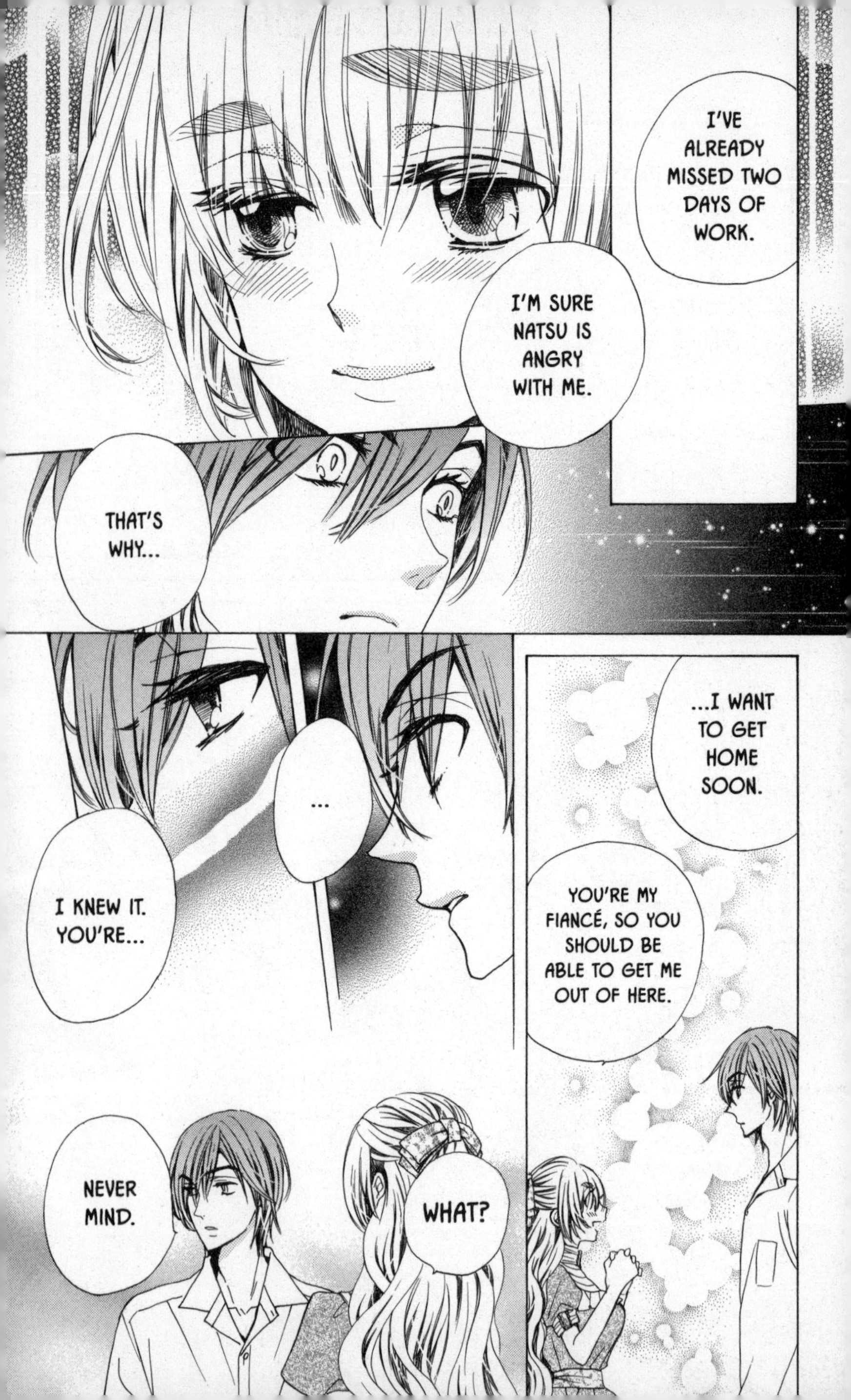
I'VE ALREADY MISSED TWO DAYS OF WORK.
I'M SURE NATSU IS ANGRY WITH ME.
THAT'S WHY...
...I WANT TO GET HOME SOON.
YOU'RE MY FIANCÉ, SO YOU SHOULD BE ABLE TO GET ME OUT OF HERE.
...
I KNEW IT. YOU'RE...
WHAT?
NEVER MIND.

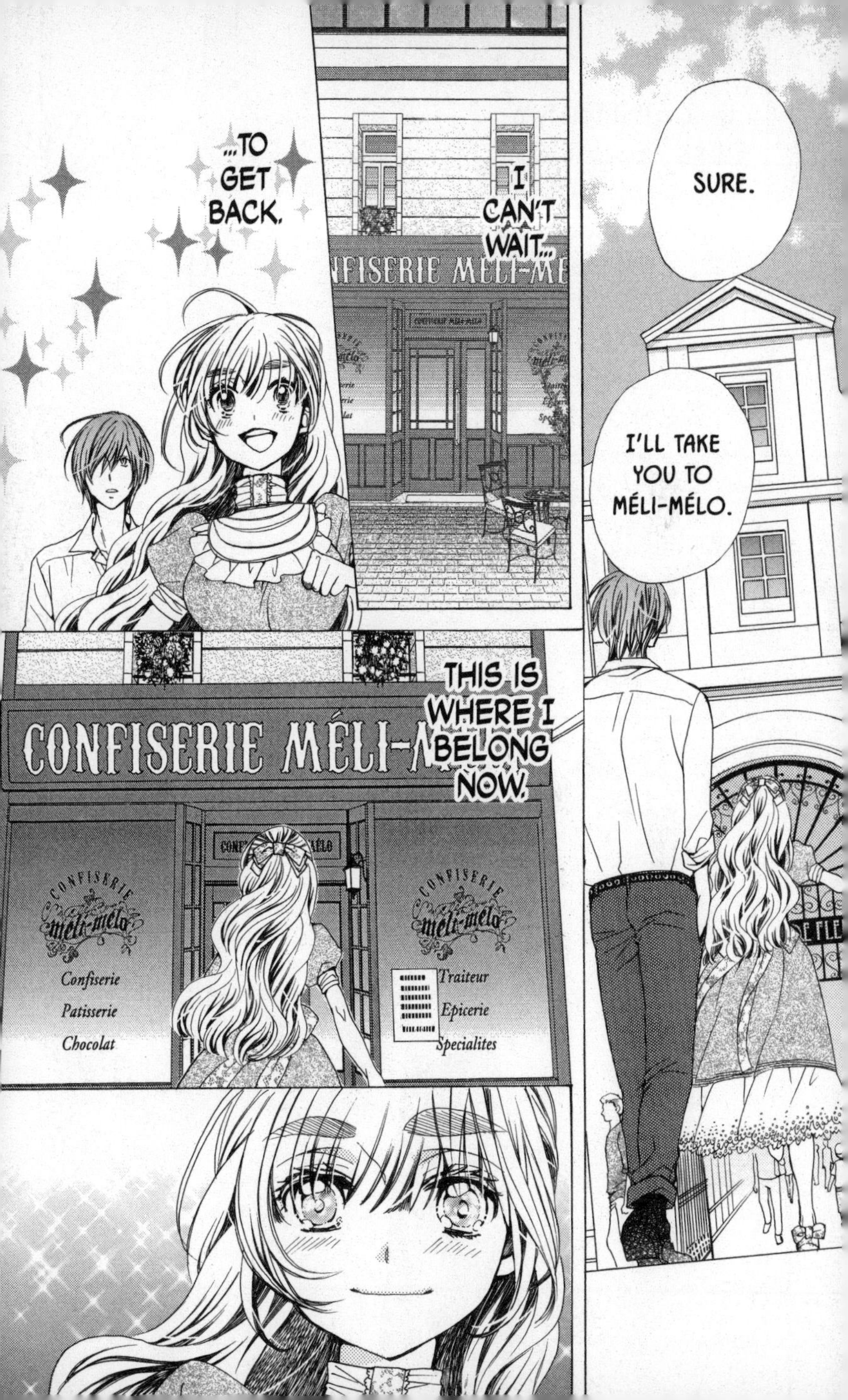
SURE.
I'LL TAKE YOU TO MÉLI-MÉLO.
I CAN'T WAIT...
...TO GET BACK.
THIS IS WHERE I BELONG NOW.
CONFISERIE
méli-mélo
Confiserie
Patisserie
Chocolat
CONFISERIE
méli-mélo
Traiteur
Epicerie
Specialites

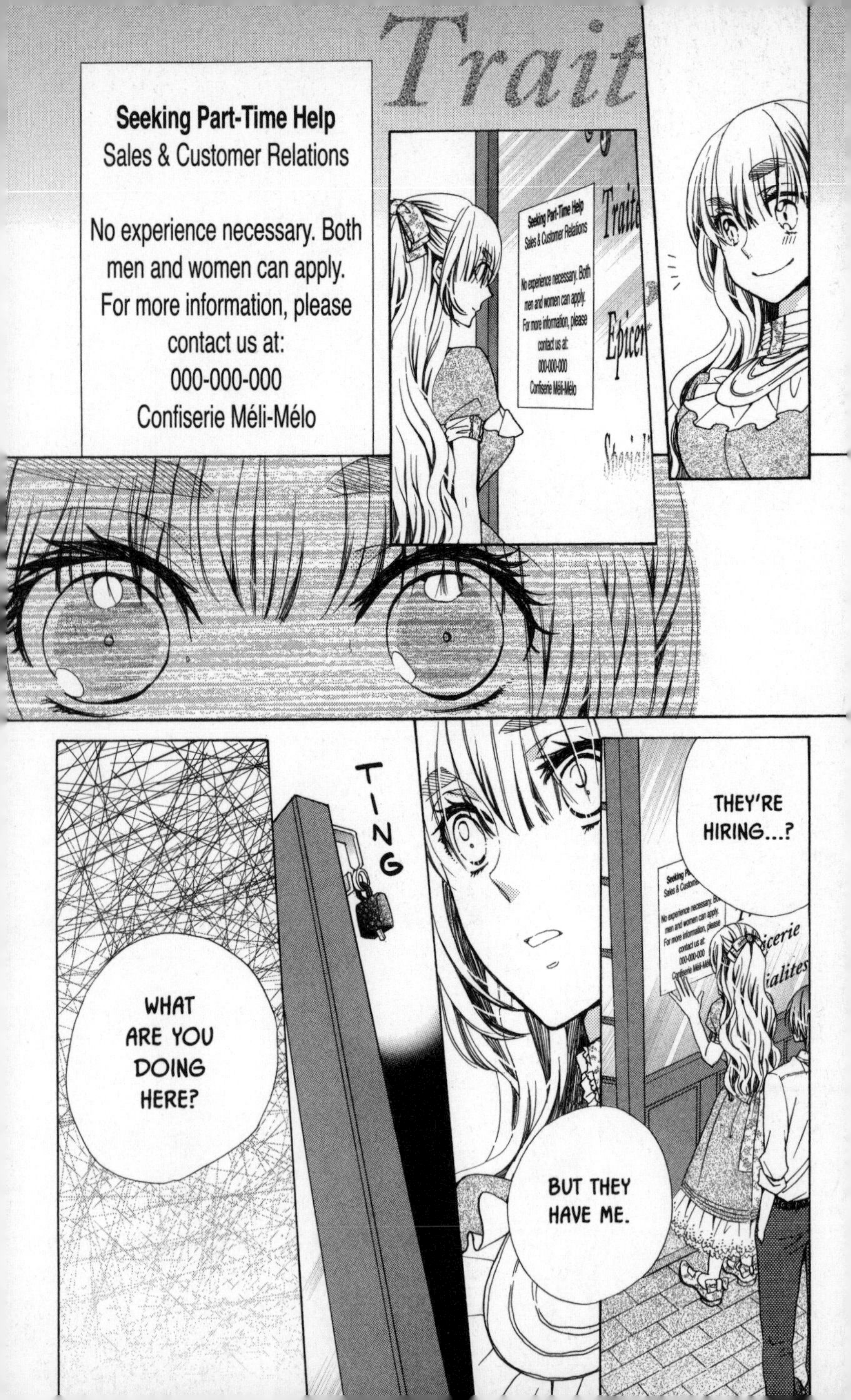
Trait
Seeking Part-Time Help
Sales & Customer Relations
No experience necessary. Both men and women can apply. For more information, please contact us at:
000-000-000
Confiserie Méli-Mélo
THEY'RE HIRING...?
BUT THEY HAVE ME.
TING
WHAT ARE YOU DOING HERE?

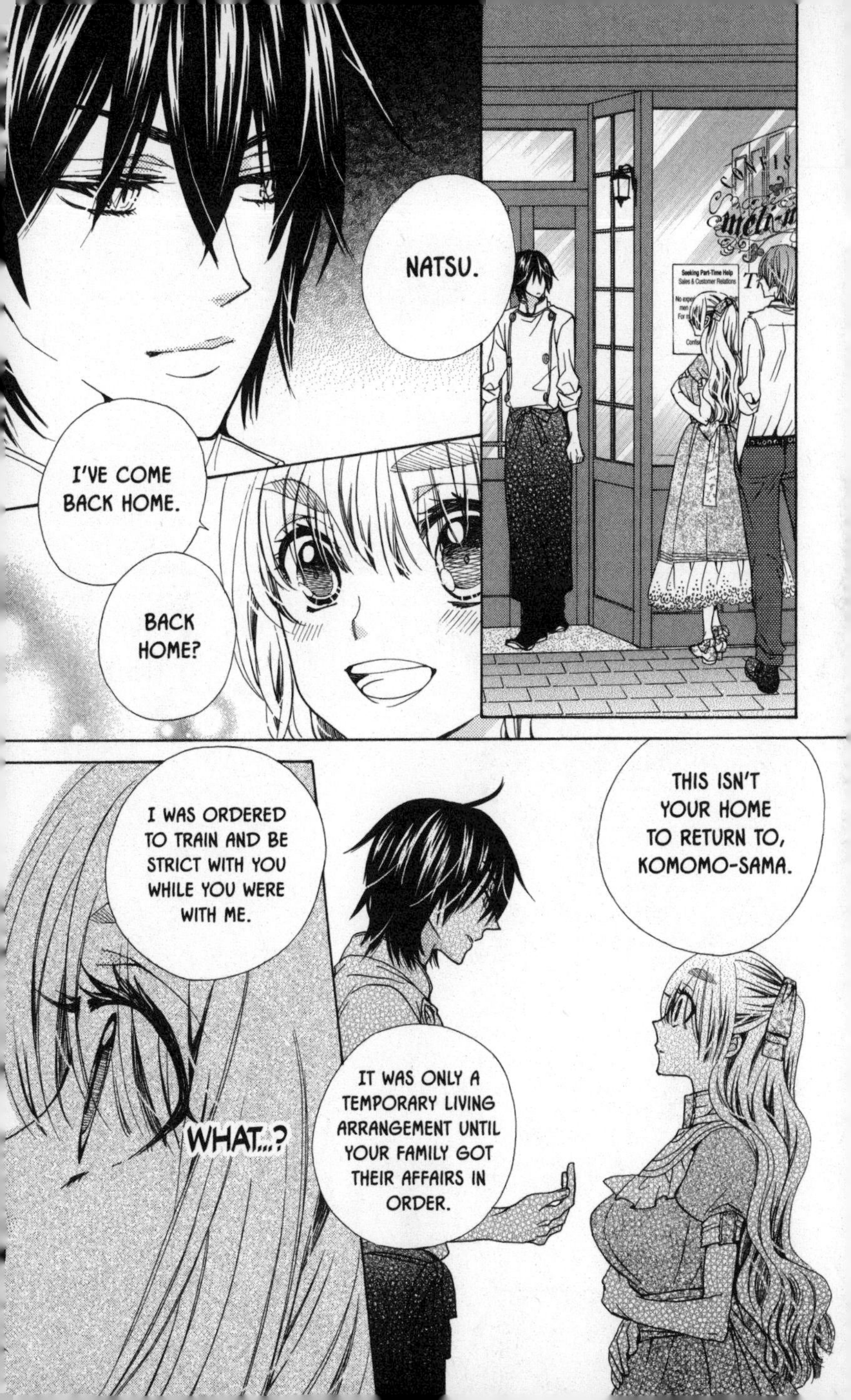
Seeking Part-Time Help
Sales & Customer Relations
NATSU.
I'VE COME BACK HOME.
BACK HOME?
THIS ISN'T YOUR HOME TO RETURN TO, KOMOMO-SAMA.
I WAS ORDERED TO TRAIN AND BE STRICT WITH YOU WHILE YOU WERE WITH ME.
IT WAS ONLY A TEMPORARY LIVING ARRANGEMENT UNTIL YOUR FAMILY GOT THEIR AFFAIRS IN ORDER.
WHAT...?

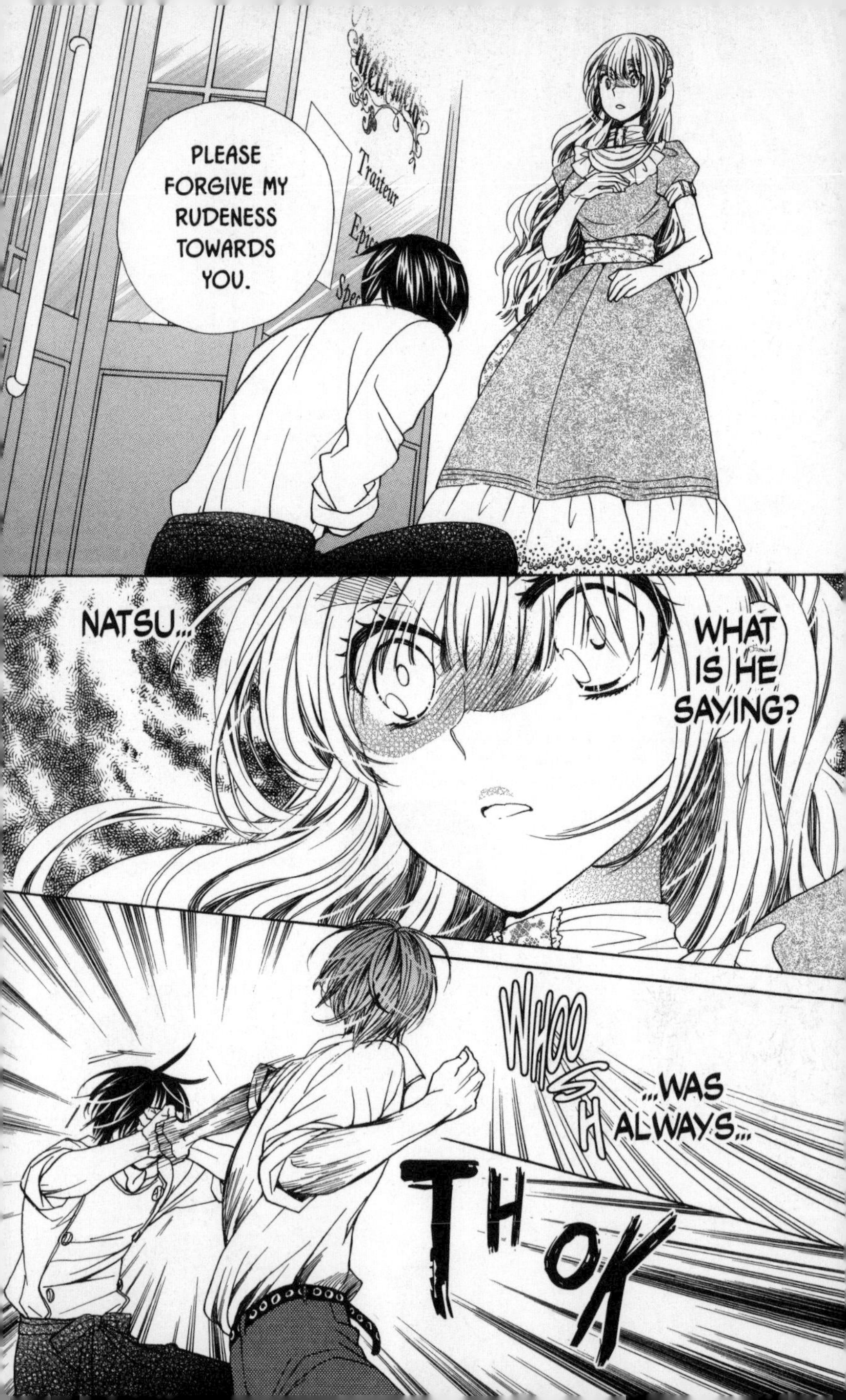
Traiteur
PLEASE FORGIVE MY RUDENESS TOWARDS YOU.
WHAT IS HE SAYING?
NATSU...
WHOOSH
...WAS ALWAYS...
THOK

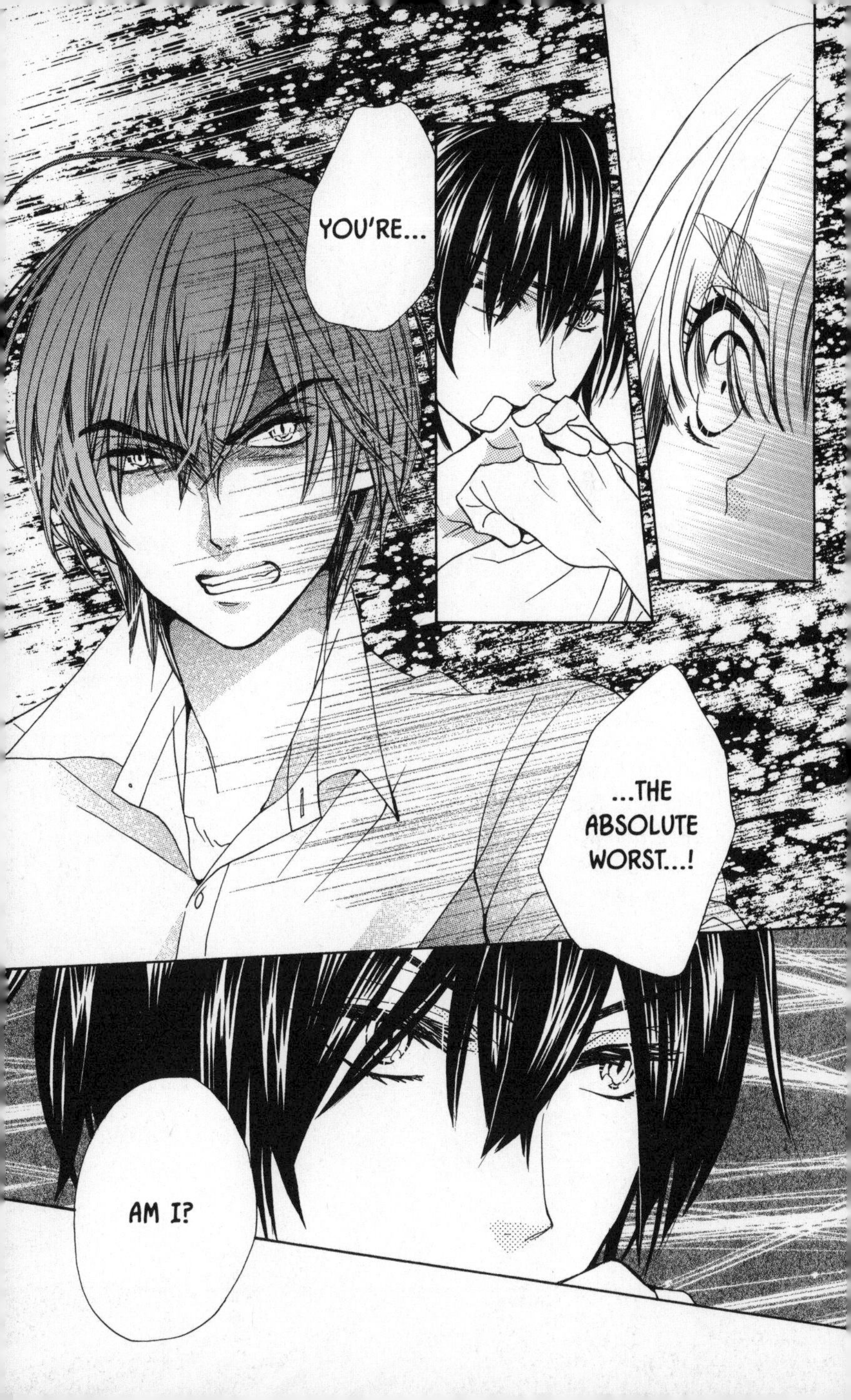
YOU'RE...
...THE ABSOLUTE WORST...!
AM I?

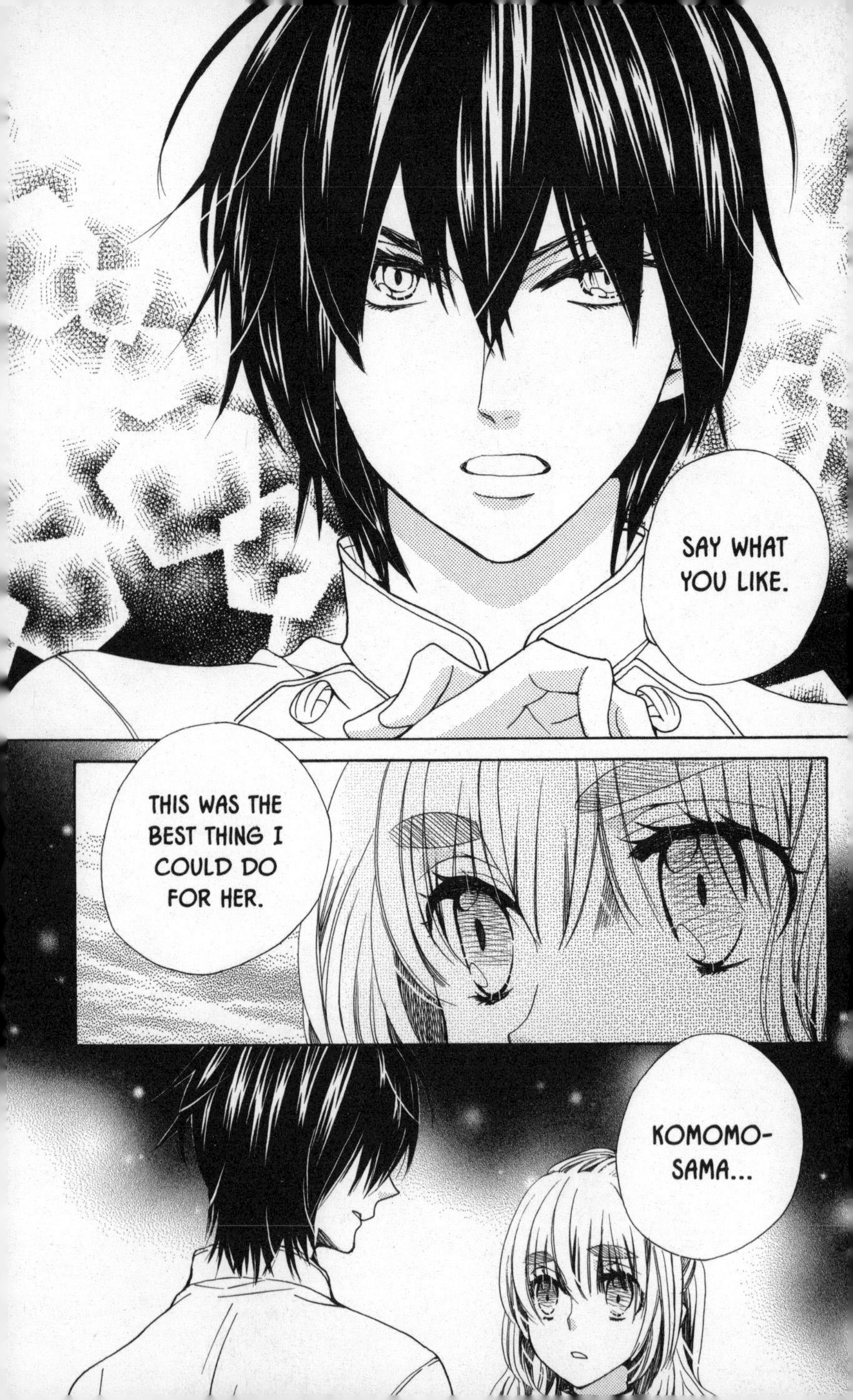
SAY WHAT YOU LIKE.
THIS WAS THE BEST THING I COULD DO FOR HER.
KOMOMO-SAMA...

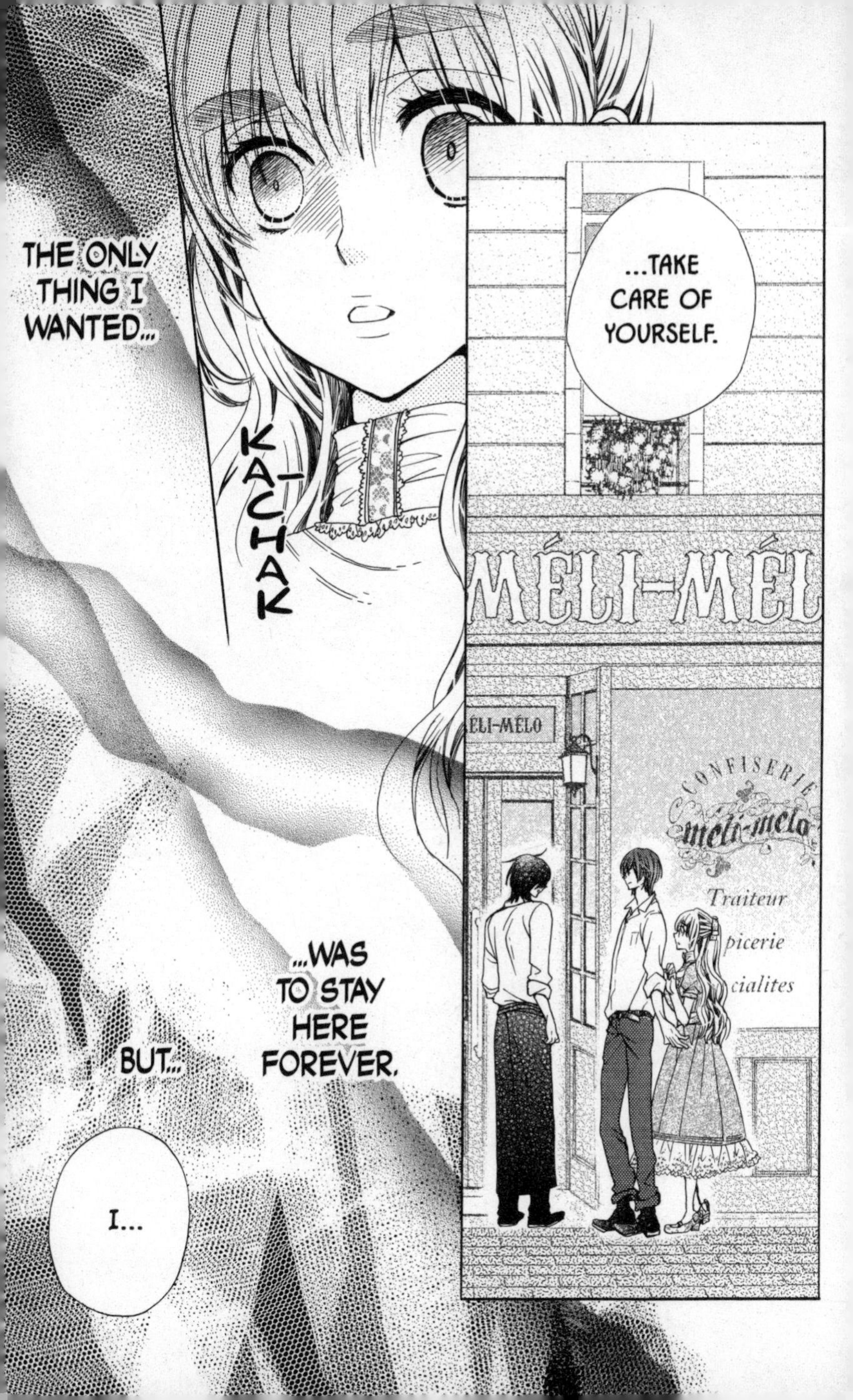
...TAKE CARE OF YOURSELF.
MÉLI-MÉL
ÉLI-MÉLO
CONFISERIE
méli-mélo
Traiteur
picerie
cialites
THE ONLY THING I WANTED...
KA-CHAK
...WAS TO STAY HERE FOREVER.
BUT...
I...

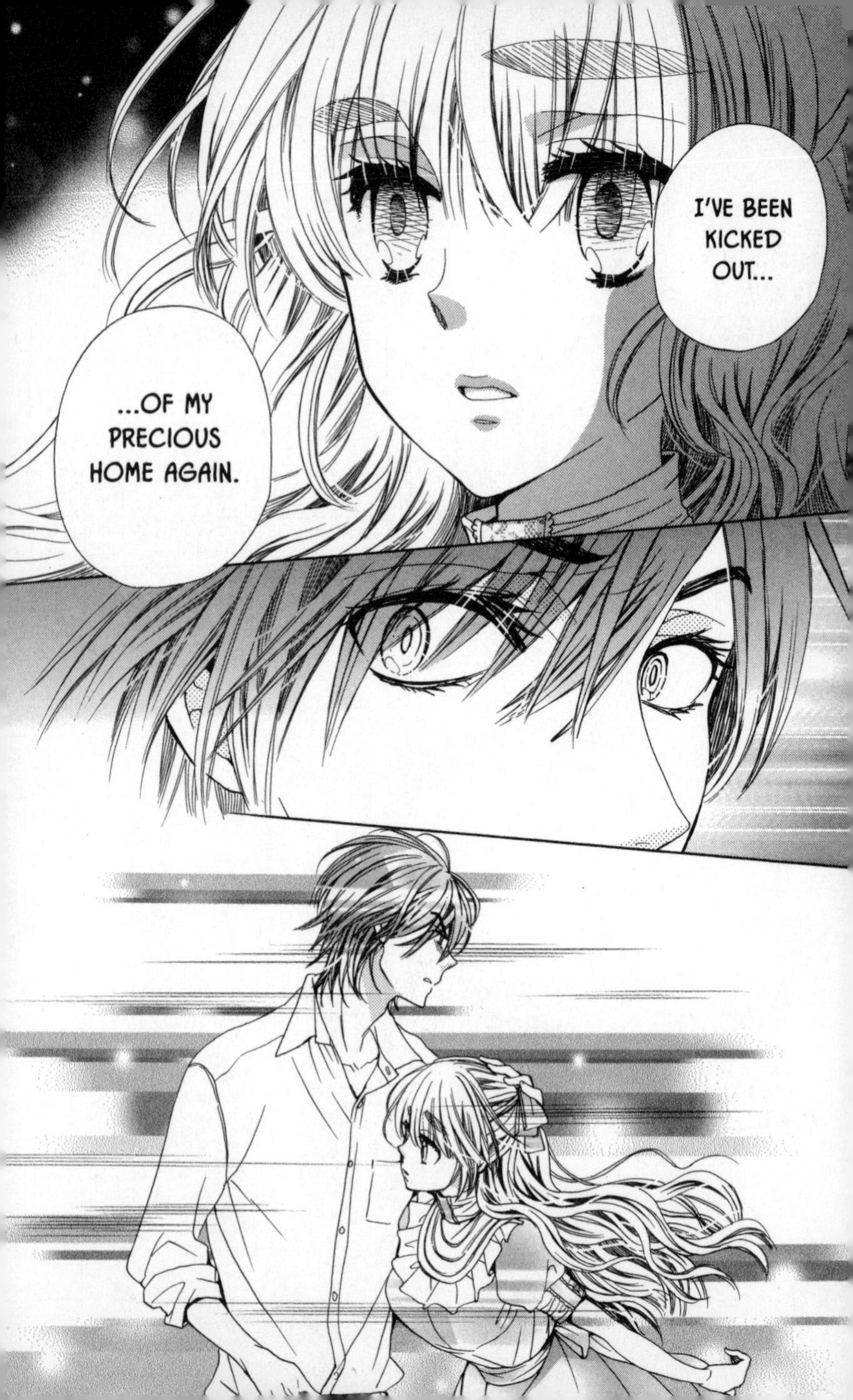
I'VE BEEN KICKED OUT...
...OF MY PRECIOUS HOME AGAIN.

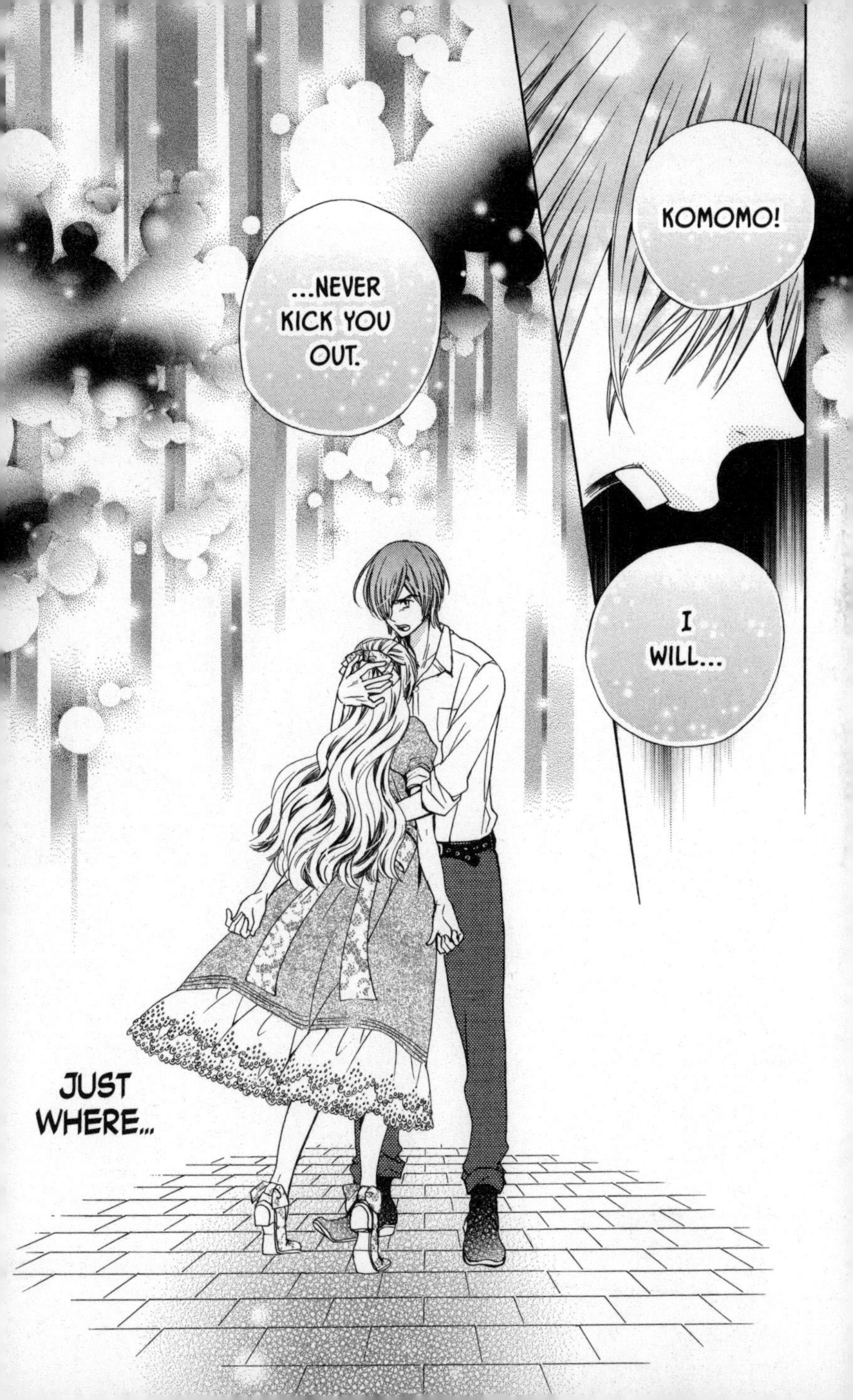
KOMOMO!
I WILL...
...NEVER KICK YOU OUT.
JUST WHERE...

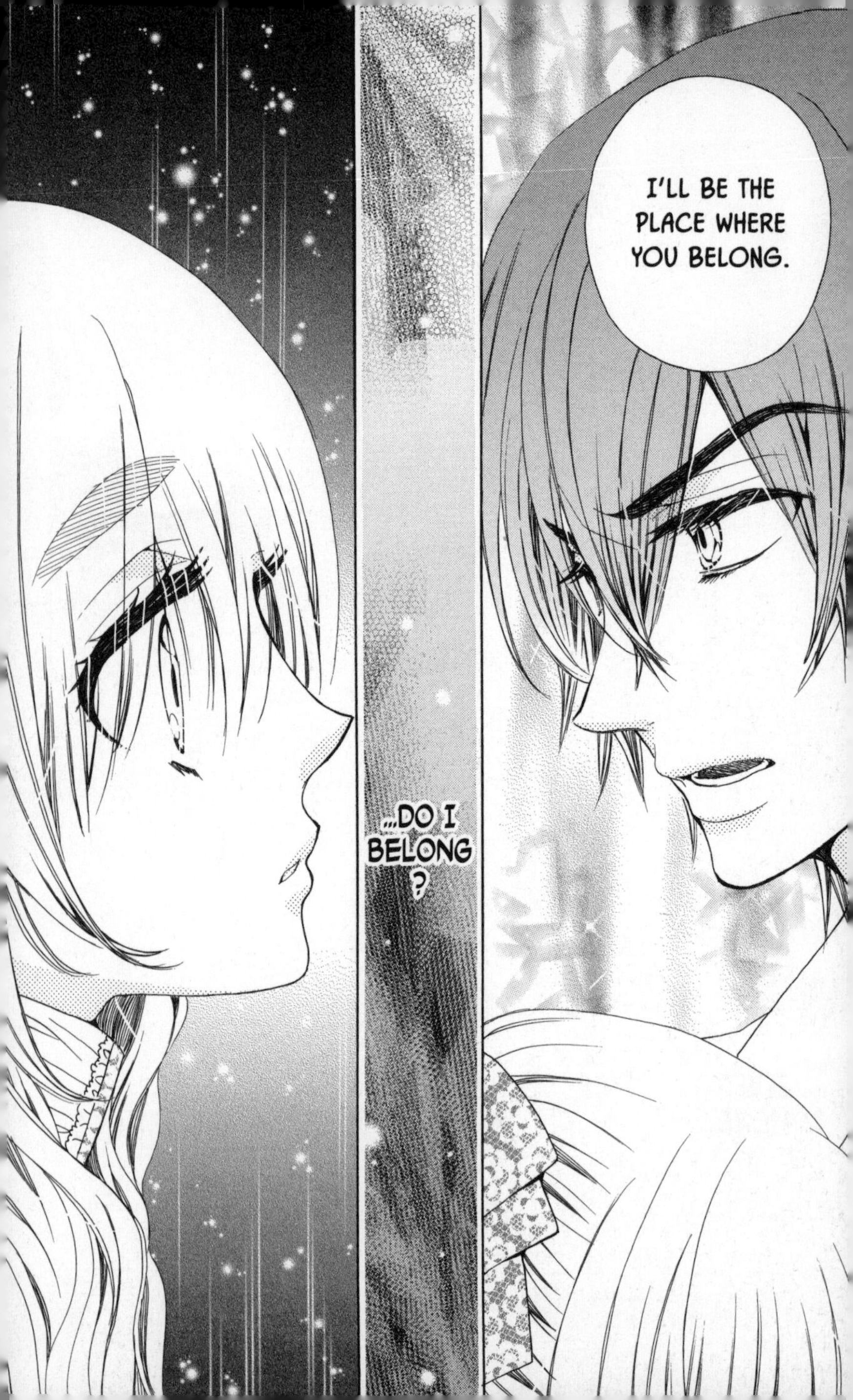
I'LL BE THE PLACE WHERE YOU BELONG.
...DO I BELONG?

CHAPTER 27

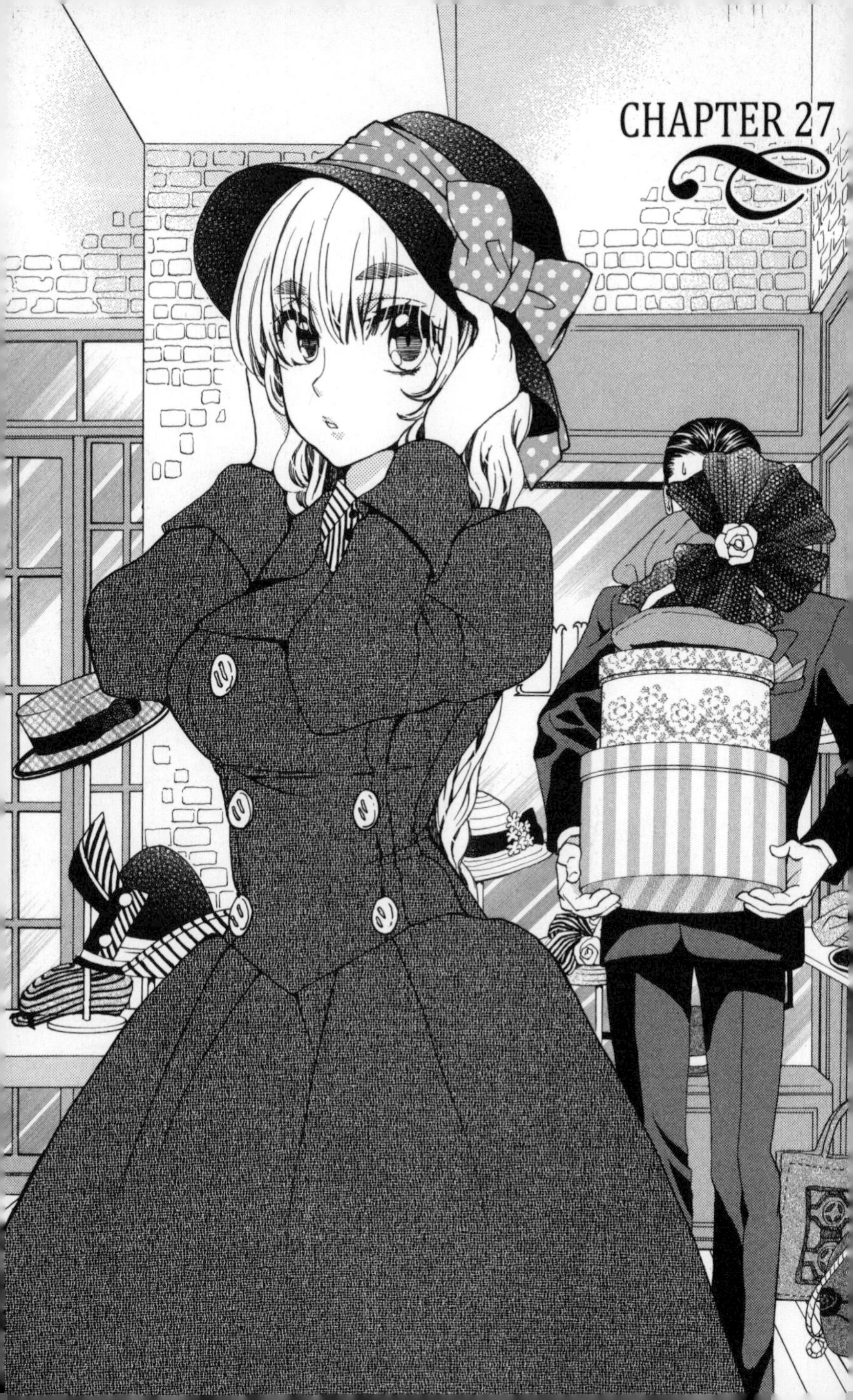

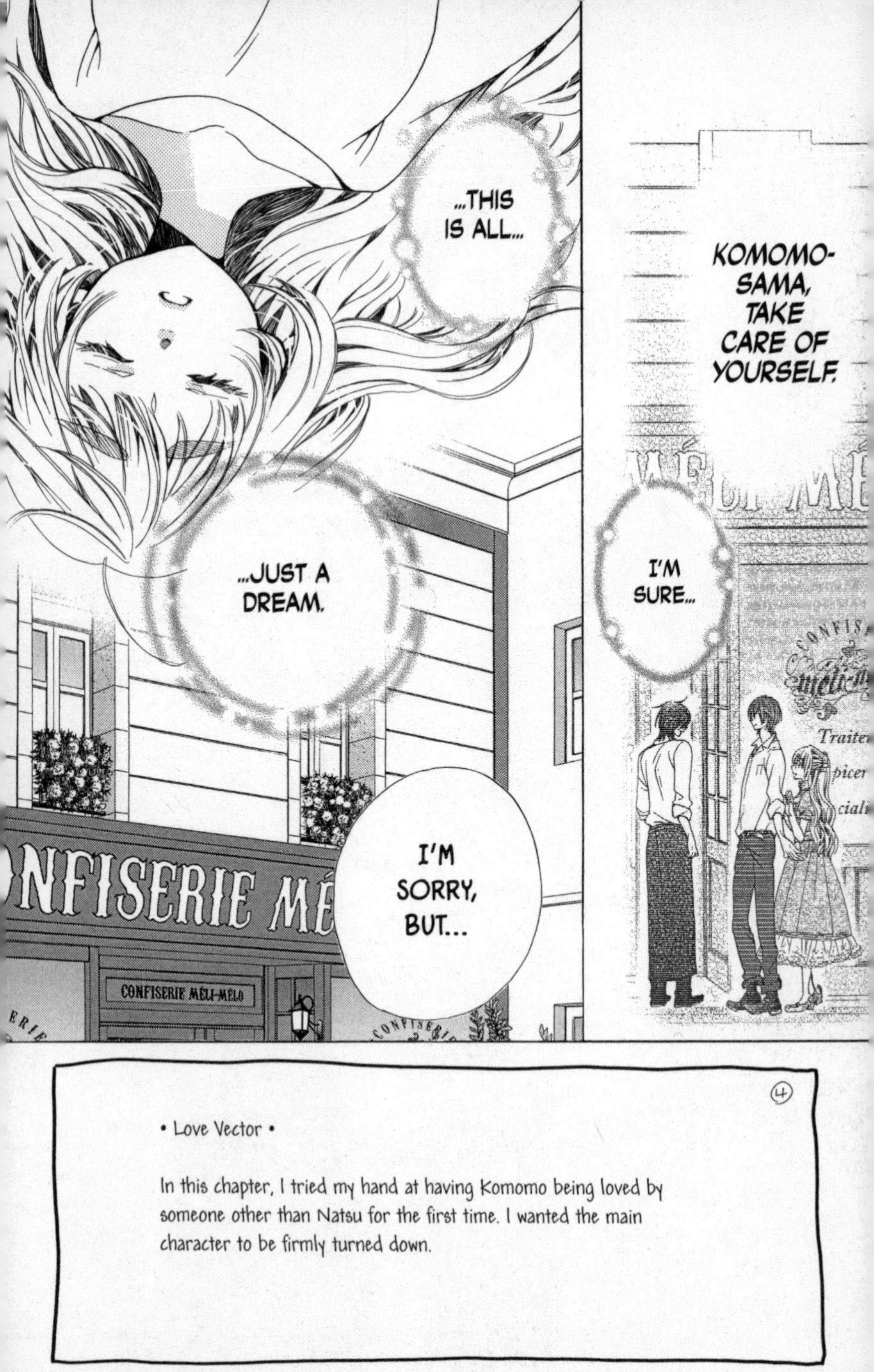
KOMOMO-SAMA, TAKE CARE OF YOURSELF.
I'M SURE...
...THIS IS ALL...
...JUST A DREAM.
I'M SORRY, BUT...
NFISERIE MÉ
CONFISERIE MÉLI-MÉLO

④

• Love Vector •

In this chapter, I tried my hand at having Komomo being loved by someone other than Natsu for the first time. I wanted the main character to be firmly turned down.

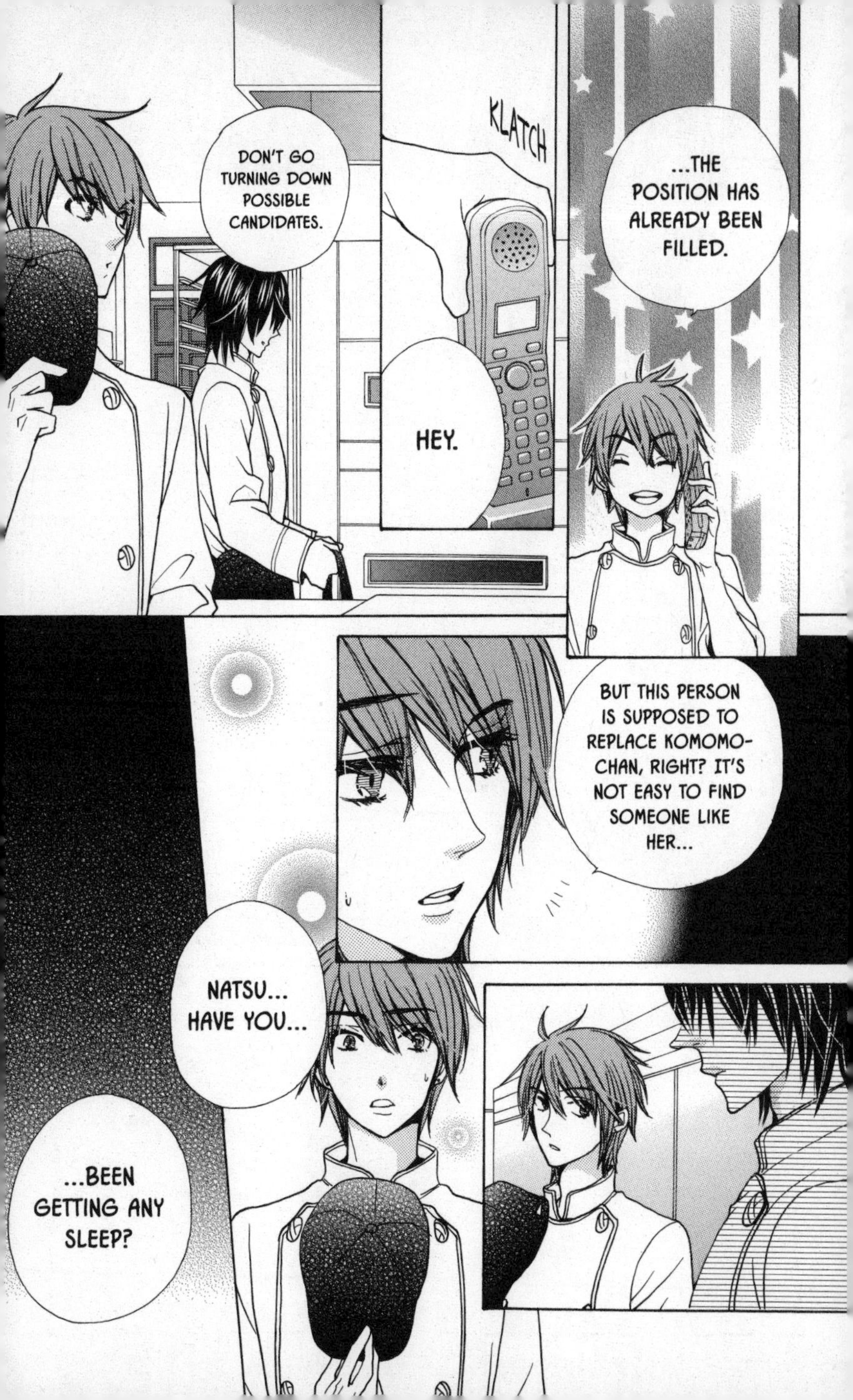
...THE POSITION HAS ALREADY BEEN FILLED.
KLATCH
HEY.
DON'T GO TURNING DOWN POSSIBLE CANDIDATES.
BUT THIS PERSON IS SUPPOSED TO REPLACE KOMOMO-CHAN, RIGHT? IT'S NOT EASY TO FIND SOMEONE LIKE HER...
NATSU... HAVE YOU...
...BEEN GETTING ANY SLEEP?

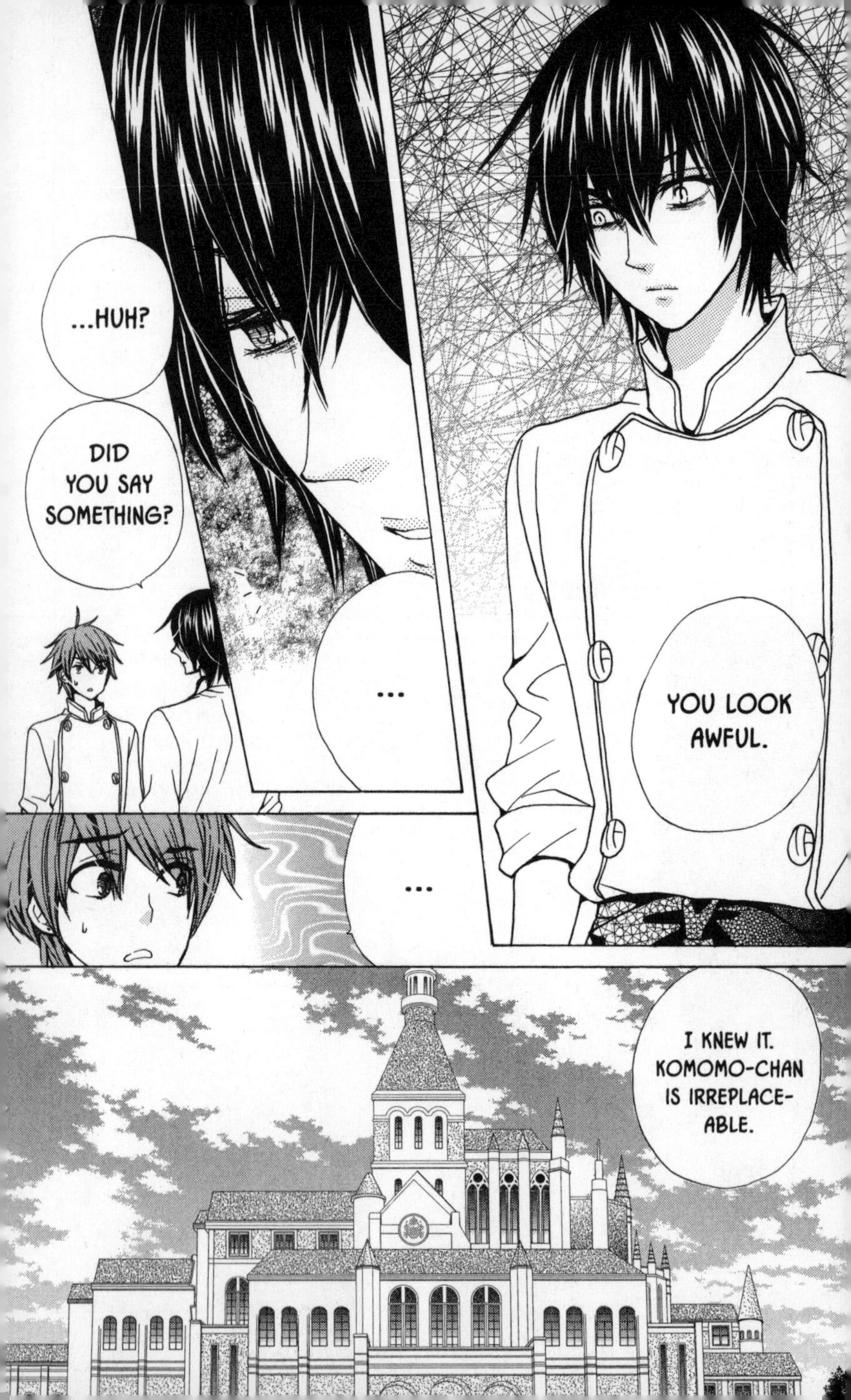
YOU LOOK AWFUL.
...
...HUH?
DID YOU SAY SOMETHING?
...
I KNEW IT. KOMOMO-CHAN IS IRREPLACE-ABLE.

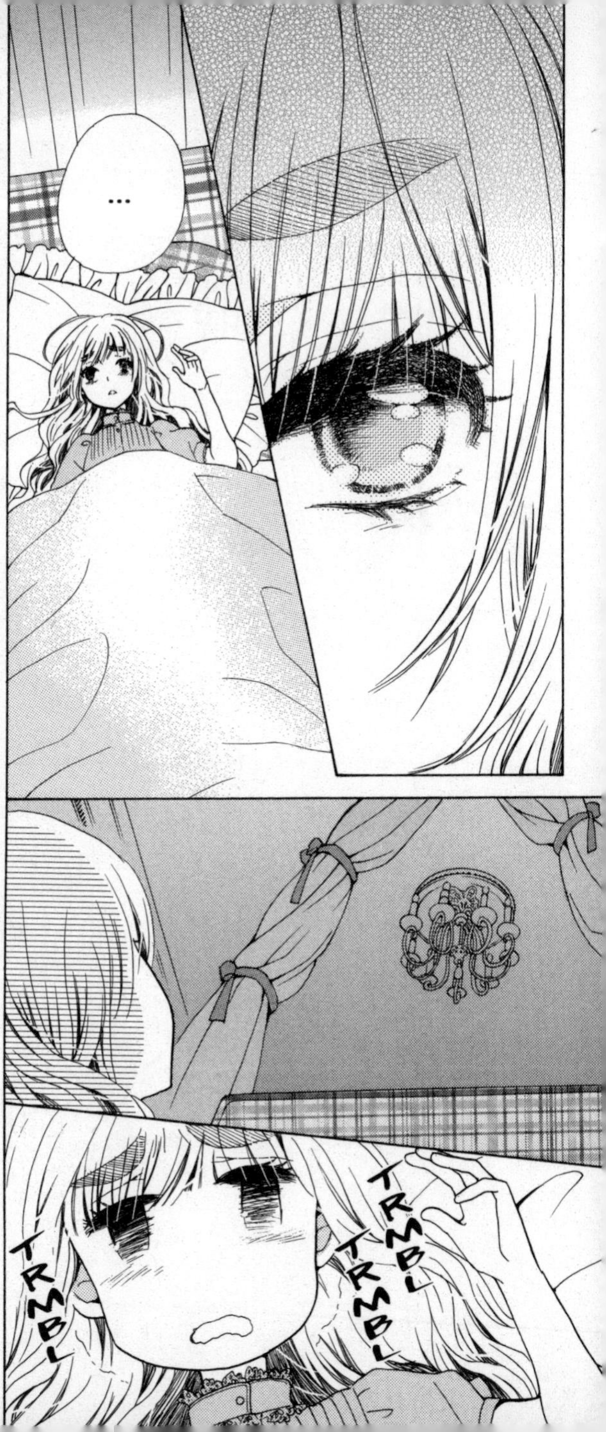
...
TRMBL TRMBL
TRMBL

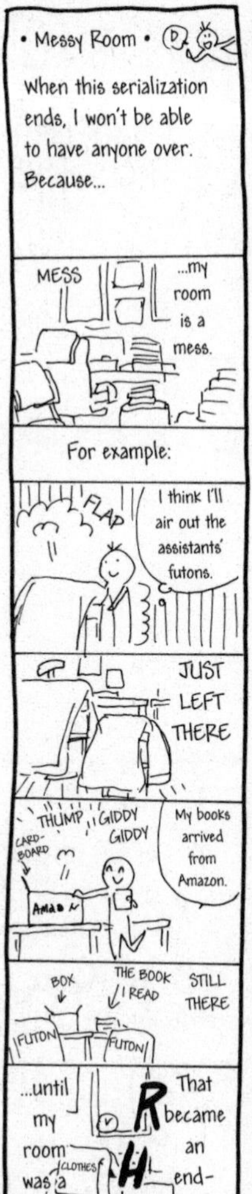
• Messy Room •
When this serialization ends, I won't be able to have anyone over. Because...
...my room is a mess.
MESS
For example:
I think I'll air out the assistants' futons.
FLAP
JUST LEFT THERE
My books arrived from Amazon.
THUMP
GIDDY GIDDY
CARD-BOARD
STILL THERE
THE BOOK I READ
BOX
FUTON
FUTON
That became an endless loop...
RHHHHM
...until my room was a disaster.
CLOTHES
AMAZON
FUTON
Of course I'll eventually clean it all up.

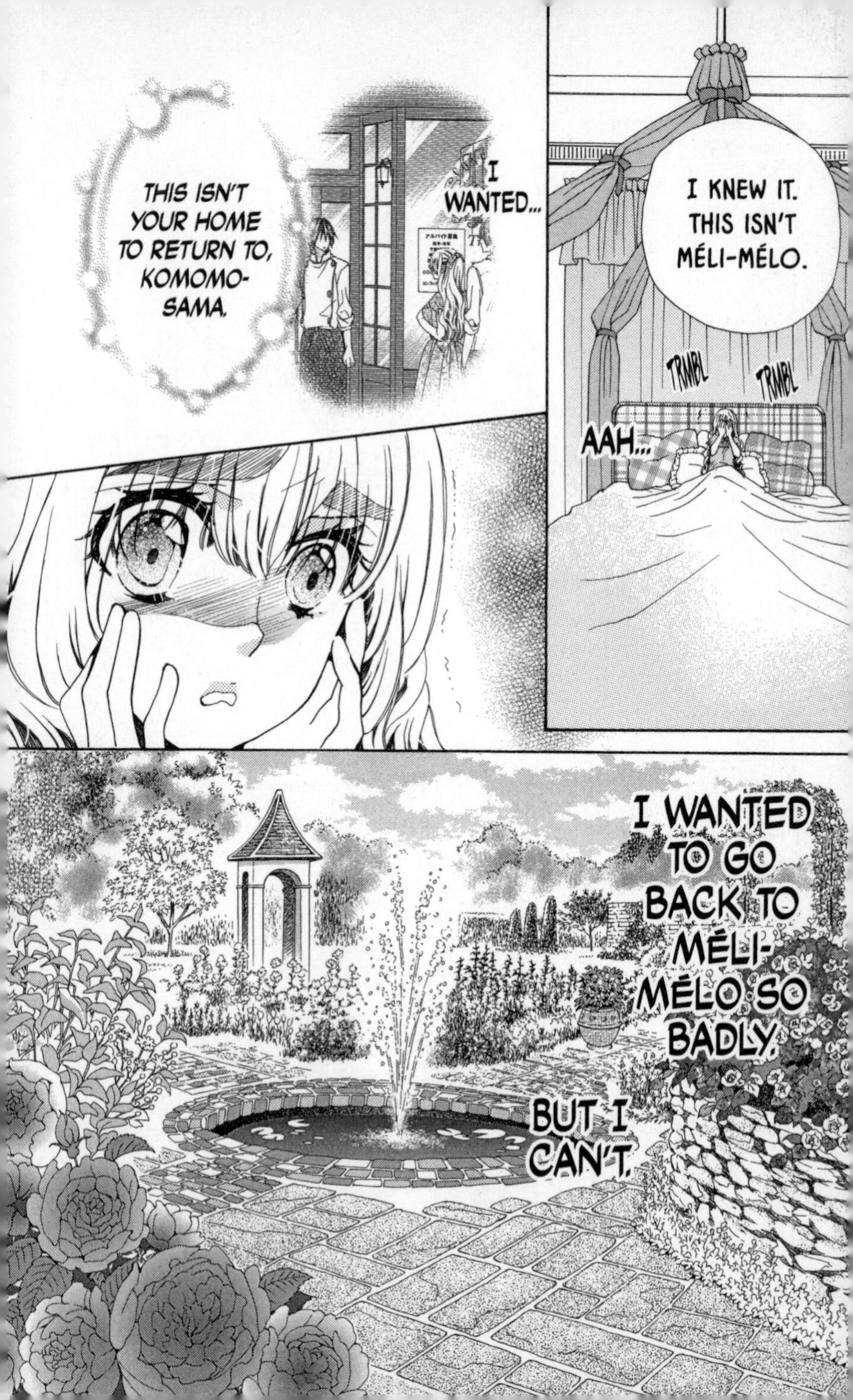
I KNEW IT. THIS ISN'T MÉLI-MÉLO.
TRMBL
TRMBL
AAH...
I WANTED...
THIS ISN'T YOUR HOME TO RETURN TO, KOMOMO-SAMA.
I WANTED TO GO BACK TO MÉLI-MÉLO SO BADLY.
BUT I CAN'T.

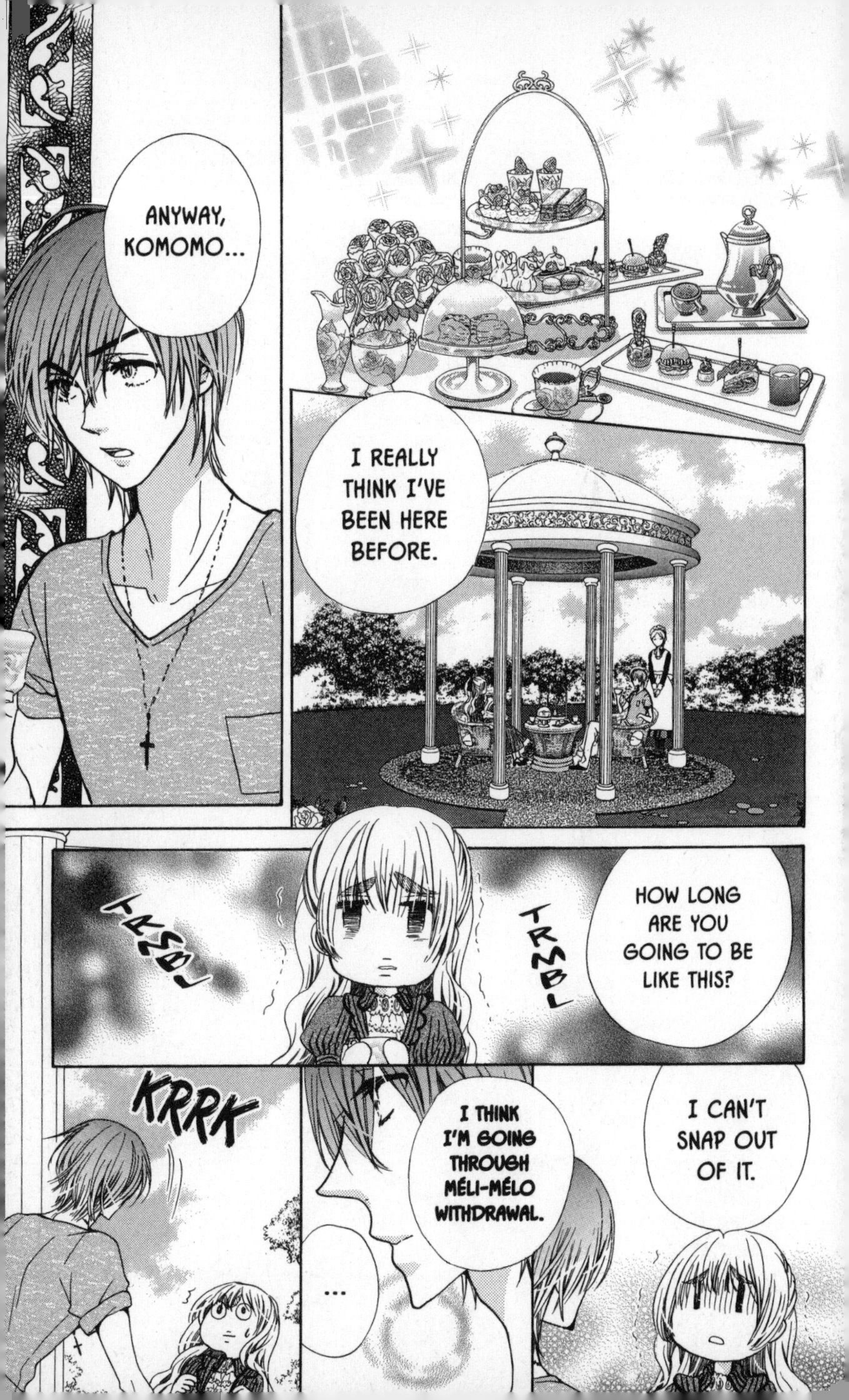
I REALLY THINK I'VE BEEN HERE BEFORE.
ANYWAY, KOMOMO...
TRMBL
TRMBL
HOW LONG ARE YOU GOING TO BE LIKE THIS?
I CAN'T SNAP OUT OF IT.
I THINK I'M GOING THROUGH MÉLI-MÉLO WITHDRAWAL.
...
KRRK

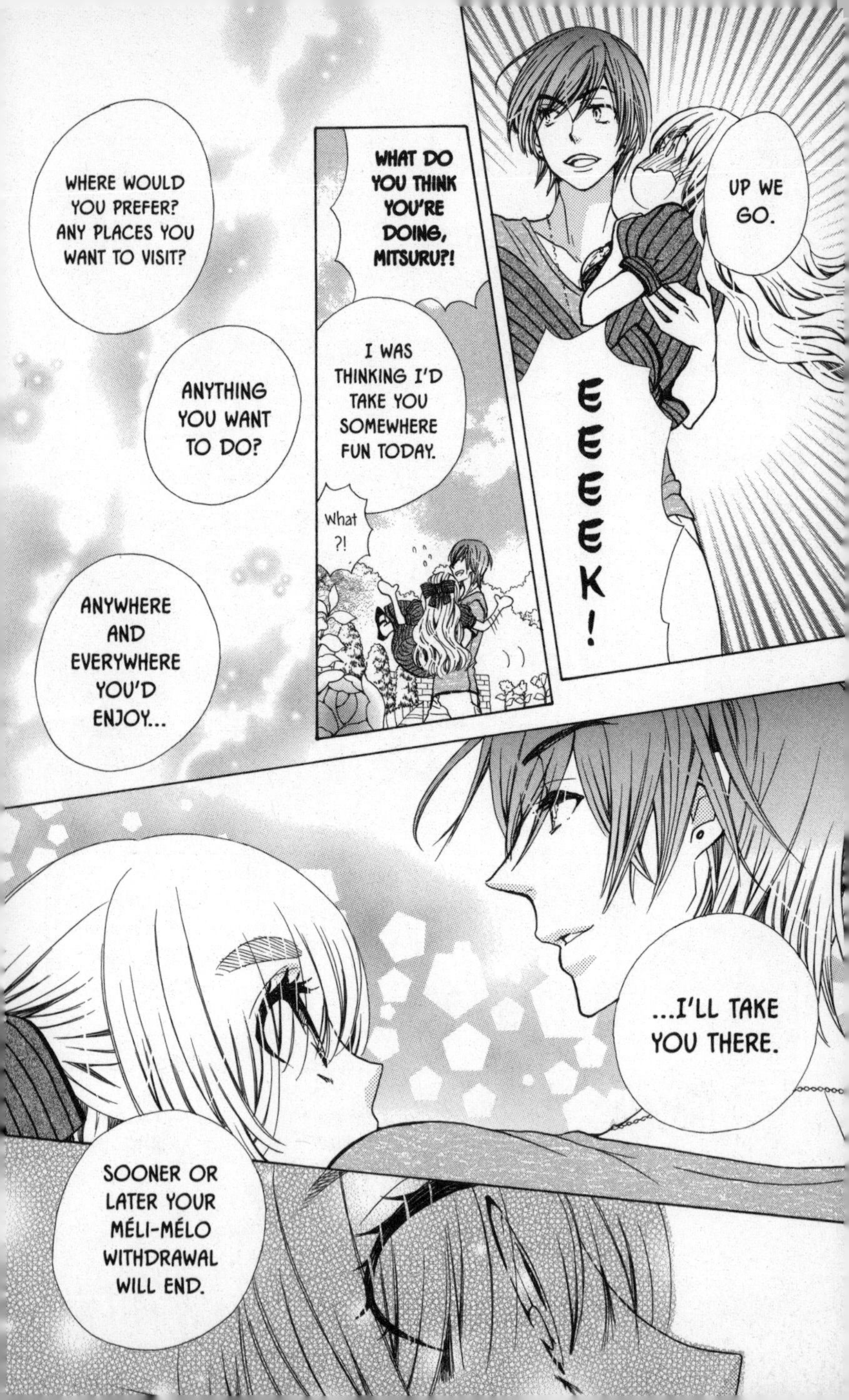
UP WE GO.
EEEEK!
WHAT DO YOU THINK YOU'RE DOING, MITSURU?!
I WAS THINKING I'D TAKE YOU SOMEWHERE FUN TODAY.
What?!
WHERE WOULD YOU PREFER? ANY PLACES YOU WANT TO VISIT?
ANYTHING YOU WANT TO DO?
ANYWHERE AND EVERYWHERE YOU'D ENJOY...
...I'LL TAKE YOU THERE.
SOONER OR LATER YOUR MÉLI-MÉLO WITHDRAWAL WILL END.

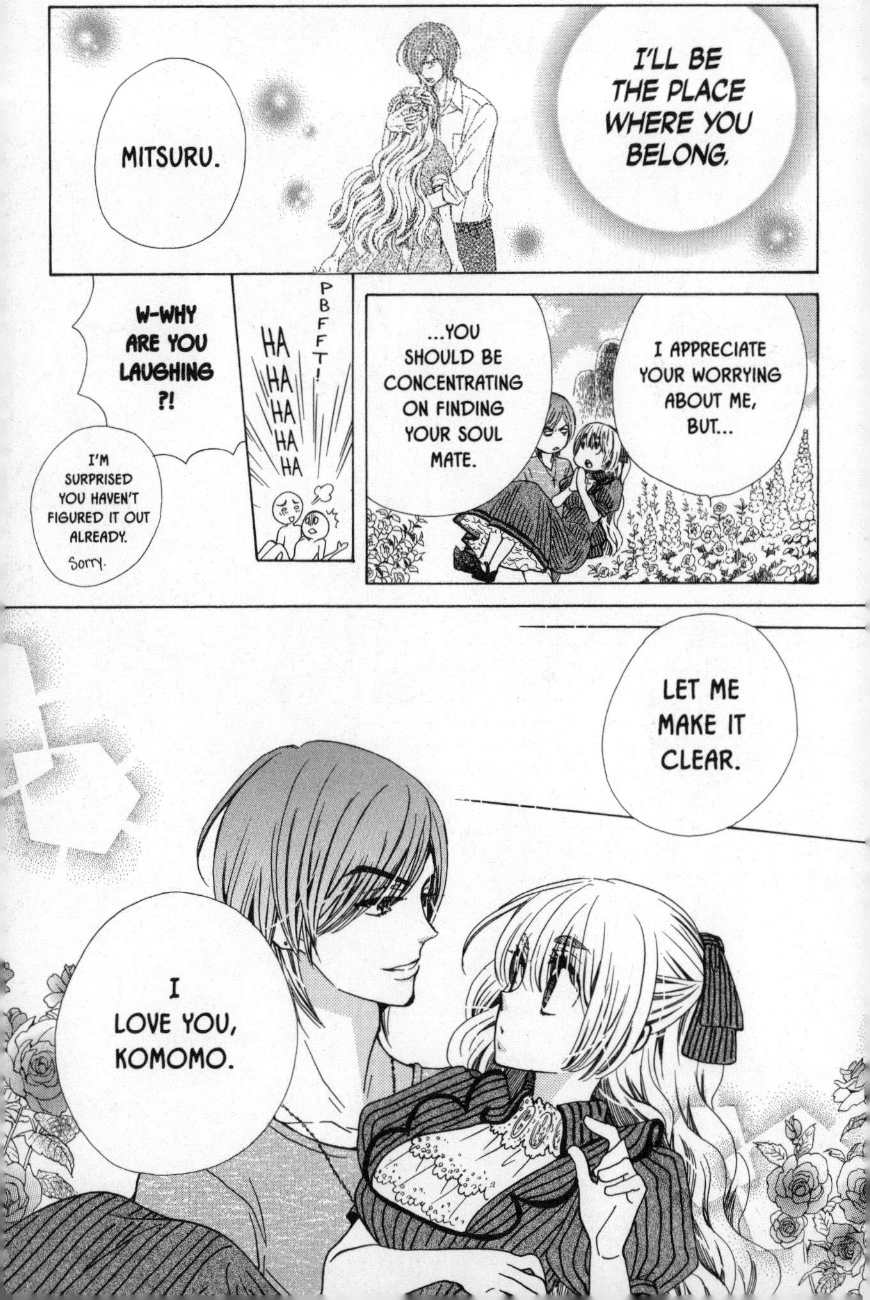
I'LL BE THE PLACE WHERE YOU BELONG.
MITSURU.
I APPRECIATE YOUR WORRYING ABOUT ME, BUT...
...YOU SHOULD BE CONCENTRATING ON FINDING YOUR SOUL MATE.
PBFFT!
HA HA HA HA HA
W-WHY ARE YOU LAUGHING ?!
I'M SURPRISED YOU HAVEN'T FIGURED IT OUT ALREADY.
Sorry.
LET ME MAKE IT CLEAR.
I LOVE YOU, KOMOMO.

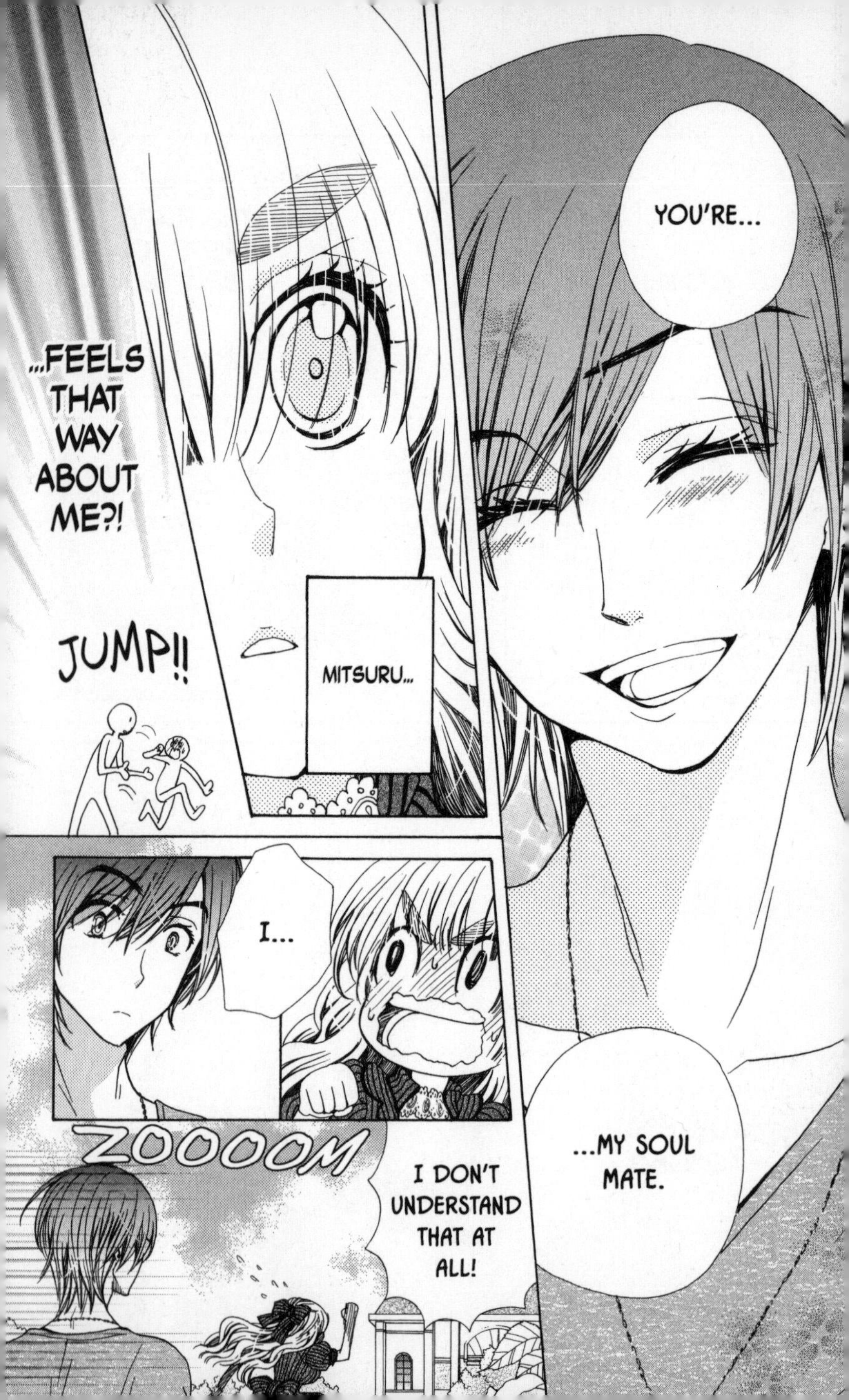
YOU'RE...
...MY SOUL MATE.
MITSURU...
...FEELS THAT WAY ABOUT ME?!
JUMP!!
I...
ZOOOOM
I DON'T UNDERSTAND THAT AT ALL!

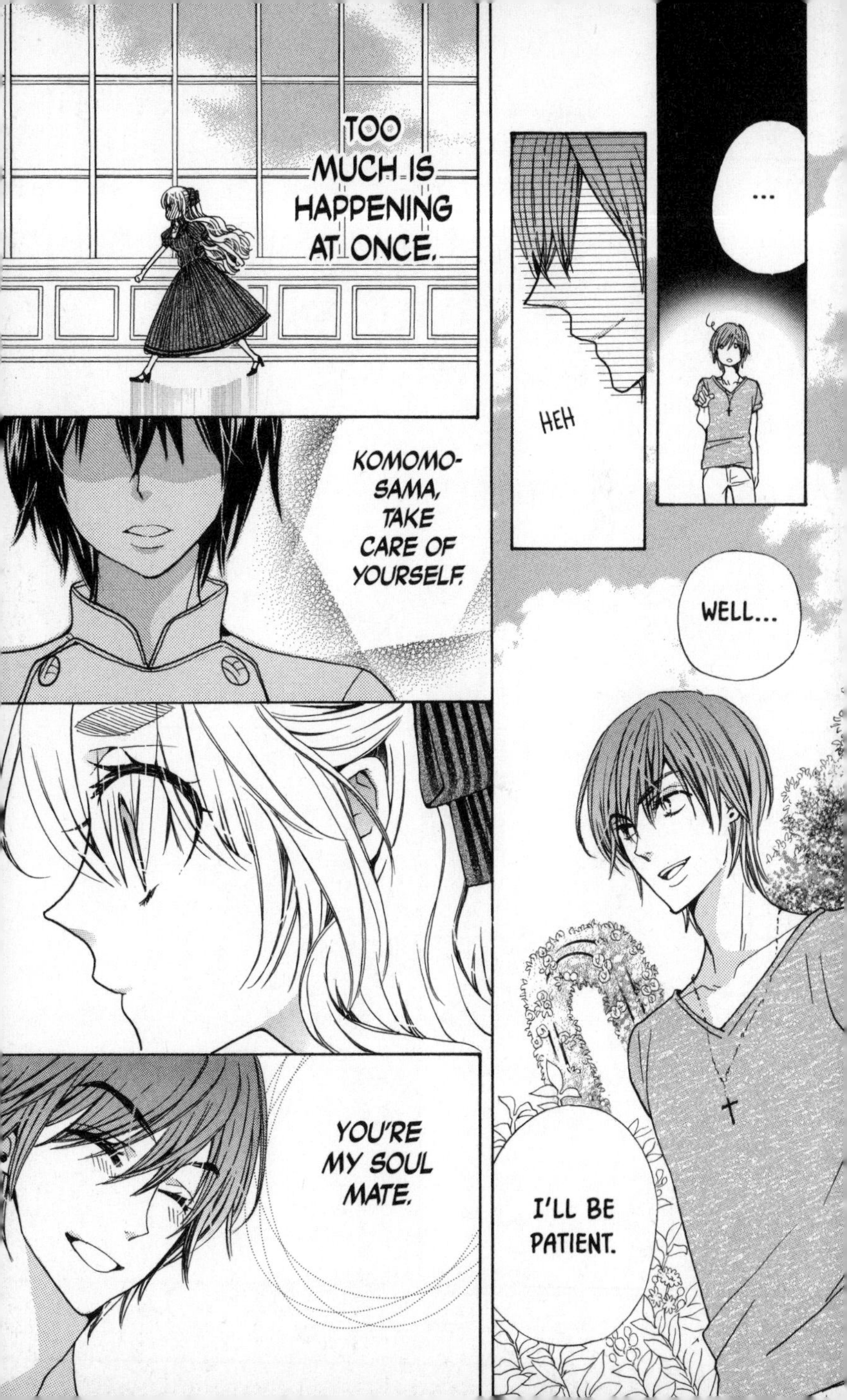
...
HEH
WELL...
I'LL BE PATIENT.
TOO MUCH IS HAPPENING AT ONCE.
KOMOMO-SAMA, TAKE CARE OF YOURSELF.
YOU'RE MY SOUL MATE.

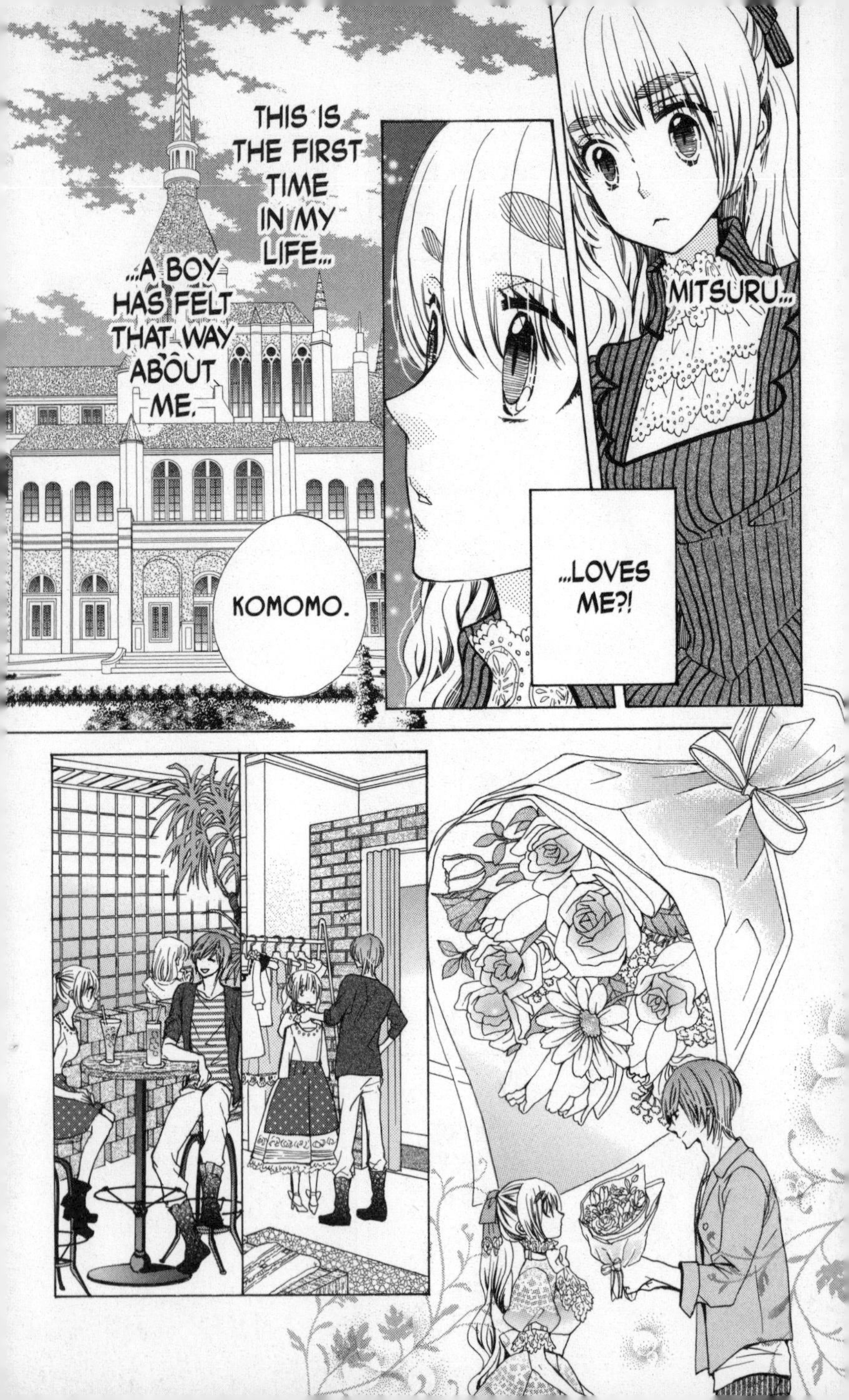
MITSURU...
...LOVES ME?!
THIS IS THE FIRST TIME IN MY LIFE...
...A BOY HAS FELT THAT WAY ABOUT ME.
KOMOMO.

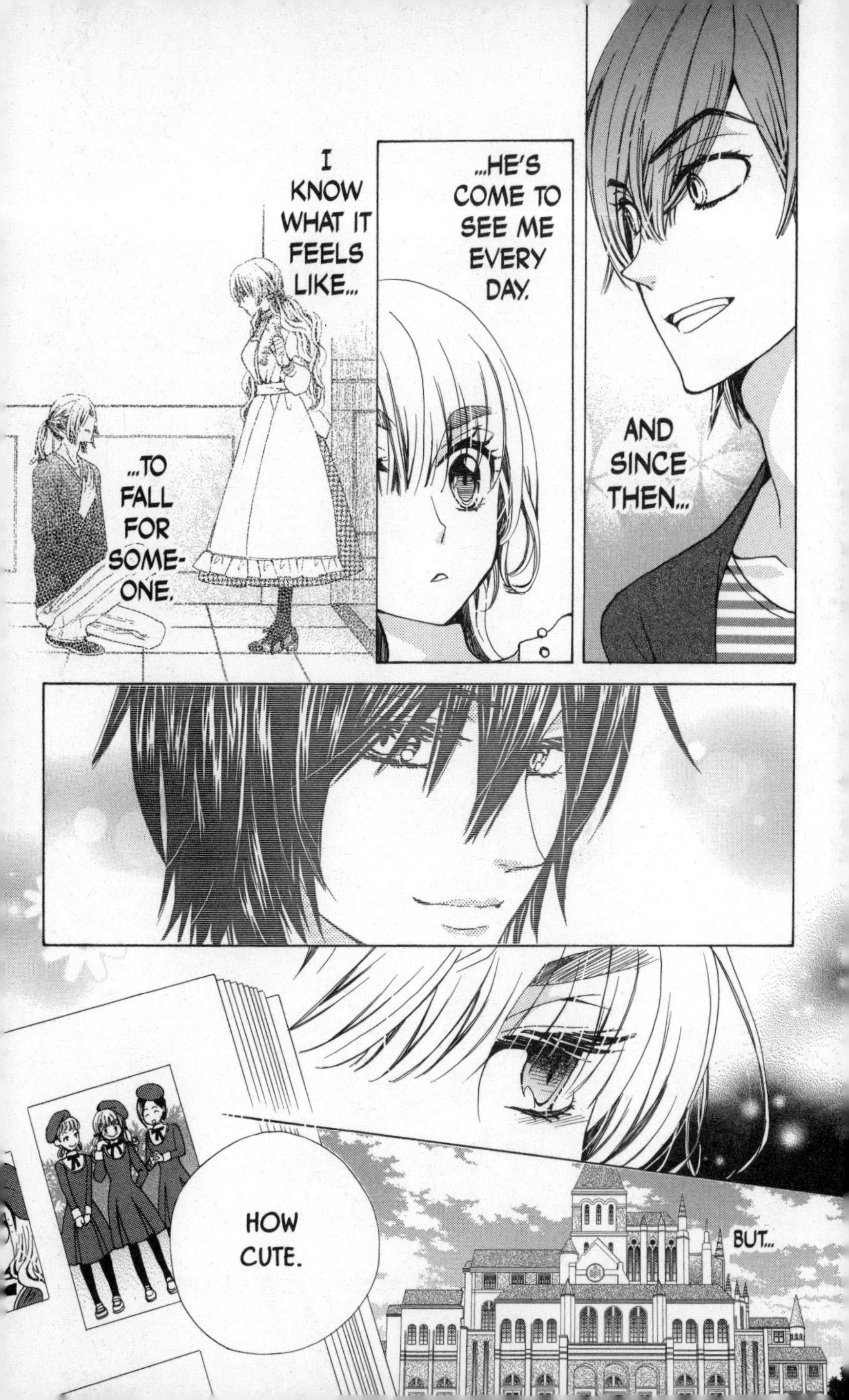
AND SINCE THEN...
...HE'S COME TO SEE ME EVERY DAY.
I KNOW WHAT IT FEELS LIKE...
...TO FALL FOR SOME-ONE.
BUT...
HOW CUTE.

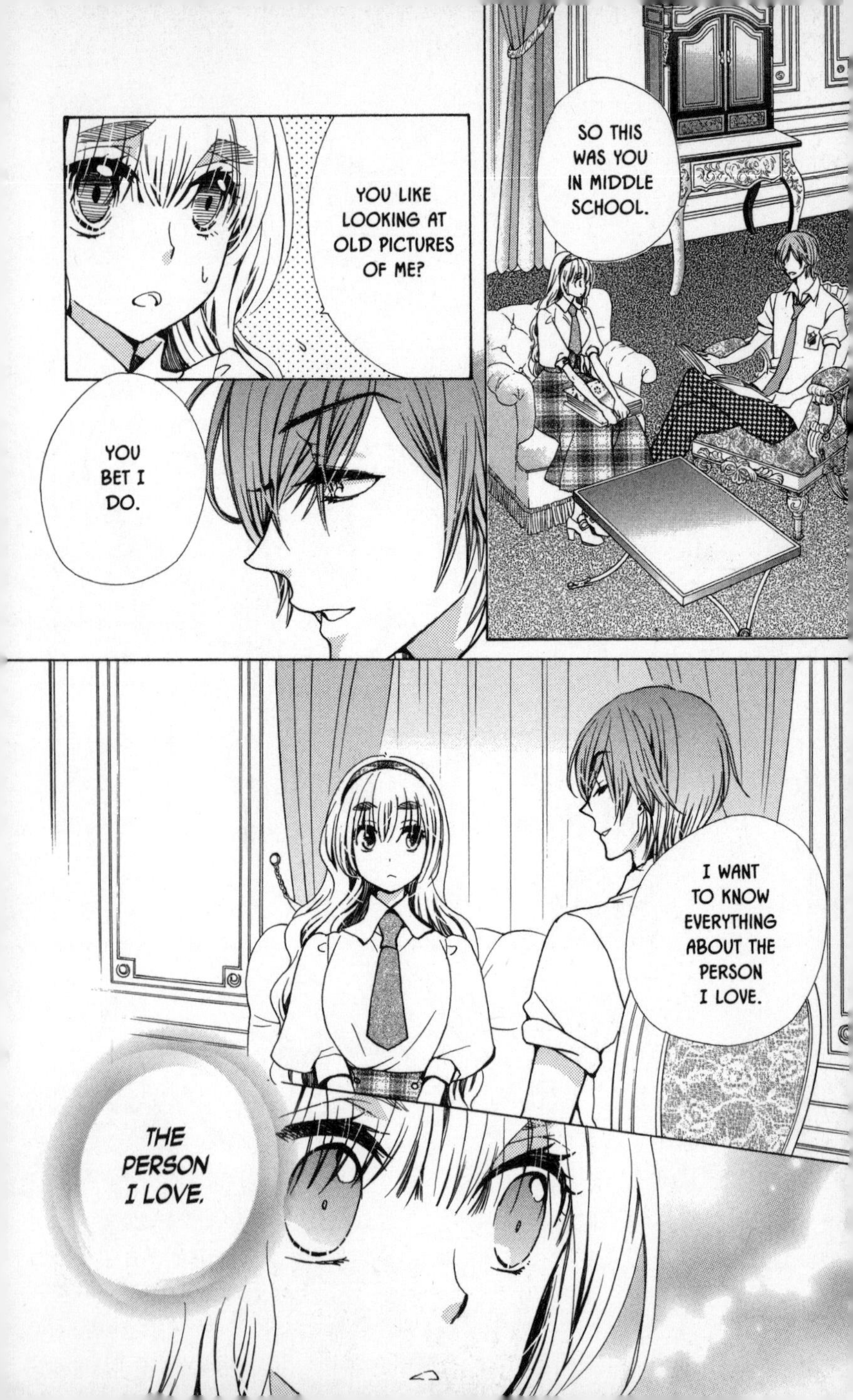
SO THIS WAS YOU IN MIDDLE SCHOOL.
YOU LIKE LOOKING AT OLD PICTURES OF ME?
YOU BET I DO.
I WANT TO KNOW EVERYTHING ABOUT THE PERSON I LOVE.
THE PERSON I LOVE.

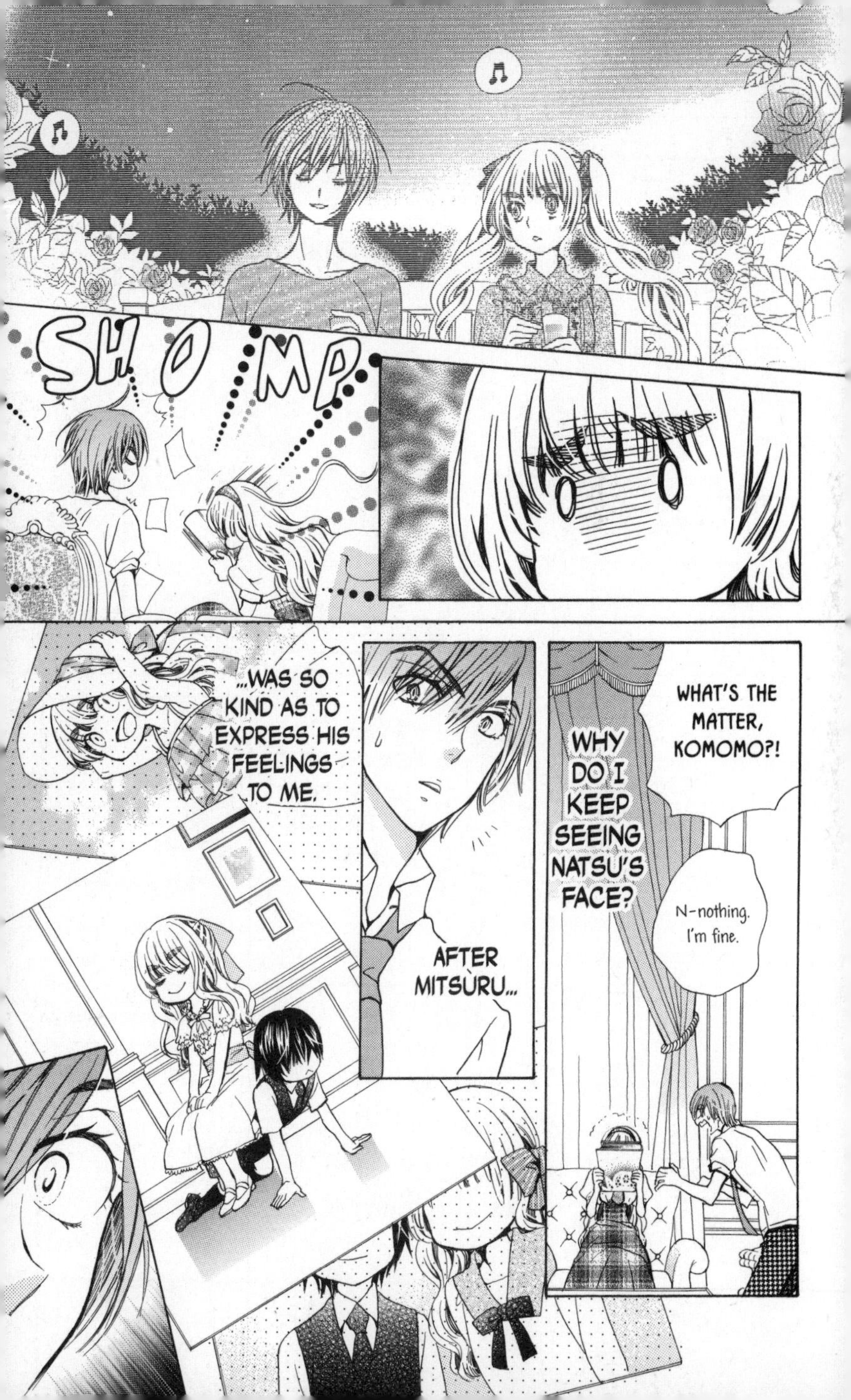
SHOMP
WHAT'S THE MATTER, KOMOMO?!
WHY DO I KEEP SEEING NATSU'S FACE?
N-nothing. I'm fine.
AFTER MITSURU...
...WAS SO KIND AS TO EXPRESS HIS FEELINGS TO ME.

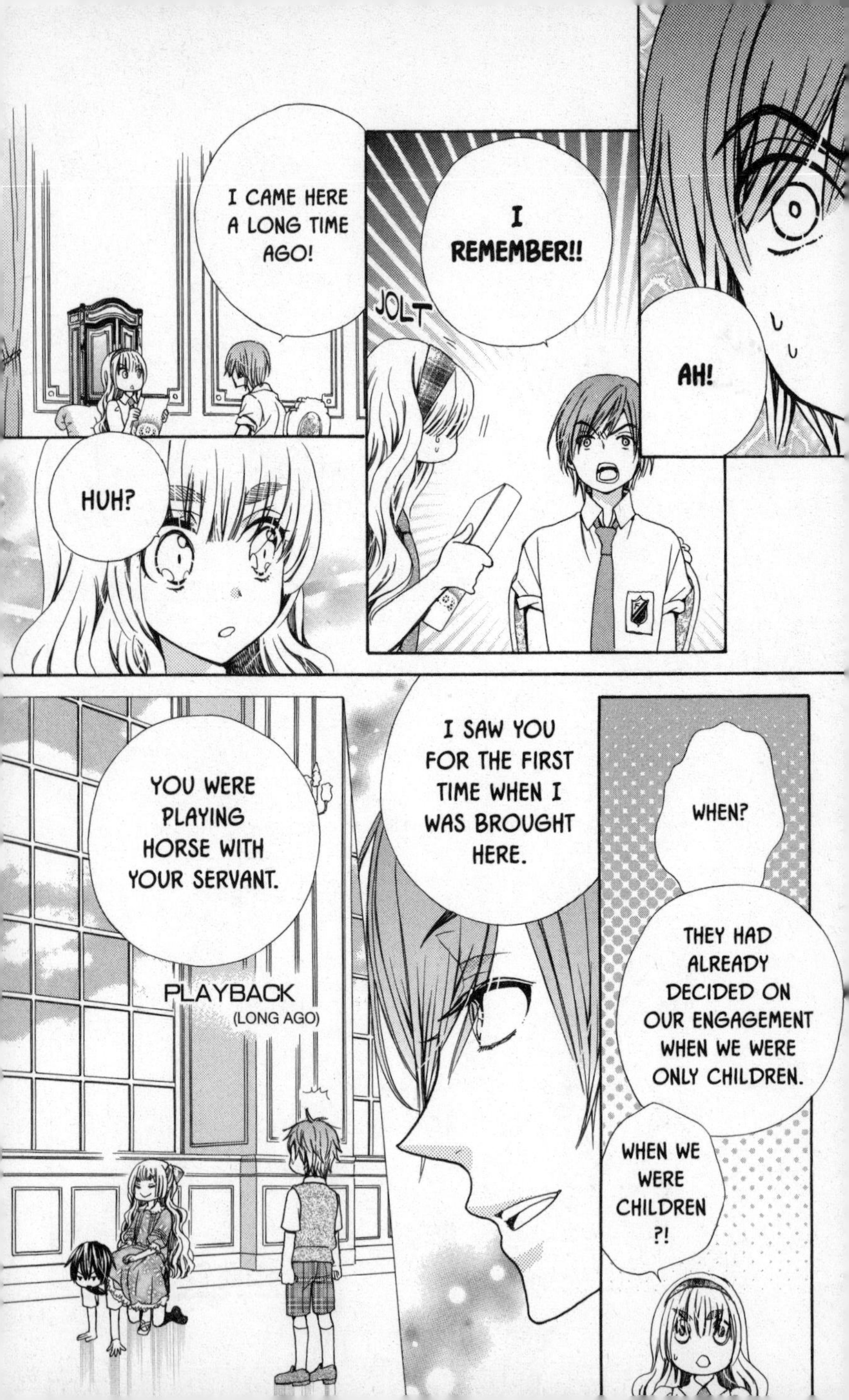
AH!
I REMEMBER!!
JOLT
I CAME HERE A LONG TIME AGO!
HUH?
WHEN?
THEY HAD ALREADY DECIDED ON OUR ENGAGEMENT WHEN WE WERE ONLY CHILDREN.
WHEN WE WERE CHILDREN ?!
I SAW YOU FOR THE FIRST TIME WHEN I WAS BROUGHT HERE.
YOU WERE PLAYING HORSE WITH YOUR SERVANT.
PLAYBACK
(LONG AGO)

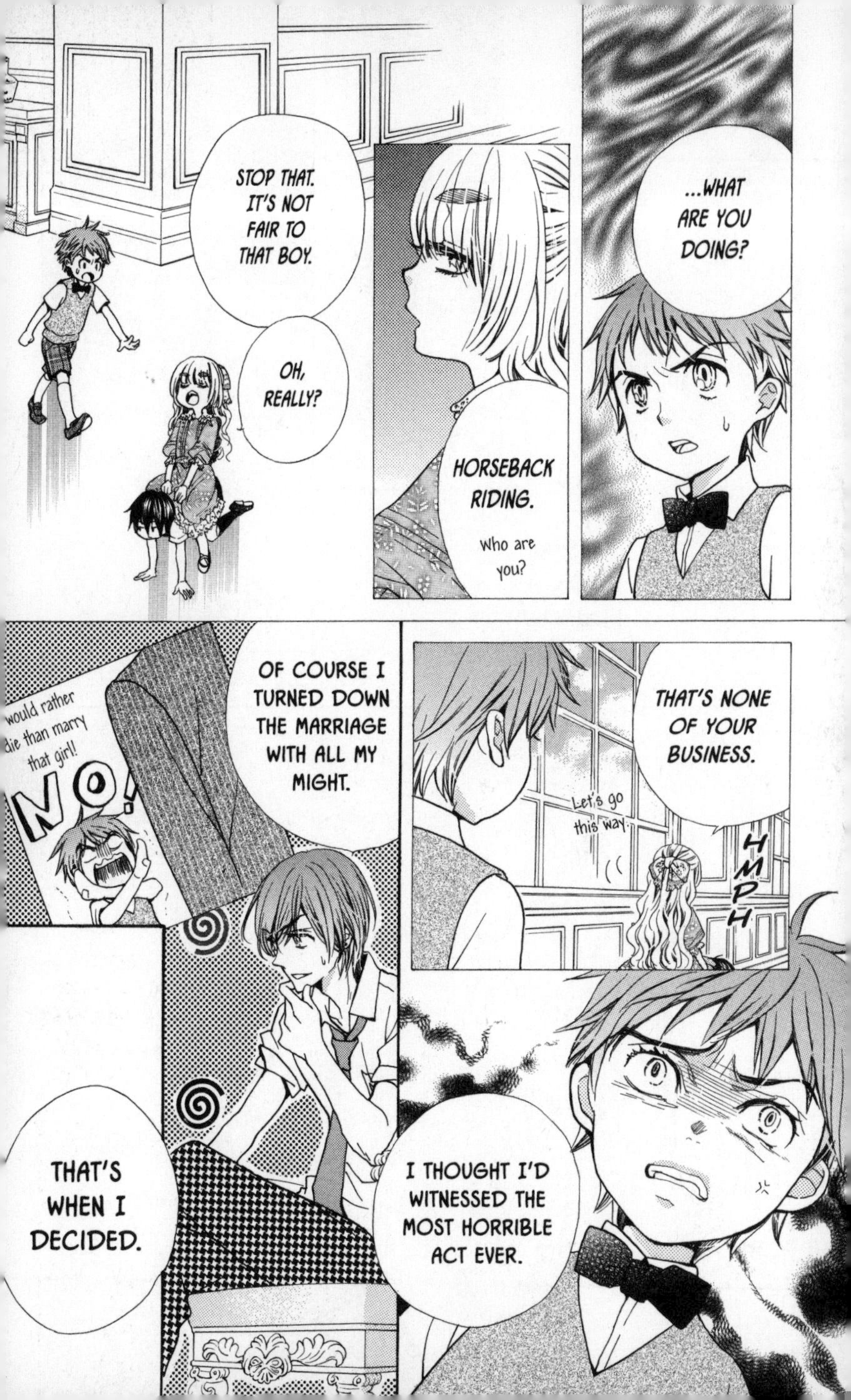

...WHAT ARE YOU DOING?
HORSEBACK RIDING.
Who are you?
STOP THAT. IT'S NOT FAIR TO THAT BOY.
OH, REALLY?
THAT'S NONE OF YOUR BUSINESS.
Let's go this way.
HMPH
OF COURSE I TURNED DOWN THE MARRIAGE WITH ALL MY MIGHT.
would rather die than marry that girl!
NO!
I THOUGHT I'D WITNESSED THE MOST HORRIBLE ACT EVER.
THAT'S WHEN I DECIDED.

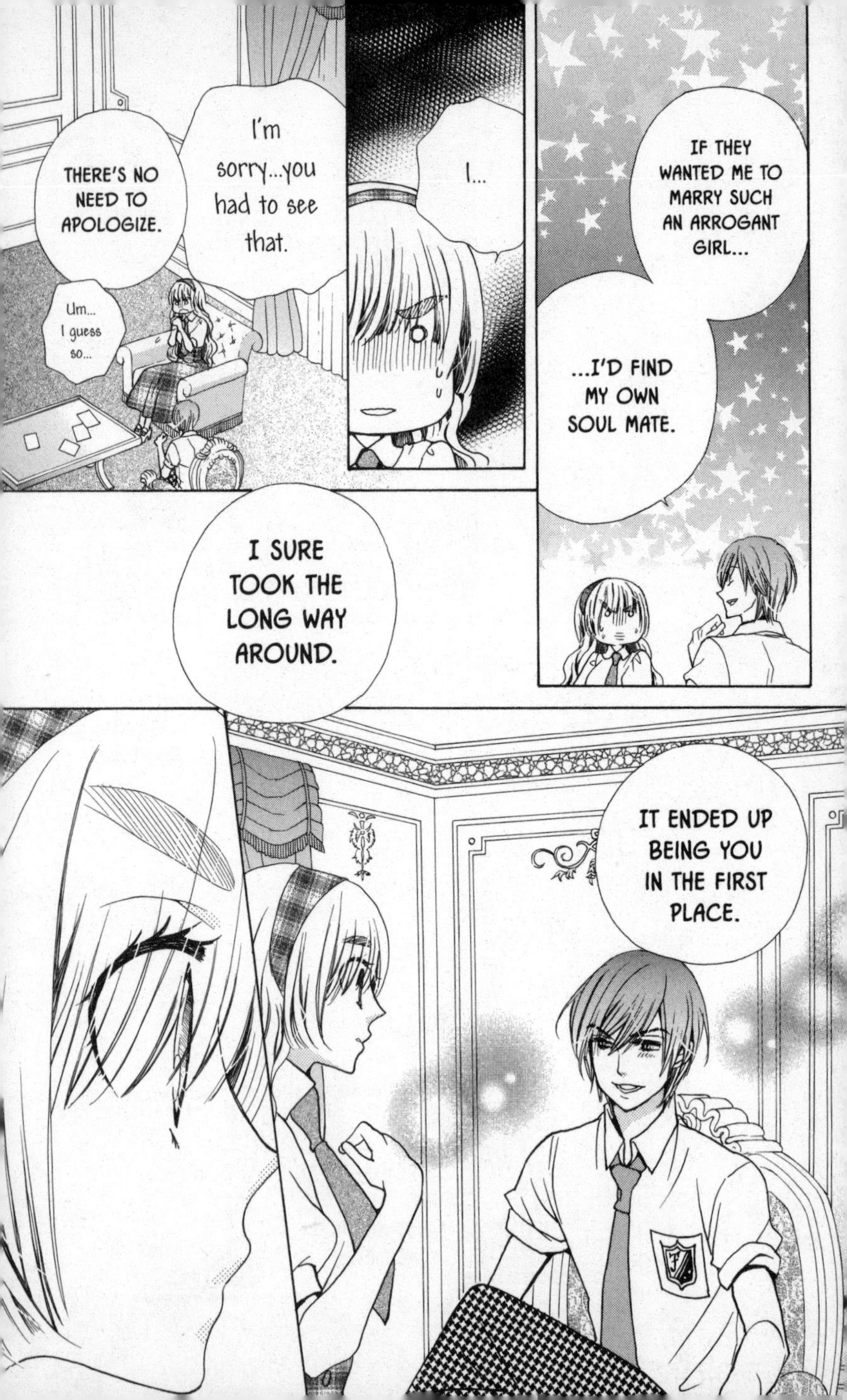
IF THEY WANTED ME TO MARRY SUCH AN ARROGANT GIRL...
...I'D FIND MY OWN SOUL MATE.
I...
I'm sorry...you had to see that.
THERE'S NO NEED TO APOLOGIZE.
Um... I guess so...
I SURE TOOK THE LONG WAY AROUND.
IT ENDED UP BEING YOU IN THE FIRST PLACE.

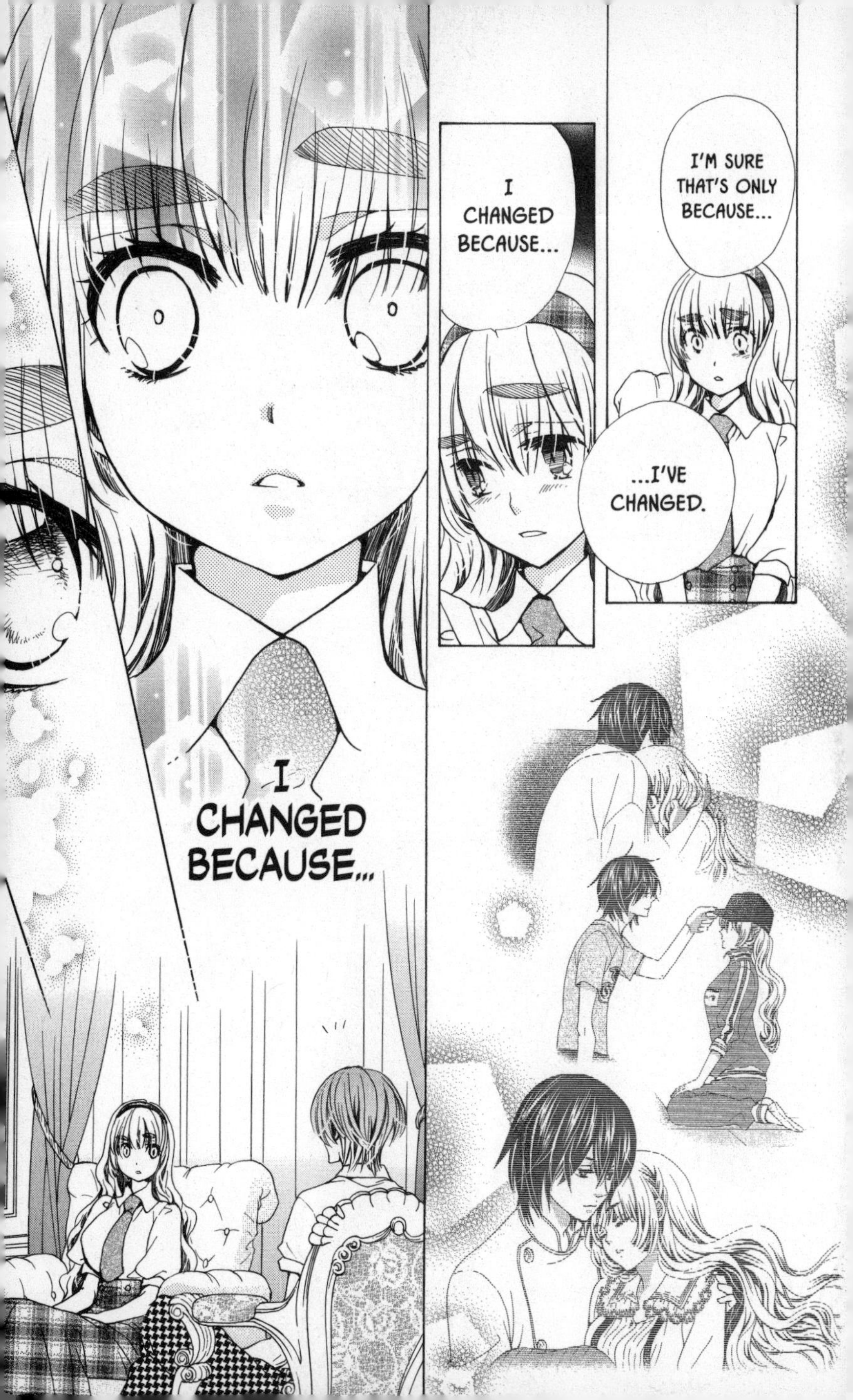
I'M SURE THAT'S ONLY BECAUSE...
...I'VE CHANGED.
I CHANGED BECAUSE...
I CHANGED BECAUSE...

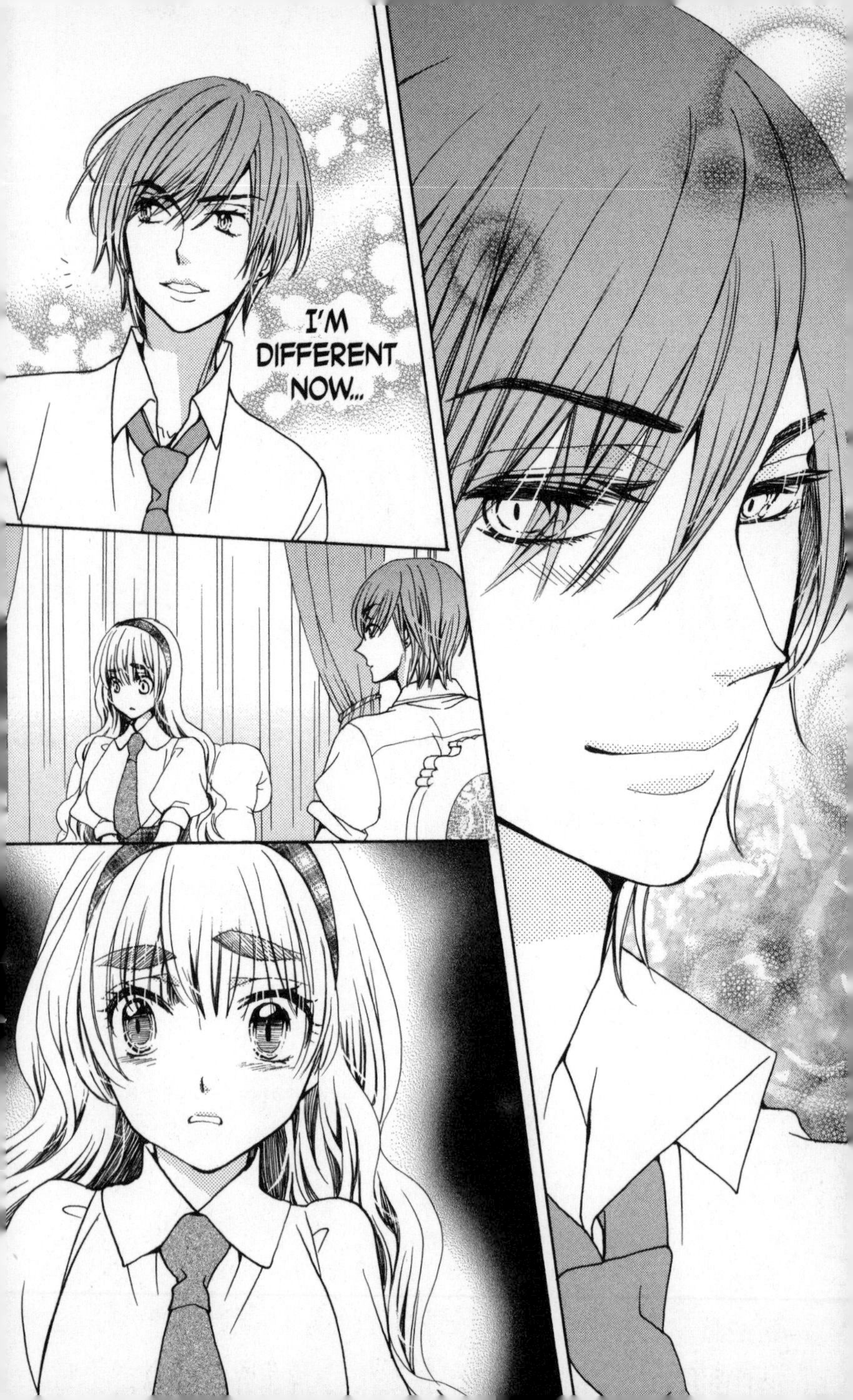
I'M DIFFERENT NOW...

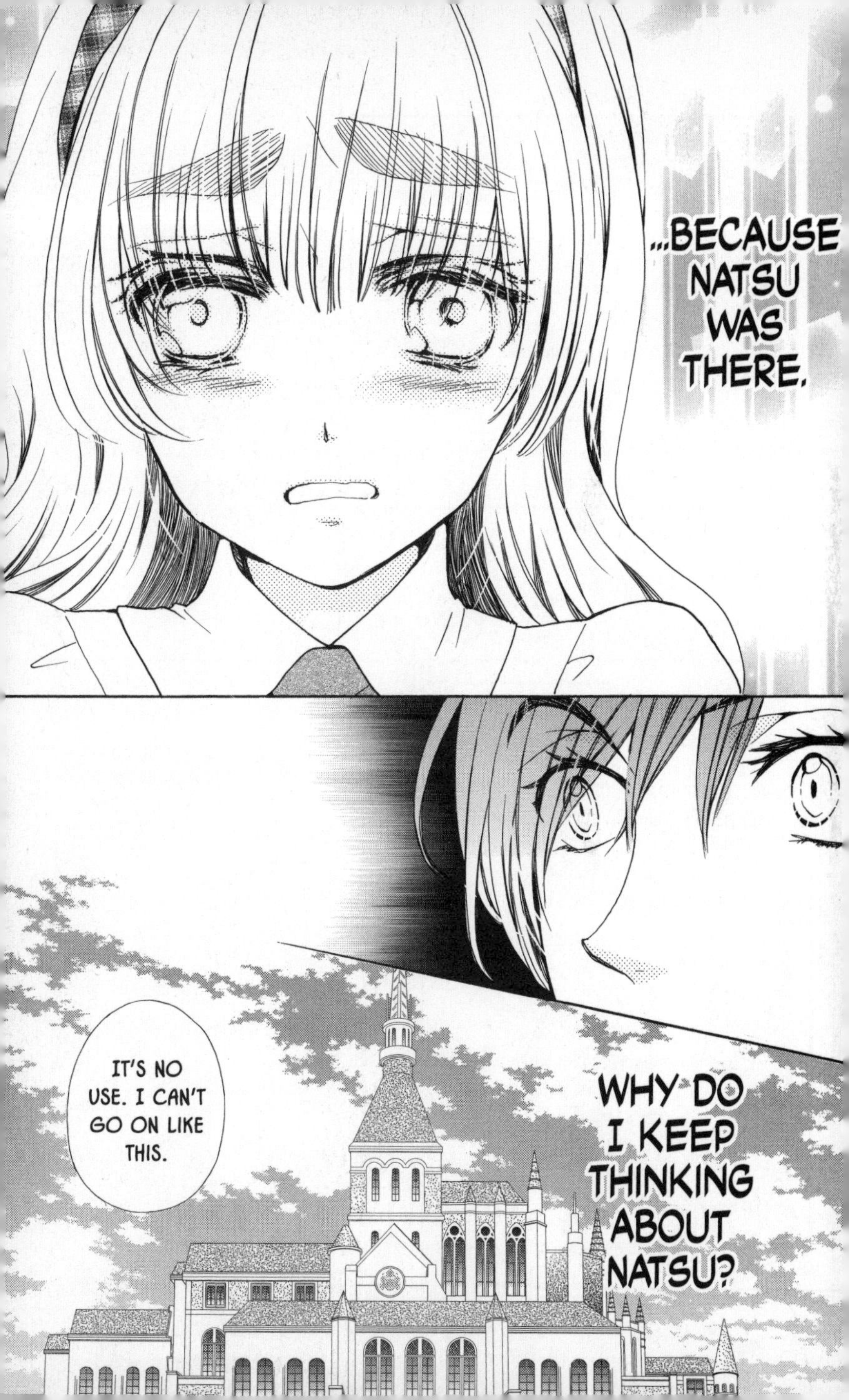
...BECAUSE NATSU WAS THERE.
WHY DO I KEEP THINKING ABOUT NATSU?
IT'S NO USE. I CAN'T GO ON LIKE THIS.

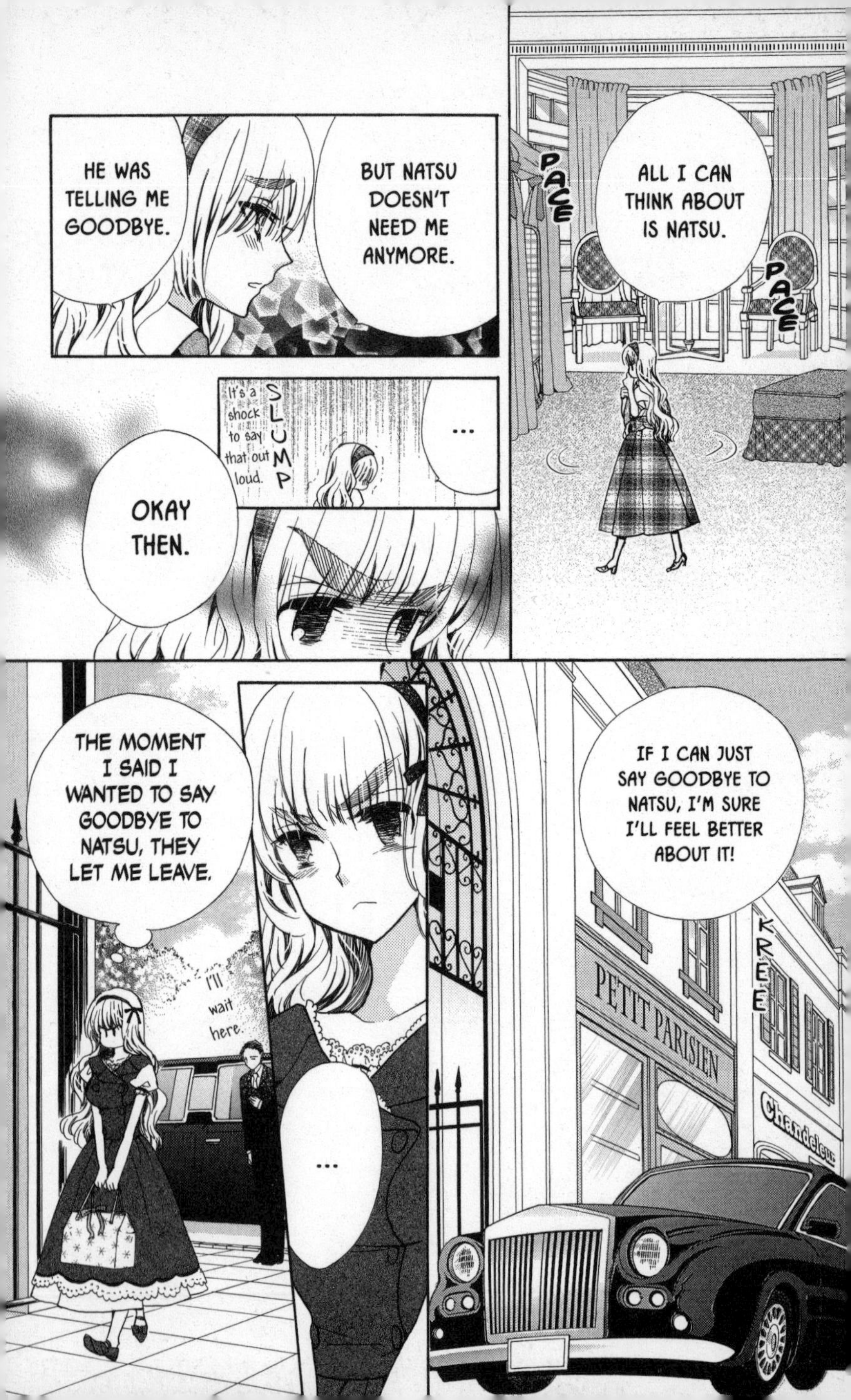
PACE
ALL I CAN THINK ABOUT IS NATSU.
PACE
BUT NATSU DOESN'T NEED ME ANYMORE.
HE WAS TELLING ME GOODBYE.
...
SLUMP
It's a shock to say that out loud.
OKAY THEN.
IF I CAN JUST SAY GOODBYE TO NATSU, I'M SURE I'LL FEEL BETTER ABOUT IT!
KREE
PETIT PARISIEN
...
THE MOMENT I SAID I WANTED TO SAY GOODBYE TO NATSU, THEY LET ME LEAVE.
I'll wait here.

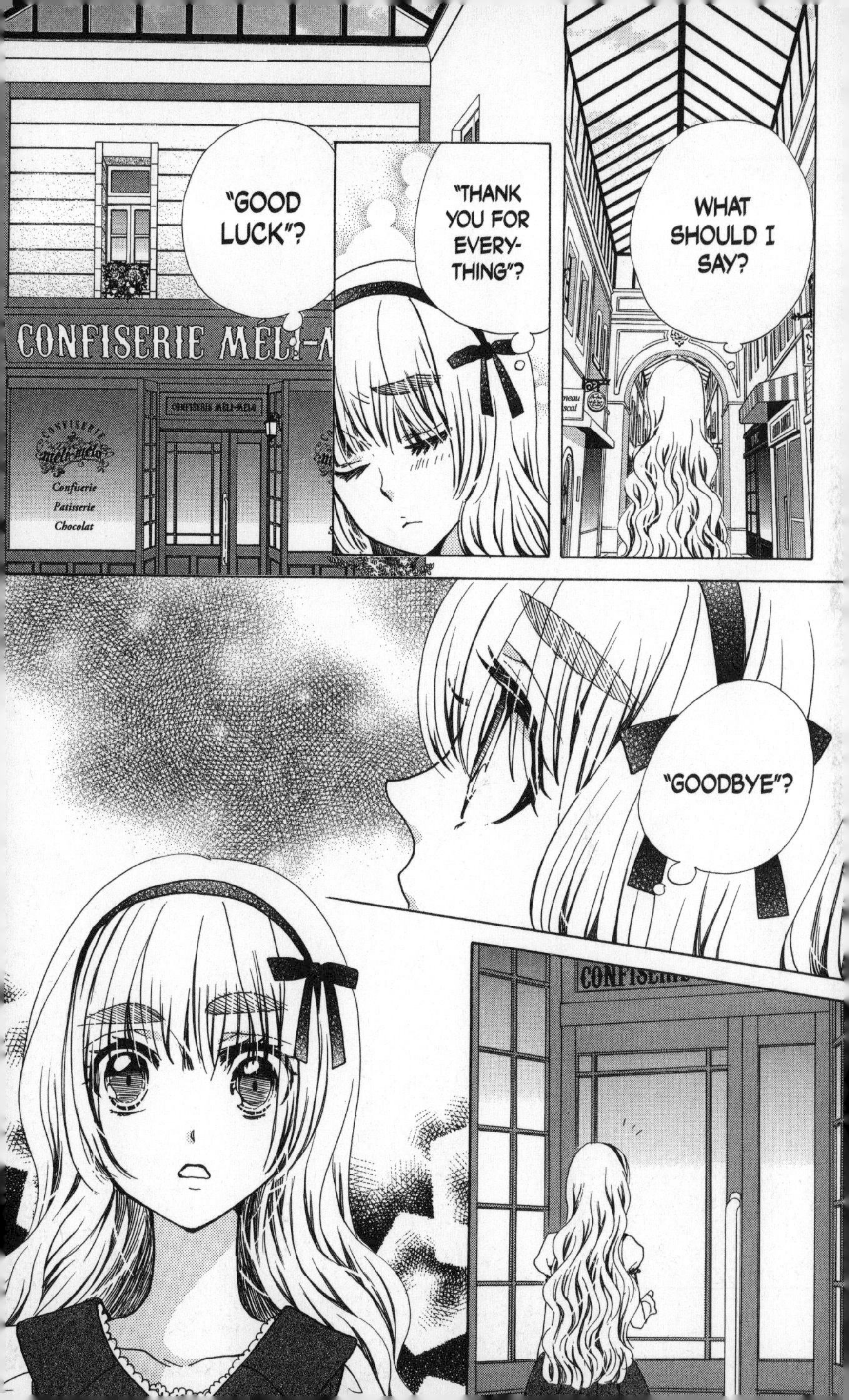
WHAT SHOULD I SAY?
"THANK YOU FOR EVERY-THING"?
"GOOD LUCK"?
CONFISERIE MÉLI-MÉLO
Confiserie
Patisserie
Chocolat
"GOODBYE"?

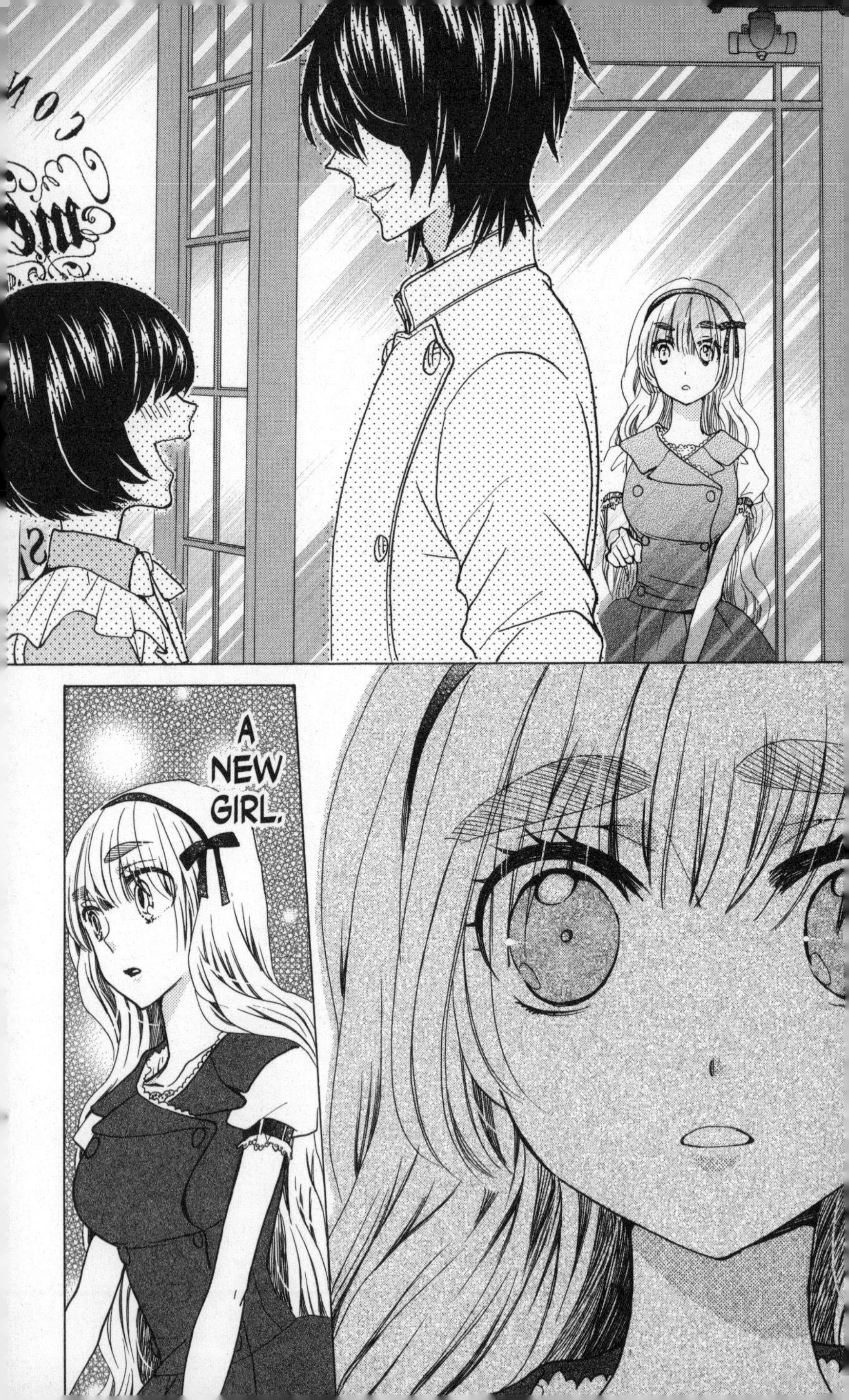
A NEW GIRL.

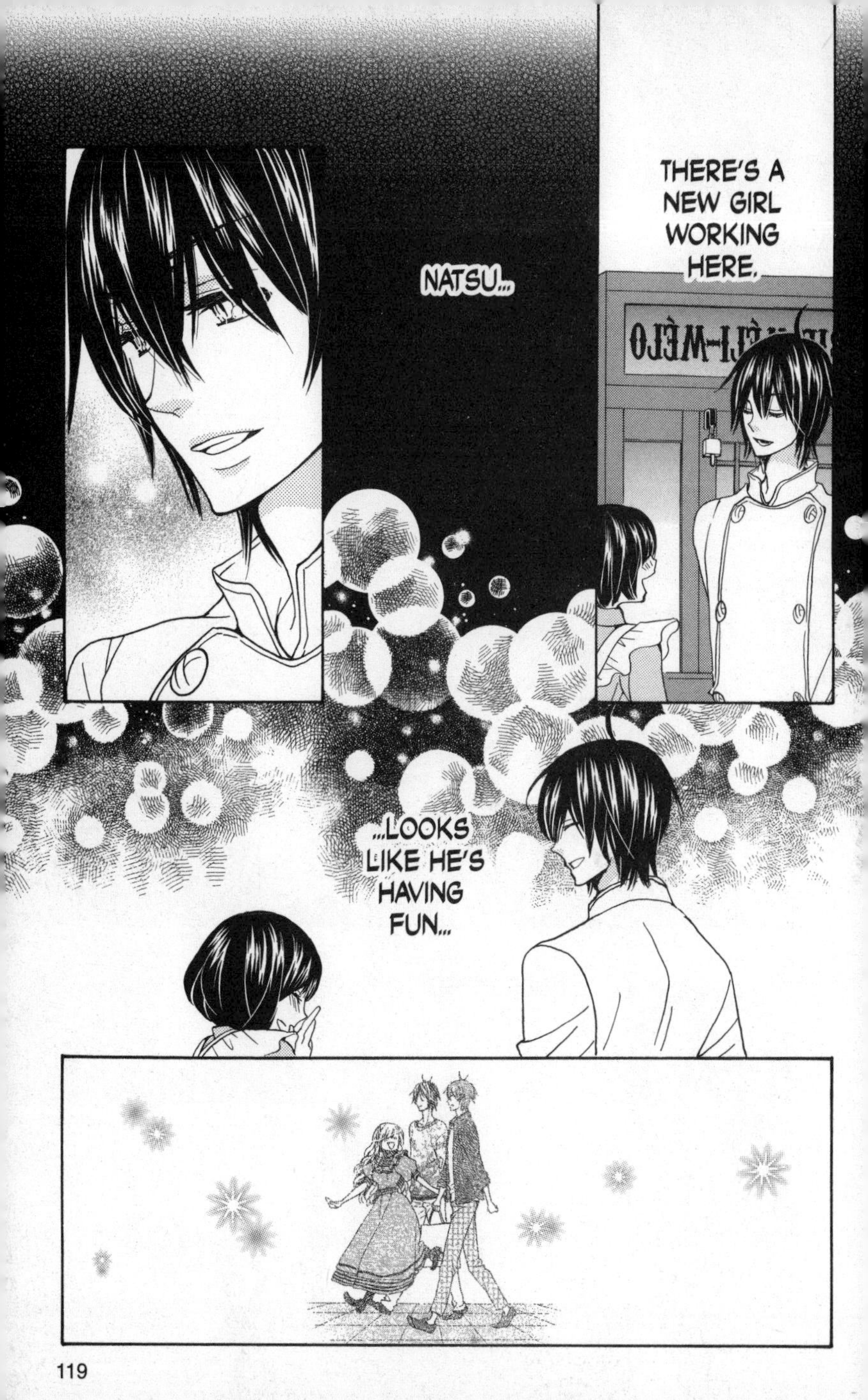
THERE'S A NEW GIRL WORKING HERE.
NATSU...
...LOOKS LIKE HE'S HAVING FUN...

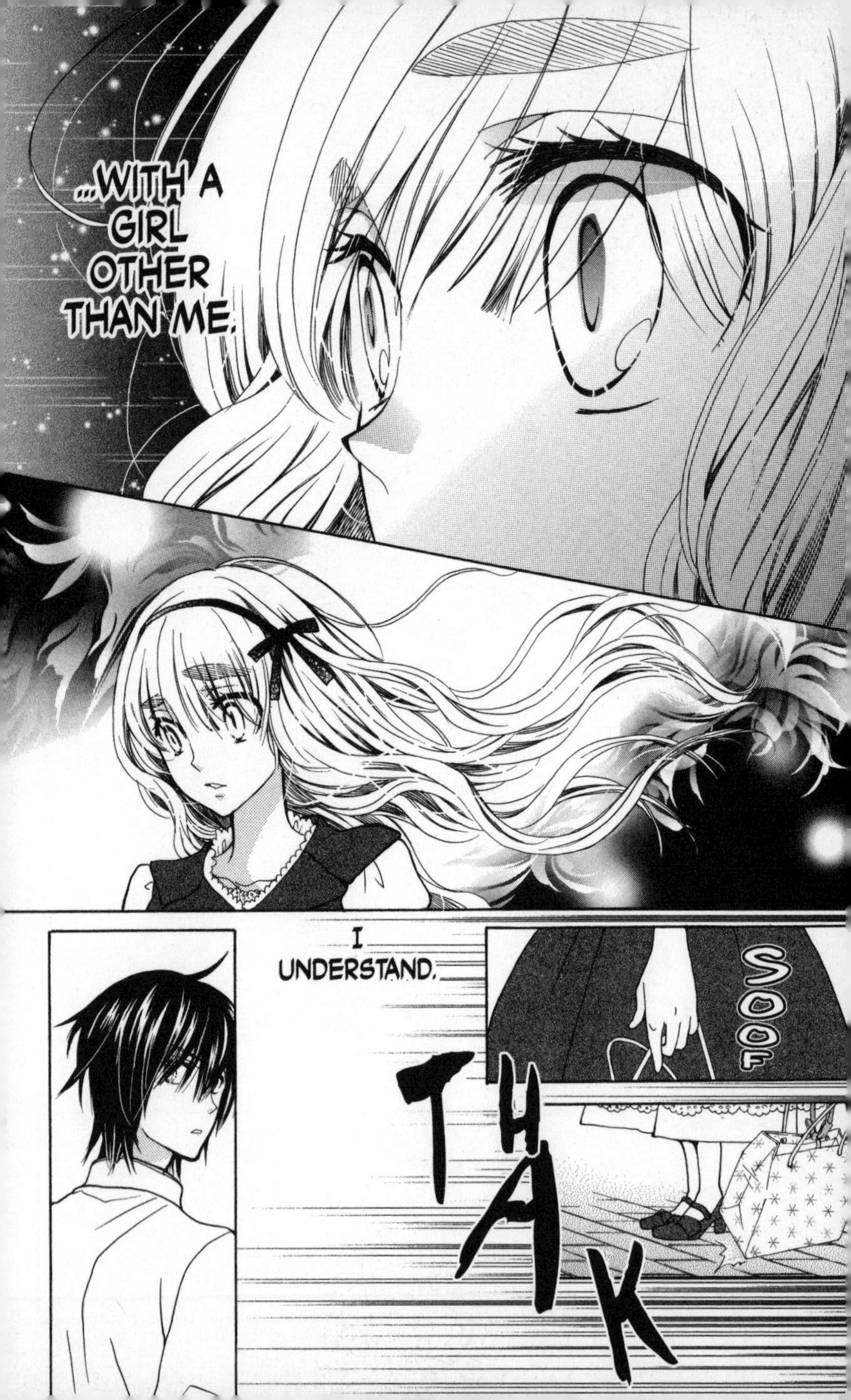
...WITH A GIRL OTHER THAN ME.
SOOF
THAK
I UNDERSTAND.

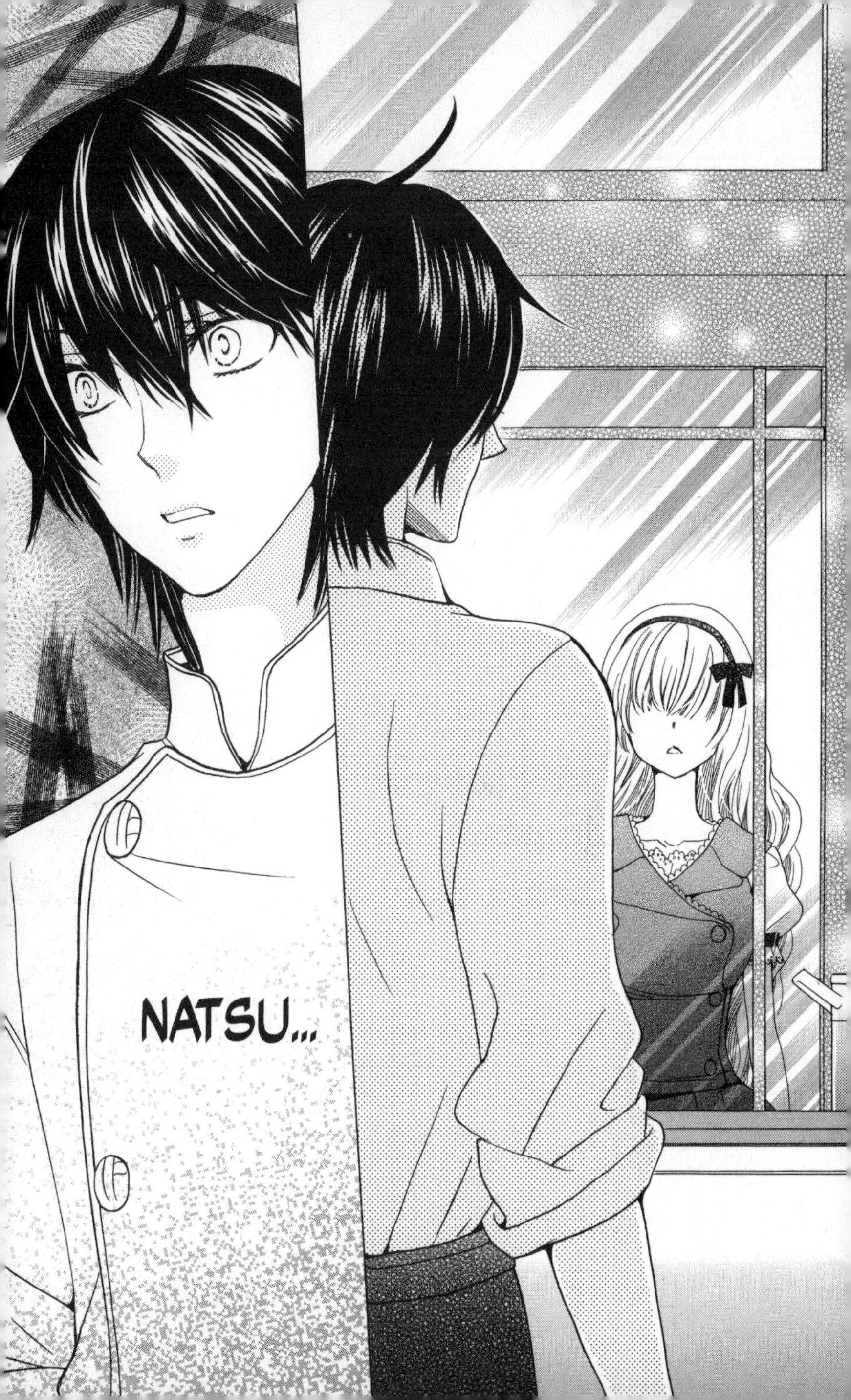
NATSU...

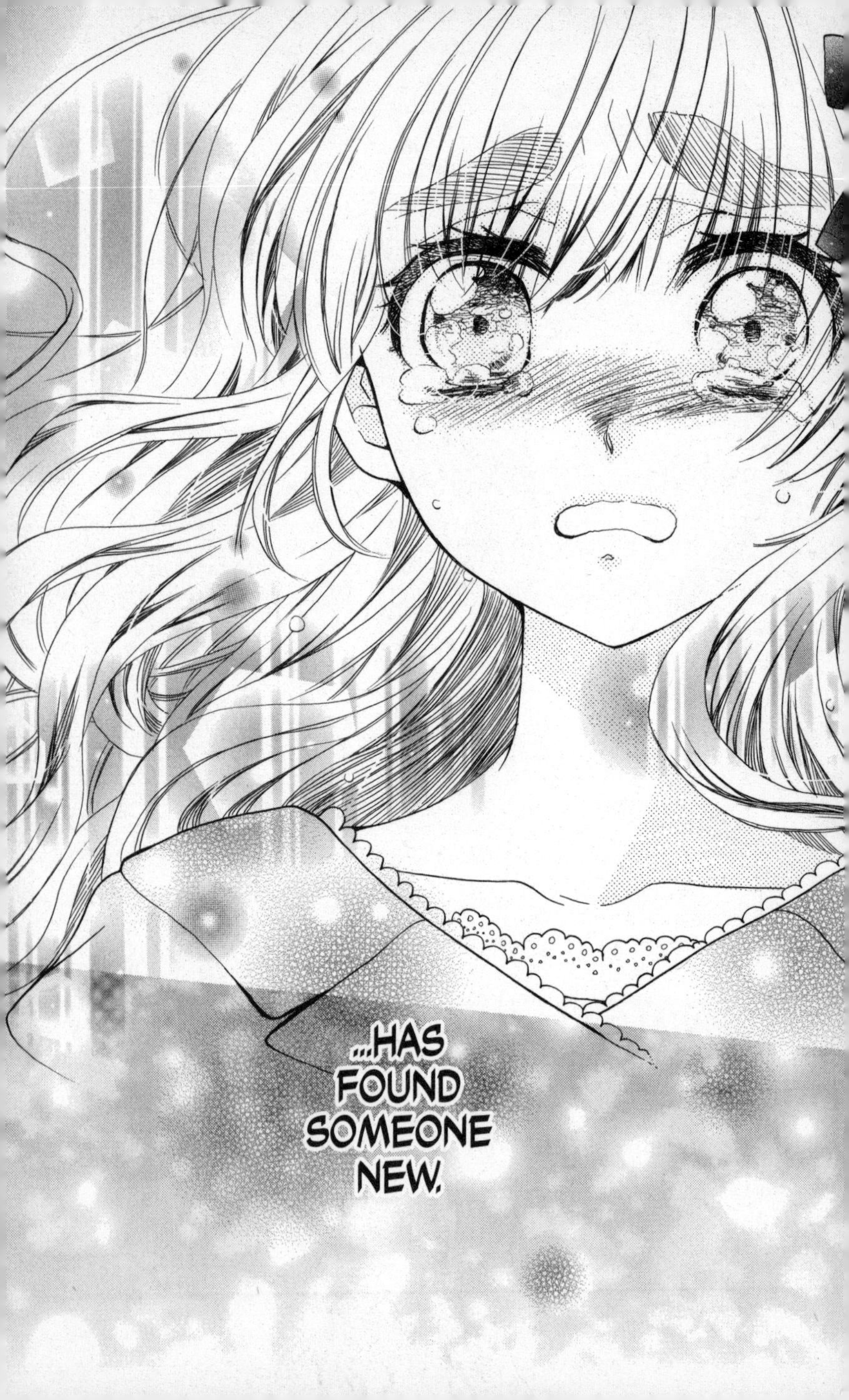
...HAS FOUND SOMEONE NEW.

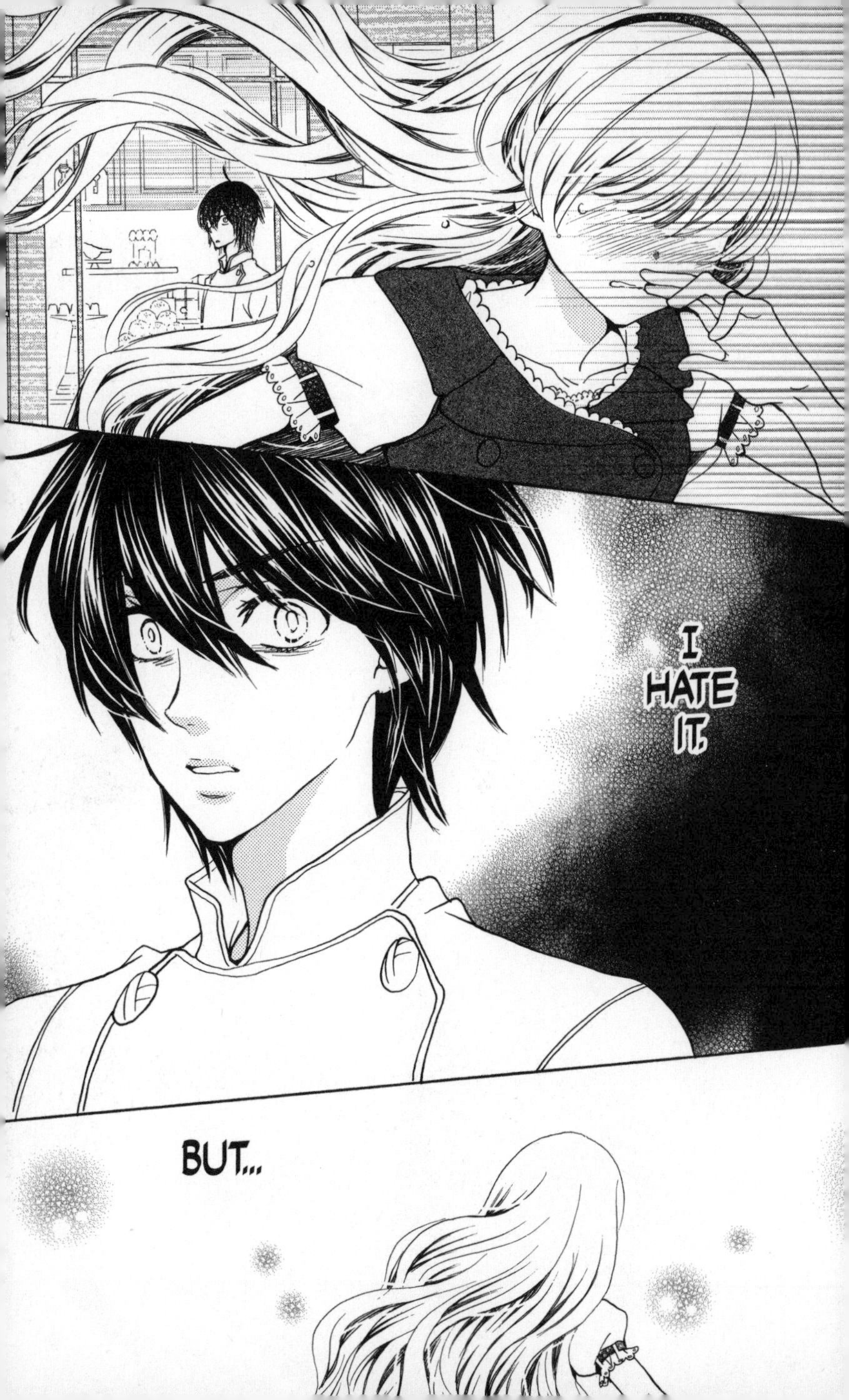
I HATE IT.
BUT...

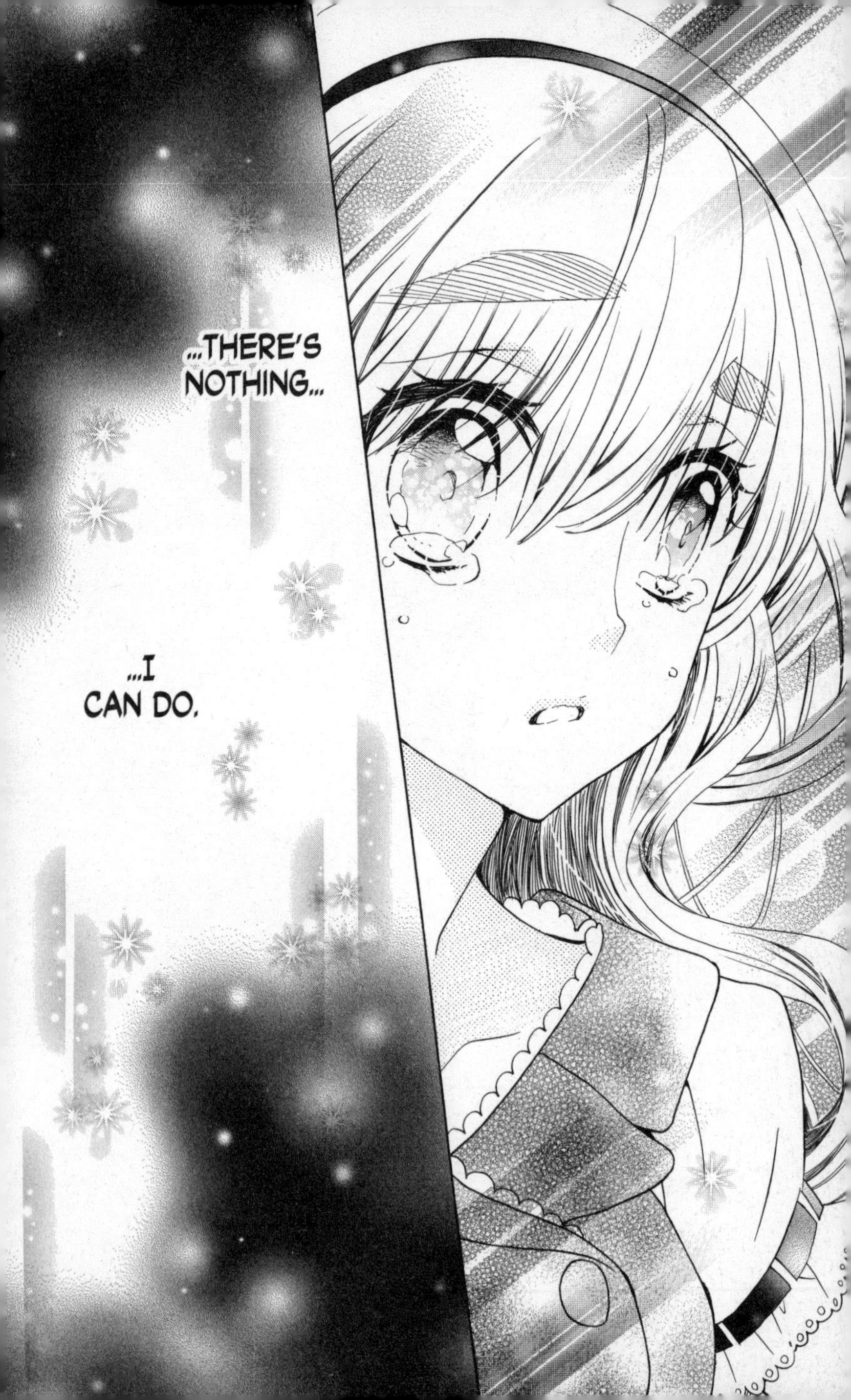
...THERE'S NOTHING...
...I CAN DO.

CHAPTER 28

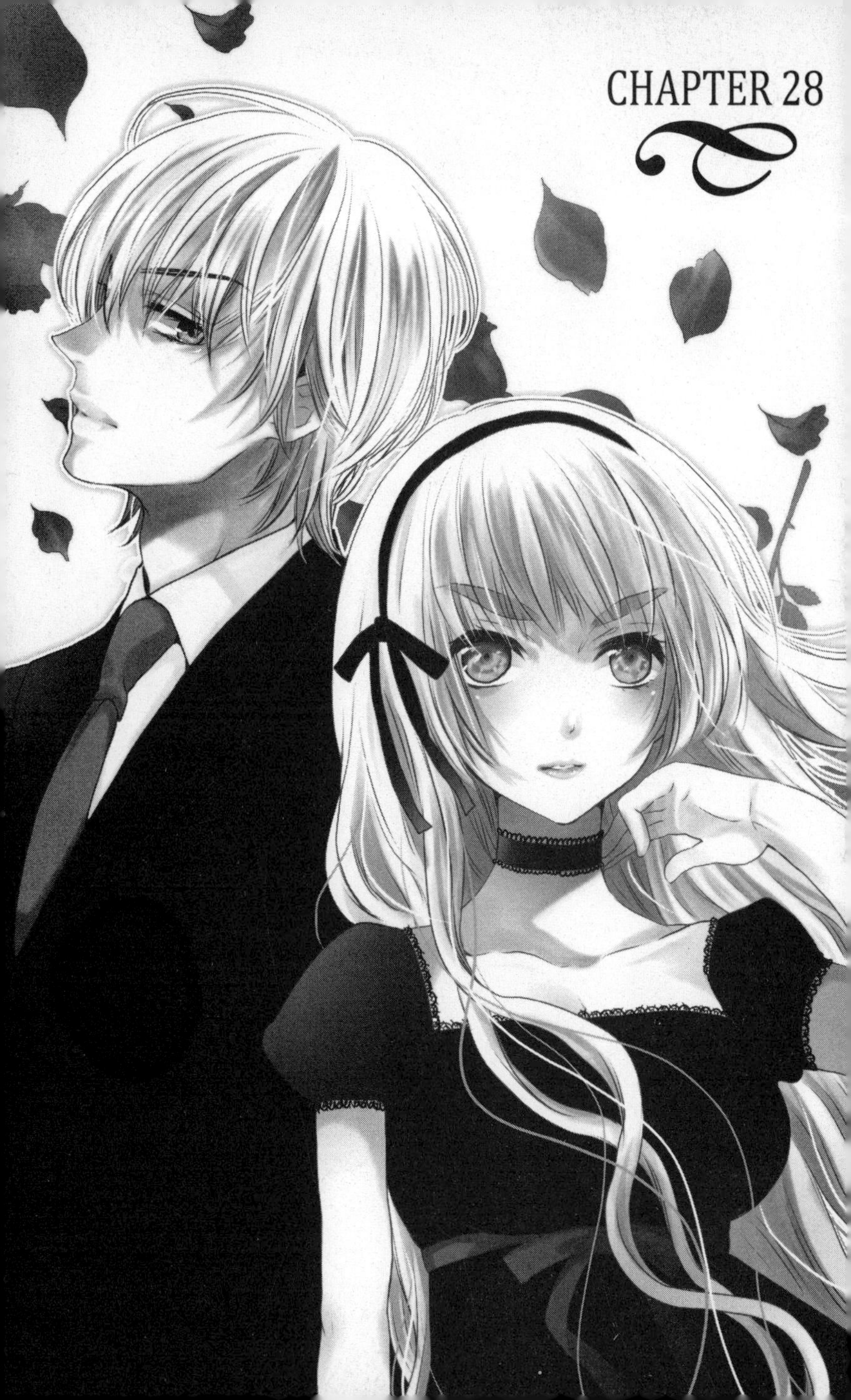

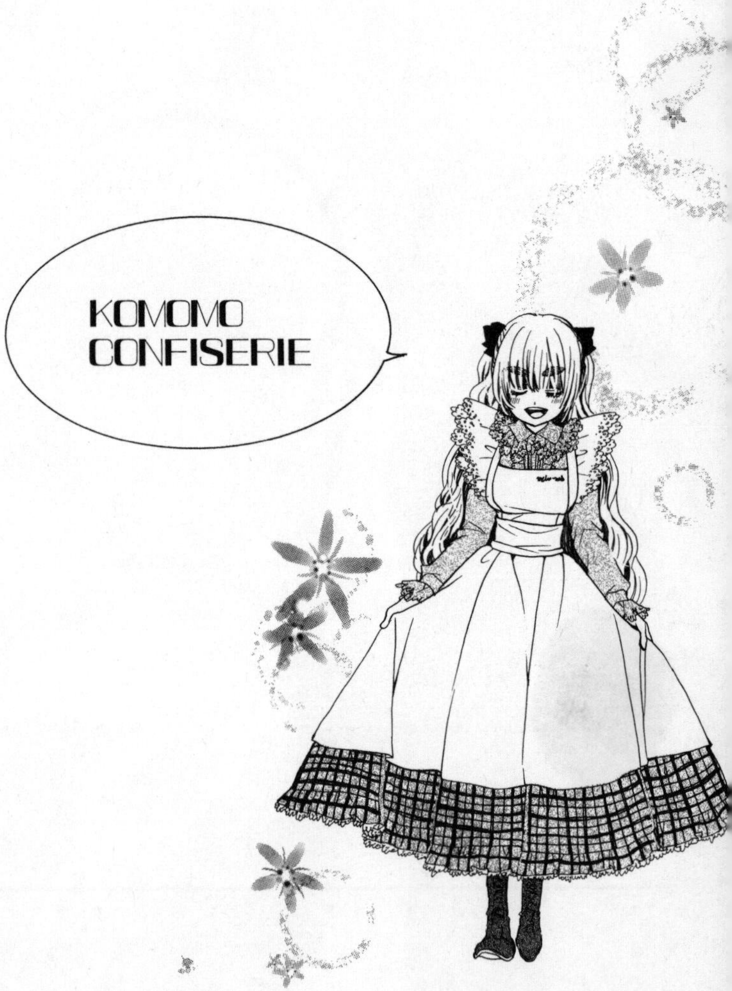
KOMOMO CONFISERIE

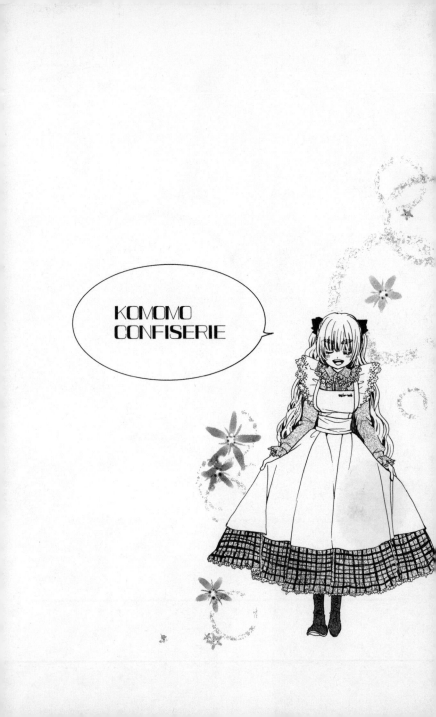

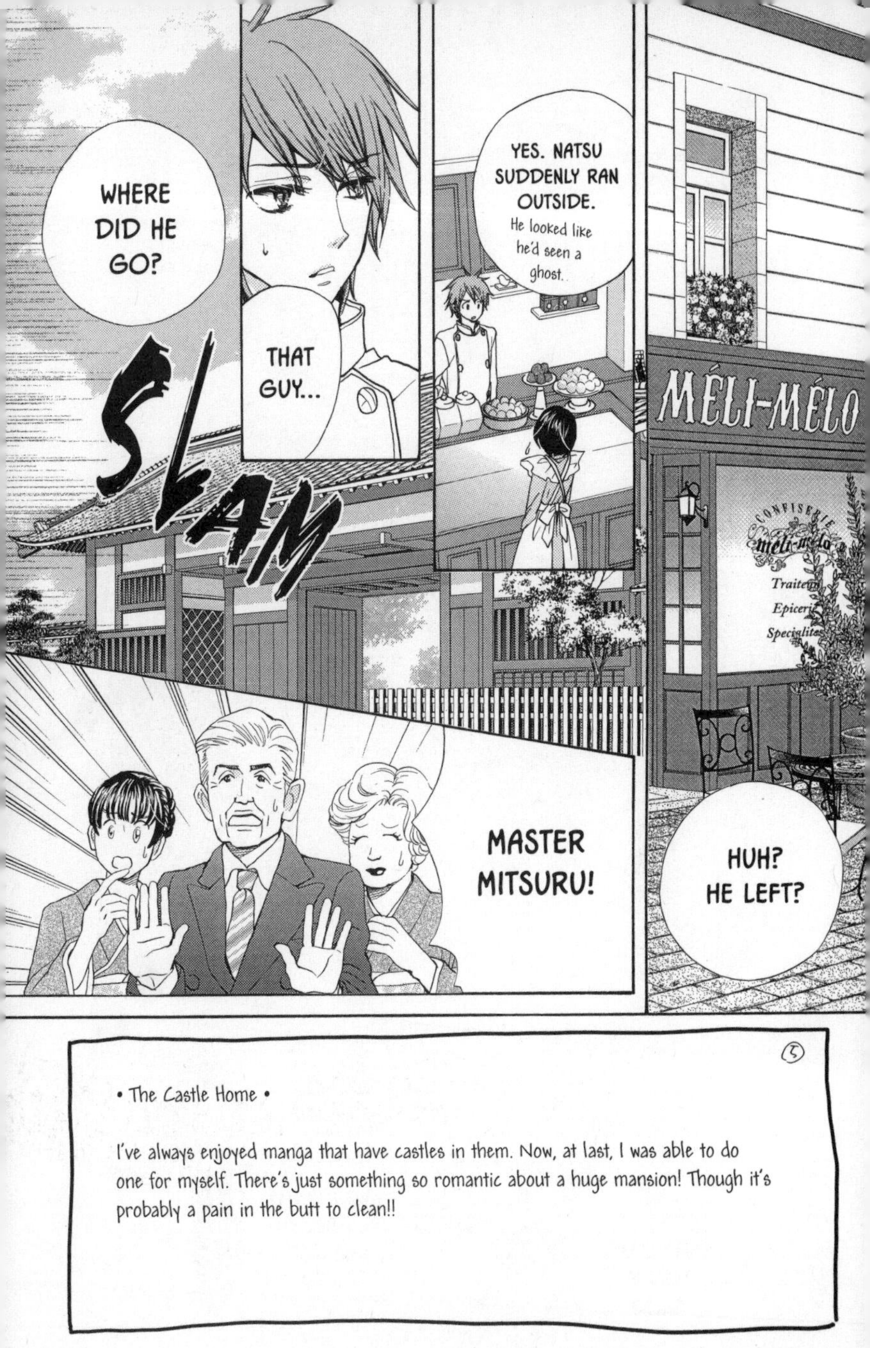
MÉLI-MÉLO
CONFISERIE
méli-mélo
HUH? HE LEFT?
YES. NATSU SUDDENLY RAN OUTSIDE. He looked like he'd seen a ghost.
THAT GUY...
WHERE DID HE GO?
SLAM
MASTER MITSURU!

(5)

• The Castle Home •

I've always enjoyed manga that have castles in them. Now, at last, I was able to do one for myself. There's just something so romantic about a huge mansion! Though it's probably a pain in the butt to clean!!

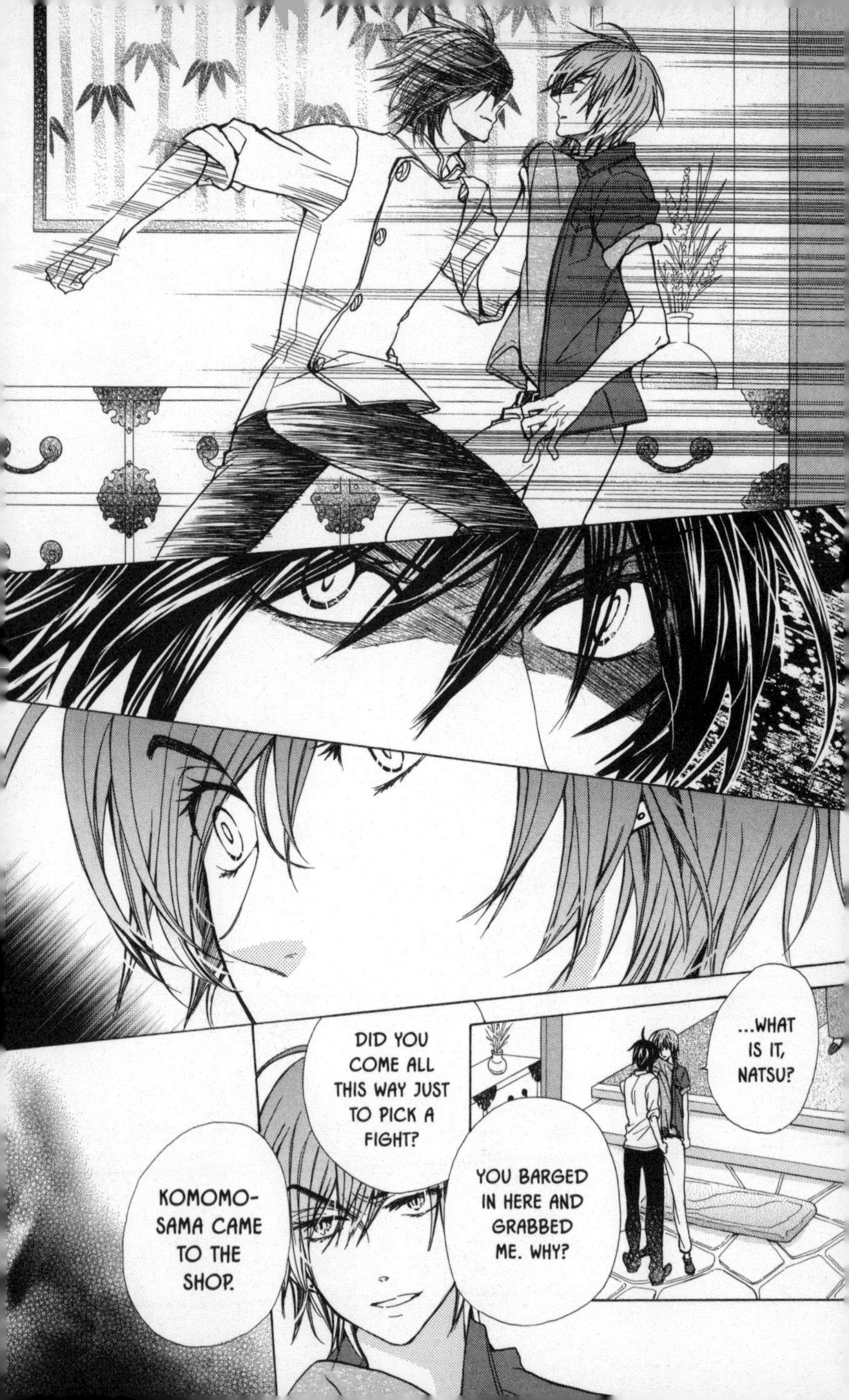
...WHAT IS IT, NATSU?
DID YOU COME ALL THIS WAY JUST TO PICK A FIGHT?
YOU BARGED IN HERE AND GRABBED ME. WHY?
KOMOMO-SAMA CAME TO THE SHOP.

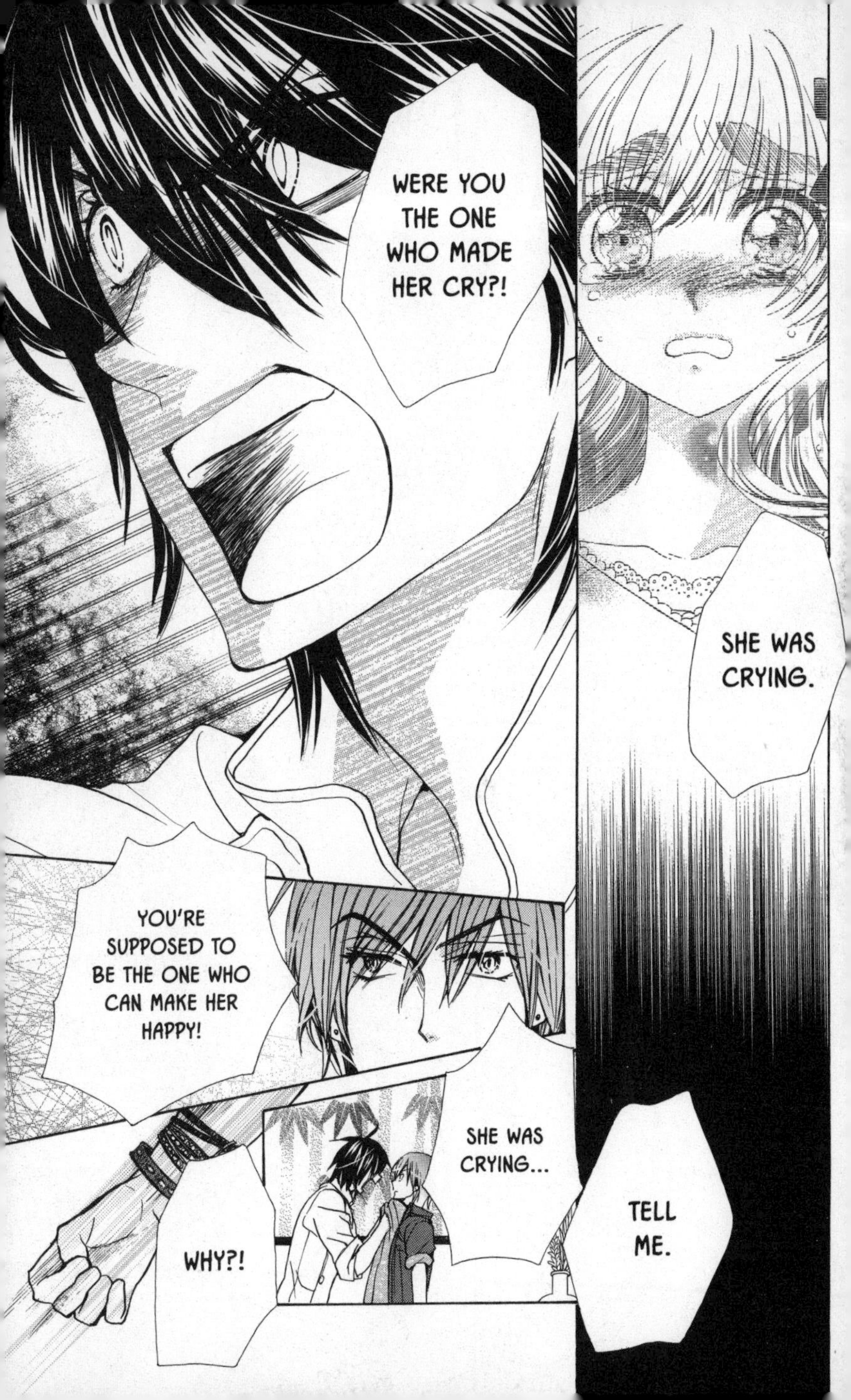
SHE WAS CRYING.
TELL ME.
WERE YOU THE ONE WHO MADE HER CRY?!
YOU'RE SUPPOSED TO BE THE ONE WHO CAN MAKE HER HAPPY!
SHE WAS CRYING...
WHY?!

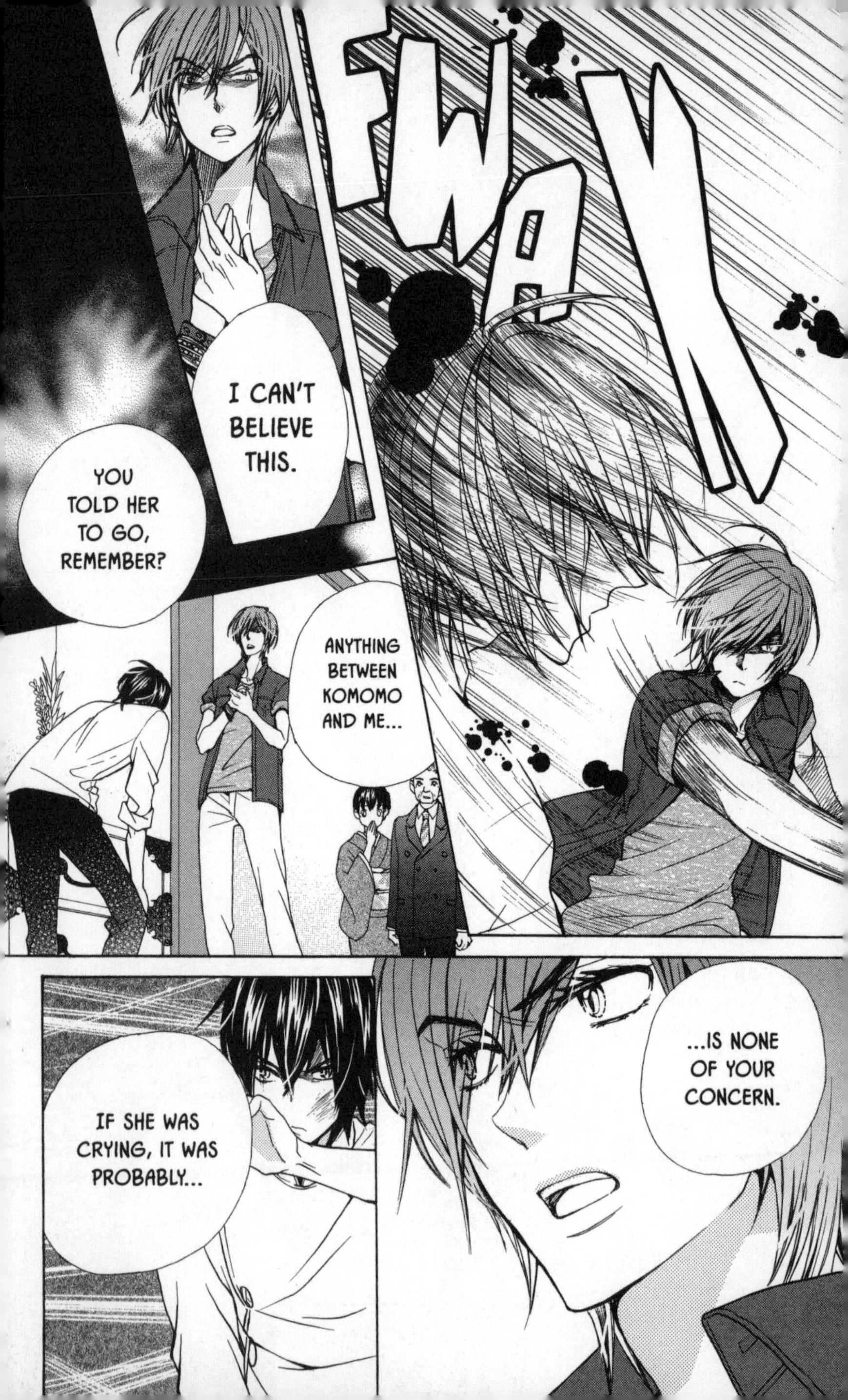
FWAK
I CAN'T BELIEVE THIS.
YOU TOLD HER TO GO, REMEMBER?
ANYTHING BETWEEN KOMOMO AND ME...
...IS NONE OF YOUR CONCERN.
IF SHE WAS CRYING, IT WAS PROBABLY...

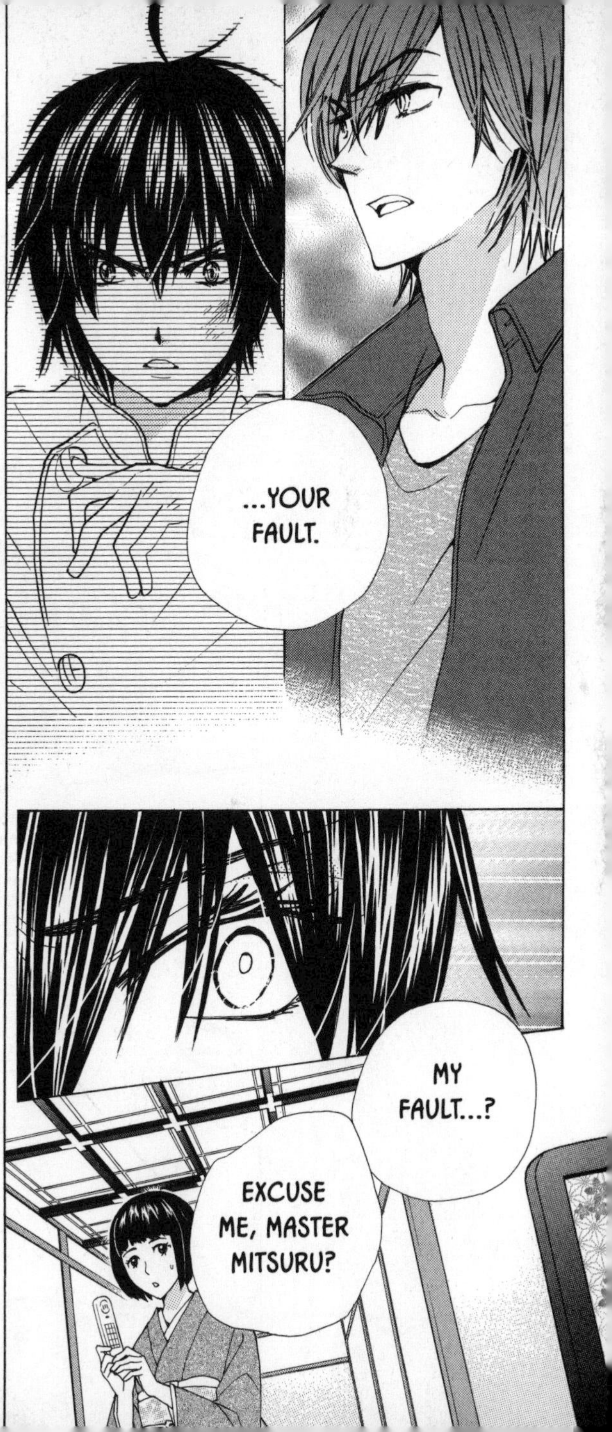
...YOUR FAULT.
MY FAULT...?
EXCUSE ME, MASTER MITSURU?

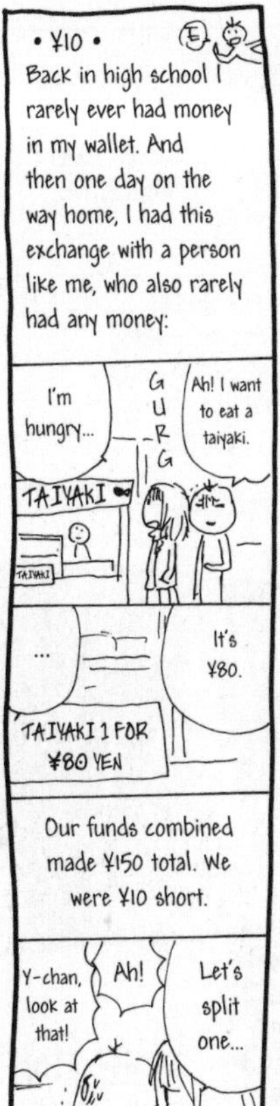
• ¥10 •
Back in high school I rarely ever had money in my wallet. And then one day on the way home, I had this exchange with a person like me, who also rarely had any money:
I'm hungry...
GURG
Ah! I want to eat a taiyaki.
TAIYAKI
...
It's ¥80.
TAIYAKI 1 FOR ¥80 YEN
Our funds combined made ¥150 total. We were ¥10 short.
Y-chan, look at that!
Ah!
Let's split one...
W-what?!
There's a ¥10 coin under that vending machine!!
GURG
Though it was on the ground.
Now...
...we can buy two.
I'll let you imagine the rest.

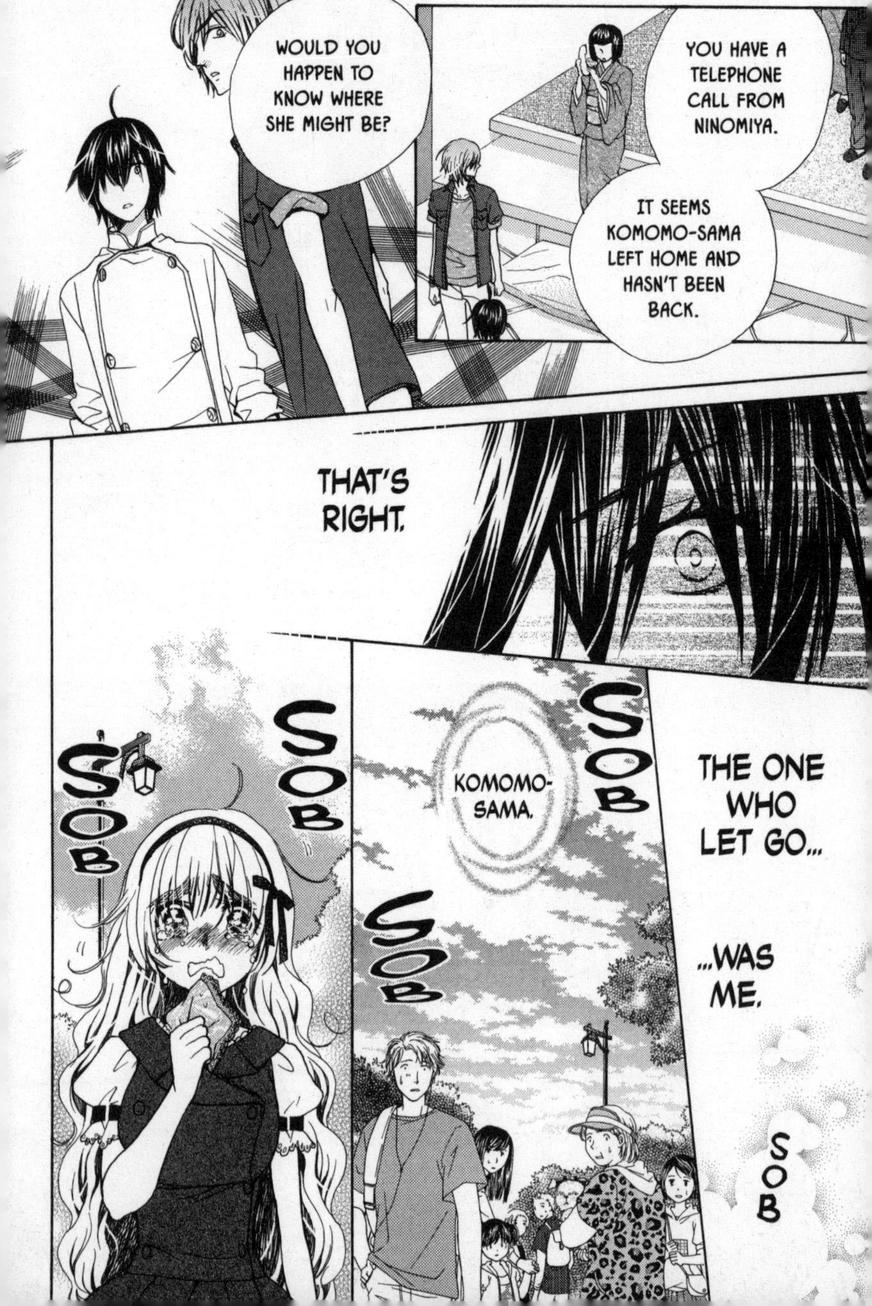
YOU HAVE A TELEPHONE CALL FROM NINOMIYA.
IT SEEMS KOMOMO-SAMA LEFT HOME AND HASN'T BEEN BACK.
WOULD YOU HAPPEN TO KNOW WHERE SHE MIGHT BE?
THAT'S RIGHT.
THE ONE WHO LET GO...
...WAS ME.
SOB
SOB
KOMOMO-SAMA.
SOB
SOB
SOB

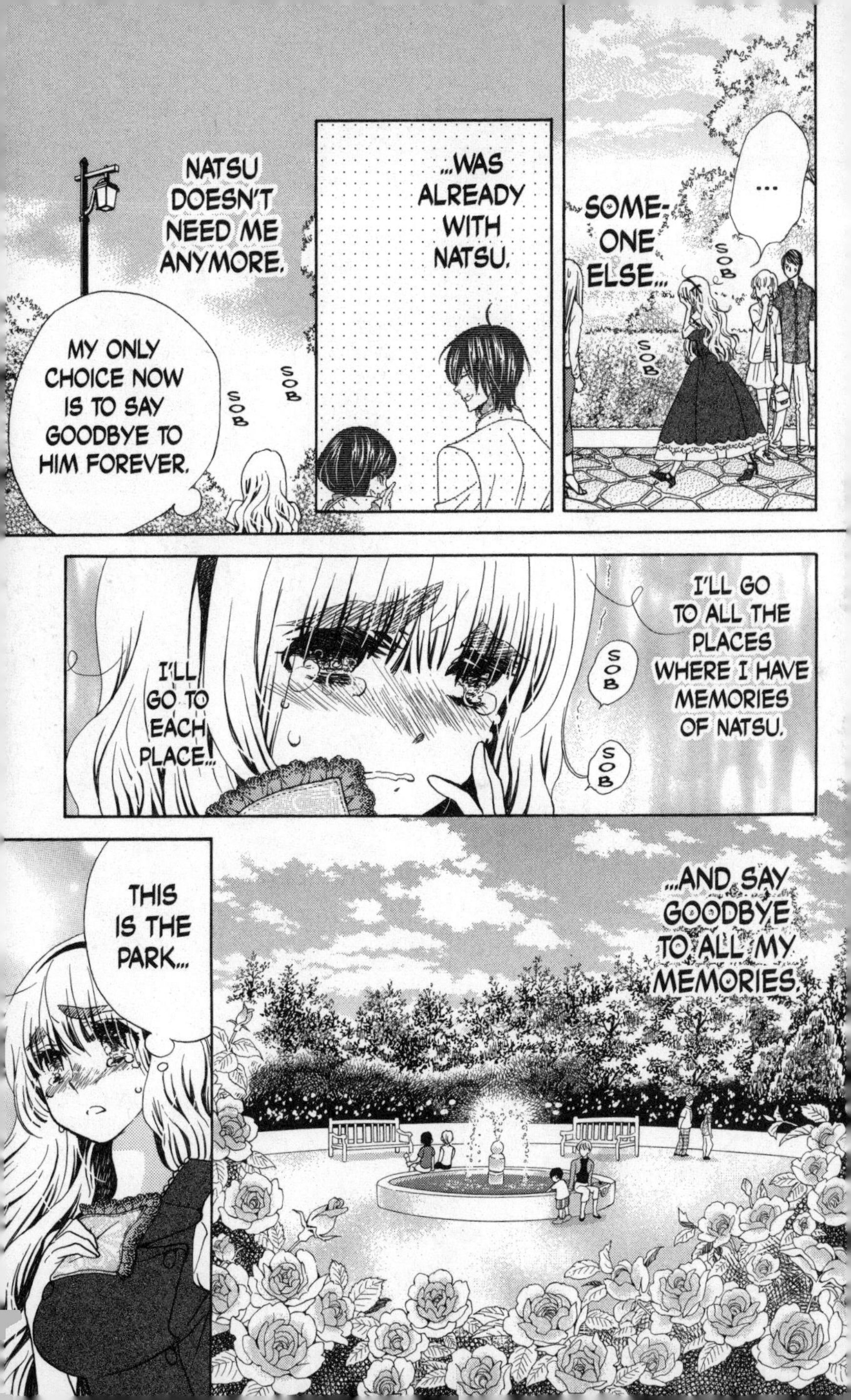
...
SOME-ONE ELSE...
SOB
SOB
...WAS ALREADY WITH NATSU.
NATSU DOESN'T NEED ME ANYMORE.
SOB
SOB
MY ONLY CHOICE NOW IS TO SAY GOODBYE TO HIM FOREVER.
I'LL GO TO ALL THE PLACES WHERE I HAVE MEMORIES OF NATSU.
SOB
SOB
I'LL GO TO EACH PLACE...
...AND SAY GOODBYE TO ALL MY MEMORIES.
THIS IS THE PARK...

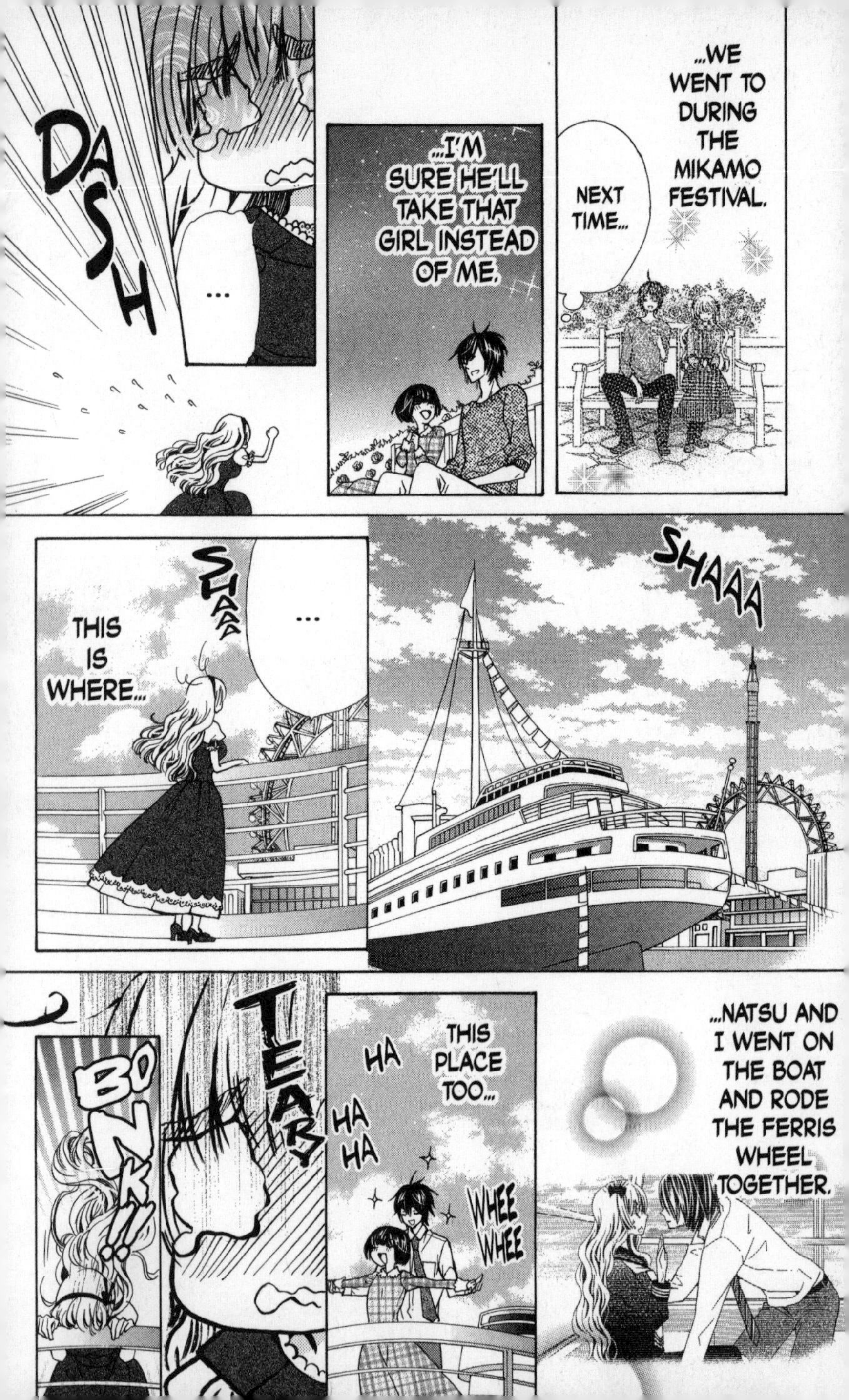
...WE WENT TO DURING THE MIKAMO FESTIVAL.
NEXT TIME...
...I'M SURE HE'LL TAKE THAT GIRL INSTEAD OF ME.
...
DASH
SHAAA
SHAAA
...
THIS IS WHERE...
...NATSU AND I WENT ON THE BOAT AND RODE THE FERRIS WHEEL TOGETHER.
THIS PLACE TOO...
HA
HA HA
WHEE WHEE
TEAR
BONK!!

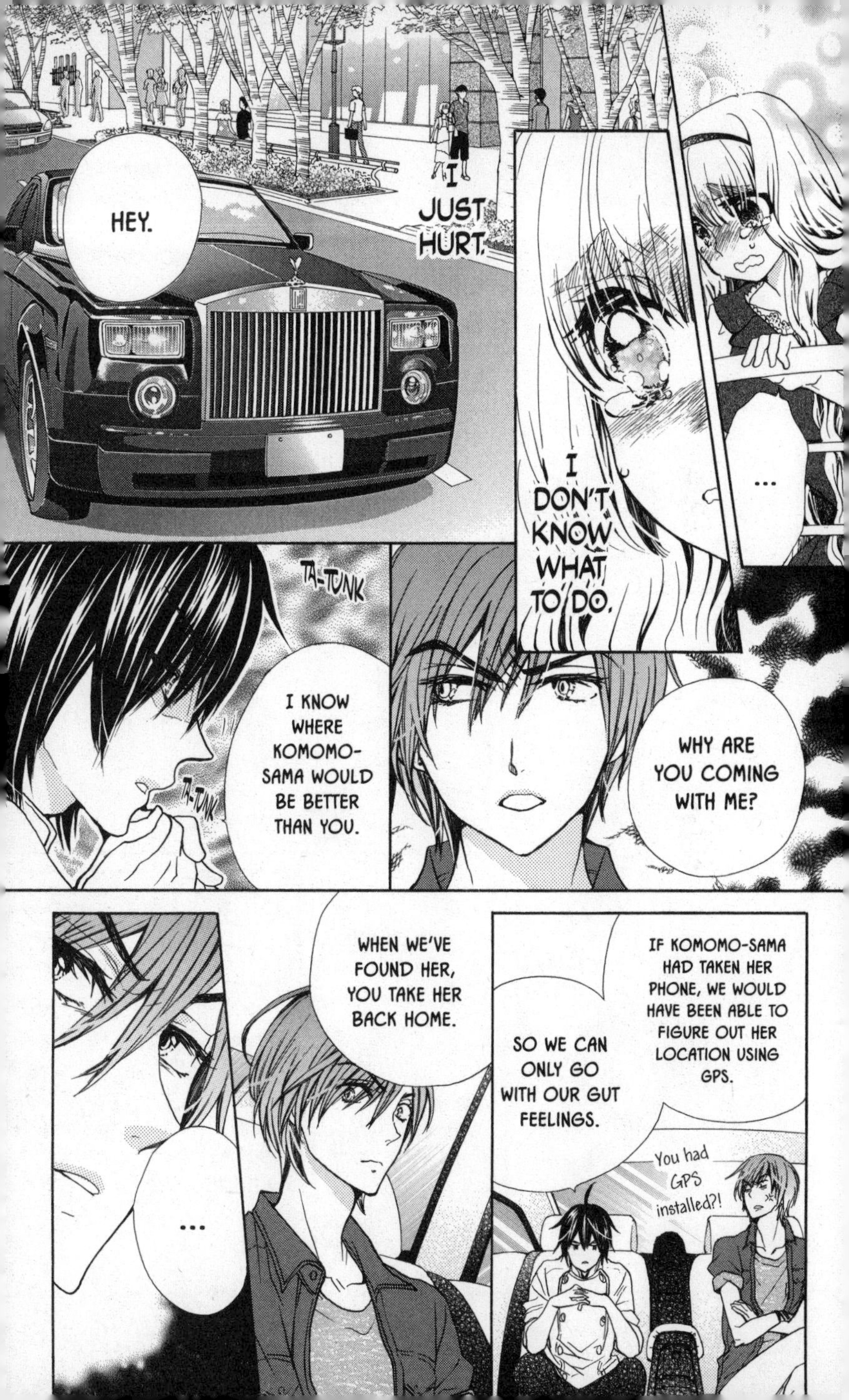
...
I DON'T KNOW WHAT TO DO.
I JUST HURT.
HEY.
WHY ARE YOU COMING WITH ME?
TA-TUNK
I KNOW WHERE KOMOMO-SAMA WOULD BE BETTER THAN YOU.
TA-TUNK
IF KOMOMO-SAMA HAD TAKEN HER PHONE, WE WOULD HAVE BEEN ABLE TO FIGURE OUT HER LOCATION USING GPS.
SO WE CAN ONLY GO WITH OUR GUT FEELINGS.
You had GPS installed?!
WHEN WE'VE FOUND HER, YOU TAKE HER BACK HOME.
...

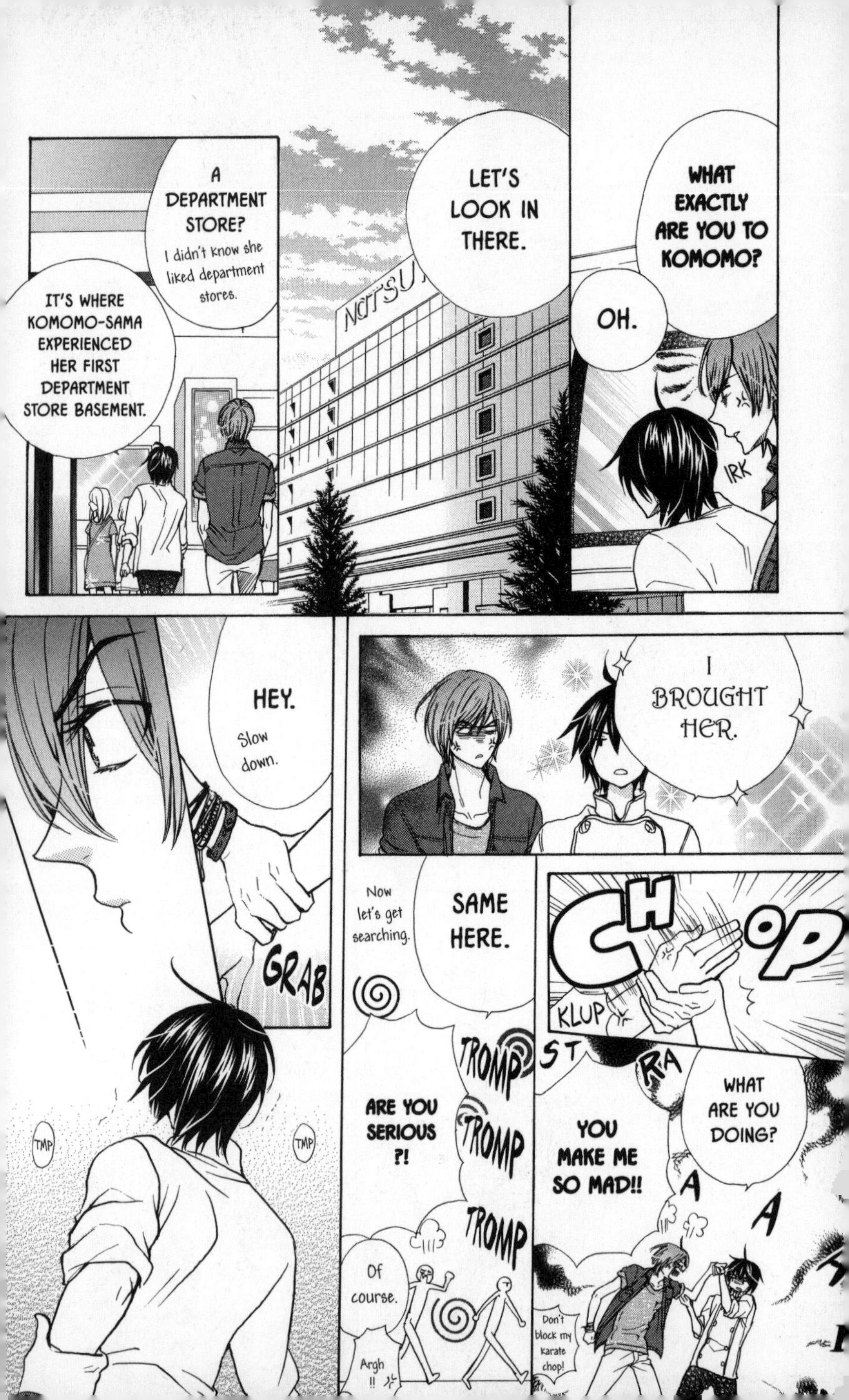
WHAT EXACTLY ARE YOU TO KOMOMO?
OH.
IRK
LET'S LOOK IN THERE.
A DEPARTMENT STORE?
I didn't know she liked department stores.
IT'S WHERE KOMOMO-SAMA EXPERIENCED HER FIRST DEPARTMENT STORE BASEMENT.
I BROUGHT HER.
CHOP
KLUP
STRAAA
WHAT ARE YOU DOING?
YOU MAKE ME SO MAD!!
Don't block my karate chop!
SAME HERE.
Now let's get searching.
TROMP
TROMP
TROMP
ARE YOU SERIOUS?!
Of course.
Argh!!
HEY.
Slow down.
GRAB
TMP
TMP

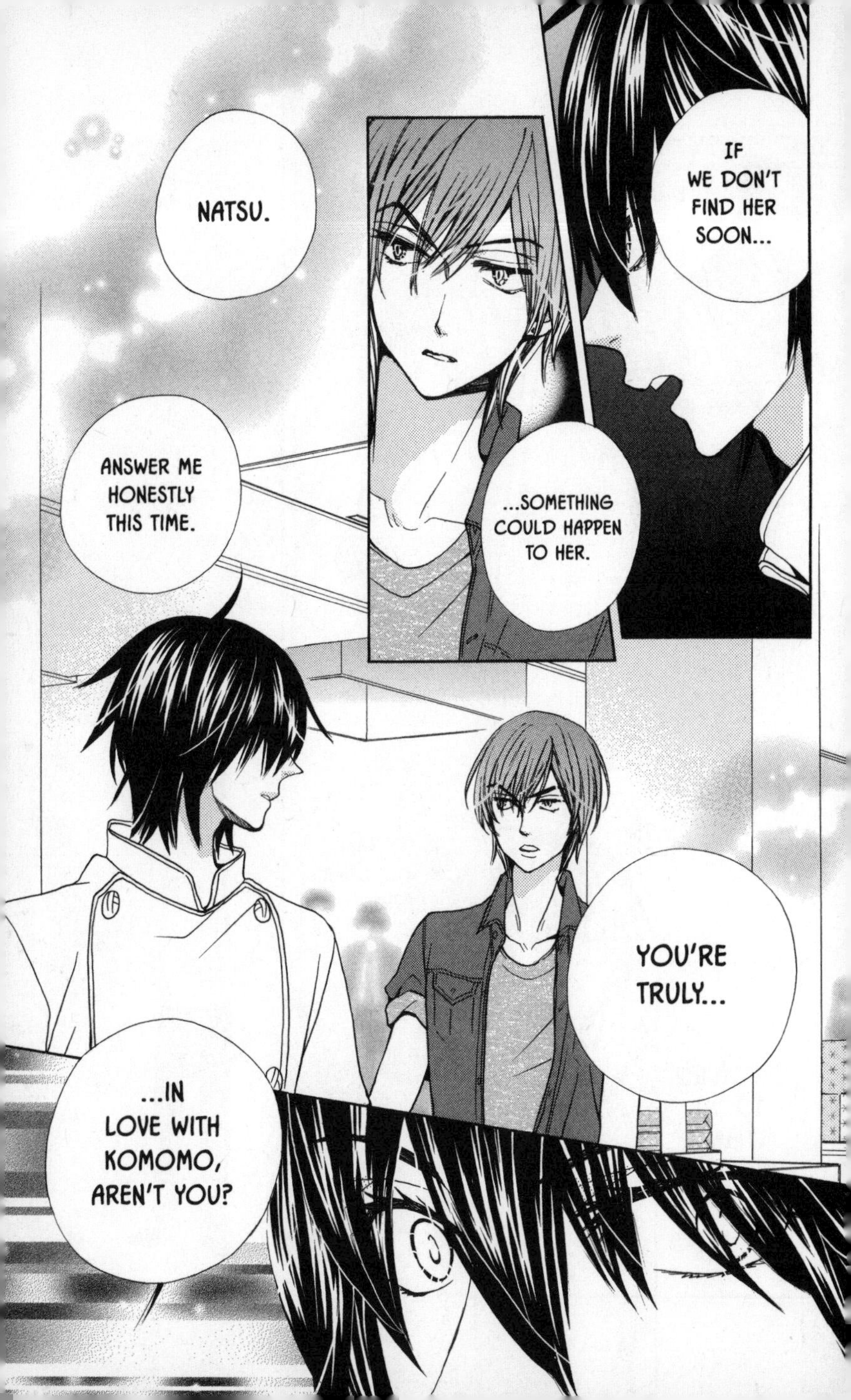
IF WE DON'T FIND HER SOON...
...SOMETHING COULD HAPPEN TO HER.
NATSU.
ANSWER ME HONESTLY THIS TIME.
YOU'RE TRULY...
...IN LOVE WITH KOMOMO, AREN'T YOU?

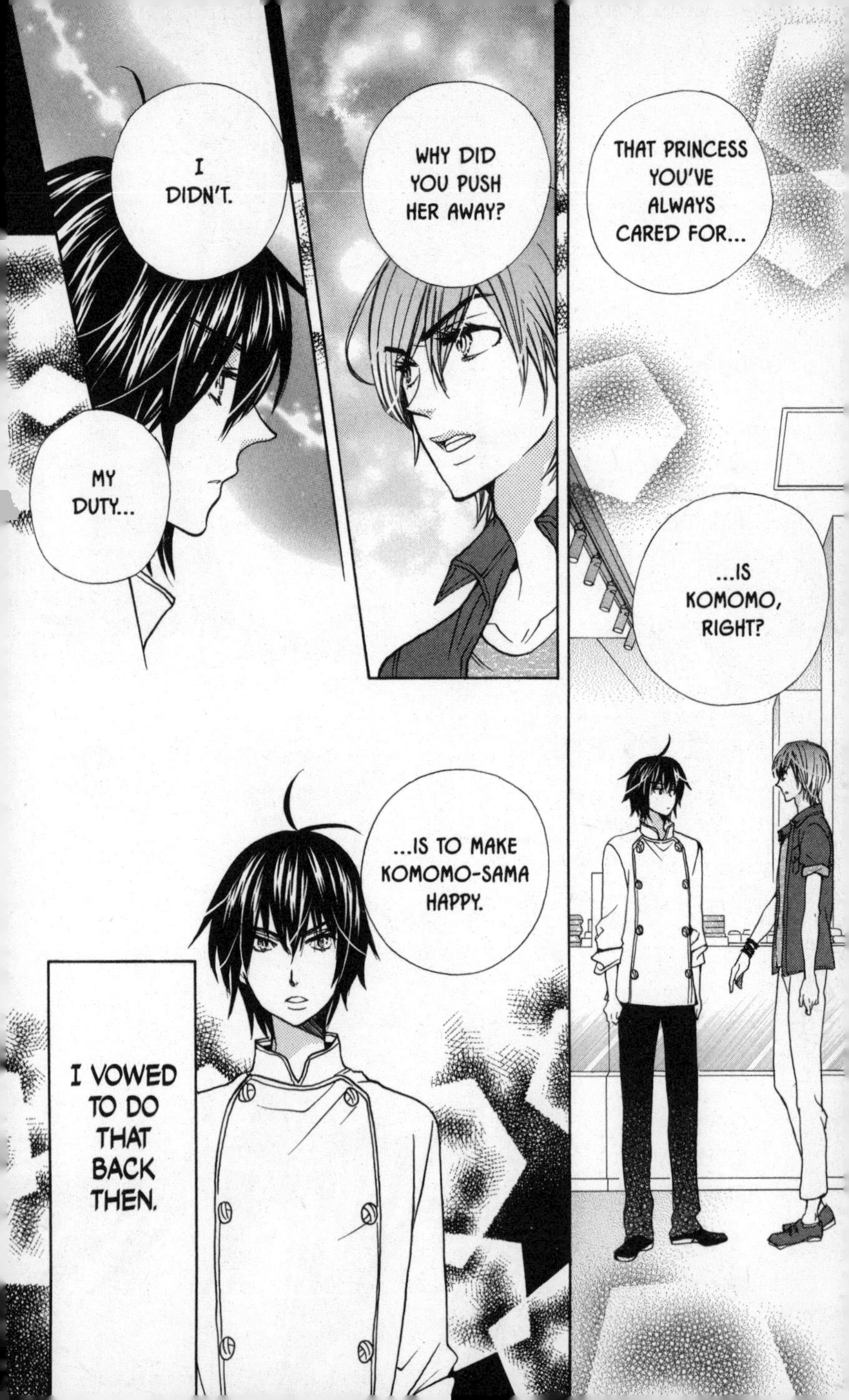
THAT PRINCESS YOU'VE ALWAYS CARED FOR...
...IS KOMOMO, RIGHT?
WHY DID YOU PUSH HER AWAY?
I DIDN'T.
MY DUTY...
...IS TO MAKE KOMOMO-SAMA HAPPY.
I VOWED TO DO THAT BACK THEN.

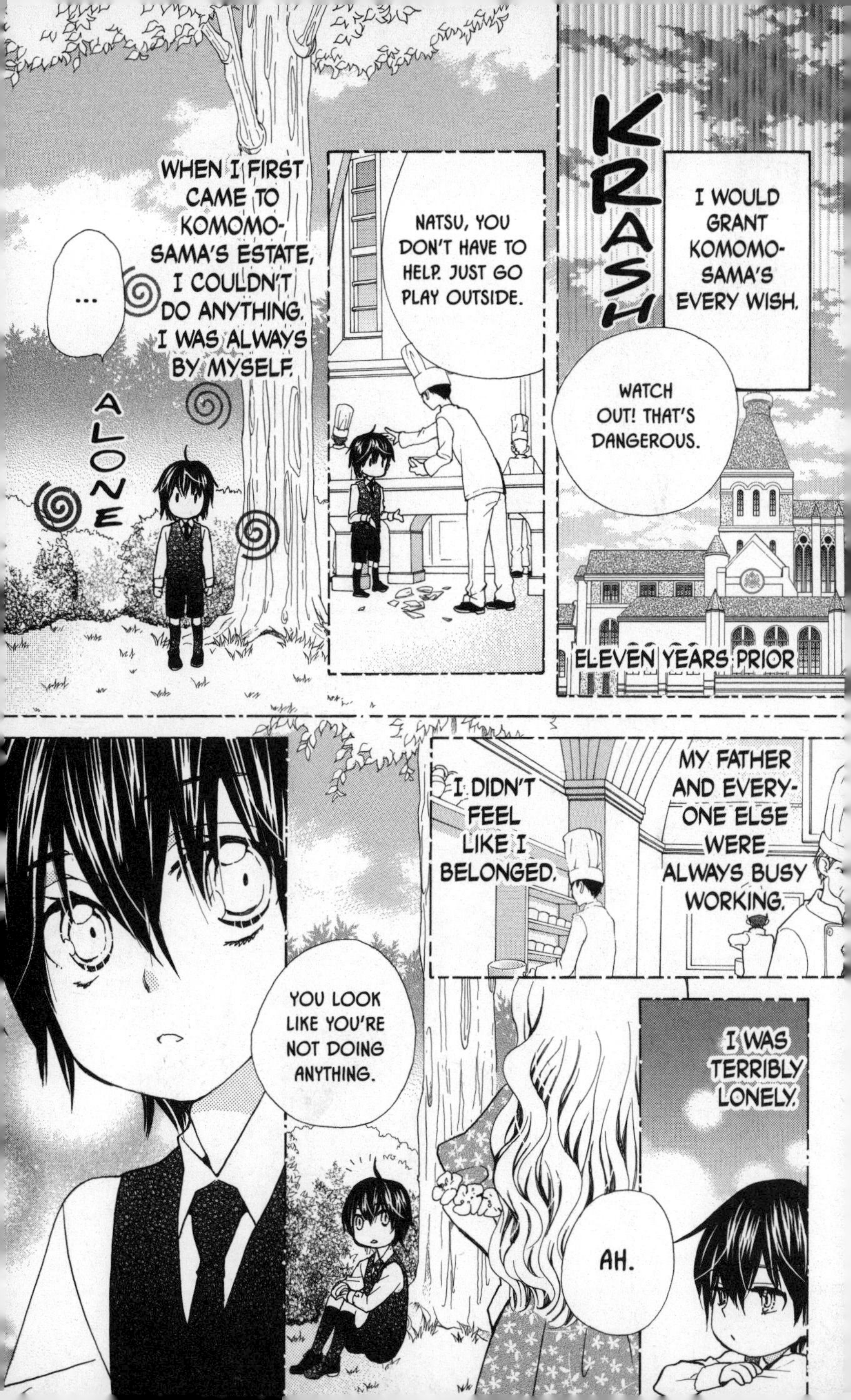
I WOULD GRANT KOMOMO-SAMA'S EVERY WISH.
KRASH
WATCH OUT! THAT'S DANGEROUS.
ELEVEN YEARS PRIOR
NATSU, YOU DON'T HAVE TO HELP. JUST GO PLAY OUTSIDE.
WHEN I FIRST CAME TO KOMOMO-SAMA'S ESTATE, I COULDN'T DO ANYTHING. I WAS ALWAYS BY MYSELF.
...
ALONE
MY FATHER AND EVERY-ONE ELSE WERE ALWAYS BUSY WORKING.
I DIDN'T FEEL LIKE I BELONGED.
I WAS TERRIBLY LONELY.
AH.
YOU LOOK LIKE YOU'RE NOT DOING ANYTHING.

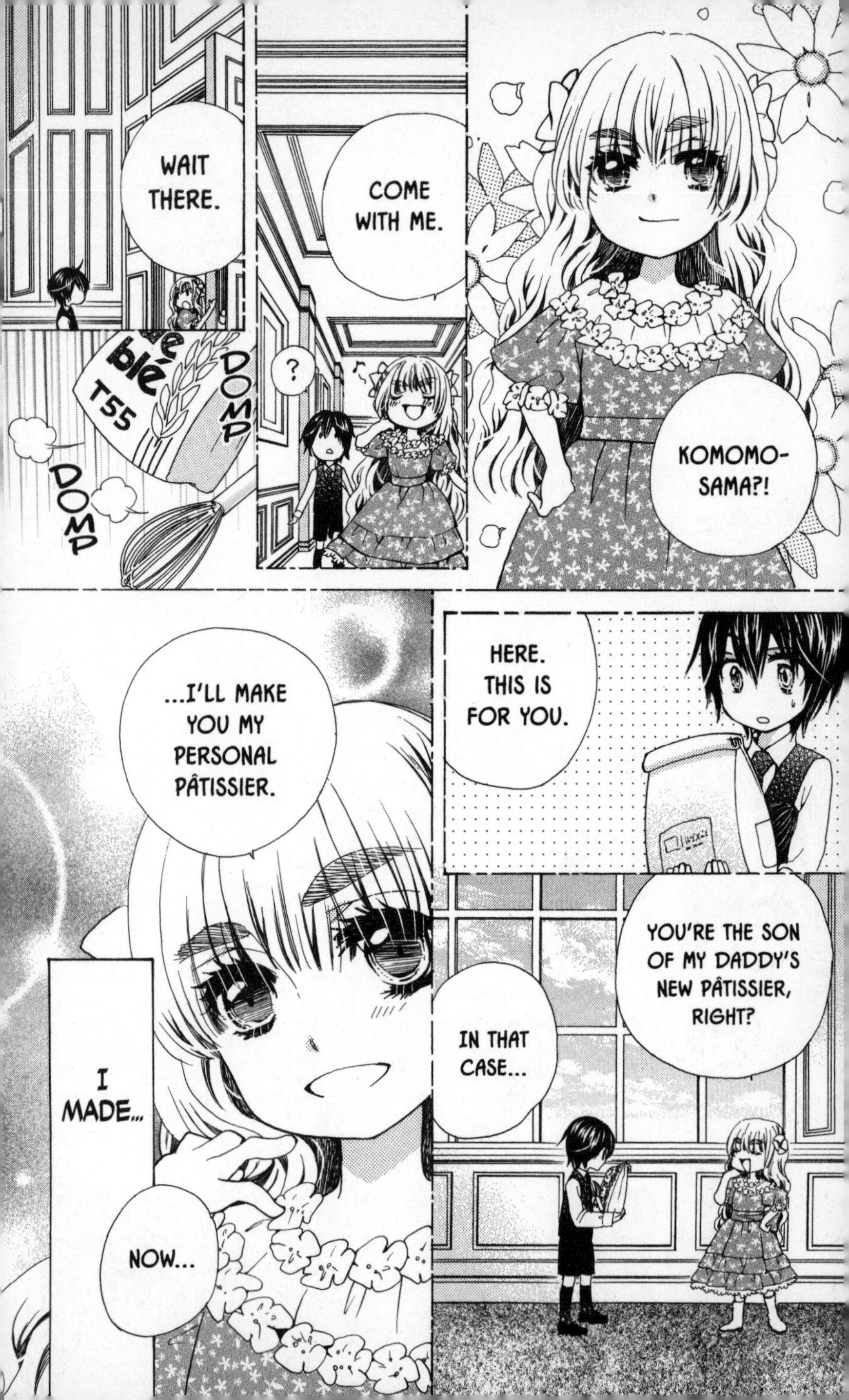

KOMOMO-SAMA?!
COME WITH ME.
?
WAIT THERE.
blé
T55
DOMP
DOMP
HERE. THIS IS FOR YOU.
YOU'RE THE SON OF MY DADDY'S NEW PÂTISSIER, RIGHT?
IN THAT CASE...
...I'LL MAKE YOU MY PERSONAL PÂTISSIER.
I MADE...
NOW...

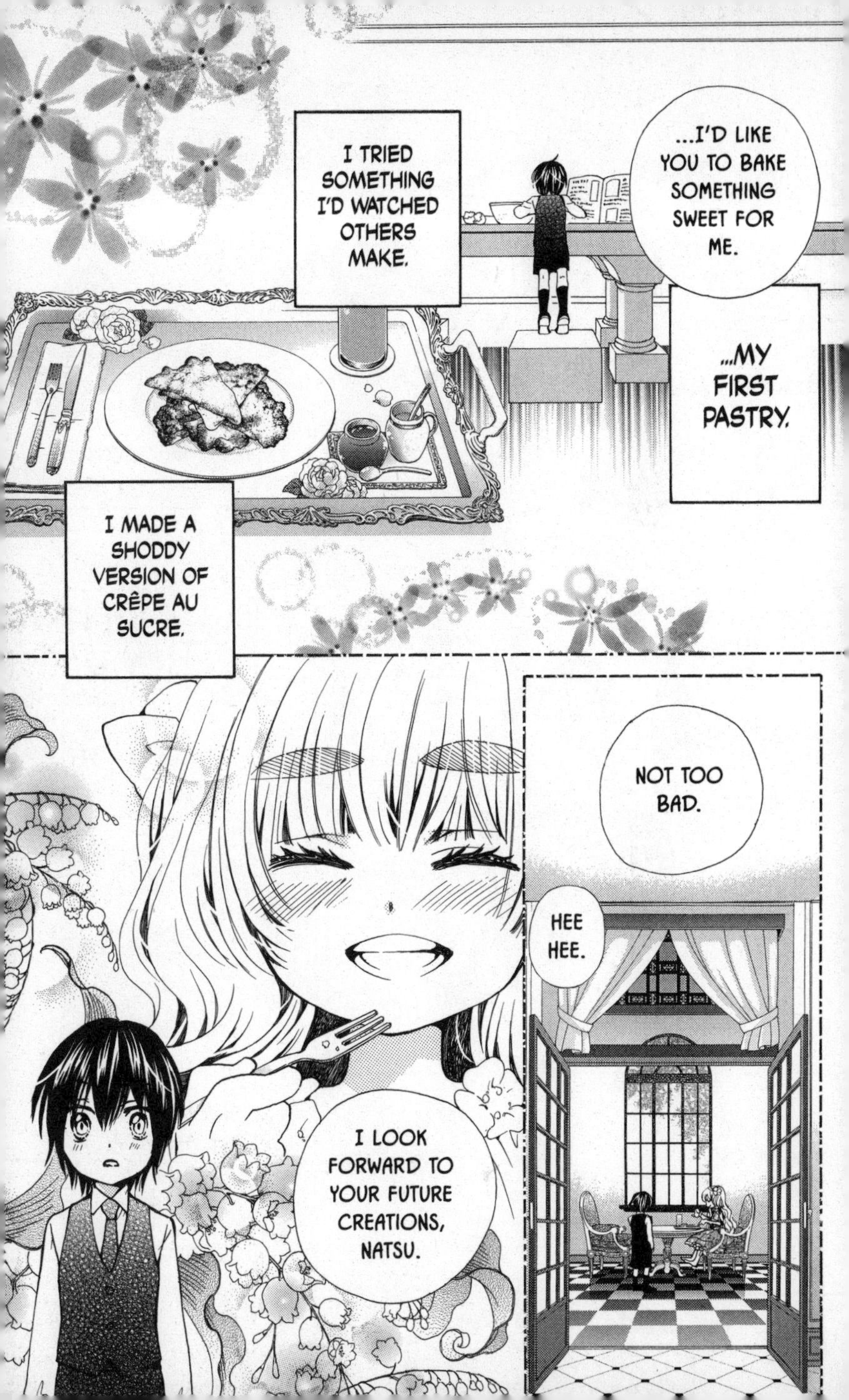

...I'D LIKE YOU TO BAKE SOMETHING SWEET FOR ME.
I TRIED SOMETHING I'D WATCHED OTHERS MAKE.
...MY FIRST PASTRY.
I MADE A SHODDY VERSION OF CRÊPE AU SUCRE.
NOT TOO BAD.
HEE HEE.
I LOOK FORWARD TO YOUR FUTURE CREATIONS, NATSU.

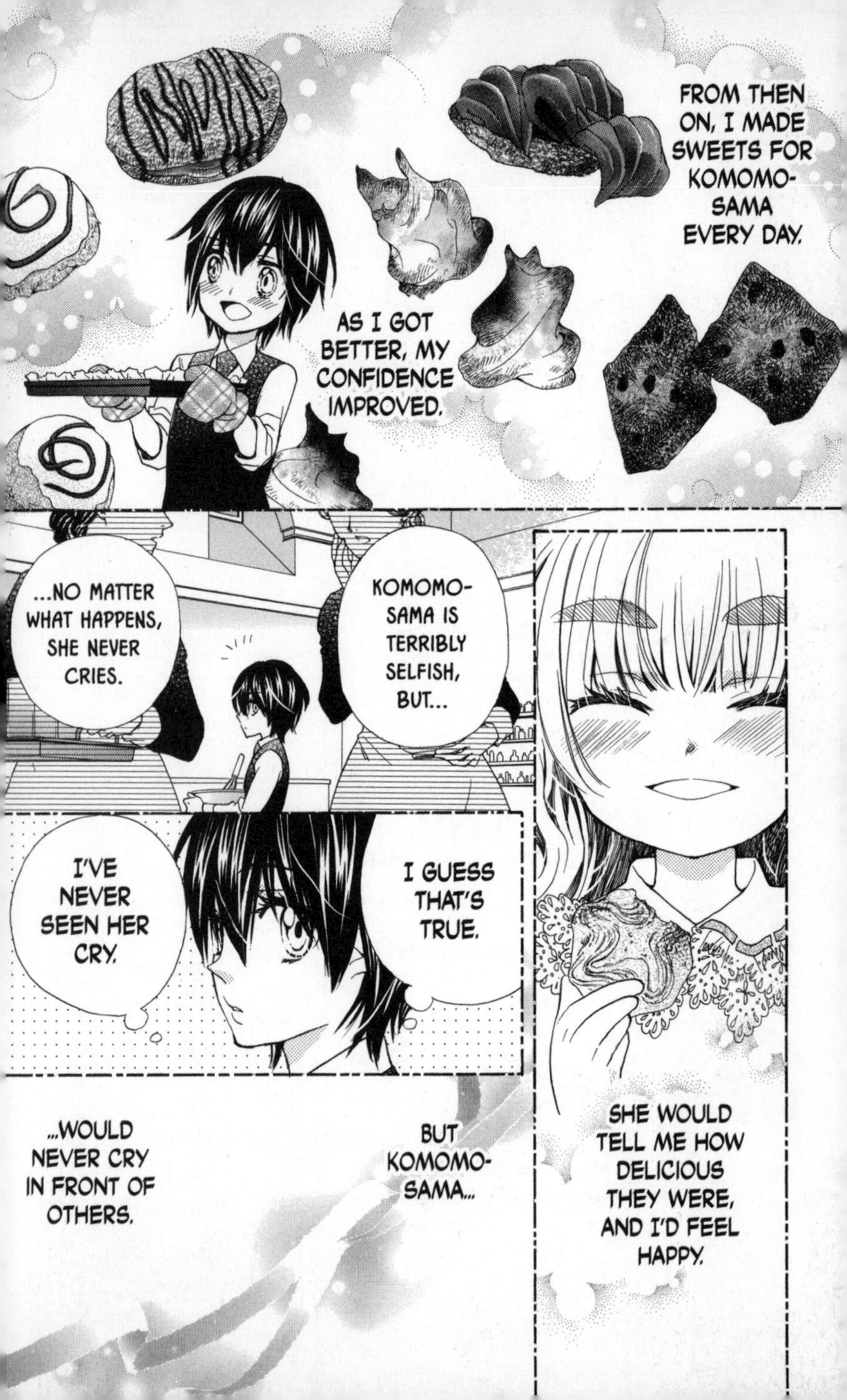
FROM THEN ON, I MADE SWEETS FOR KOMOMO-SAMA EVERY DAY.
AS I GOT BETTER, MY CONFIDENCE IMPROVED.
SHE WOULD TELL ME HOW DELICIOUS THEY WERE, AND I'D FEEL HAPPY.
KOMOMO-SAMA IS TERRIBLY SELFISH, BUT...
...NO MATTER WHAT HAPPENS, SHE NEVER CRIES.
I GUESS THAT'S TRUE.
I'VE NEVER SEEN HER CRY.
BUT KOMOMO-SAMA...
...WOULD NEVER CRY IN FRONT OF OTHERS.

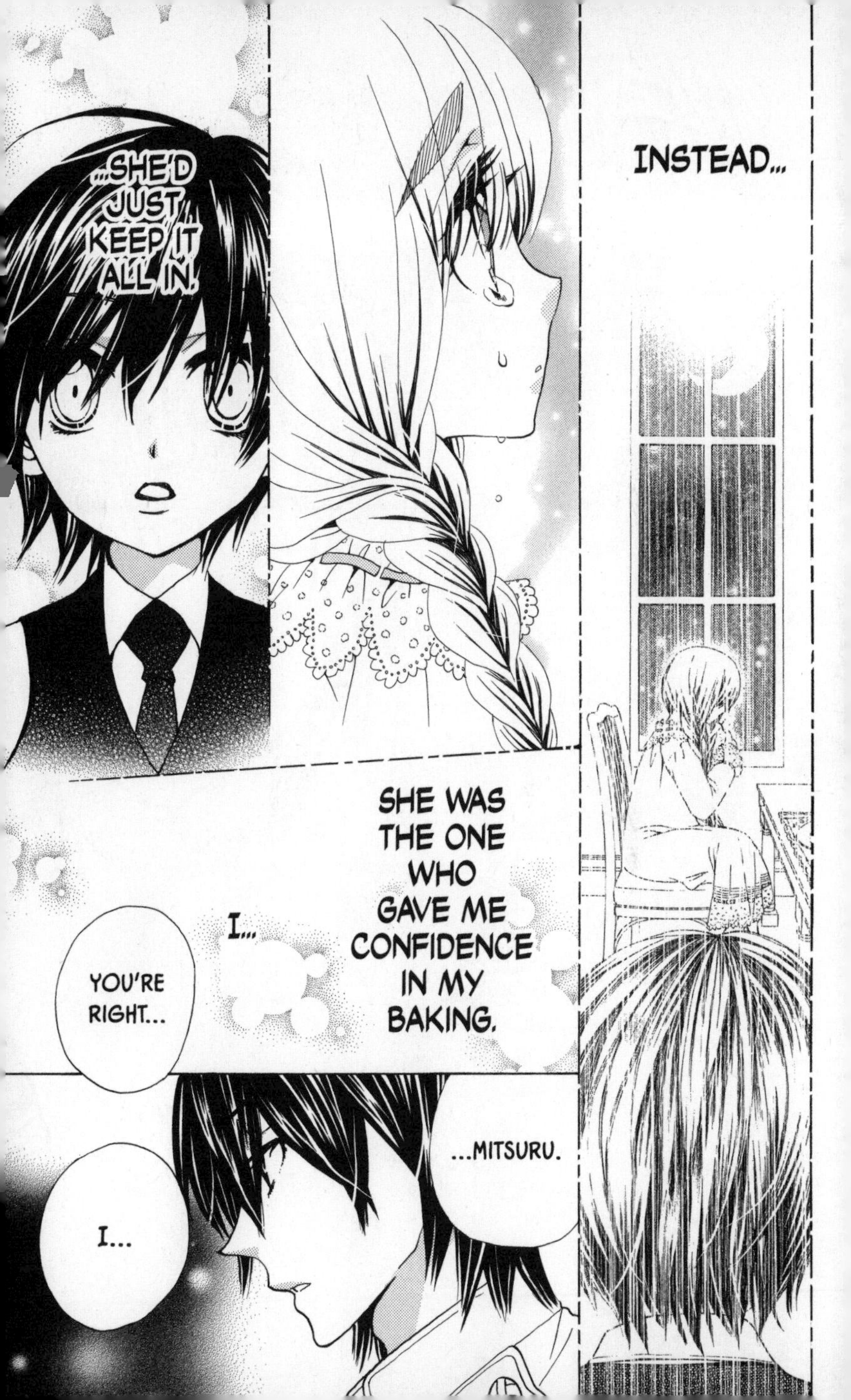
INSTEAD...
...SHE'D JUST KEEP IT ALL IN.
SHE WAS THE ONE WHO GAVE ME CONFIDENCE IN MY BAKING.
I...
YOU'RE RIGHT...
...MITSURU.
I...

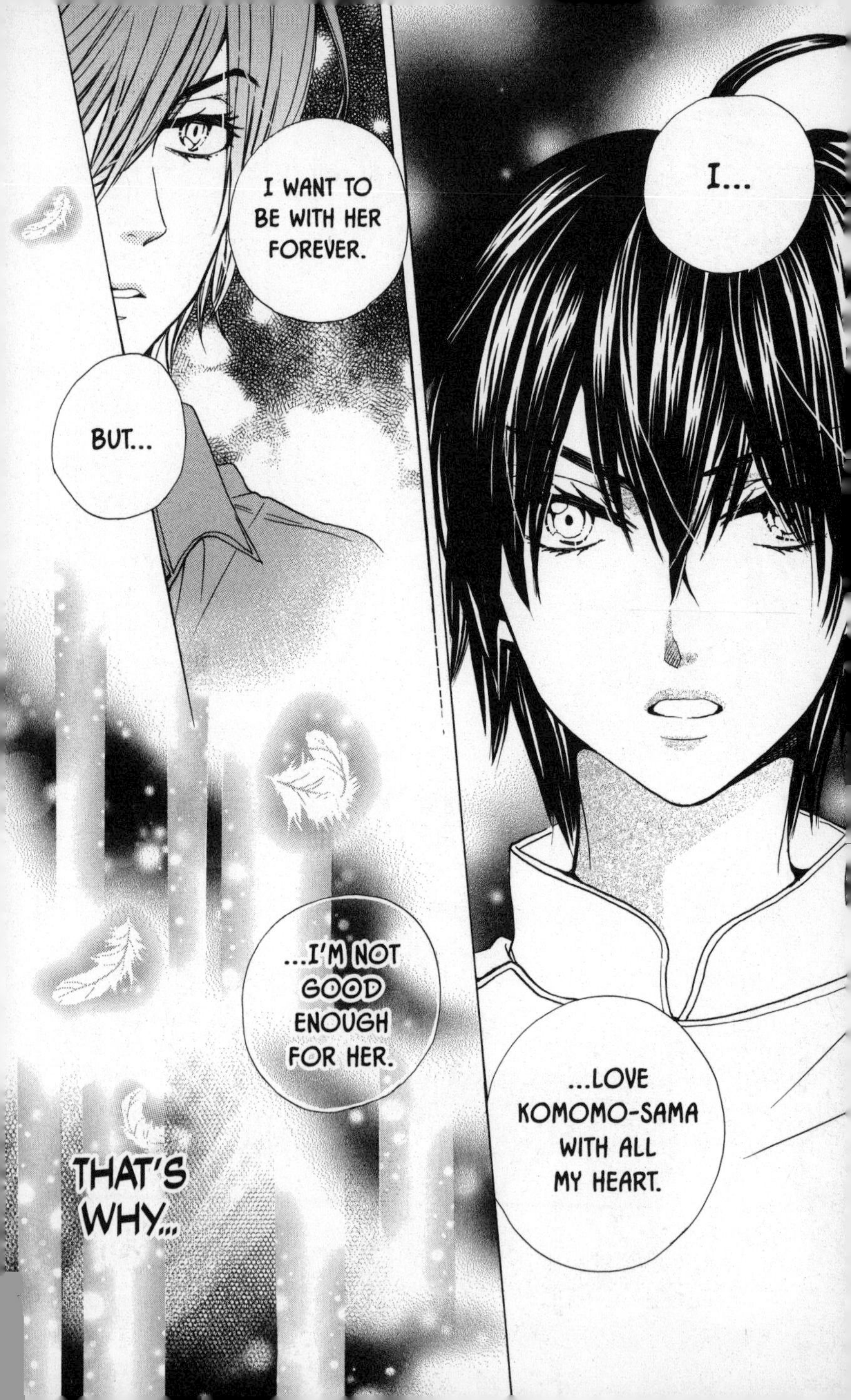
I...
...LOVE KOMOMO-SAMA WITH ALL MY HEART.
I WANT TO BE WITH HER FOREVER.
BUT...
...I'M NOT GOOD ENOUGH FOR HER.
THAT'S WHY...

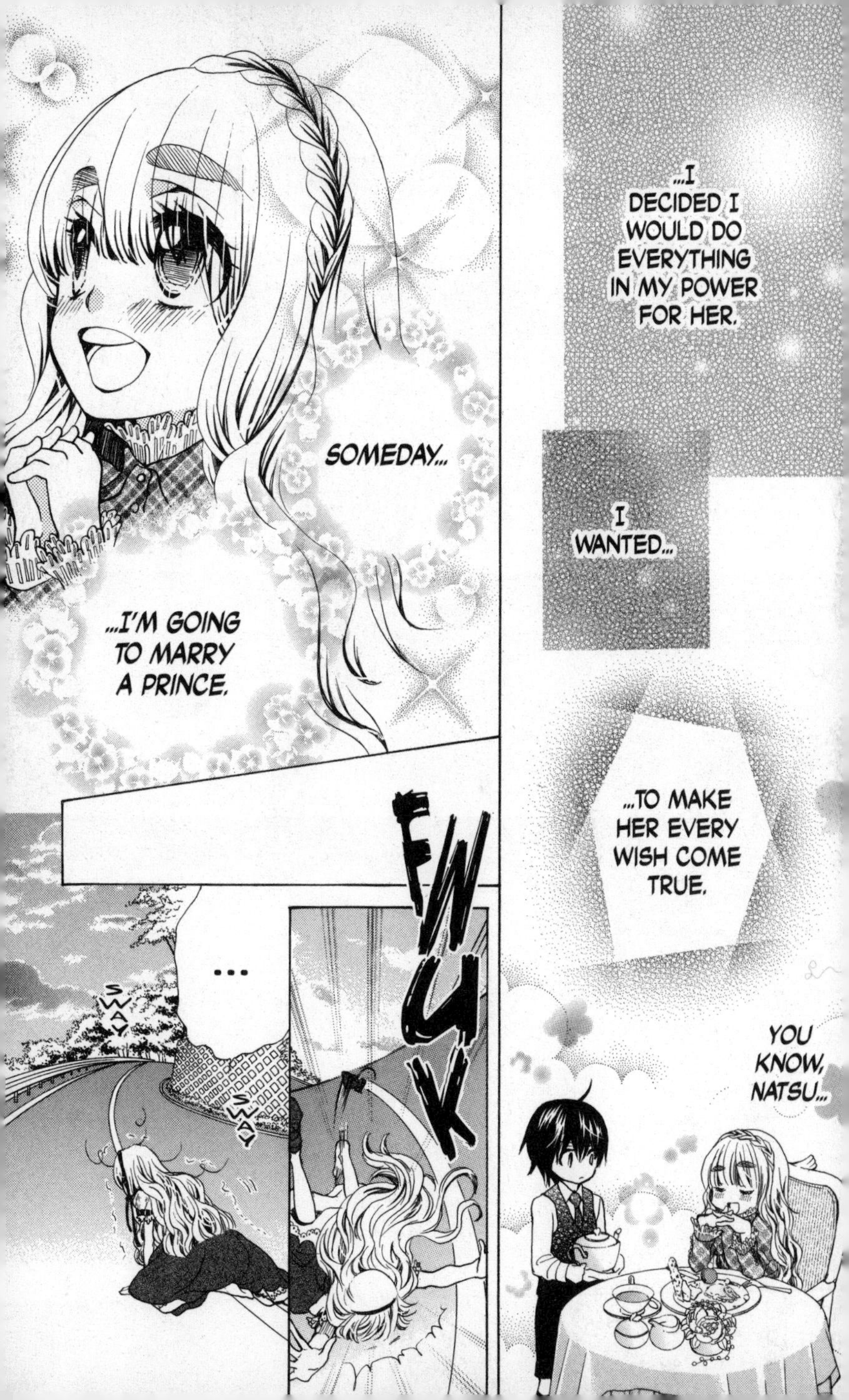
...I DECIDED I WOULD DO EVERYTHING IN MY POWER FOR HER.
I WANTED...
...TO MAKE HER EVERY WISH COME TRUE.
YOU KNOW, NATSU...
SOMEDAY...
...I'M GOING TO MARRY A PRINCE.
FWUK
...
SWAY
SWAY

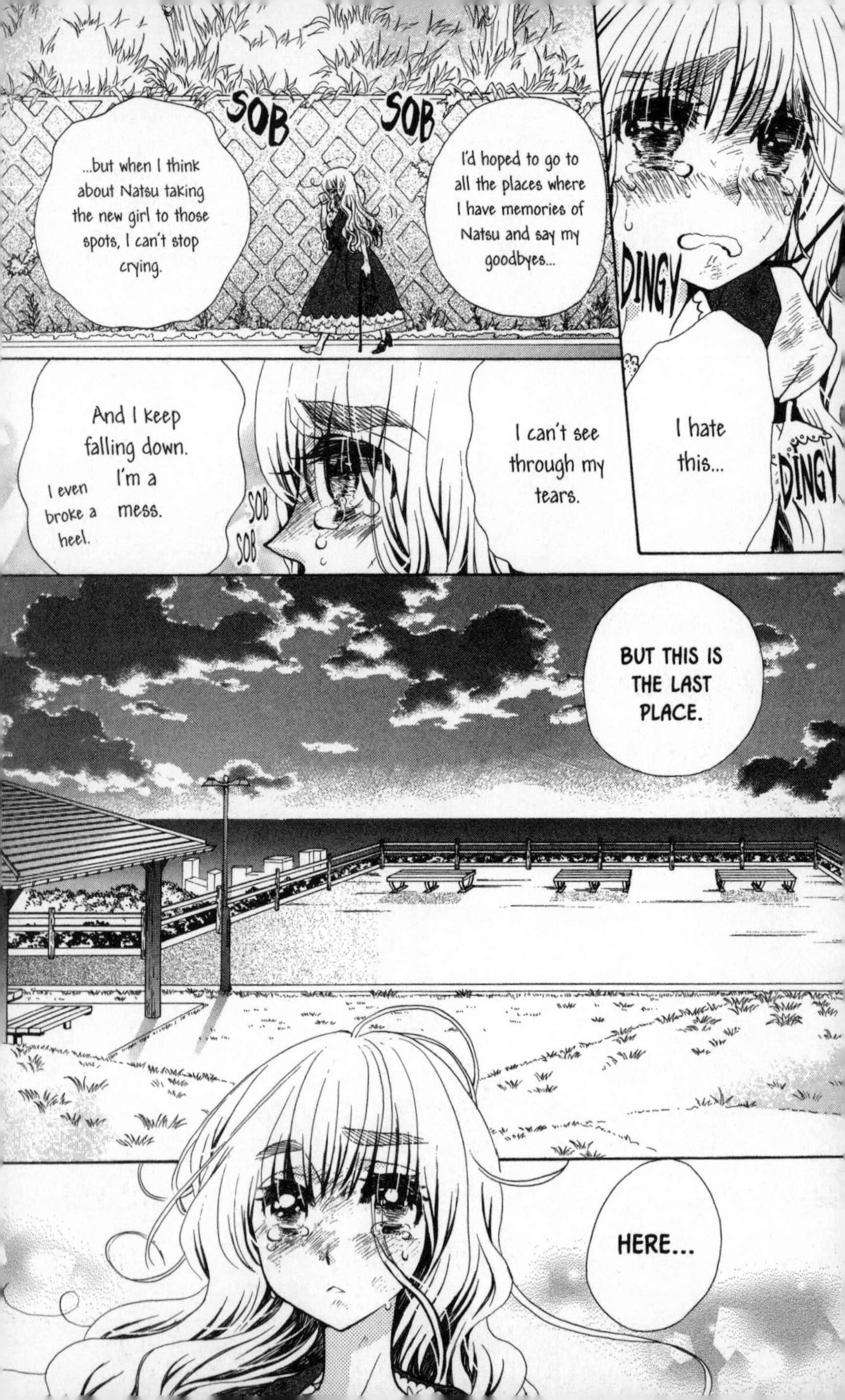
DINGY
I hate this...
DINGY
SOB SOB
I'd hoped to go to all the places where I have memories of Natsu and say my goodbyes...
...but when I think about Natsu taking the new girl to those spots, I can't stop crying.
I can't see through my tears.
SOB SOB
And I keep falling down. I'm a mess.
I even broke a heel.
BUT THIS IS THE LAST PLACE.
HERE...

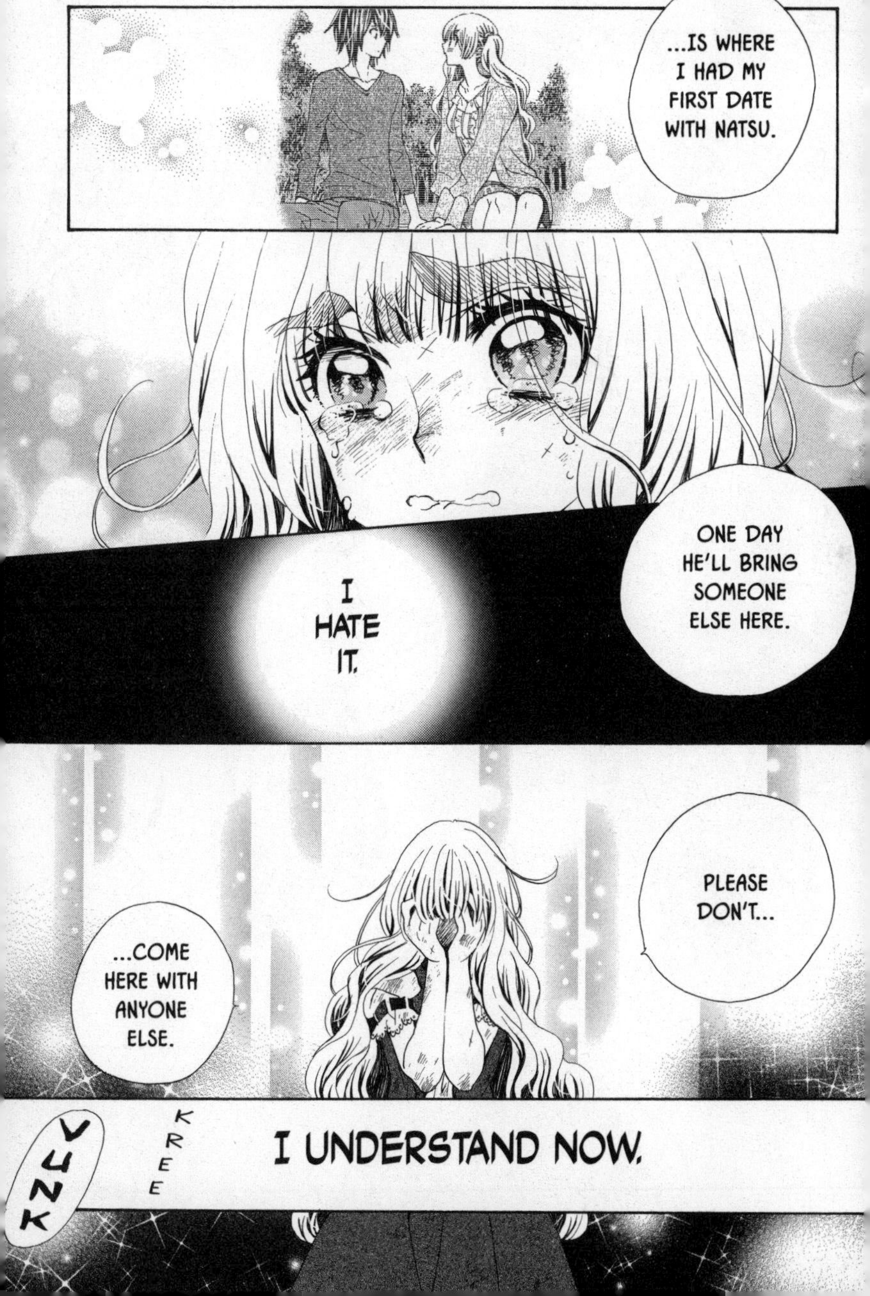
...IS WHERE I HAD MY FIRST DATE WITH NATSU.
ONE DAY HE'LL BRING SOMEONE ELSE HERE.
I HATE IT.
PLEASE DON'T...
...COME HERE WITH ANYONE ELSE.
I UNDERSTAND NOW.
KREE
VUNK

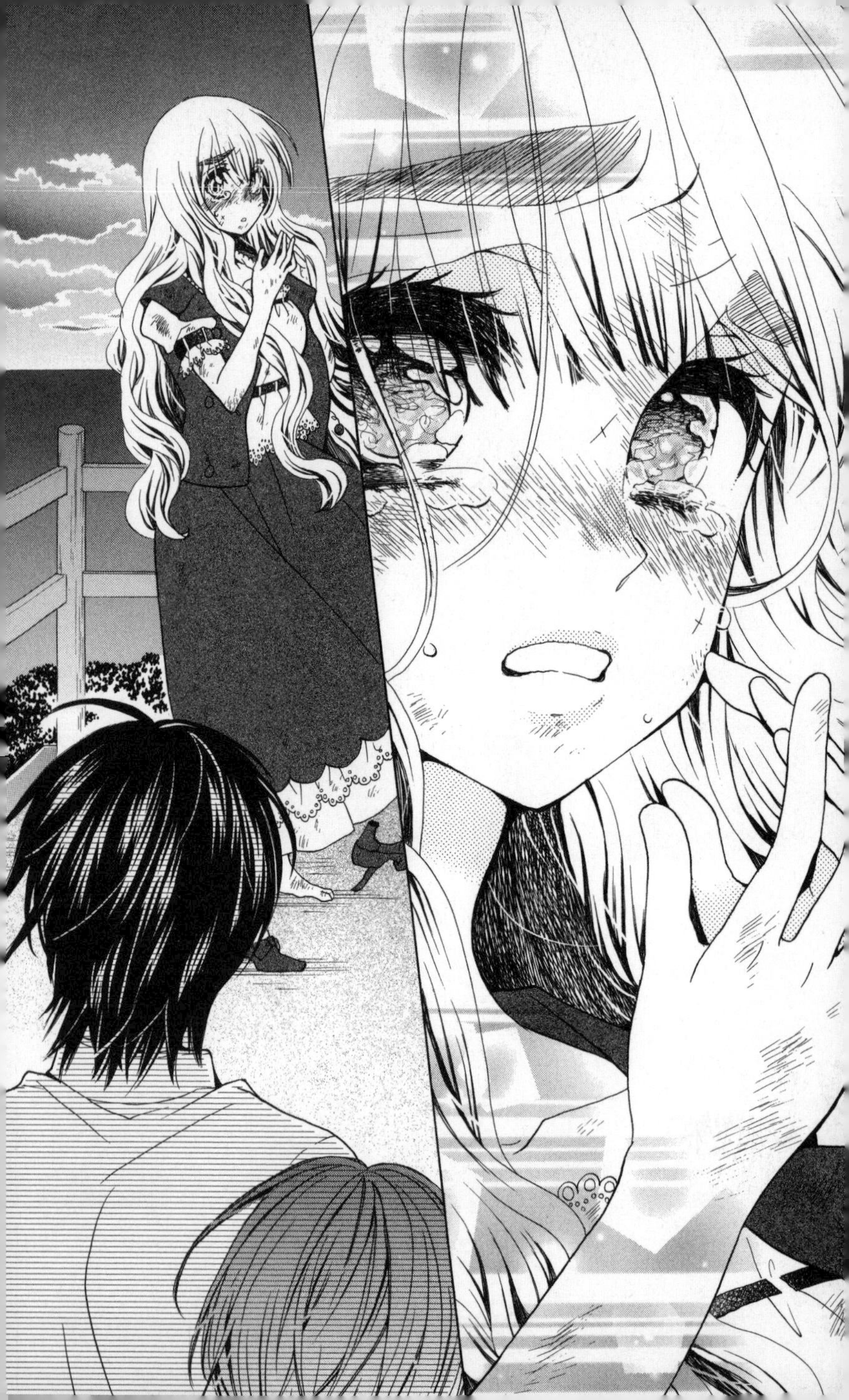

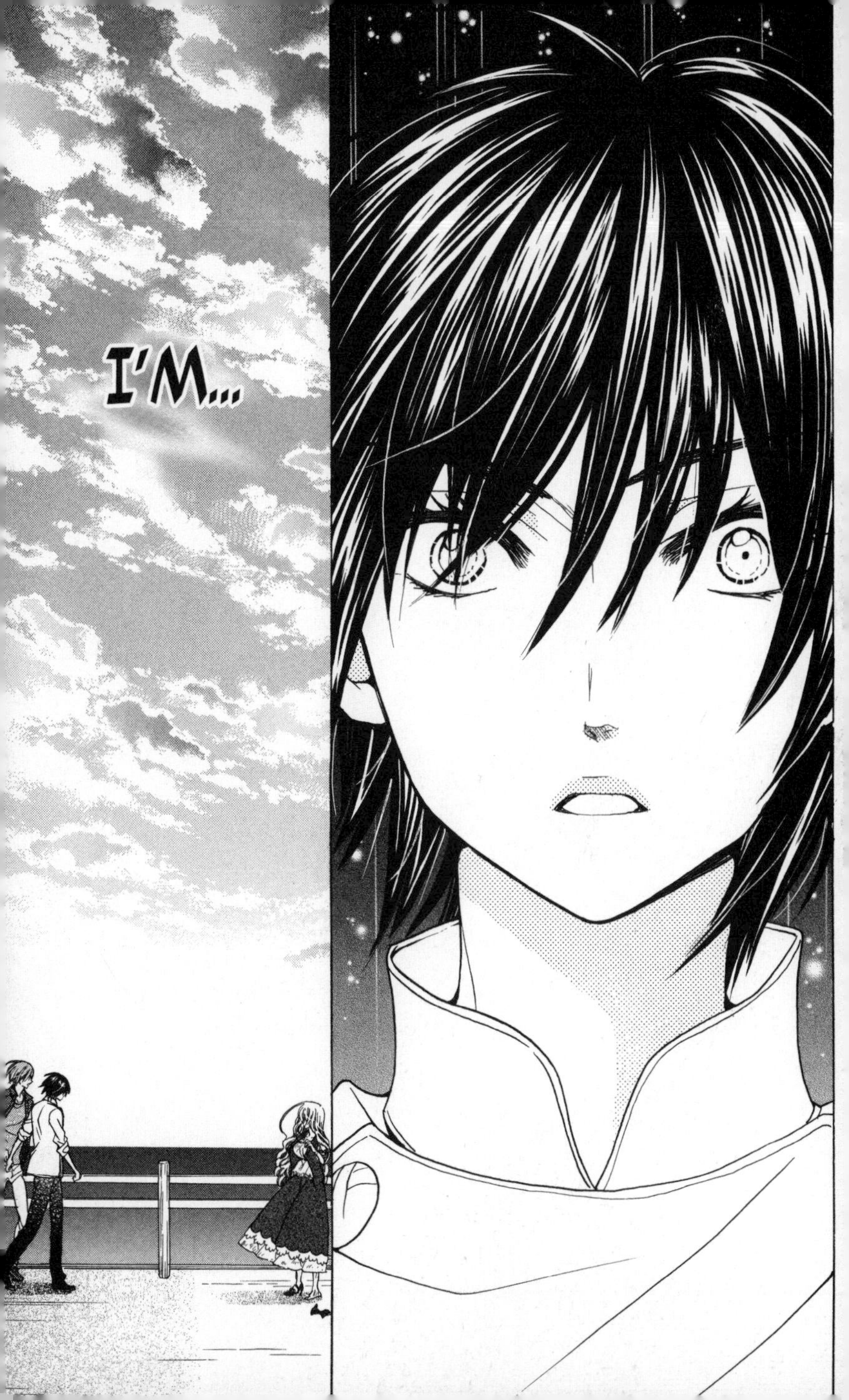
I'M...

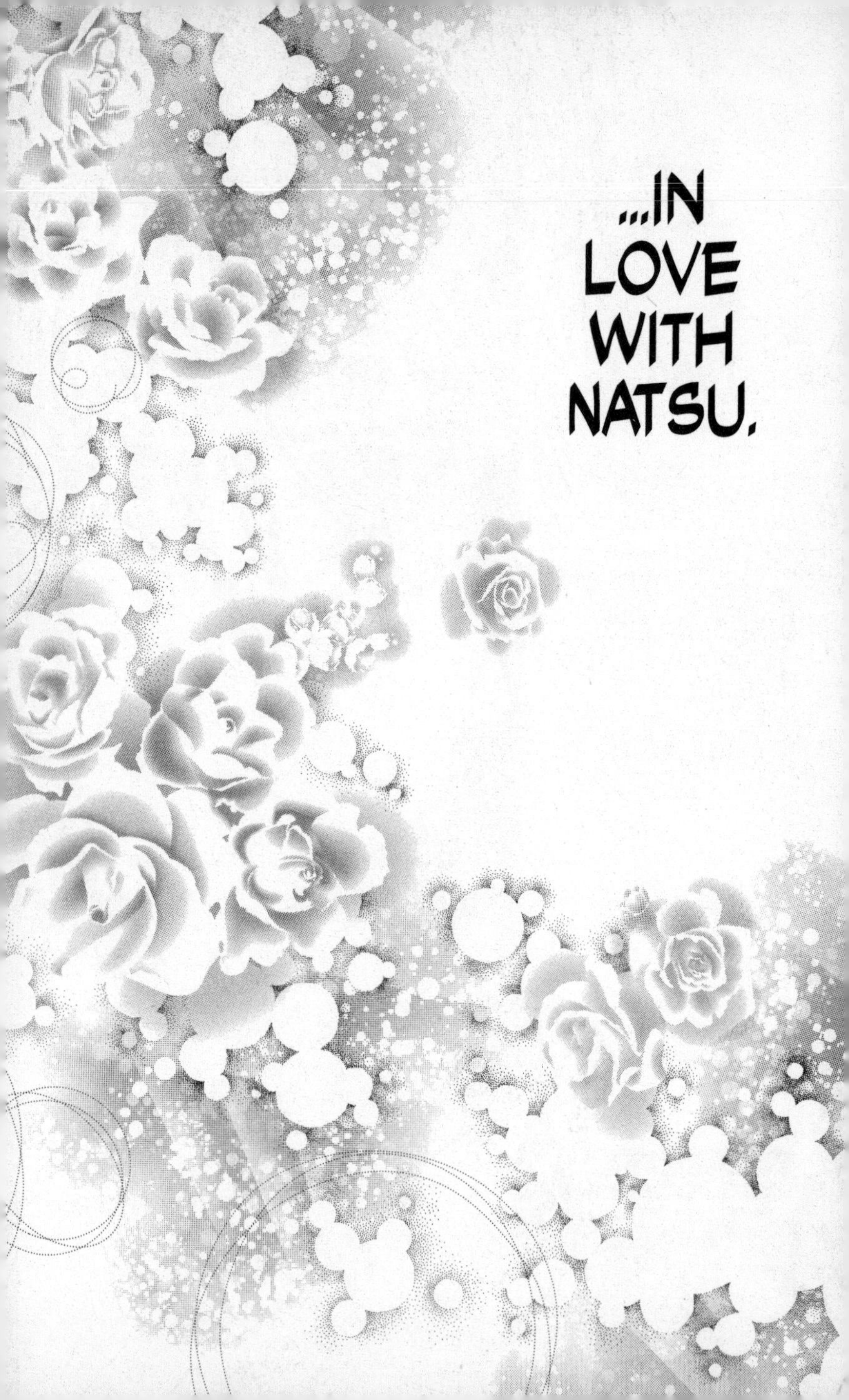
...IN LOVE WITH NATSU.

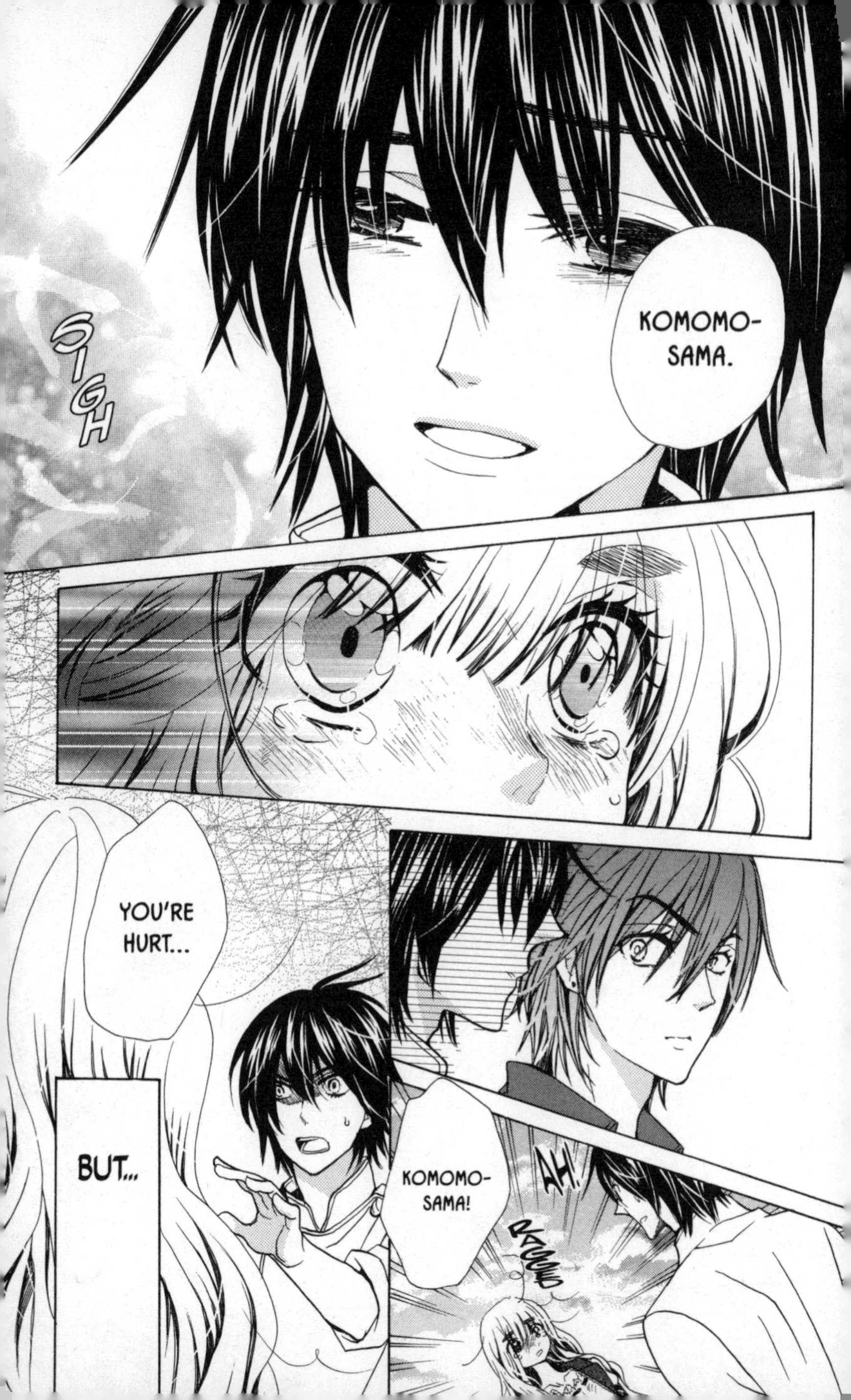
KOMOMO-SAMA.
SIGH
AH.
KOMOMO-SAMA!
YOU'RE HURT...
BUT...

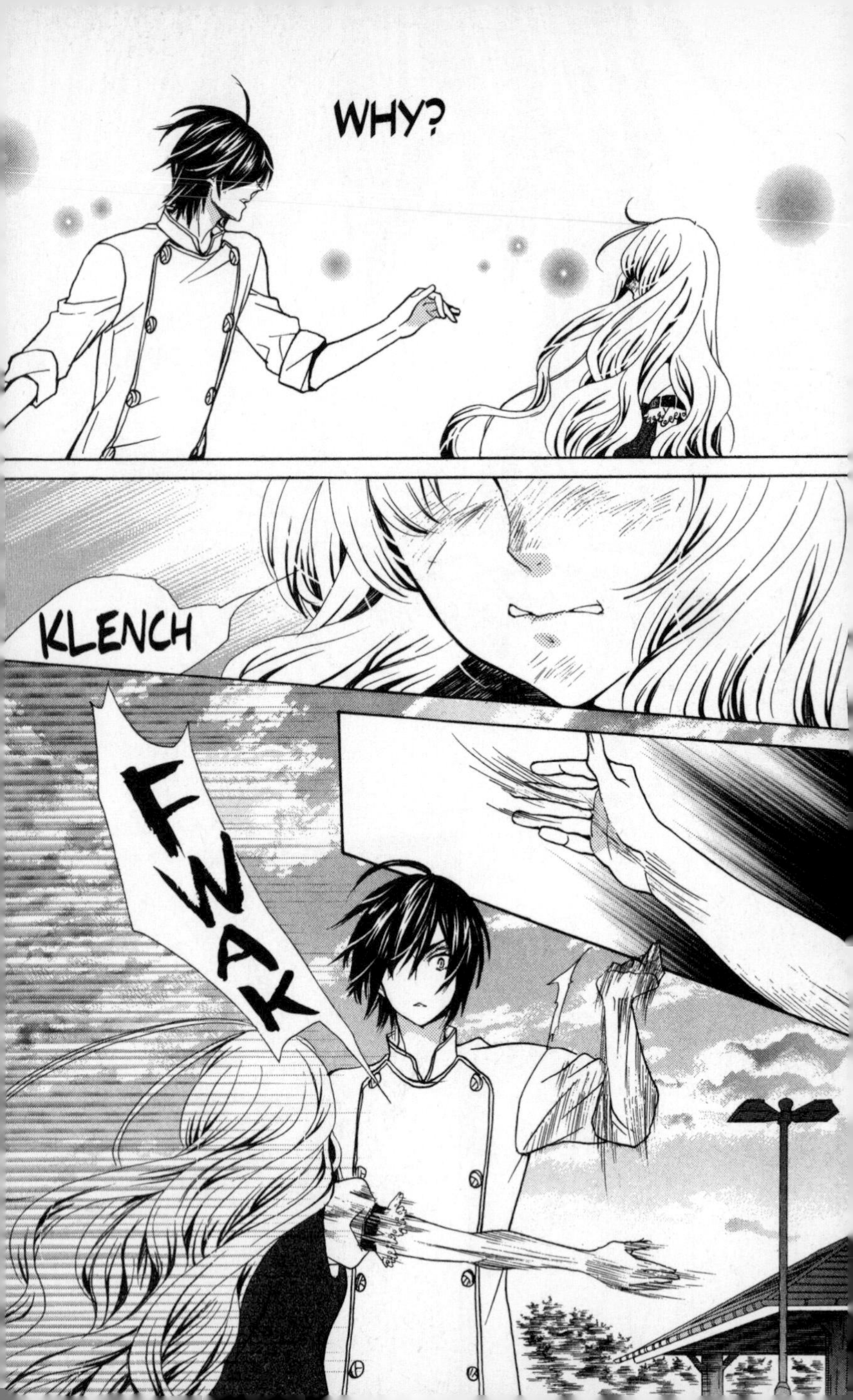
WHY?
KLENCH
FWAK

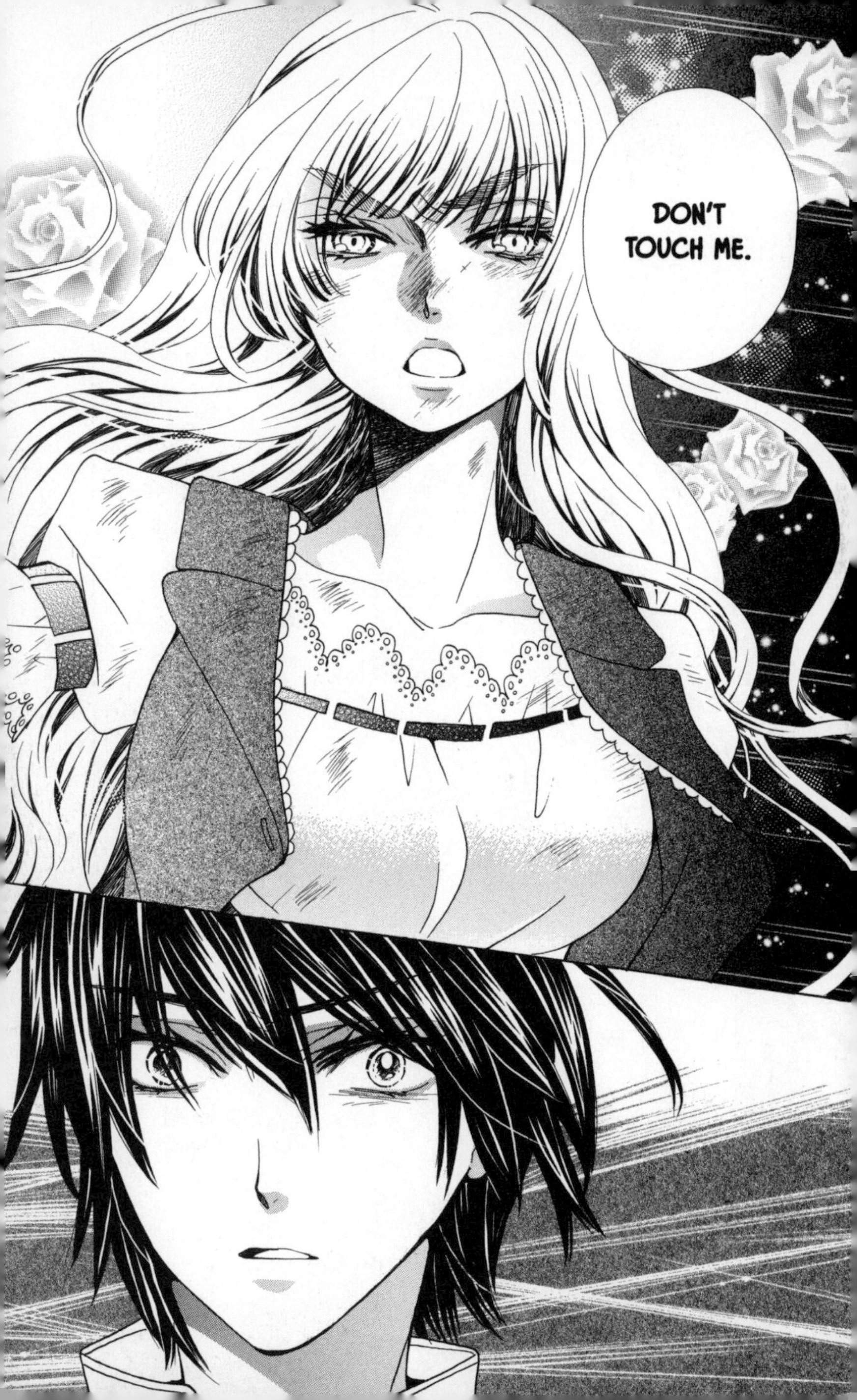
DON'T TOUCH ME.

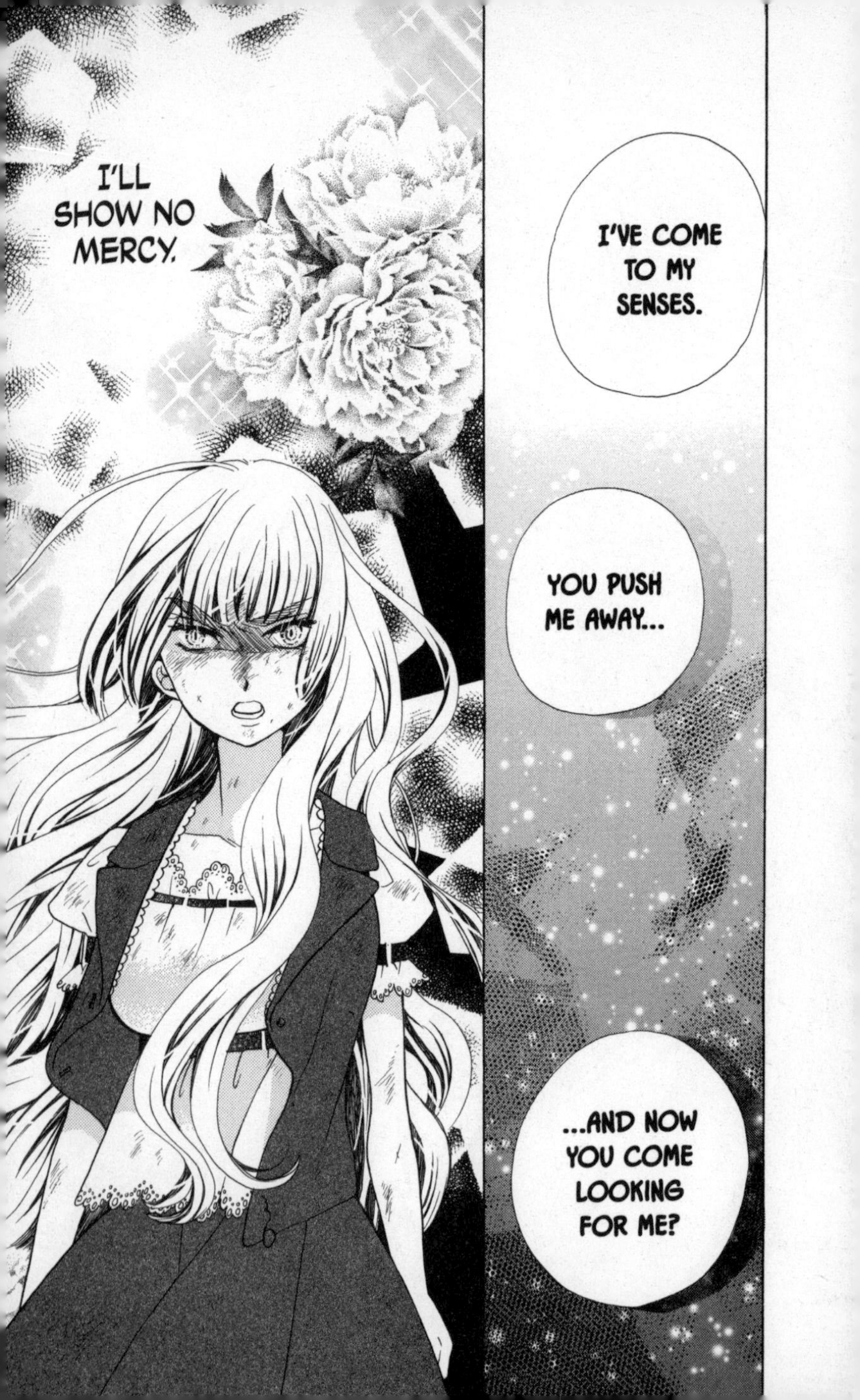
I'VE COME TO MY SENSES.
YOU PUSH ME AWAY...
...AND NOW YOU COME LOOKING FOR ME?
I'LL SHOW NO MERCY.

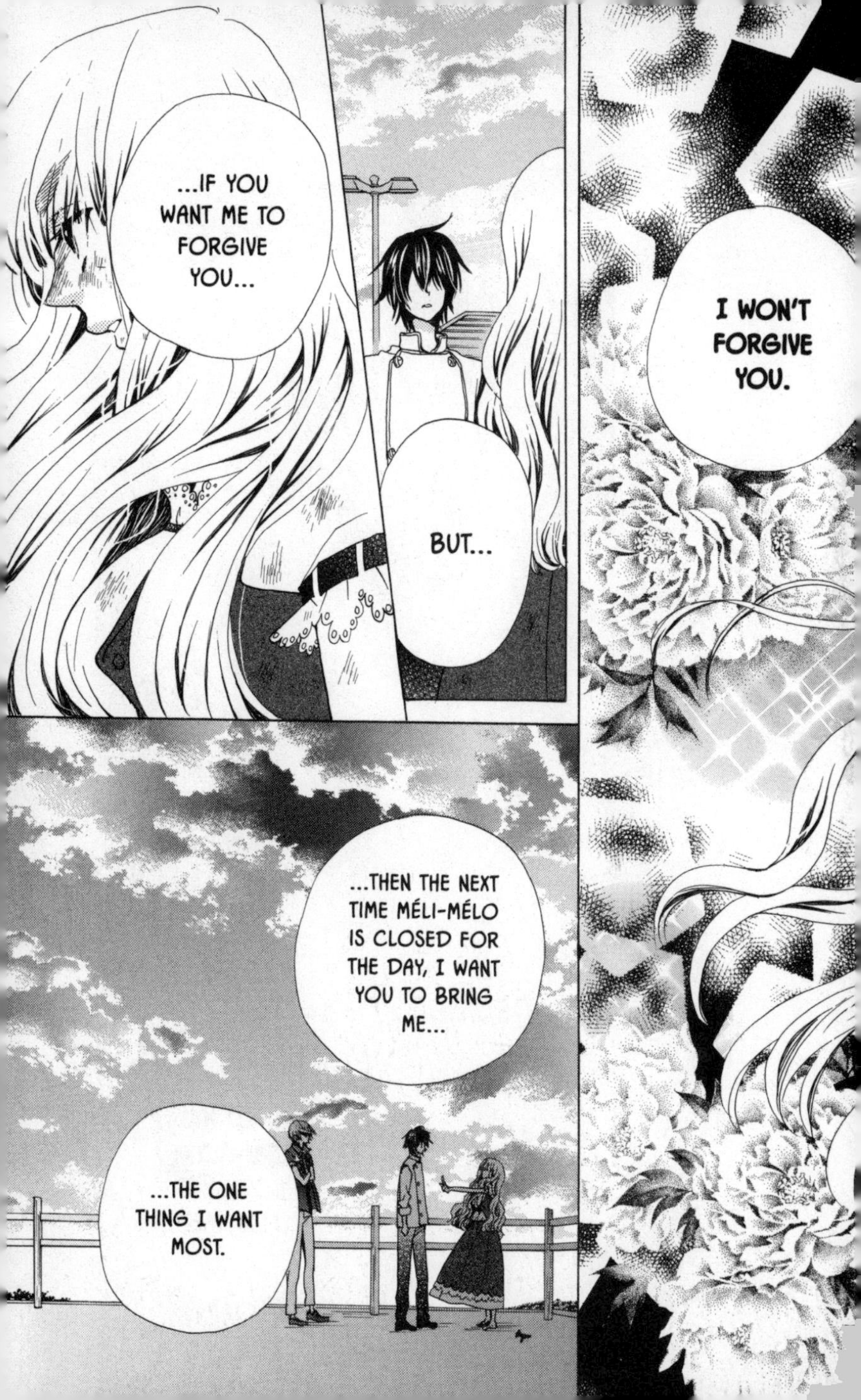
I WON'T FORGIVE YOU.
BUT...
...IF YOU WANT ME TO FORGIVE YOU...
...THEN THE NEXT TIME MÉLI-MÉLO IS CLOSED FOR THE DAY, I WANT YOU TO BRING ME...
...THE ONE THING I WANT MOST.

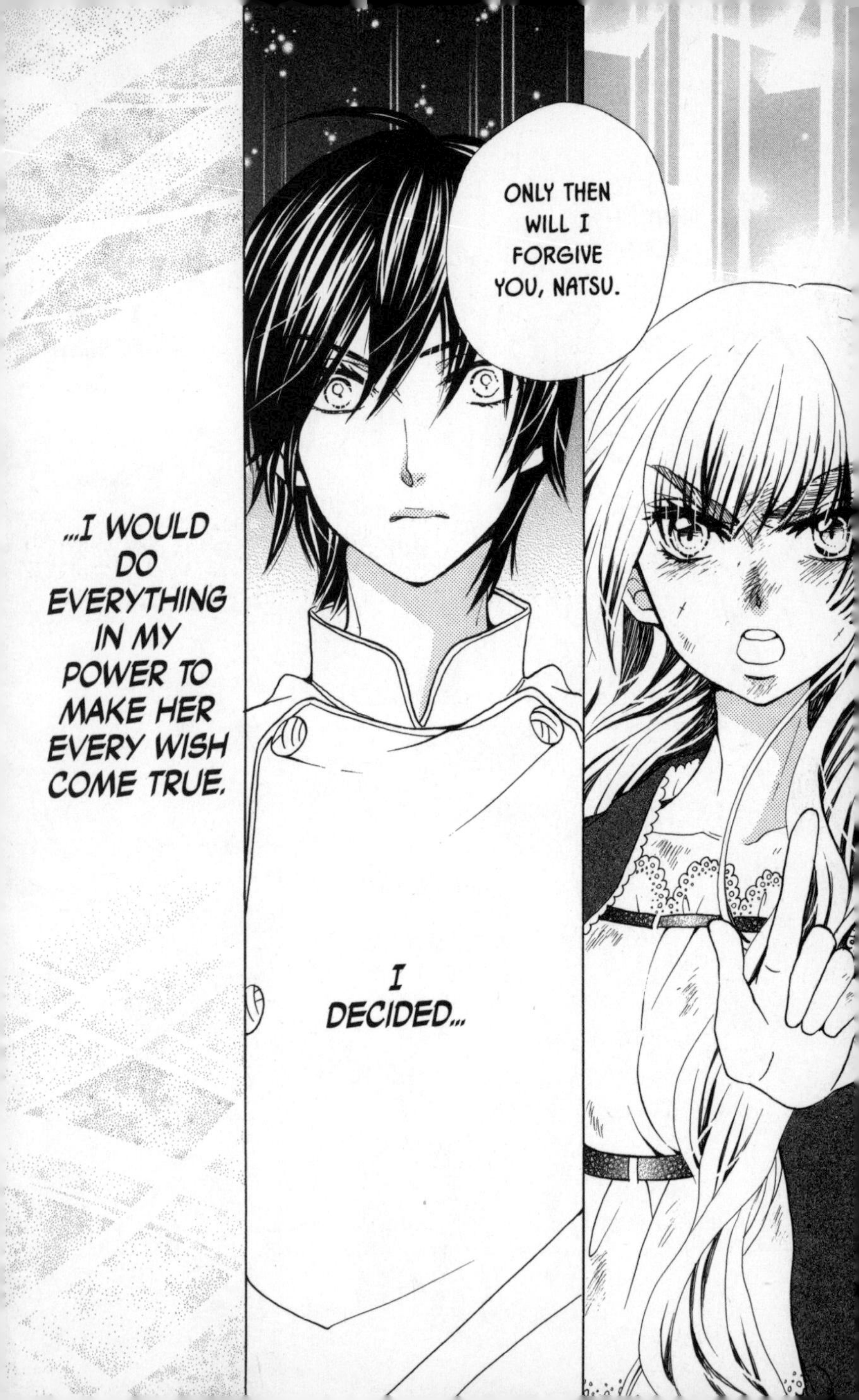
ONLY THEN WILL I FORGIVE YOU, NATSU.
I DECIDED...
...I WOULD DO EVERYTHING IN MY POWER TO MAKE HER EVERY WISH COME TRUE.

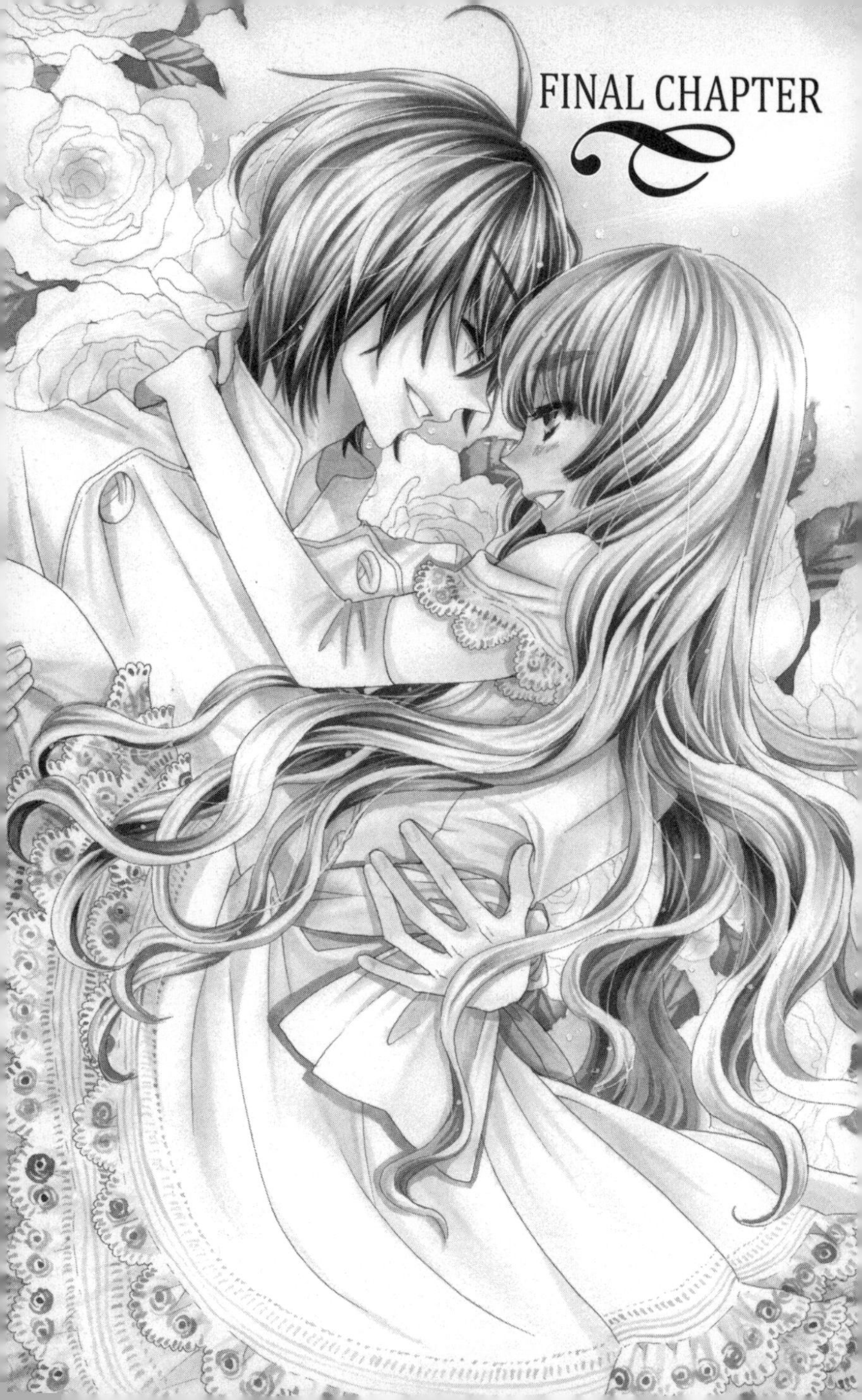
FINAL CHAPTER

~ My Personal Takes on Different Pastries ~

~ Tarte Tatin ~

This apple pie is an accidental creation from the Hotel Tatin. I can't help but prefer Tatin that's been plenty burned. I want to eat it with whipped cream or vanilla icing!

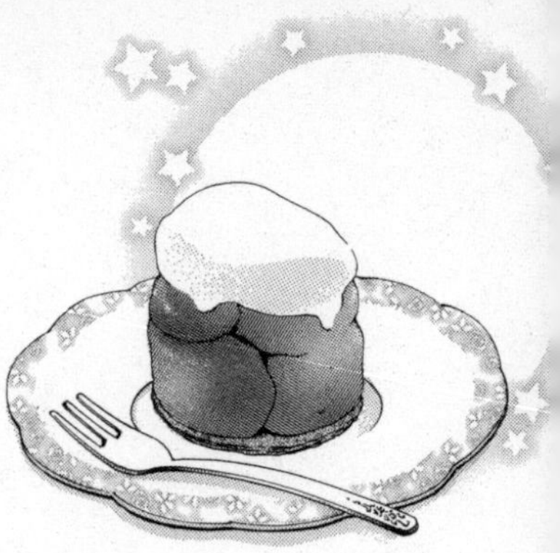

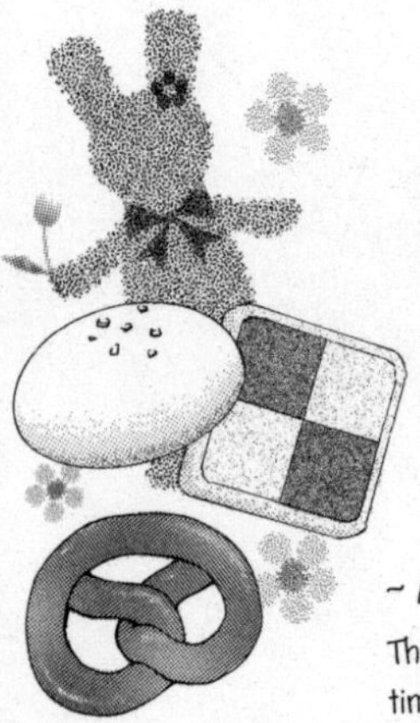

~ Gâteau Sec ~

This is a cookie or other such biscuit that is baked dry. When you go to any French pastry shop, you can see a whole variety of gâteau secs. I like the kind with jam in them. It's a naughty cookie that you will find yourself gorging on.

~ Afternoon Tea ~

This is a meal that came from the English tea time. It's not French! It's a fun little set with sweets or sandwiches and such! Depending on the place, the contents differ, making it really very fun. The way the plates are stacked in three tiers really builds tension! And for meaning to be only a snack, it can be incredibly filling!

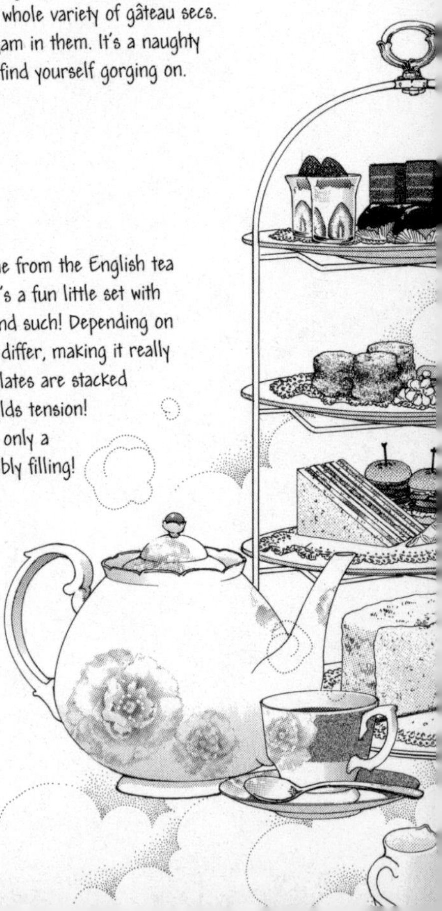

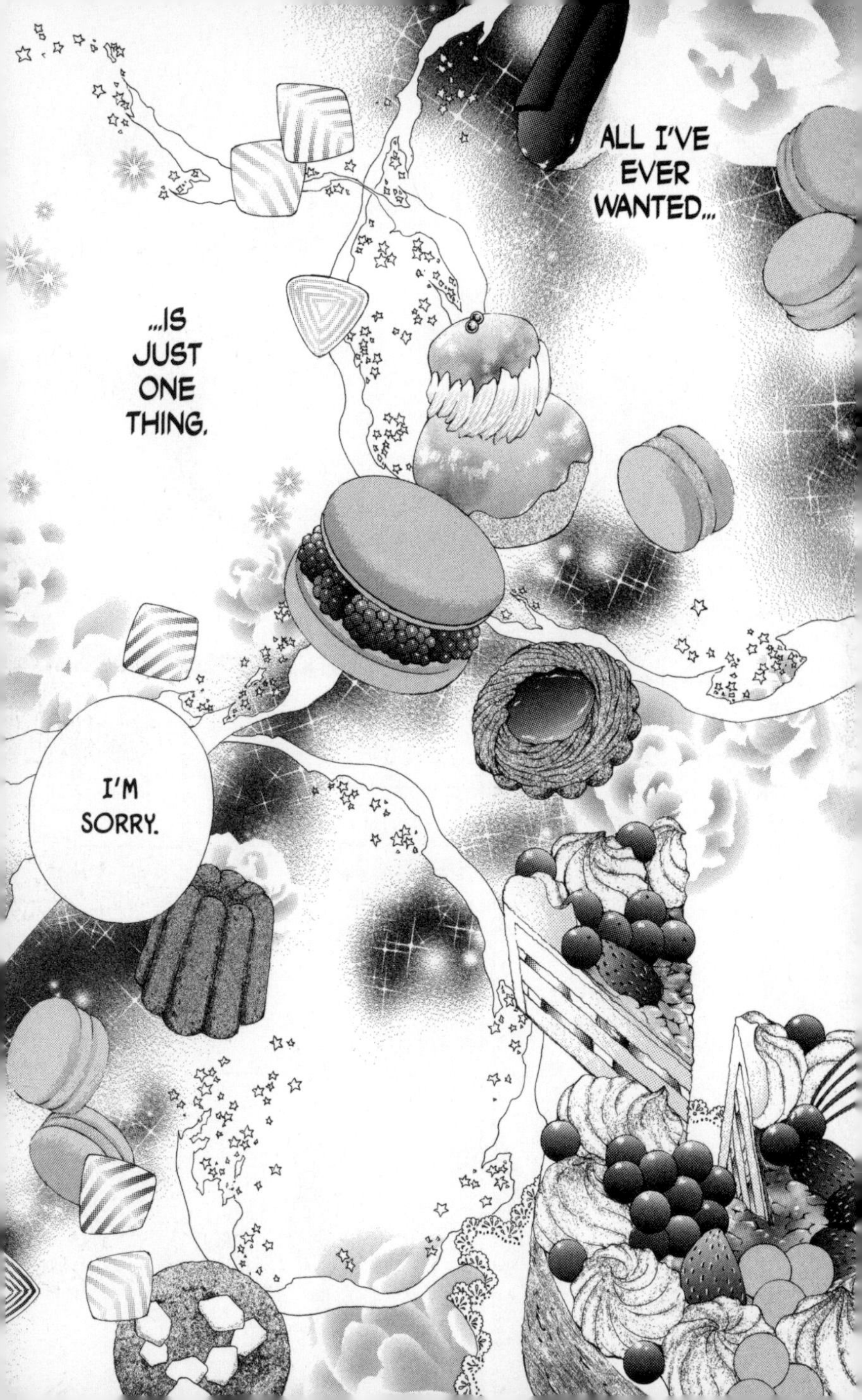
ALL I'VE EVER WANTED...
...IS JUST ONE THING.
I'M SORRY.

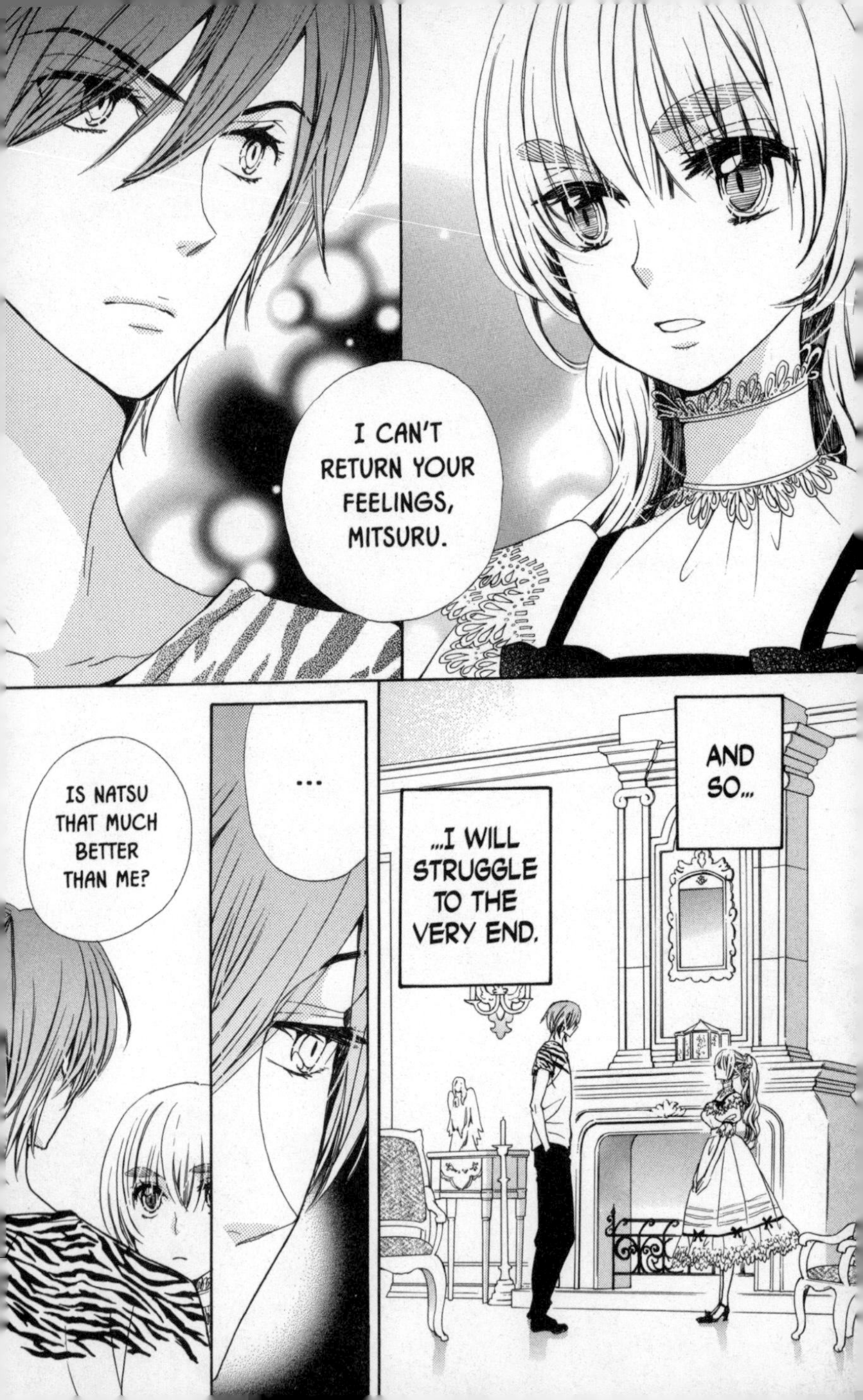
I CAN'T RETURN YOUR FEELINGS, MITSURU.
AND SO...
...I WILL STRUGGLE TO THE VERY END.
...
IS NATSU THAT MUCH BETTER THAN ME?

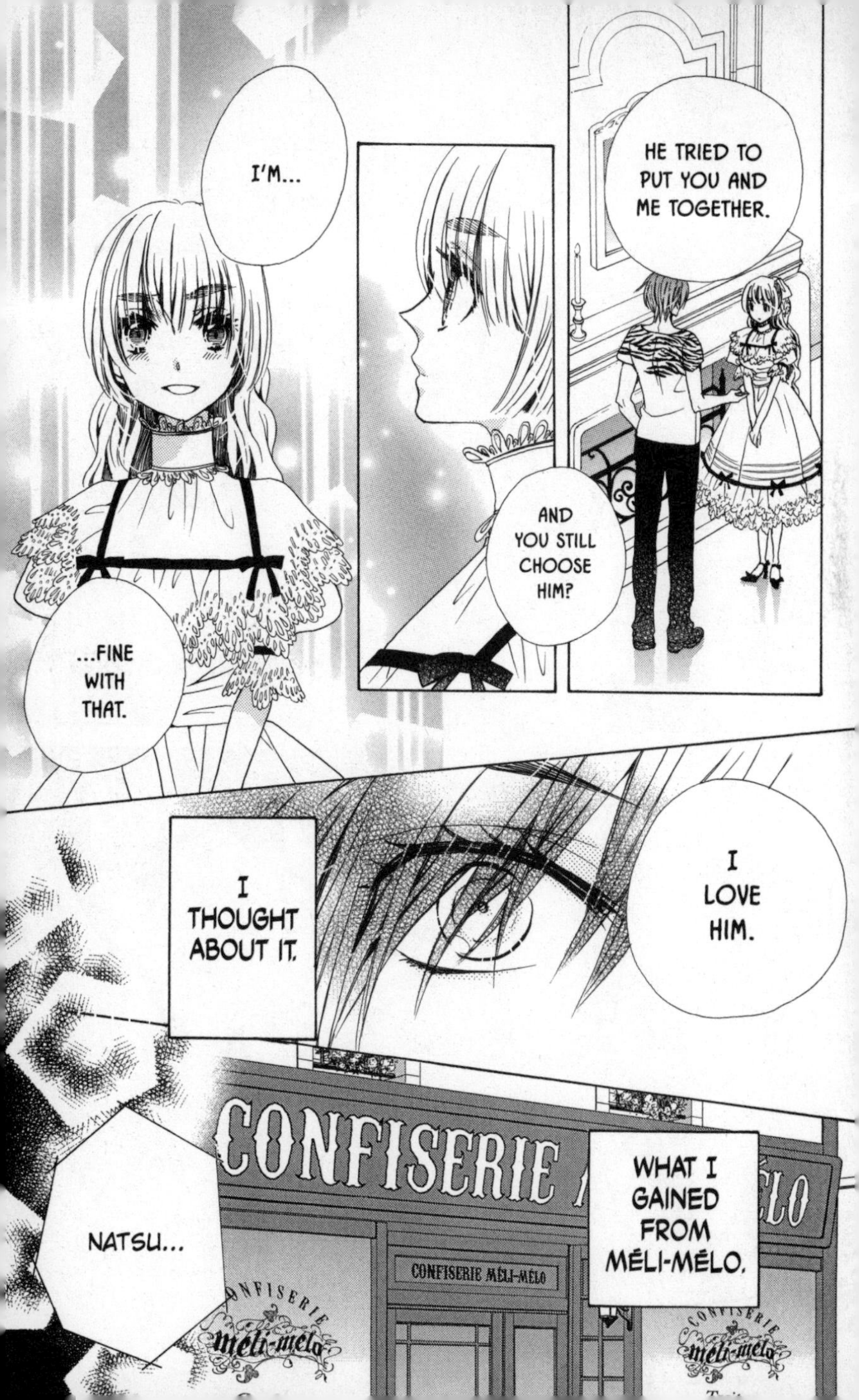
HE TRIED TO PUT YOU AND ME TOGETHER.
AND YOU STILL CHOOSE HIM?
I'M...
...FINE WITH THAT.
I LOVE HIM.
I THOUGHT ABOUT IT.
CONFISERIE
WHAT I GAINED FROM MÉLI-MÉLO.
CONFISERIE MÉLI-MÉLO
NATSU...

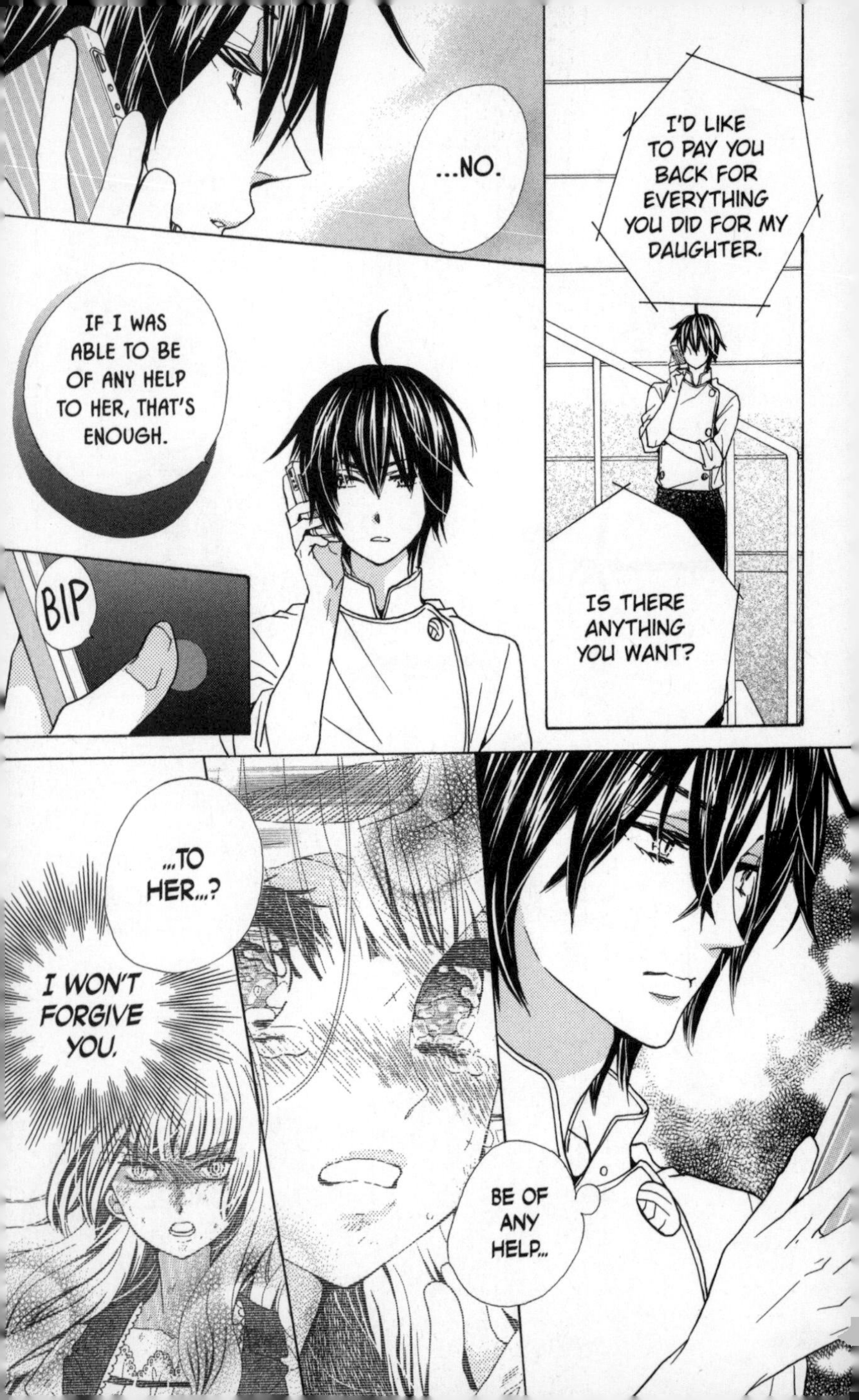
I'D LIKE TO PAY YOU BACK FOR EVERYTHING YOU DID FOR MY DAUGHTER.
IS THERE ANYTHING YOU WANT?
...NO.
IF I WAS ABLE TO BE OF ANY HELP TO HER, THAT'S ENOUGH.
BIP
BE OF ANY HELP...
...TO HER...?
I WON'T FORGIVE YOU.

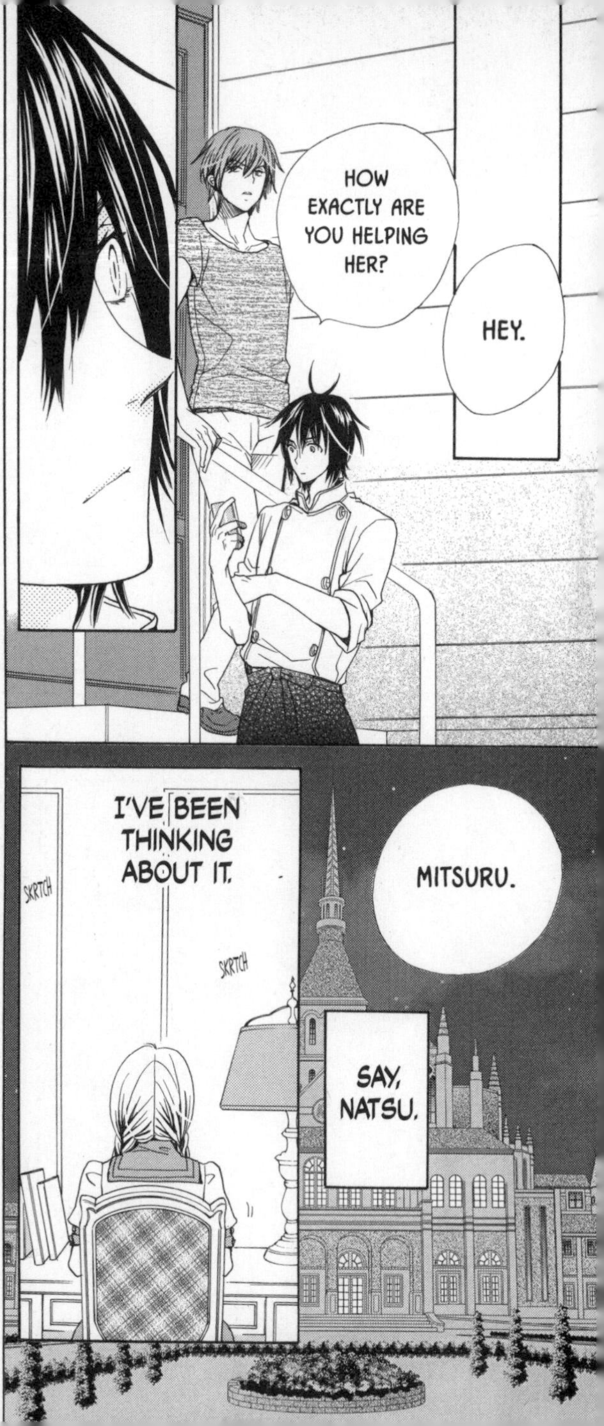
HEY.
HOW EXACTLY ARE YOU HELPING HER?
MITSURU.
SAY, NATSU.
I'VE BEEN THINKING ABOUT IT.
SKRTCH
SKRTCH

• Etc. •

This is my last sidebar. Thank you so much for sticking with me all this time!

I'm very glad I was able to finish this story to its end. I was able to enjoy drawing it while gazing at all my favorite sweets.

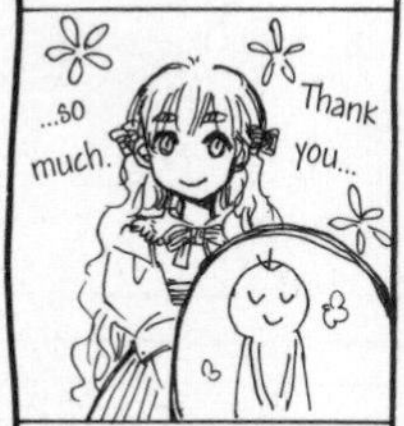
Thank you...
...so much.

I hope we meet again in my next work. Until then, thank you!

Thank you to everyone who has read this far, all my assistants who always help me out, my editors, Kosaka-sama for helping me collect reference materials, everyone from Tsujicho Cooking School, Blondir-sama, my friends, Kamio Sensei and my family. Thank you so much!

-Maki Minami ♥

With all my love.

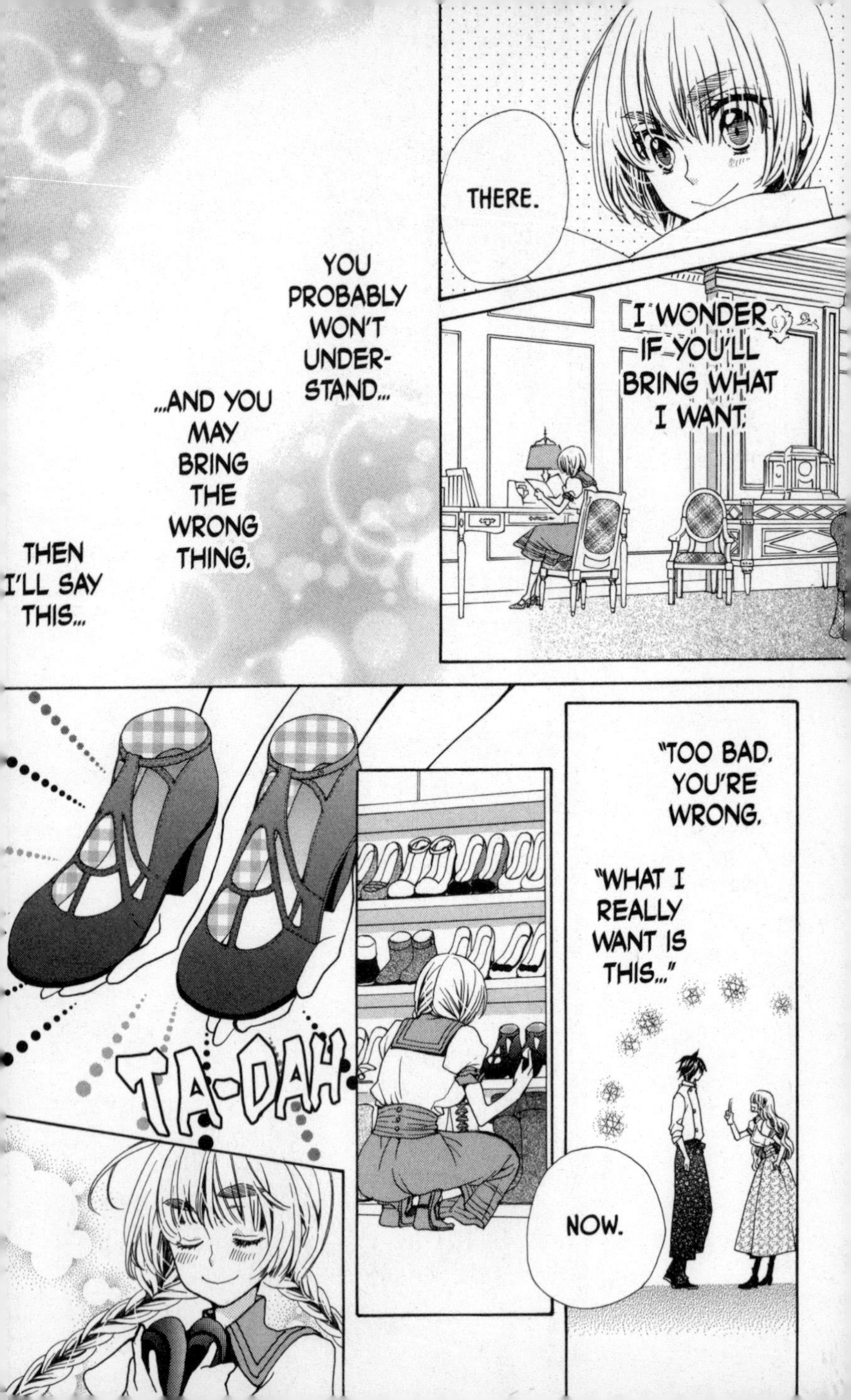
THERE.
I WONDER IF YOU'LL BRING WHAT I WANT.
YOU PROBABLY WON'T UNDER-STAND...
...AND YOU MAY BRING THE WRONG THING.
THEN I'LL SAY THIS...
"TOO BAD. YOU'RE WRONG.
"WHAT I REALLY WANT IS THIS..."
NOW.
TA-DAH

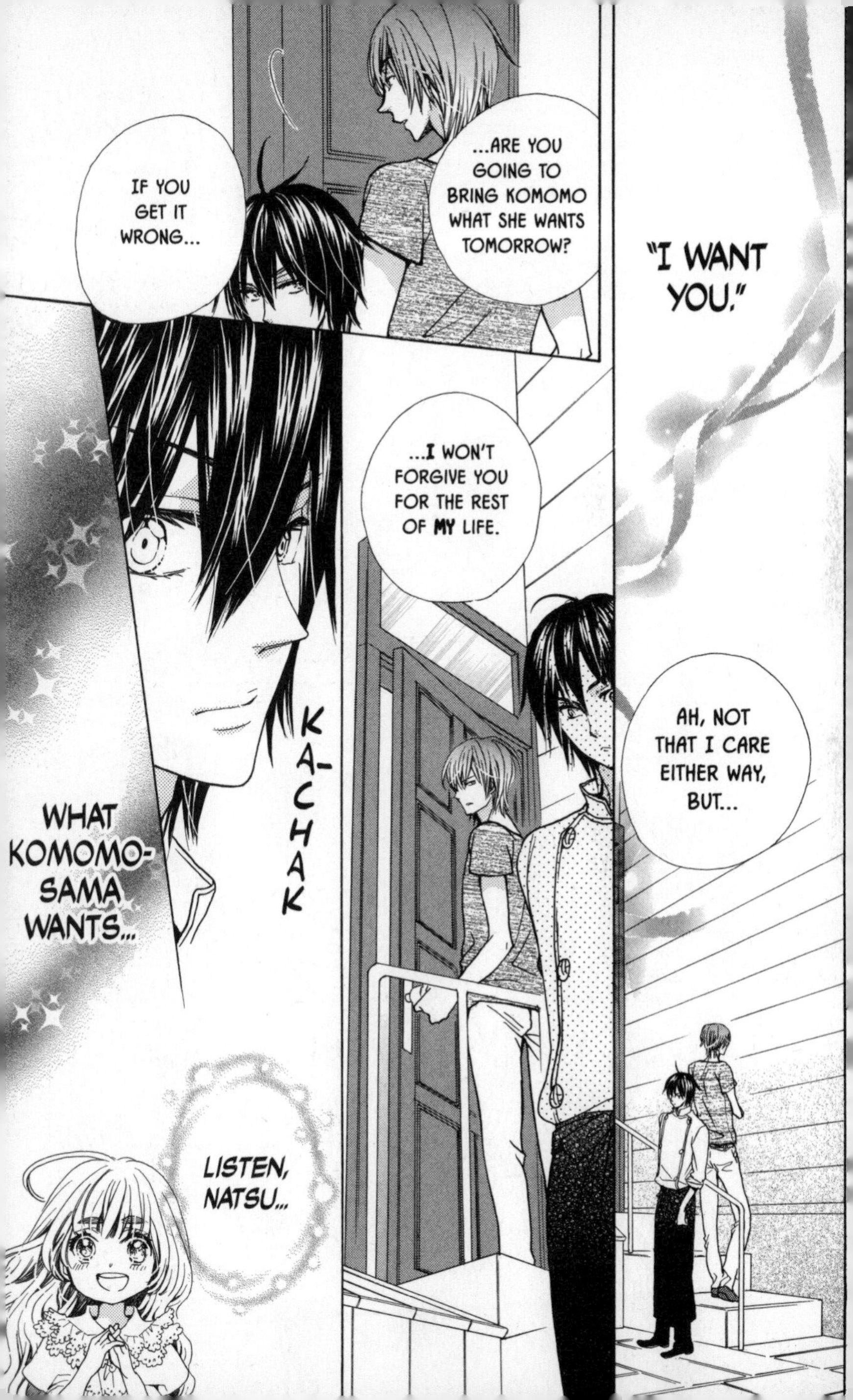
"I WANT YOU."
AH, NOT THAT I CARE EITHER WAY, BUT...
...ARE YOU GOING TO BRING KOMOMO WHAT SHE WANTS TOMORROW?
IF YOU GET IT WRONG...
...I WON'T FORGIVE YOU FOR THE REST OF **MY** LIFE.
KA-CHAK
WHAT KOMOMO-SAMA WANTS...
LISTEN, NATSU...

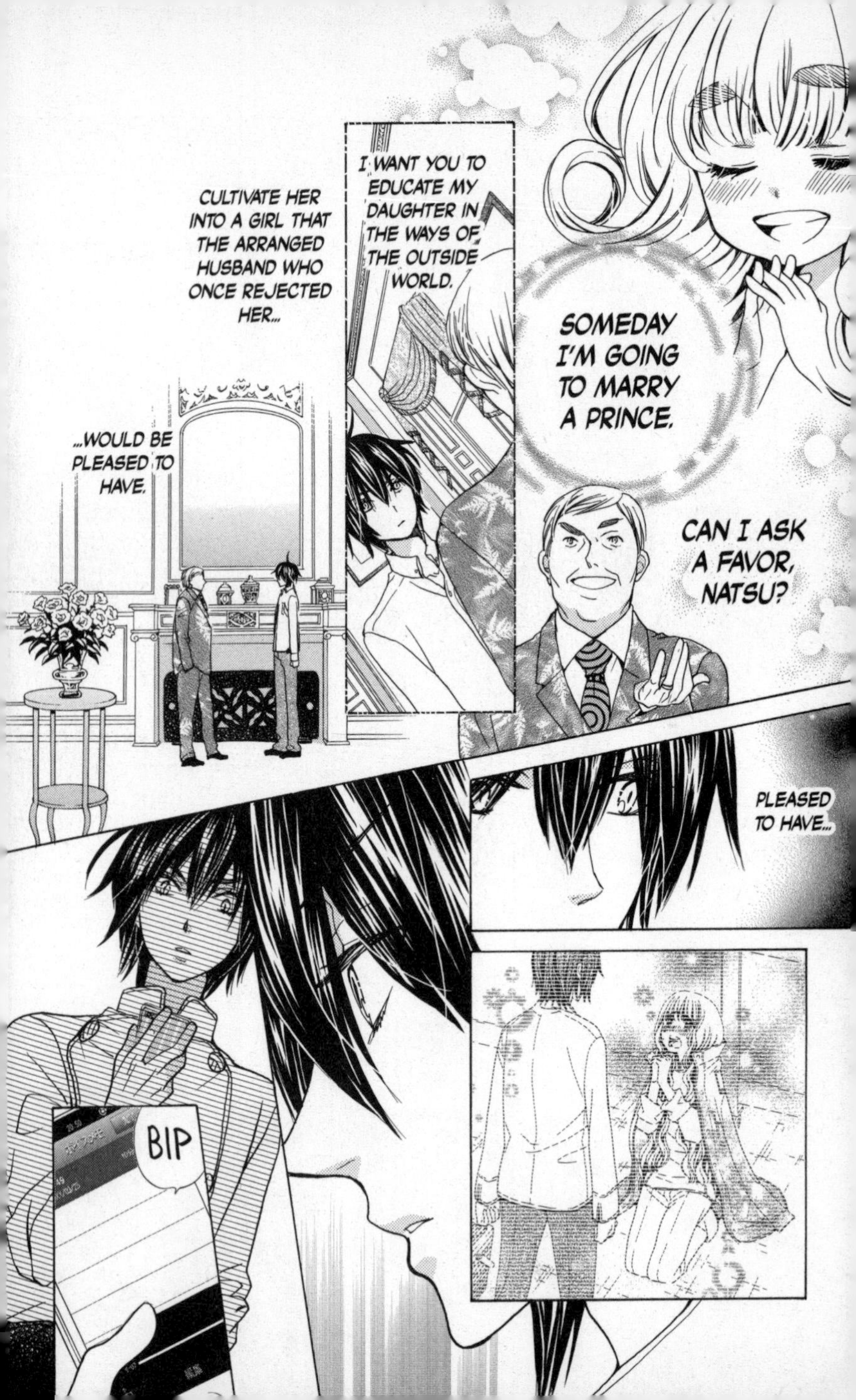
SOMEDAY I'M GOING TO MARRY A PRINCE.
CAN I ASK A FAVOR, NATSU?
I WANT YOU TO EDUCATE MY DAUGHTER IN THE WAYS OF THE OUTSIDE WORLD.
CULTIVATE HER INTO A GIRL THAT THE ARRANGED HUSBAND WHO ONCE REJECTED HER...
...WOULD BE PLEASED TO HAVE.
PLEASED TO HAVE...
BIP

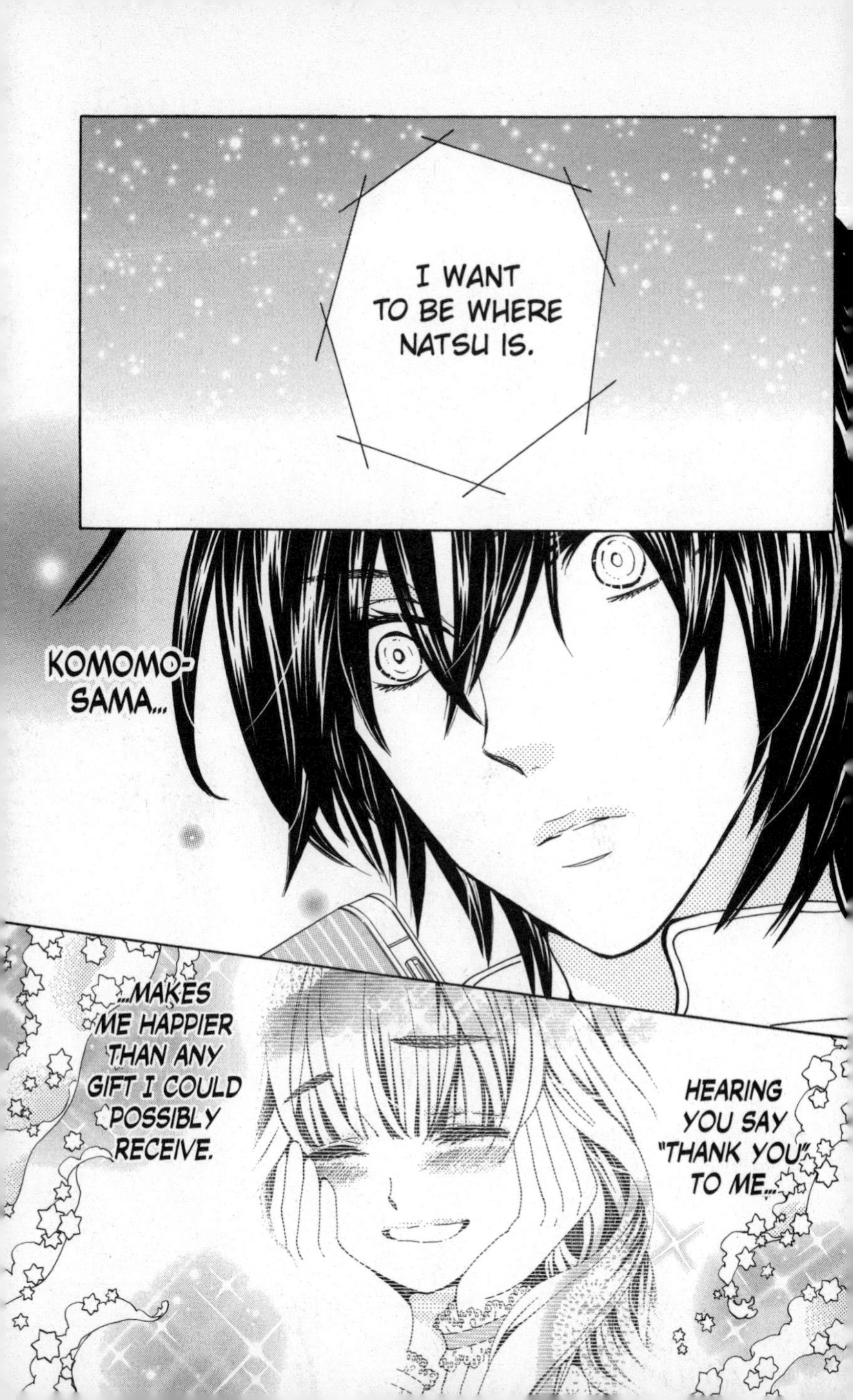
I WANT TO BE WHERE NATSU IS.
KOMOMO-SAMA...
HEARING YOU SAY "THANK YOU" TO ME...
...MAKES ME HAPPIER THAN ANY GIFT I COULD POSSIBLY RECEIVE.

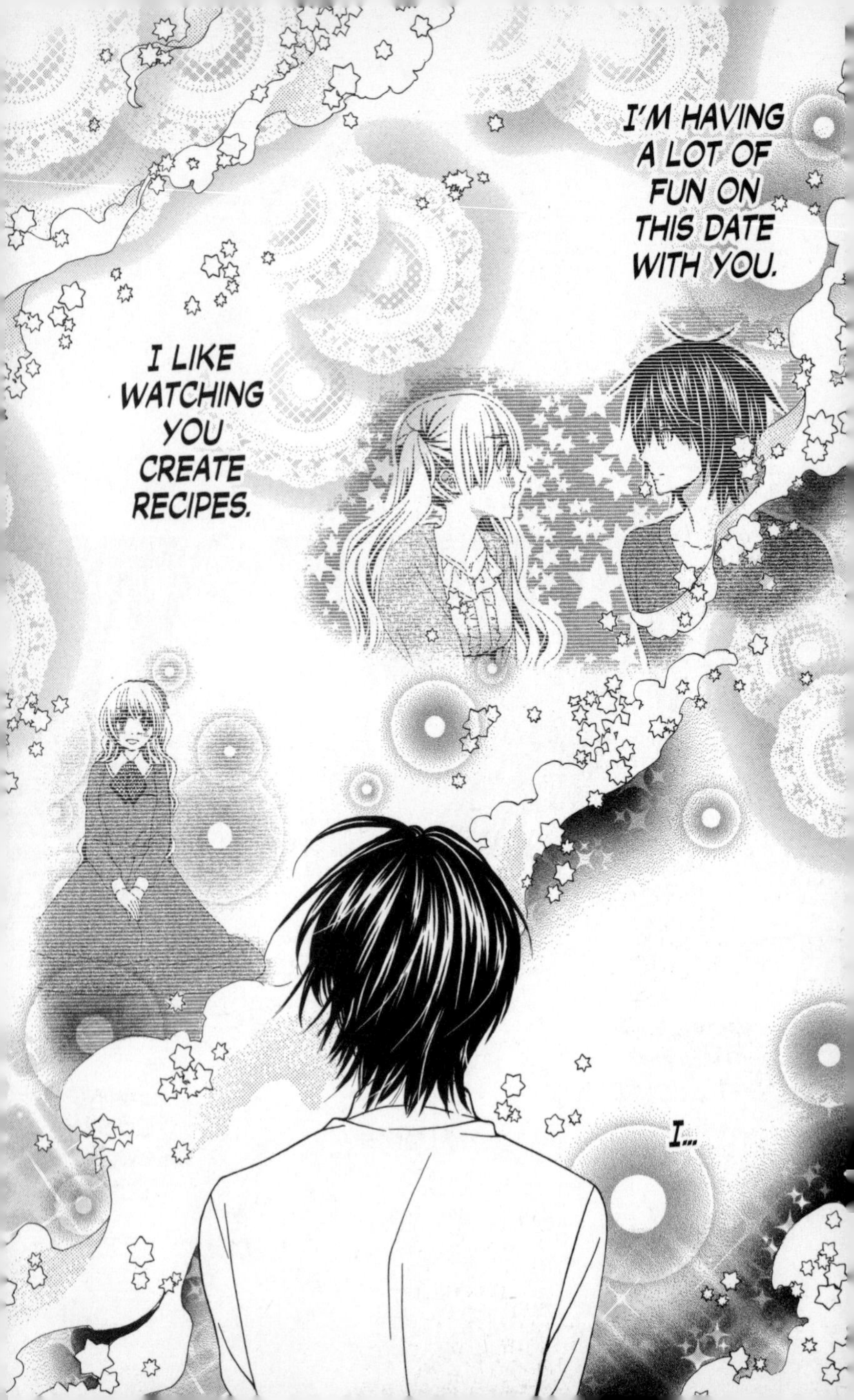
I'M HAVING A LOT OF FUN ON THIS DATE WITH YOU.
I LIKE WATCHING YOU CREATE RECIPES.
I...

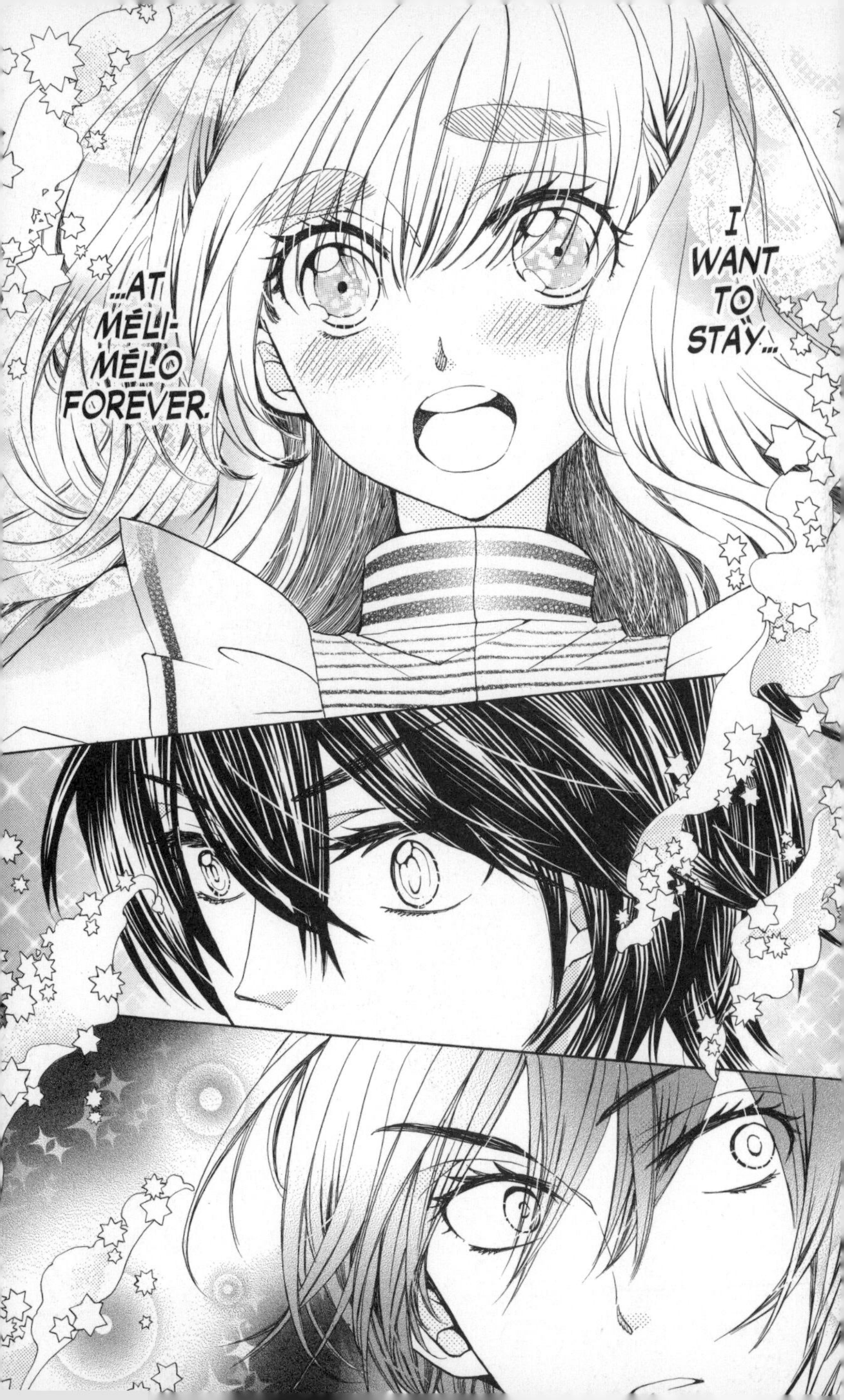
I WANT TO STAY...
...AT MÉLI-MÉLO FOREVER.

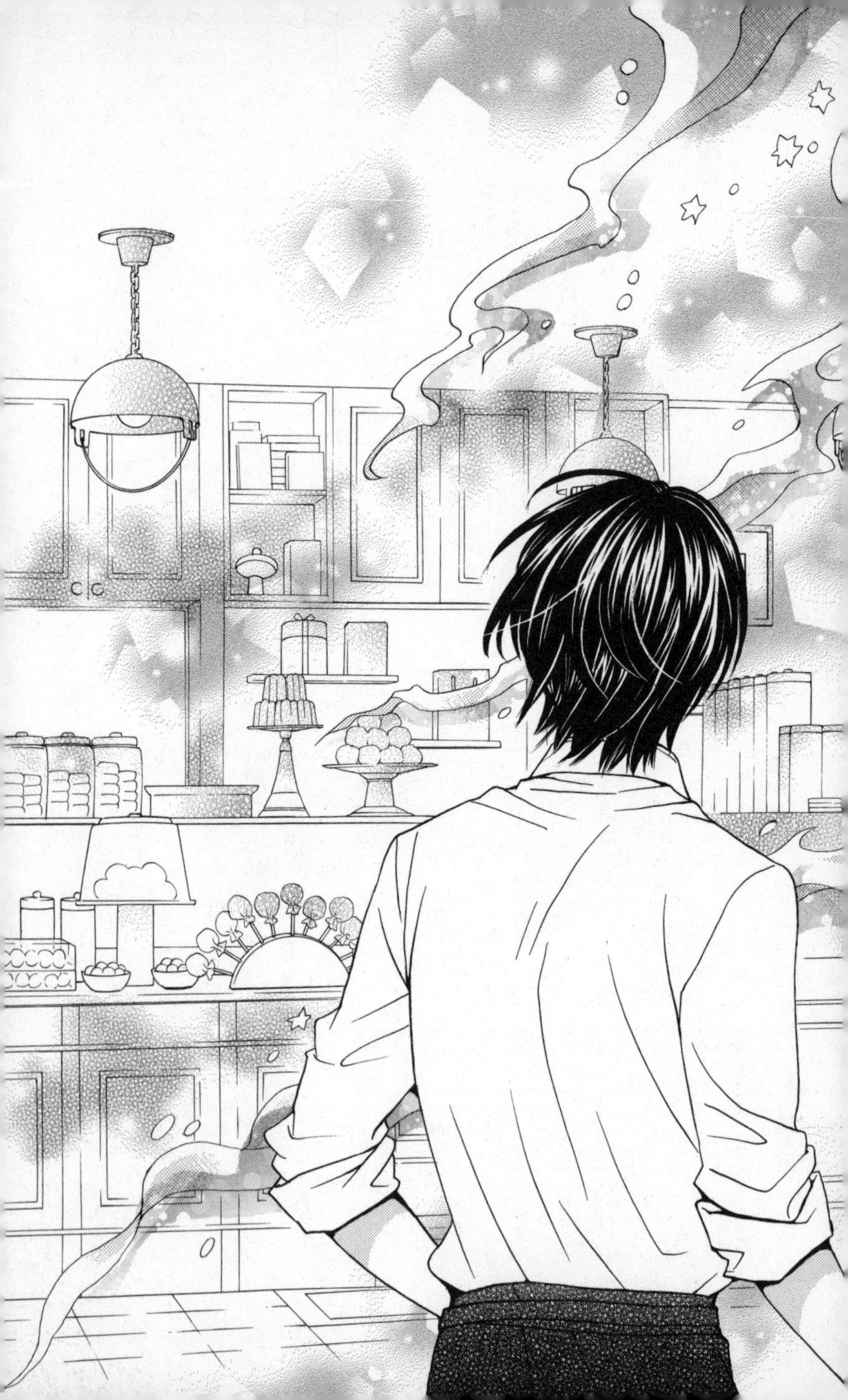

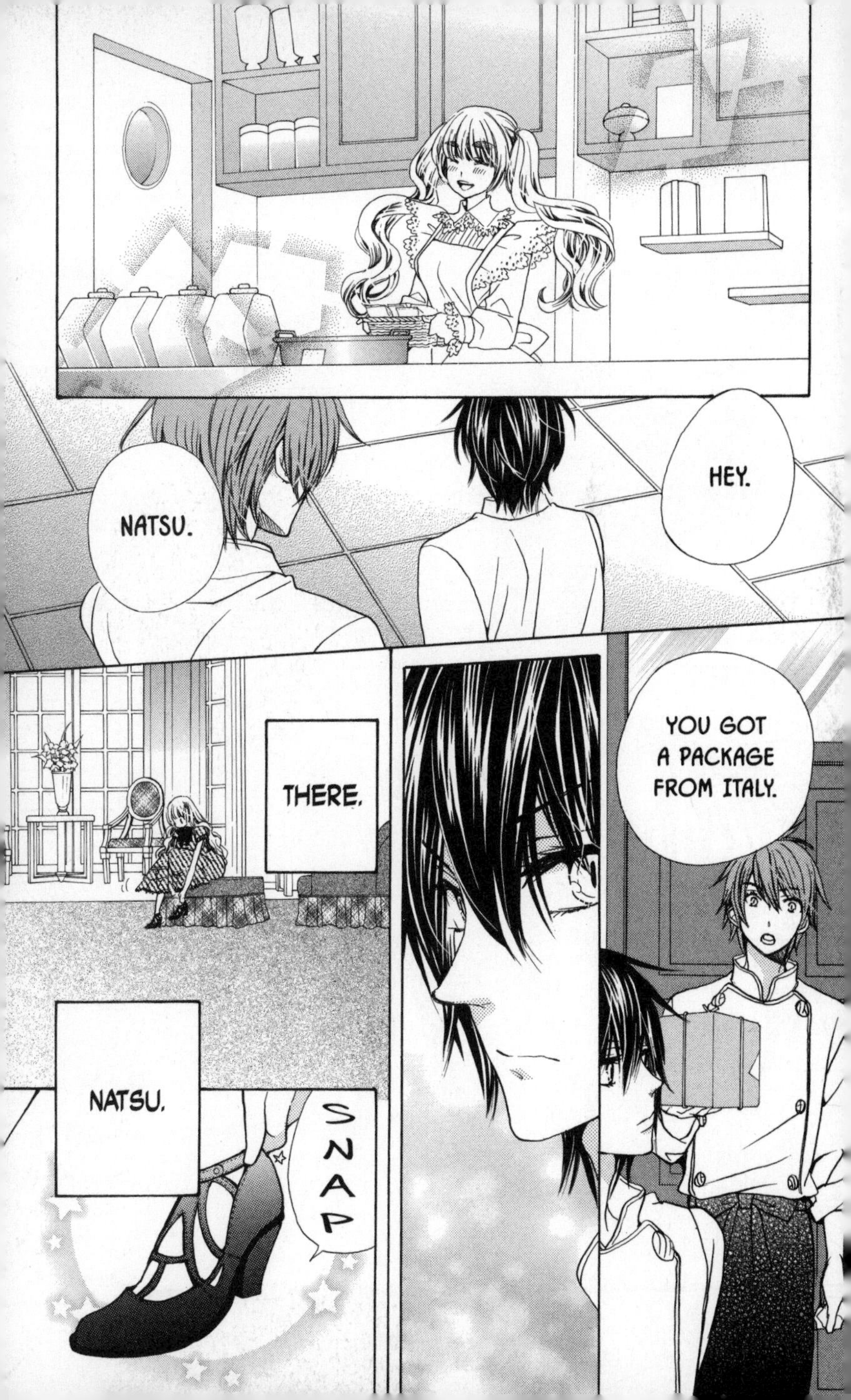
HEY.
NATSU.
YOU GOT A PACKAGE FROM ITALY.
THERE.
NATSU.
SNAP

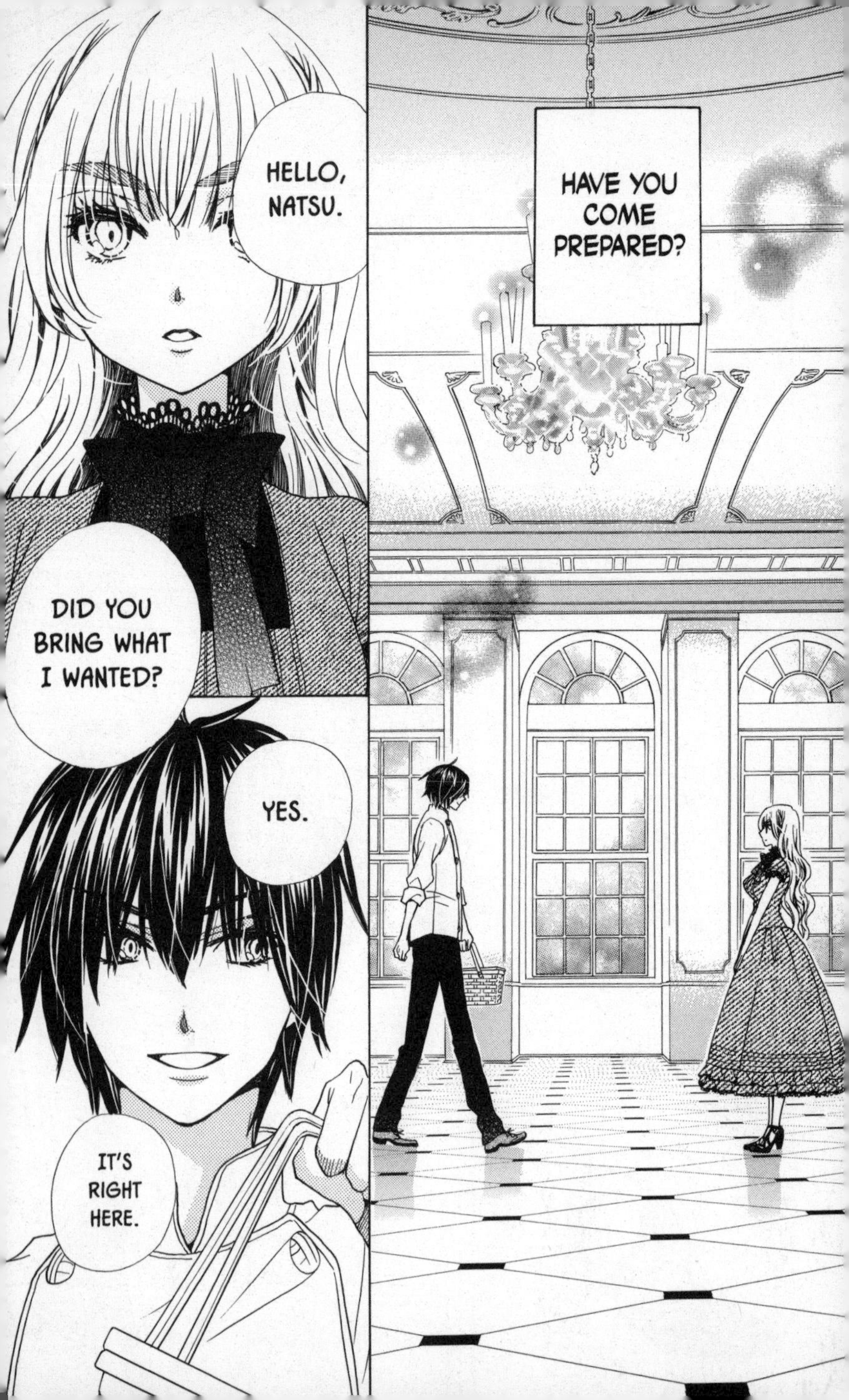
HAVE YOU COME PREPARED?
HELLO, NATSU.
DID YOU BRING WHAT I WANTED?
YES.
IT'S RIGHT HERE.

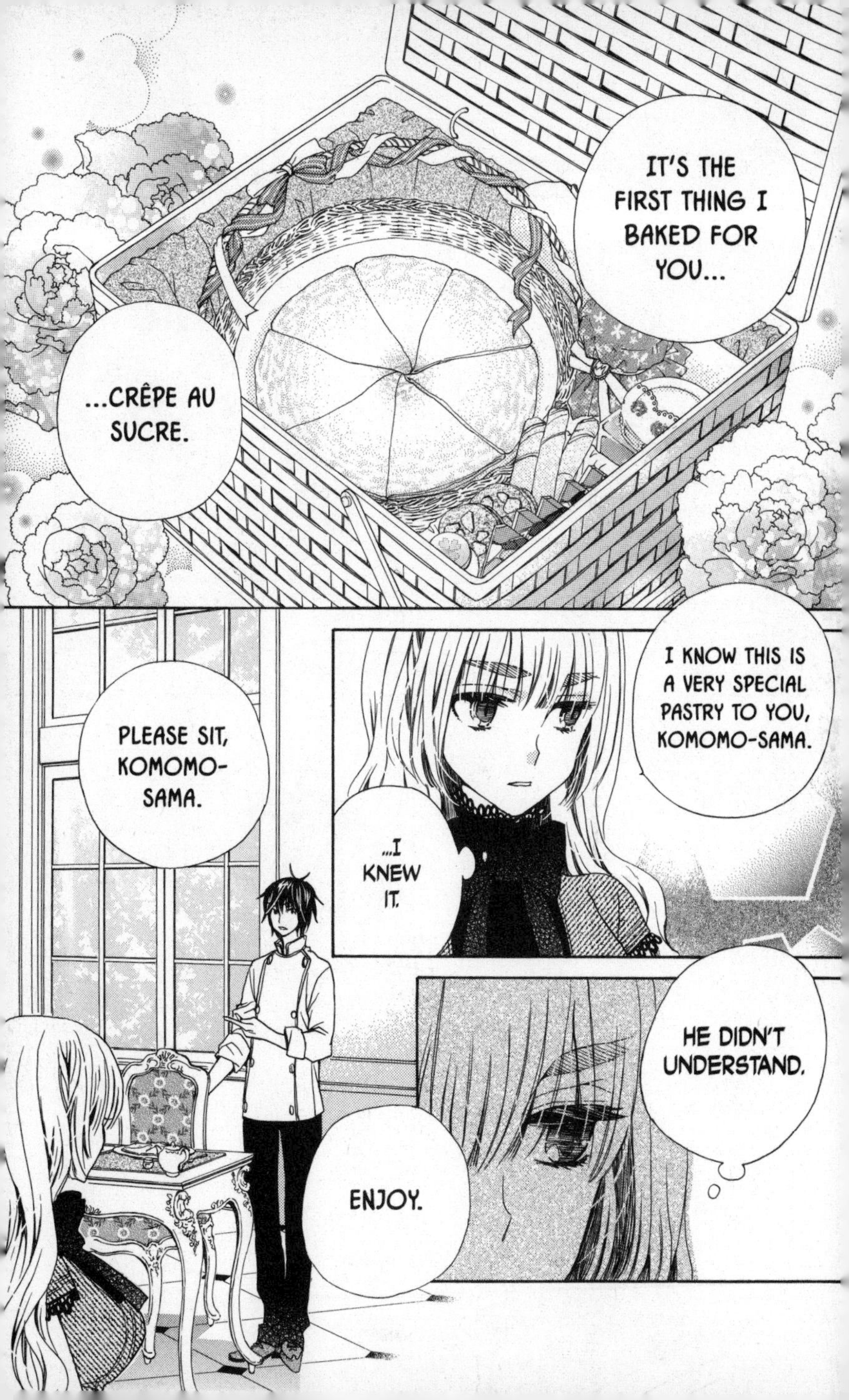
IT'S THE FIRST THING I BAKED FOR YOU...
...CRÊPE AU SUCRE.
I KNOW THIS IS A VERY SPECIAL PASTRY TO YOU, KOMOMO-SAMA.
...I KNEW IT.
HE DIDN'T UNDERSTAND.
PLEASE SIT, KOMOMO-SAMA.
ENJOY.

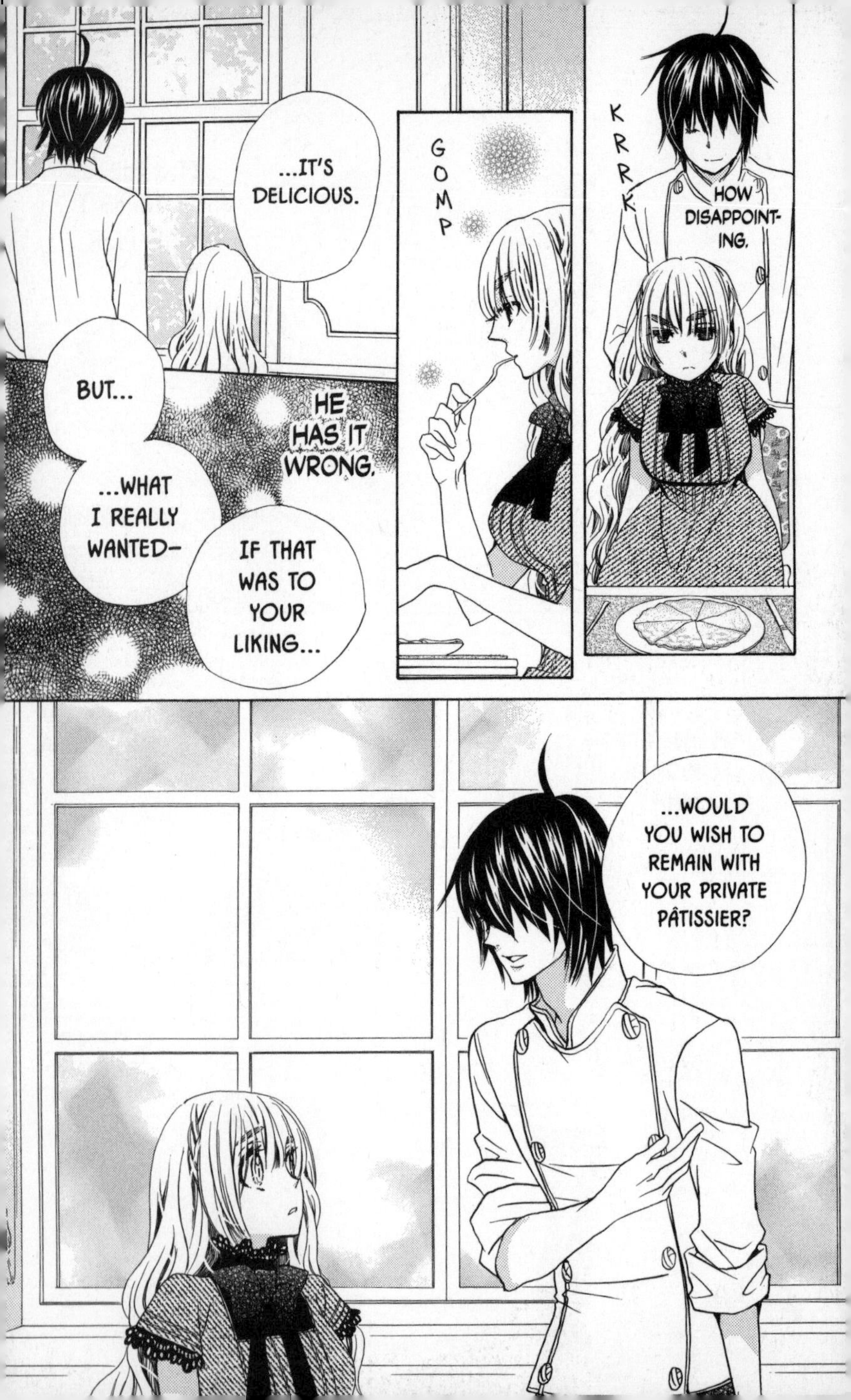
KRRK
HOW DISAPPOINT-ING.
GOMP
...IT'S DELICIOUS.
HE HAS IT WRONG.
BUT...
...WHAT I REALLY WANTED—
IF THAT WAS TO YOUR LIKING...
...WOULD YOU WISH TO REMAIN WITH YOUR PRIVATE PÂTISSIER?

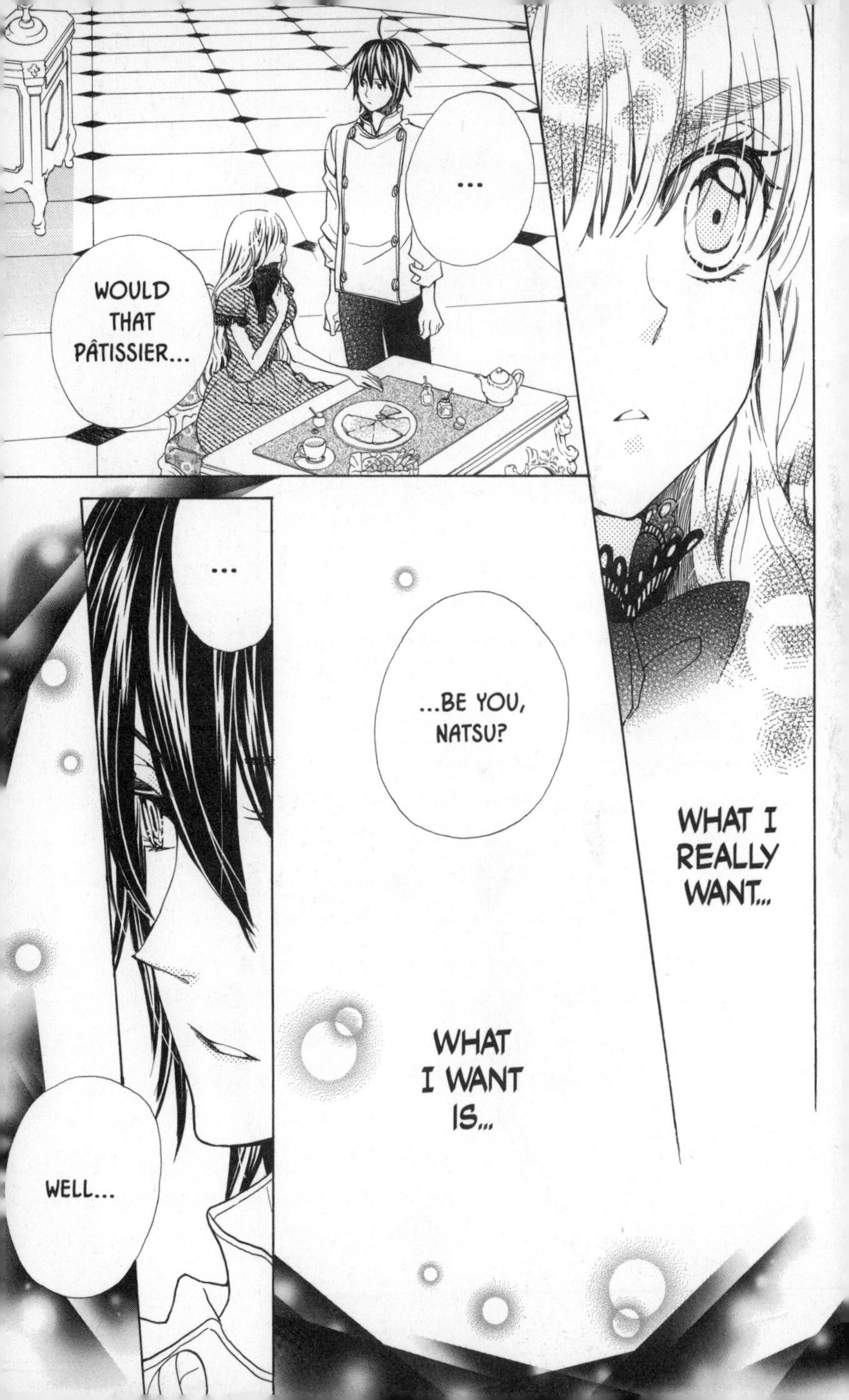
WHAT I REALLY WANT...
...
WOULD THAT PÂTISSIER...
...BE YOU, NATSU?
WHAT I WANT IS...
...
WELL...

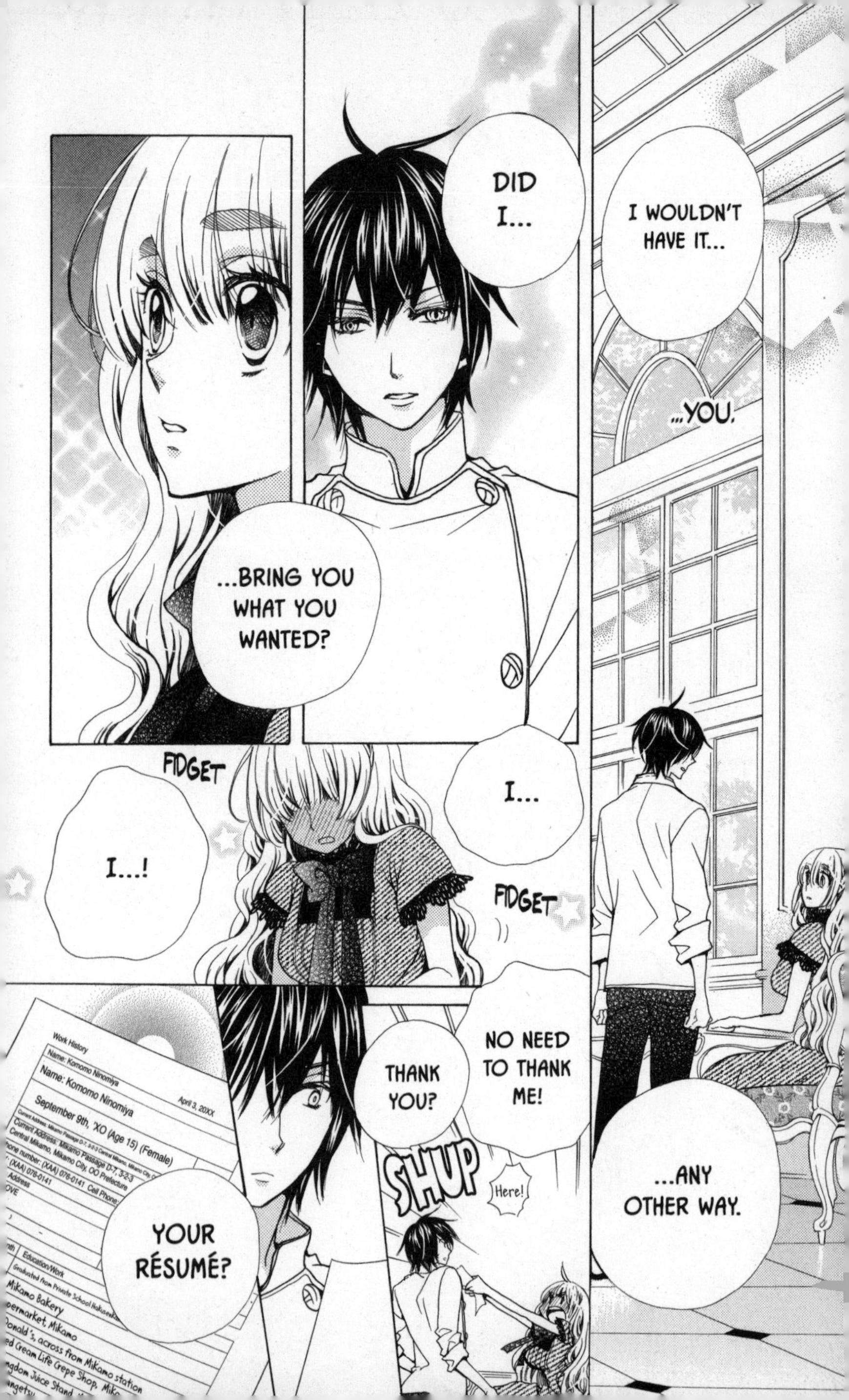
I WOULDN'T HAVE IT...
...YOU.
...ANY OTHER WAY.
DID I...
...BRING YOU WHAT YOU WANTED?
I...
FIDGET
FIDGET
I...!
NO NEED TO THANK ME!
THANK YOU?
SHUP
Here!
YOUR RÉSUMÉ?
Work History
Name: Komomo Ninomiya
April 3, 20XX
September 9th, 'XO (Age 15) (Female)
Current Address: Mikamo Passage D-7, 3-2-3
Central Mikamo, Mikamo City, OO Prefecture
Education/Work
Mikamo Bakery

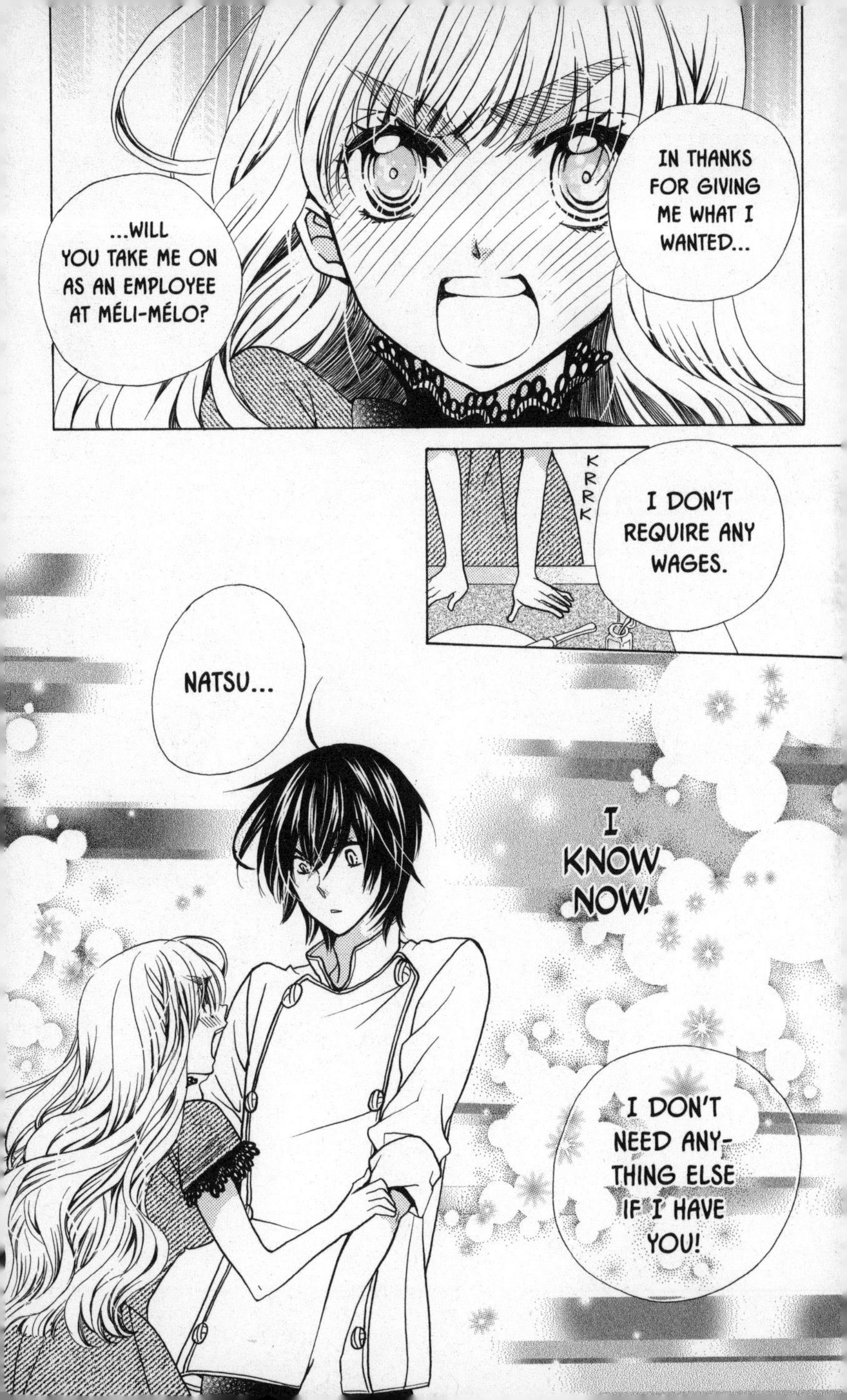
IN THANKS FOR GIVING ME WHAT I WANTED...
...WILL YOU TAKE ME ON AS AN EMPLOYEE AT MÉLI-MÉLO?
KRRK
I DON'T REQUIRE ANY WAGES.
NATSU...
I KNOW NOW.
I DON'T NEED ANY-THING ELSE IF I HAVE YOU!

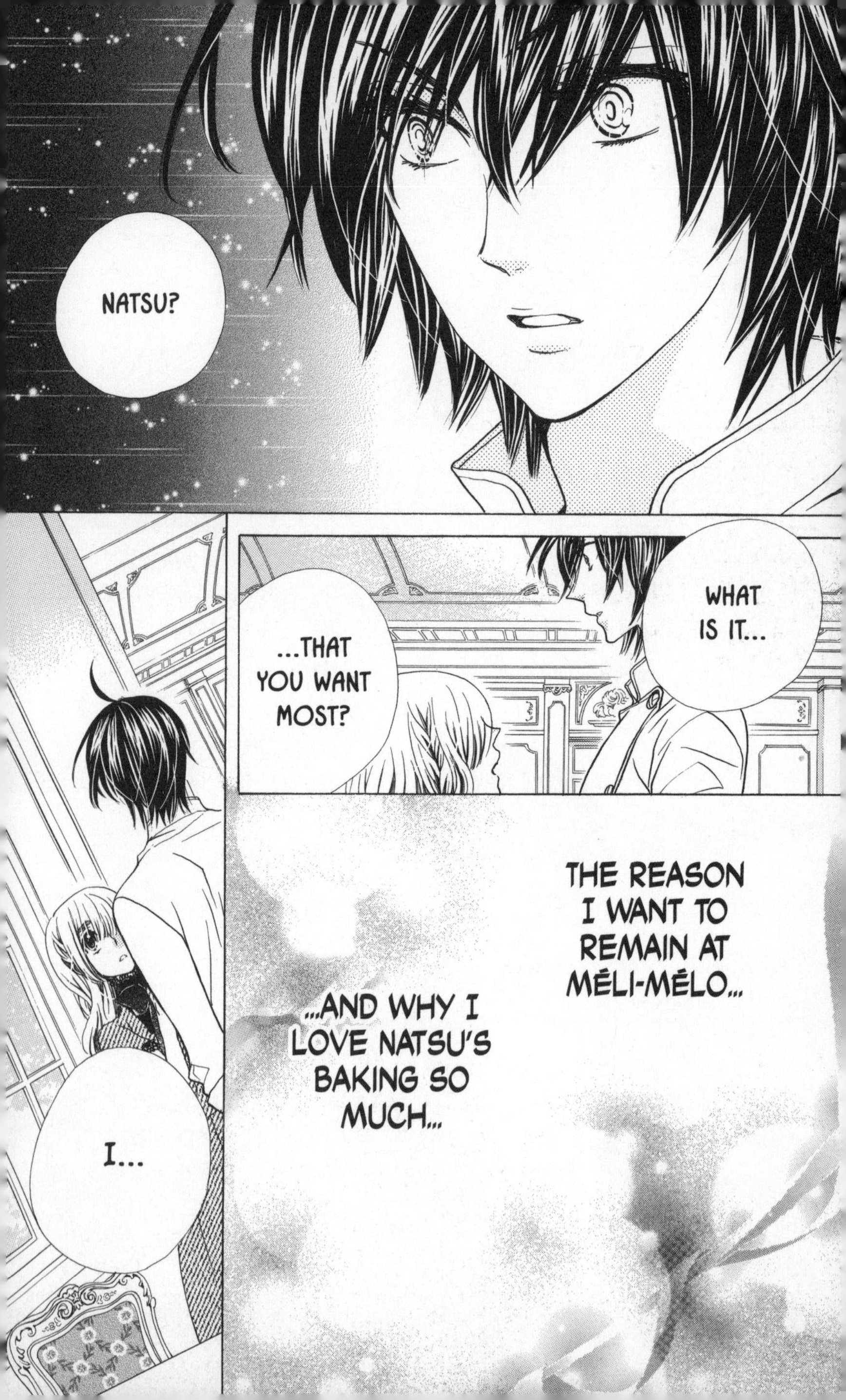
NATSU?
WHAT IS IT...
...THAT YOU WANT MOST?
THE REASON I WANT TO REMAIN AT MÉLI-MÉLO...
...AND WHY I LOVE NATSU'S BAKING SO MUCH...
I...

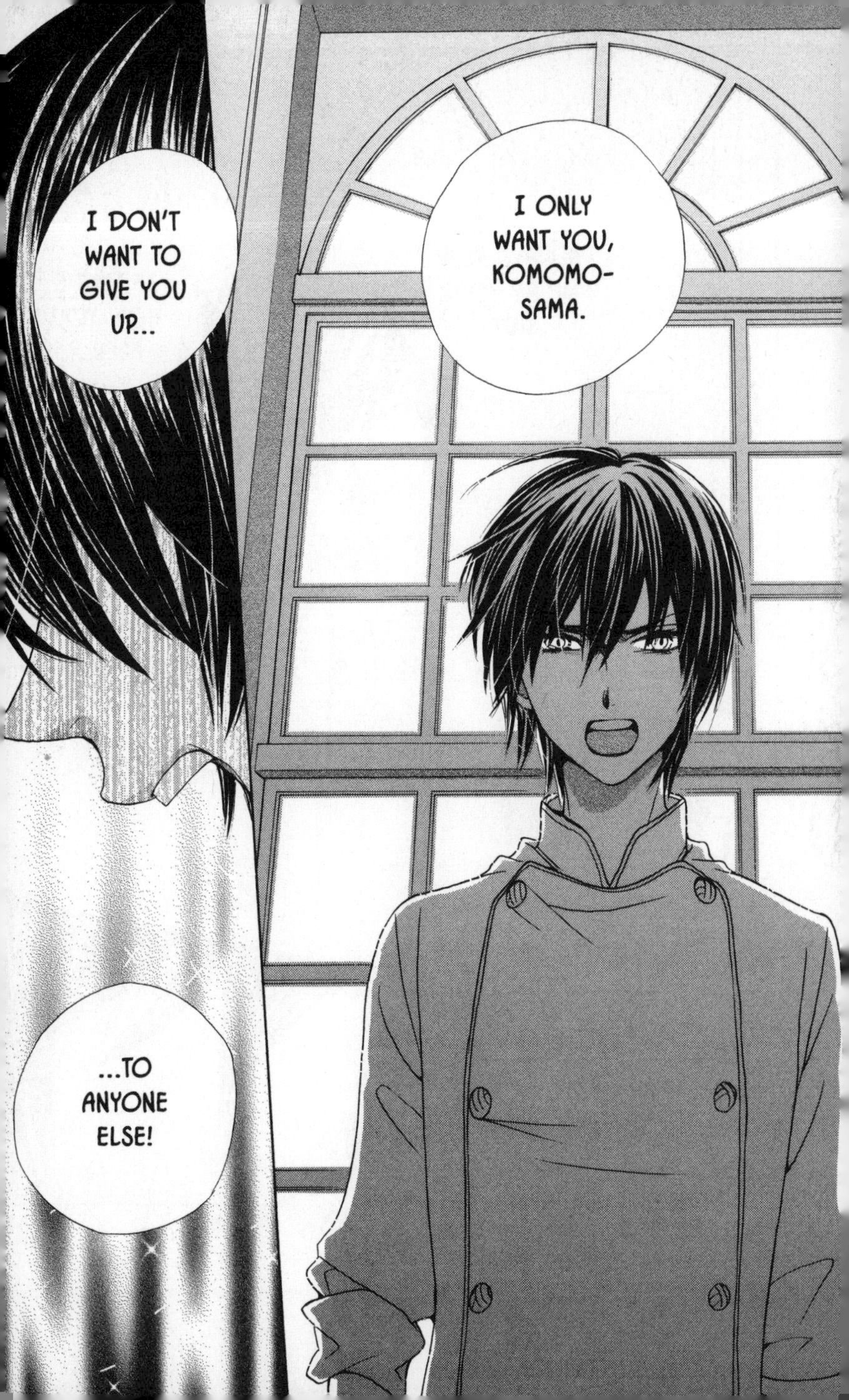
I ONLY WANT YOU, KOMOMO-SAMA.
I DON'T WANT TO GIVE YOU UP...
...TO ANYONE ELSE!

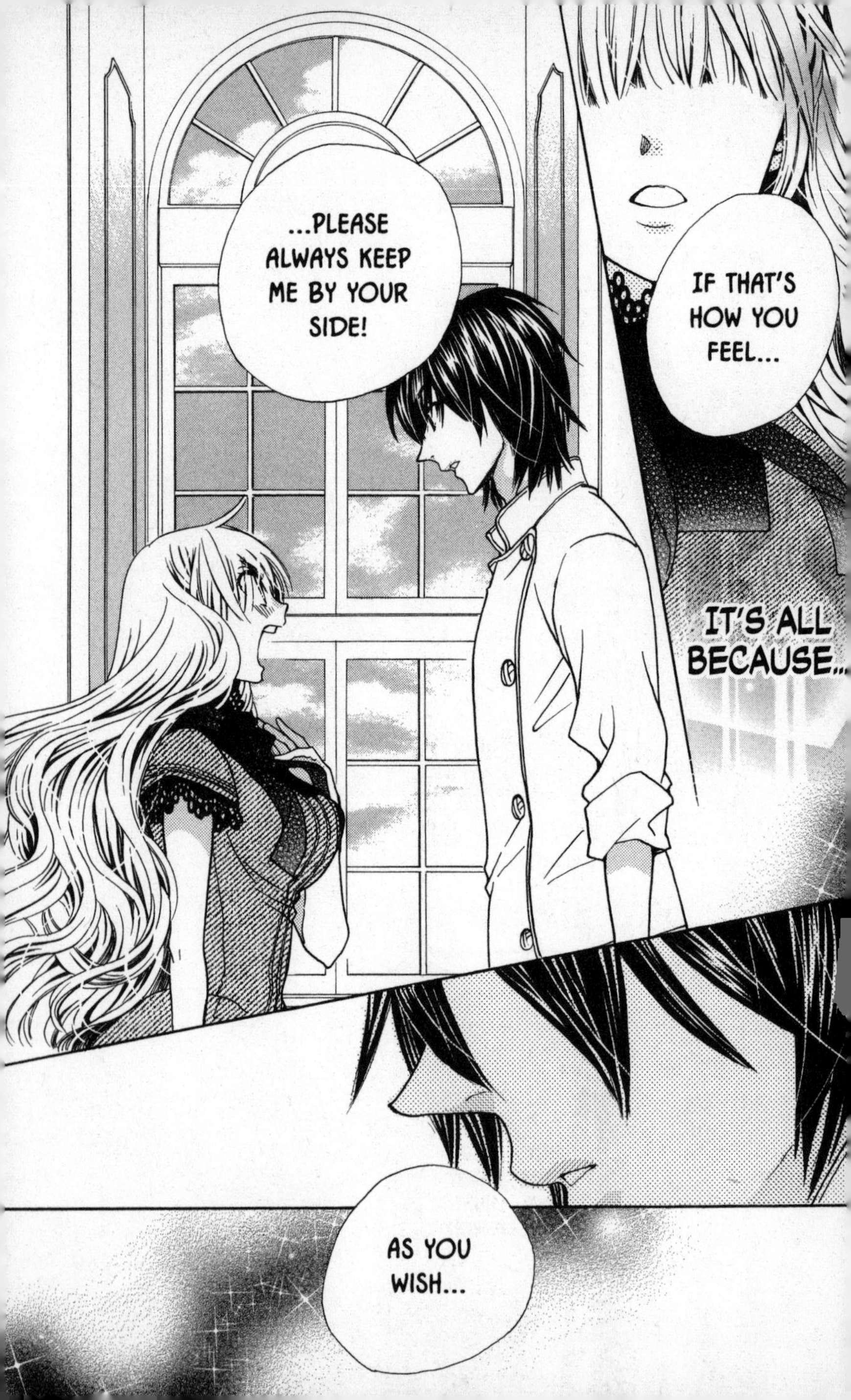

IF THAT'S HOW YOU FEEL...
IT'S ALL BECAUSE..
...PLEASE ALWAYS KEEP ME BY YOUR SIDE!
AS YOU WISH...

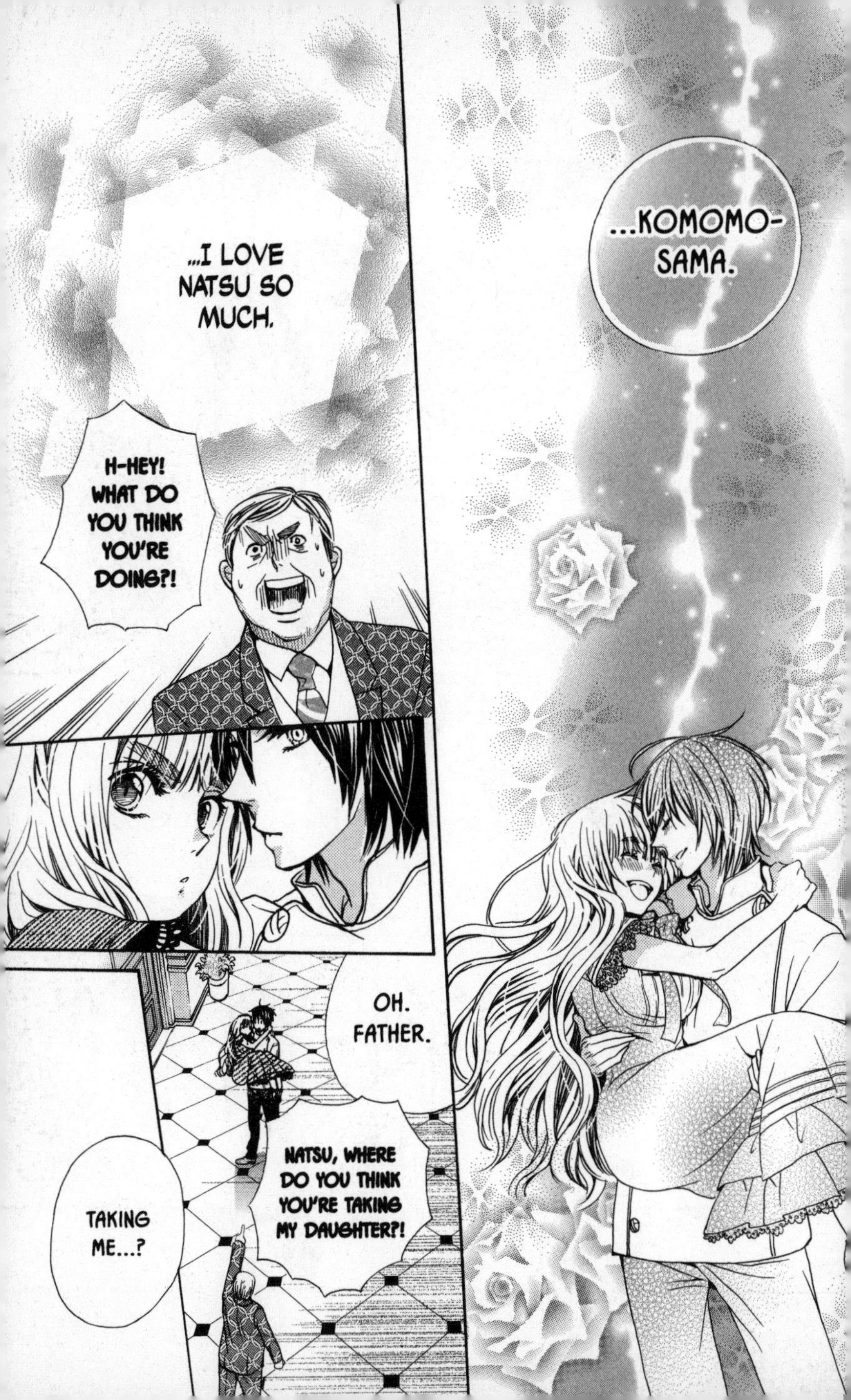
...KOMOMO-SAMA.
...I LOVE NATSU SO MUCH.
H-HEY! WHAT DO YOU THINK YOU'RE DOING?!
OH. FATHER.
NATSU, WHERE DO YOU THINK YOU'RE TAKING MY DAUGHTER?!
TAKING ME...?

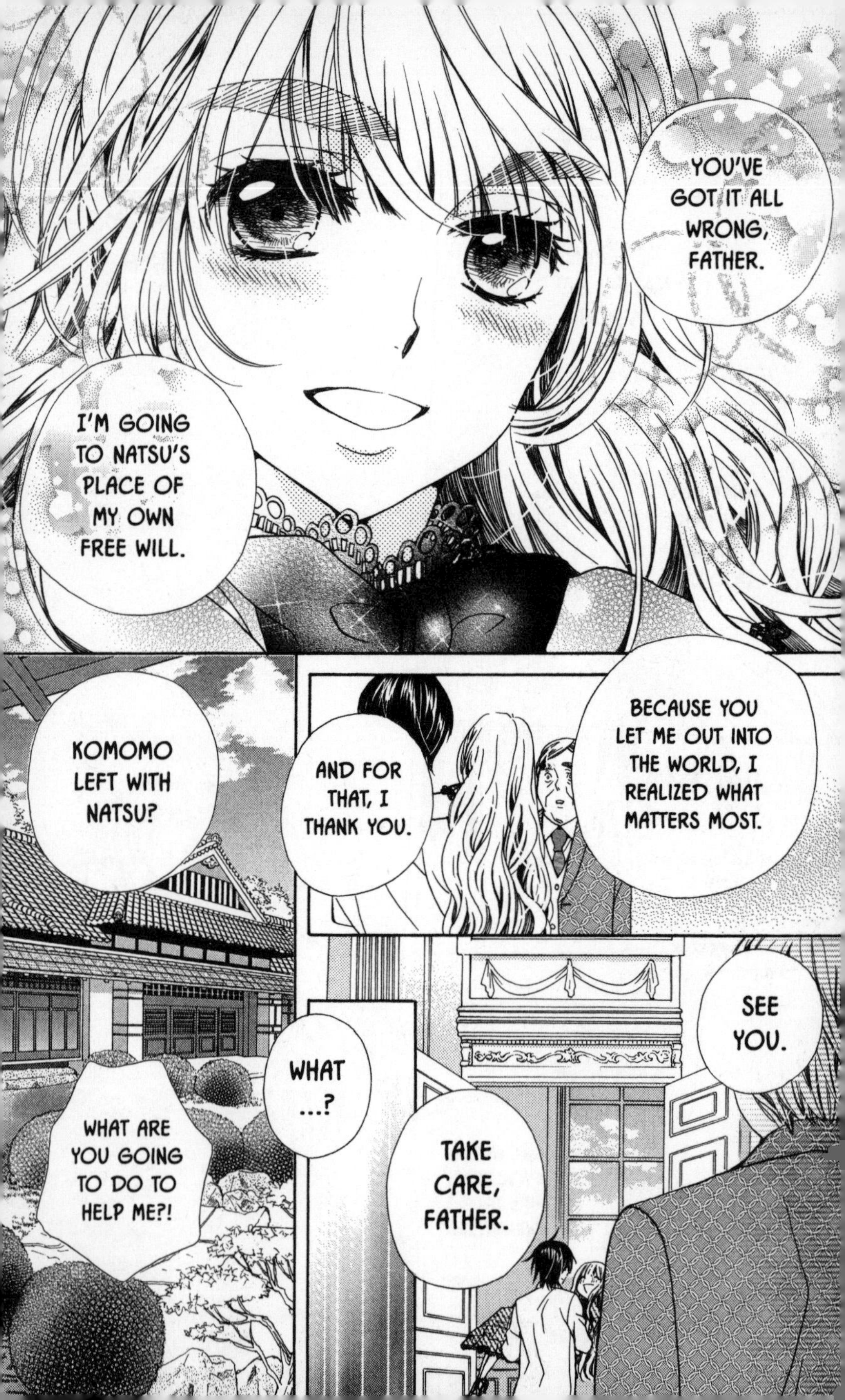
YOU'VE GOT IT ALL WRONG, FATHER.
I'M GOING TO NATSU'S PLACE OF MY OWN FREE WILL.
BECAUSE YOU LET ME OUT INTO THE WORLD, I REALIZED WHAT MATTERS MOST.
AND FOR THAT, I THANK YOU.
SEE YOU.
TAKE CARE, FATHER.
WHAT ...?
KOMOMO LEFT WITH NATSU?
WHAT ARE YOU GOING TO DO TO HELP ME?!

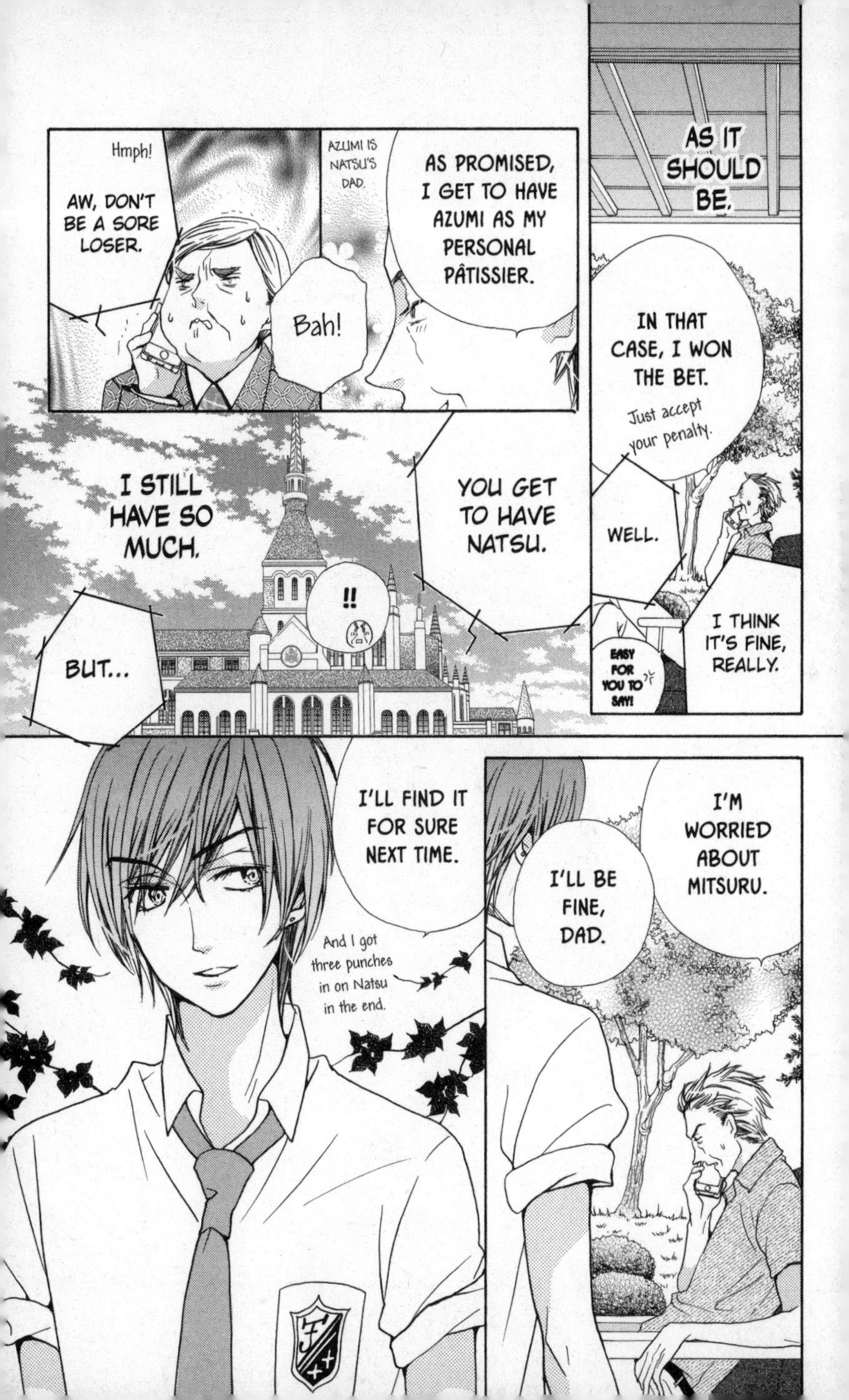
AS IT SHOULD BE.
IN THAT CASE, I WON THE BET.
Just accept your penalty.
WELL.
I THINK IT'S FINE, REALLY.
EASY FOR YOU TO SAY!
AZUMI IS NATSU'S DAD.
AS PROMISED, I GET TO HAVE AZUMI AS MY PERSONAL PÂTISSIER.
Bah!
Hmph!
AW, DON'T BE A SORE LOSER.
YOU GET TO HAVE NATSU.
!!
I STILL HAVE SO MUCH.
BUT...
I'M WORRIED ABOUT MITSURU.
I'LL BE FINE, DAD.
I'LL FIND IT FOR SURE NEXT TIME.
And I got three punches in on Natsu in the end.

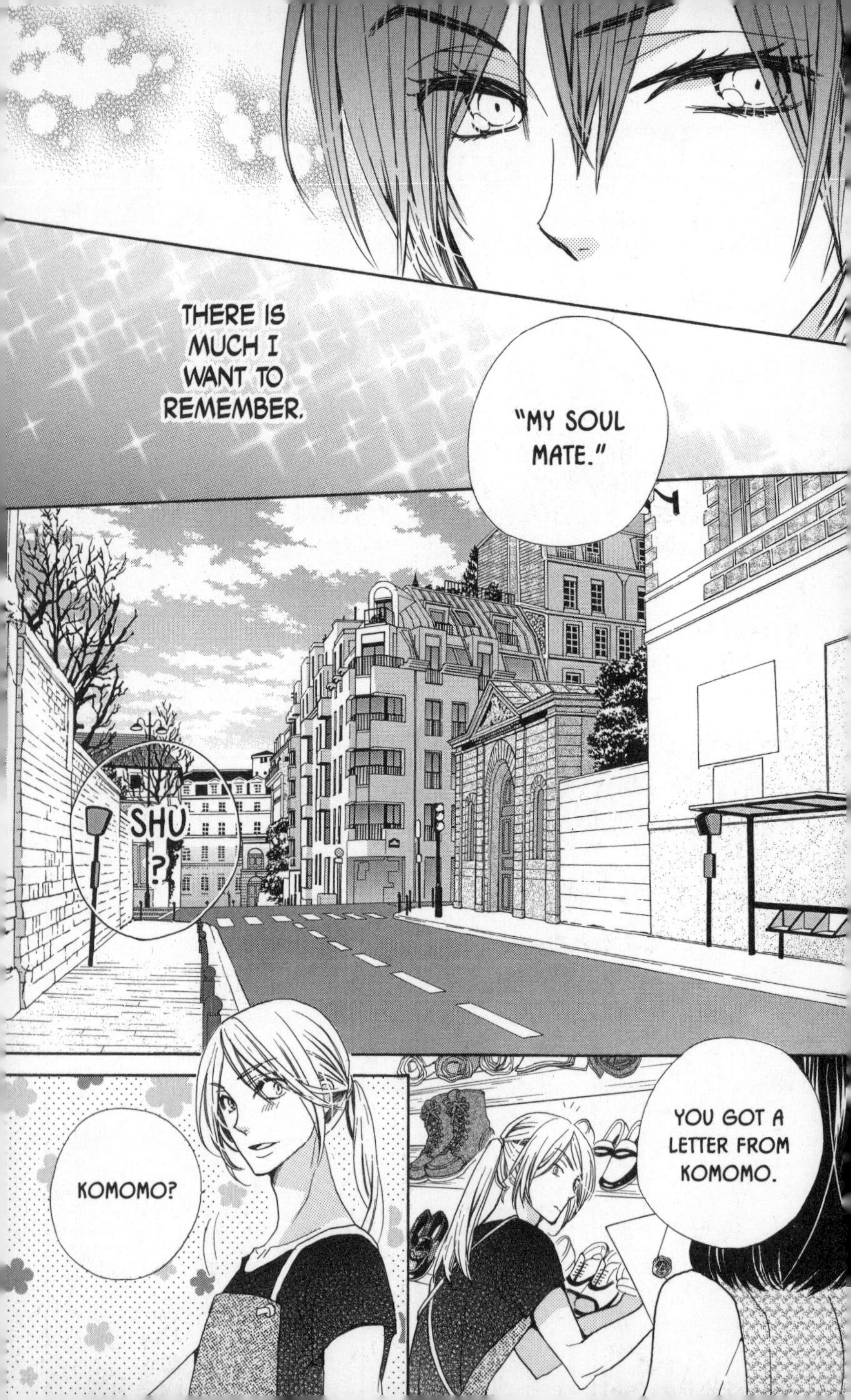
"MY SOUL MATE."
THERE IS MUCH I WANT TO REMEMBER.
SHU?
YOU GOT A LETTER FROM KOMOMO.
KOMOMO?

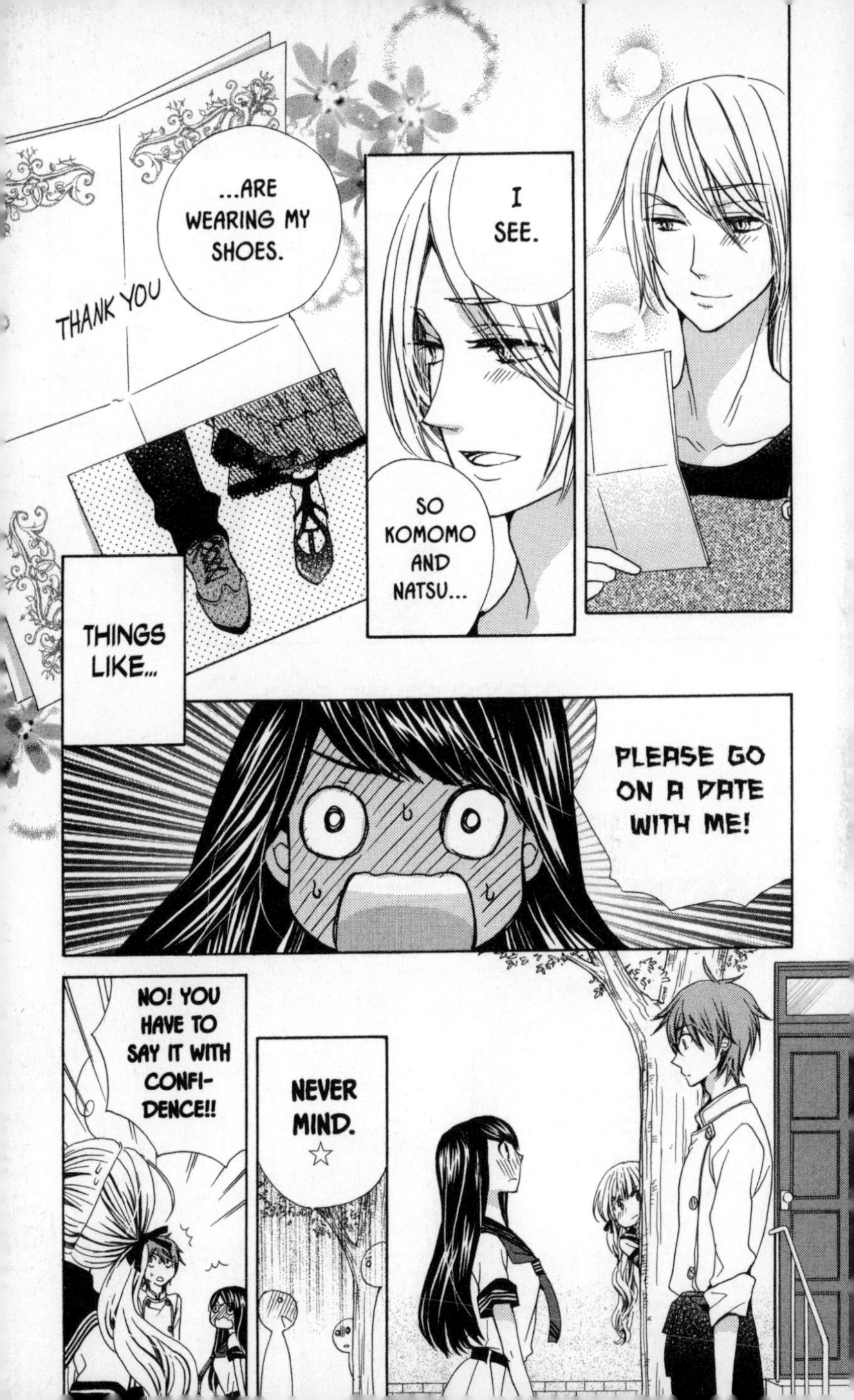
I SEE.
SO KOMOMO AND NATSU...
THANK YOU
...ARE WEARING MY SHOES.
THINGS LIKE...
PLEASE GO ON A DATE WITH ME!
NEVER MIND. ☆
NO! YOU HAVE TO SAY IT WITH CONFI- DENCE!!

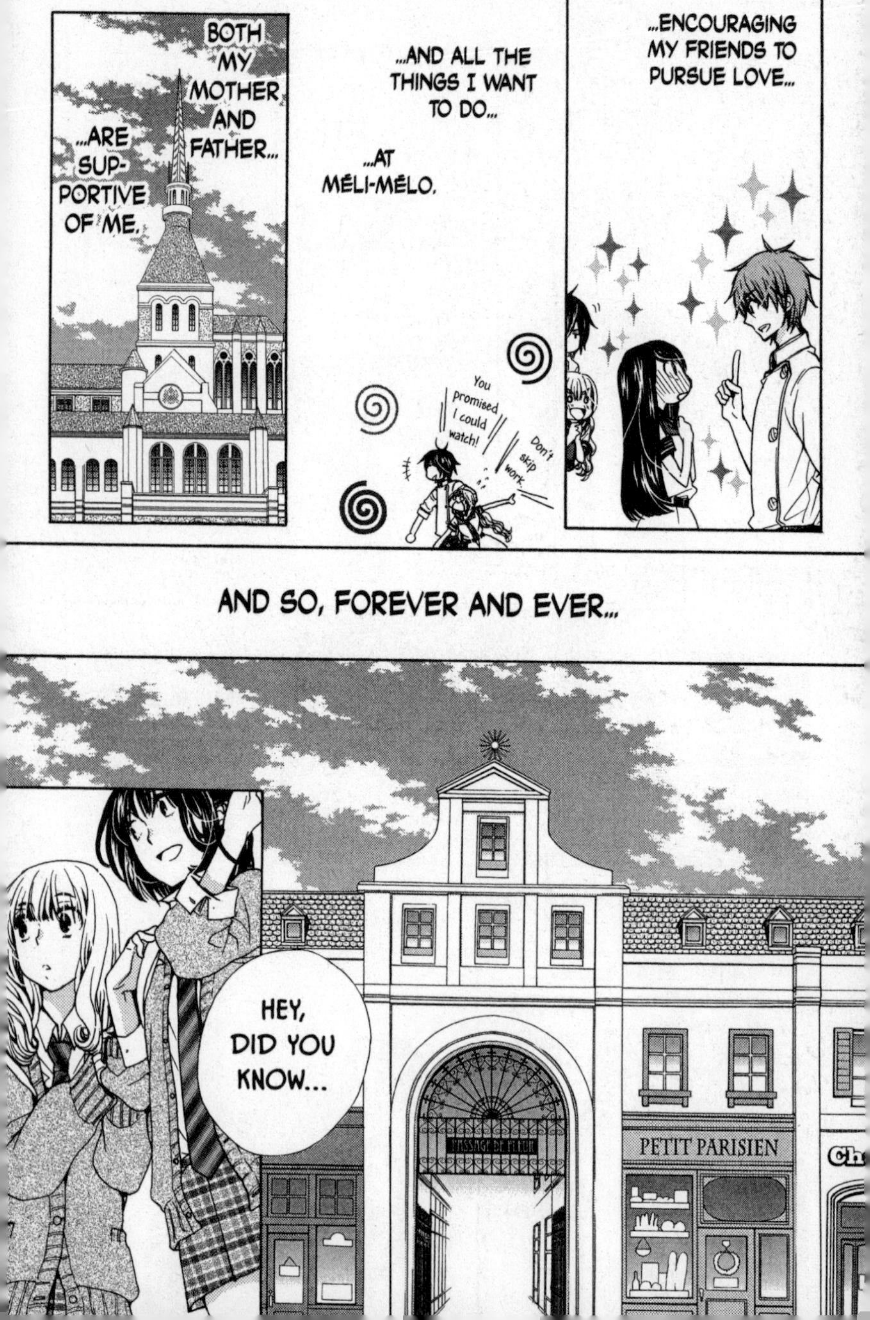
...ENCOURAGING MY FRIENDS TO PURSUE LOVE...
...AND ALL THE THINGS I WANT TO DO...
...AT MÉLI-MÉLO.
You promised I could watch!
Don't skip work.
BOTH MY MOTHER AND FATHER...
...ARE SUP-PORTIVE OF ME.
AND SO, FOREVER AND EVER...
HEY, DID YOU KNOW...
PETIT PARISIEN

...ABOUT THIS PLACE, MÉLI-MÉLO?

THEY SAY IF YOU EAT THE PASTRIES MADE HERE, YOU'LL FIND TRUE LOVE.

CONFISERIE MÉLI-MÉLO

CONFISERIE MÉLI-MÉLO

Confiserie

Patisserie

Chocolat

CONFISER
méli-me

Traite
É
Spec

TING

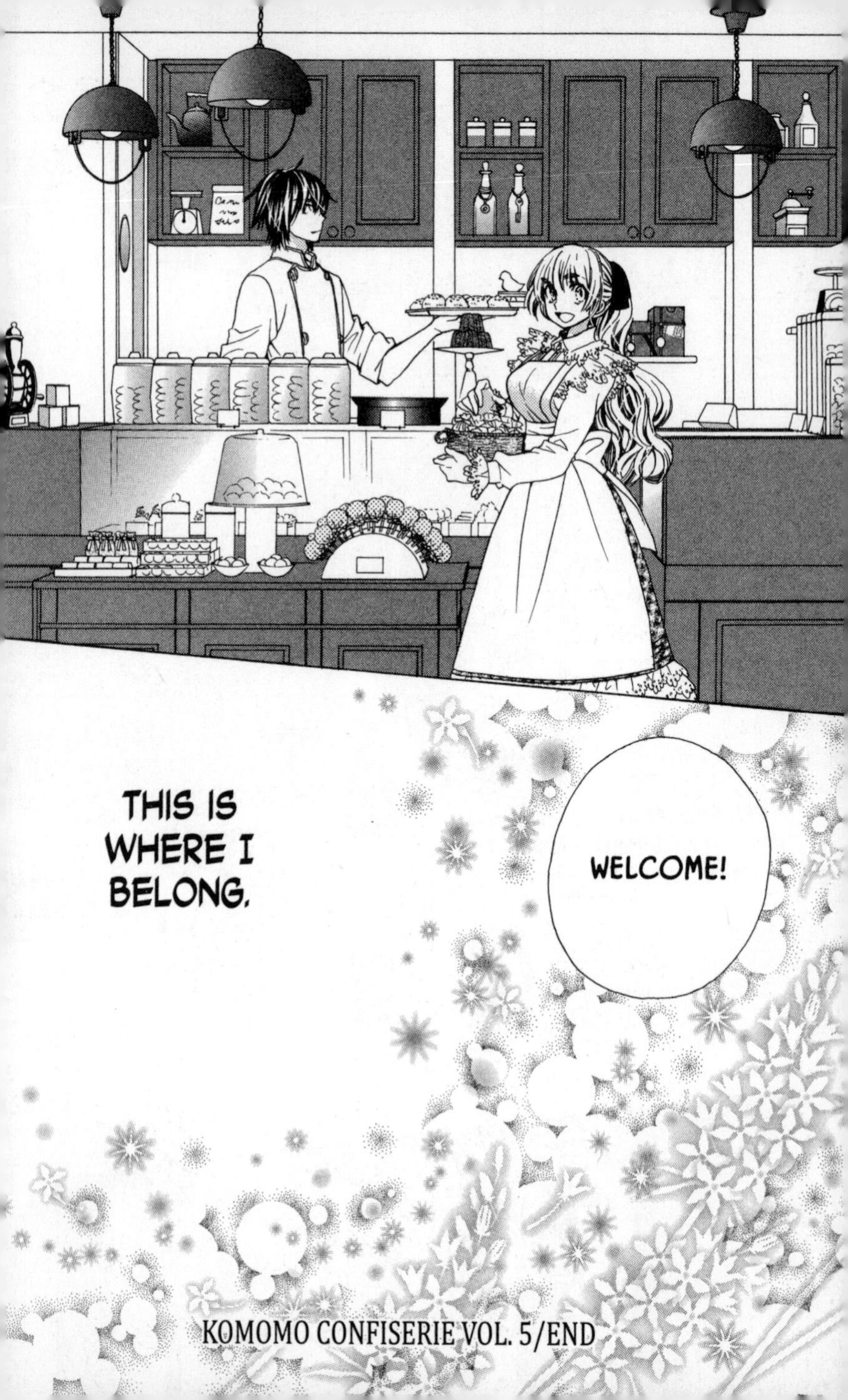
WELCOME!
THIS IS WHERE I BELONG.
KOMOMO CONFISERIE VOL. 5/END

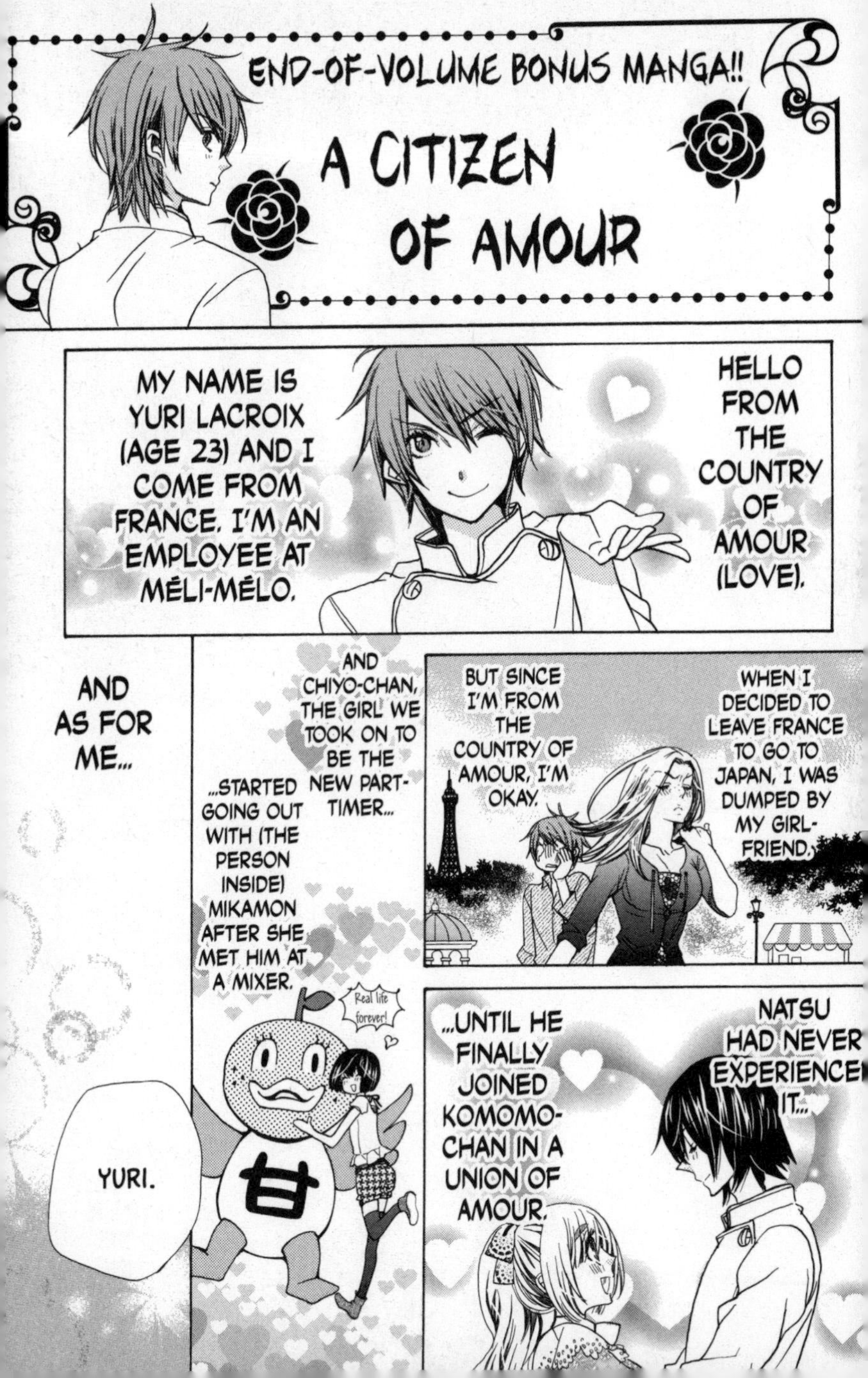
END-OF-VOLUME BONUS MANGA!!
A CITIZEN OF AMOUR
HELLO FROM THE COUNTRY OF AMOUR (LOVE).
MY NAME IS YURI LACROIX (AGE 23) AND I COME FROM FRANCE. I'M AN EMPLOYEE AT MÉLI-MÉLO.
WHEN I DECIDED TO LEAVE FRANCE TO GO TO JAPAN, I WAS DUMPED BY MY GIRL-FRIEND.
BUT SINCE I'M FROM THE COUNTRY OF AMOUR, I'M OKAY.
NATSU HAD NEVER EXPERIENCE IT...
...UNTIL HE FINALLY JOINED KOMOMO-CHAN IN A UNION OF AMOUR.
AND CHIYO-CHAN, THE GIRL WE TOOK ON TO BE THE NEW PART-TIMER...
...STARTED GOING OUT WITH (THE PERSON INSIDE) MIKAMON AFTER SHE MET HIM AT A MIXER.
Real life forever!
AND AS FOR ME...
YURI.

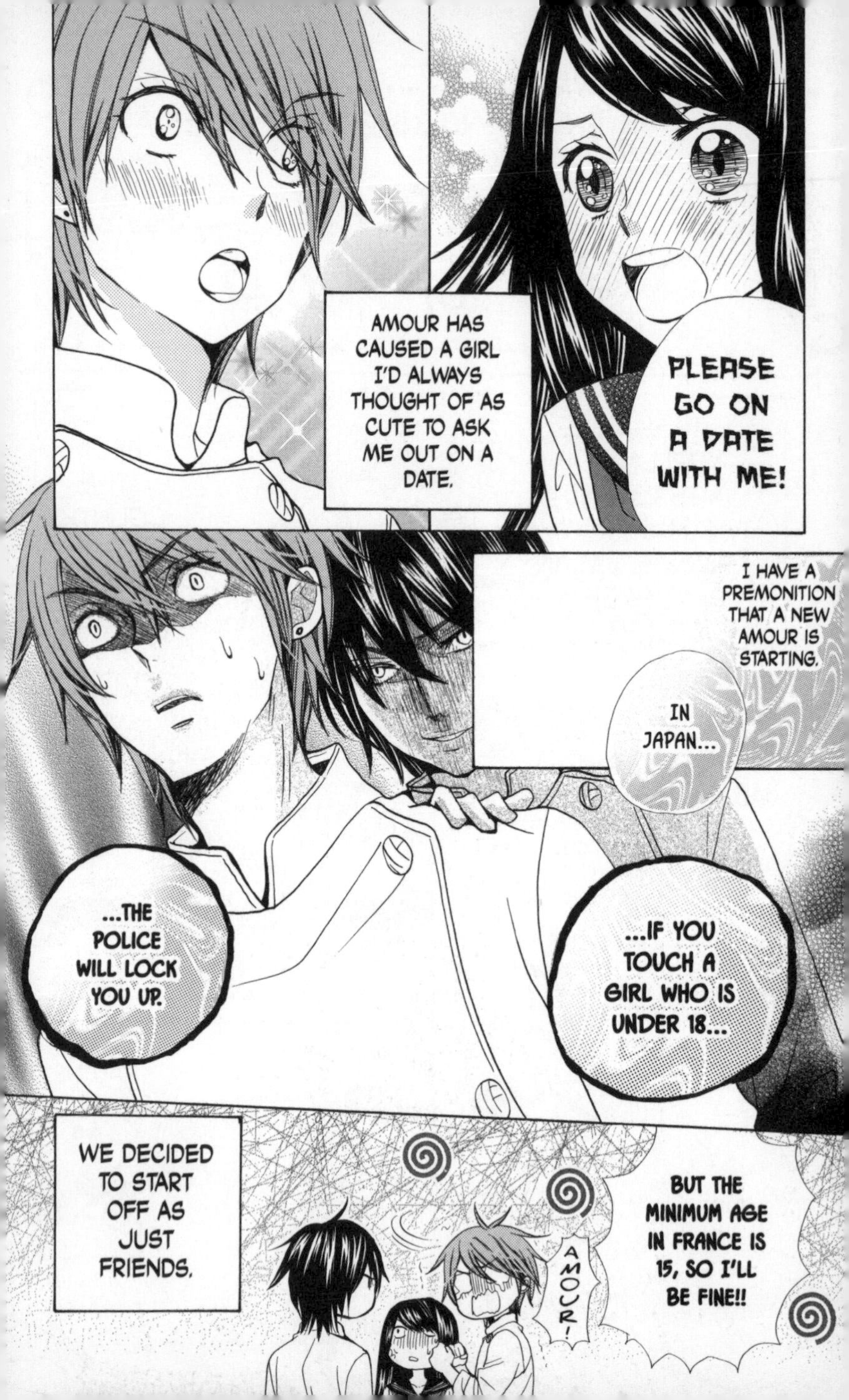
PLEASE GO ON A DATE WITH ME!
AMOUR HAS CAUSED A GIRL I'D ALWAYS THOUGHT OF AS CUTE TO ASK ME OUT ON A DATE.
I HAVE A PREMONITION THAT A NEW AMOUR IS STARTING.
IN JAPAN...
...IF YOU TOUCH A GIRL WHO IS UNDER 18...
...THE POLICE WILL LOCK YOU UP.
BUT THE MINIMUM AGE IN FRANCE IS 15, SO I'LL BE FINE!!
AMOUR!
WE DECIDED TO START OFF AS JUST FRIENDS.

Thank you, everyone!!

Thank you very much for reading through to the very end of *Komomo Confiserie*! It was fun getting to write a story about all my favorite sweets! And Komomo was a character that I truly loved from deep down! I'm glad I was able to give her a happy ending.

I wish I could've given Natsu more chapters, but I have only lack of willpower to blame.

For the record, I've stopped misspelling Natsu's name in kanji. Sorry about that, Natsu!!

I also had a lot of fun drawing Rise and Mitsuru. Oh, and Yuri too!

I also really loved Mikamon who sort of sprang up somewhere along the course of the story! Heh heh!

It was really fun discussing the shop and map of Le Passage with my assistants!

In short, I really appreciate having been given the chance to write and draw this story. Thank you all for reading it!!

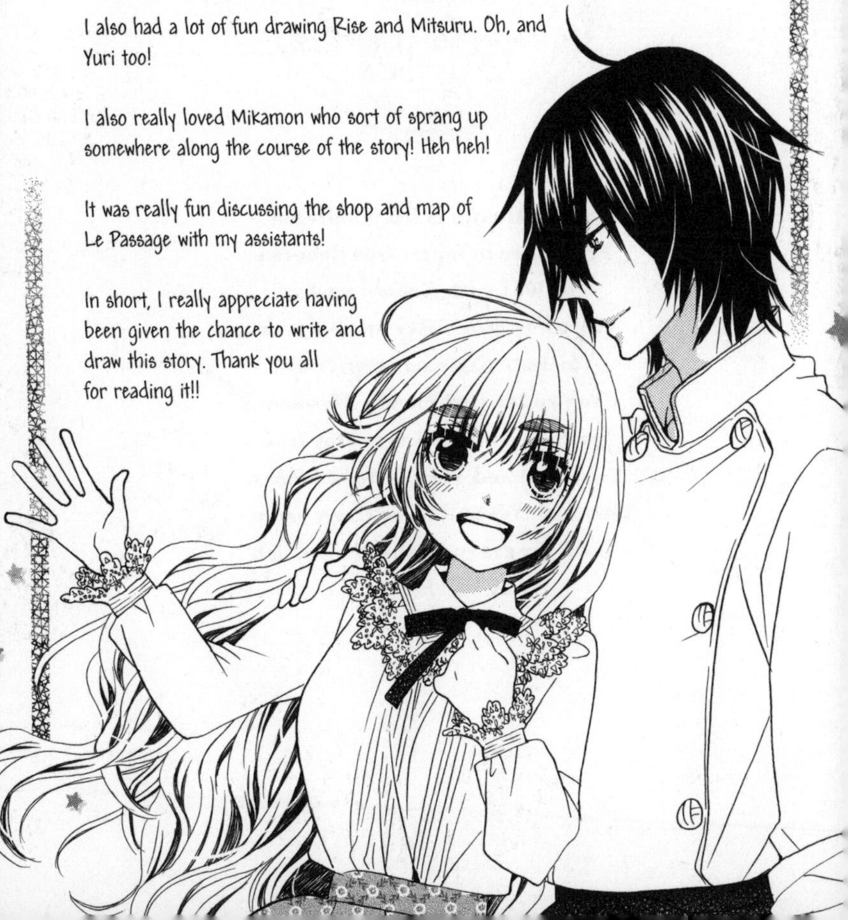

MEAT

Maki Minami is from Saitama
Prefecture in Japan. She debuted
in 2001 with *Kanata no Ao*
(Faraway Blue). Her other works
include *Kimi wa Girlfriend*
(You're My Girlfriend), *Mainichi
ga Takaramono* (Every Day Is a
Treasure) and *Yuki Atataka* (Warm
Winter). *S•A* and *Voice Over! Seiyu
Academy* are published in English
by VIZ Media.

Komomo Confiserie
Shojo Beat Edition
Volume 5

STORY AND ART BY
Maki Minami

Supervisor: Tsuji Shizuo Ryori Kyoiku Kenkyujo/Hiromi Kosaka
Special thanks to Tsujicho Group

Translation/Christine Dashiell
Touch-Up Art & Lettering/John Hunt
Design/Yukiko Whitley, Sarah Richardson
Editor/Nancy Thistlethwaite

Komomo Confiserie by Maki Minami
© Maki Minami 2015
All rights reserved.
First published in Japan in 2015 by HAKUSENSHA, Inc., Tokyo.
English language translation rights arranged with HAKUSENSHA, Inc.,
Tokyo.

Printed in the U.S.A.

Published by VIZ Media, LLC
P.O. Box 77010
San Francisco, CA 94107

10 9 8 7 6 5 4 3 2 1
First printing, September 2016

www.viz.com   www.shojobeat.com

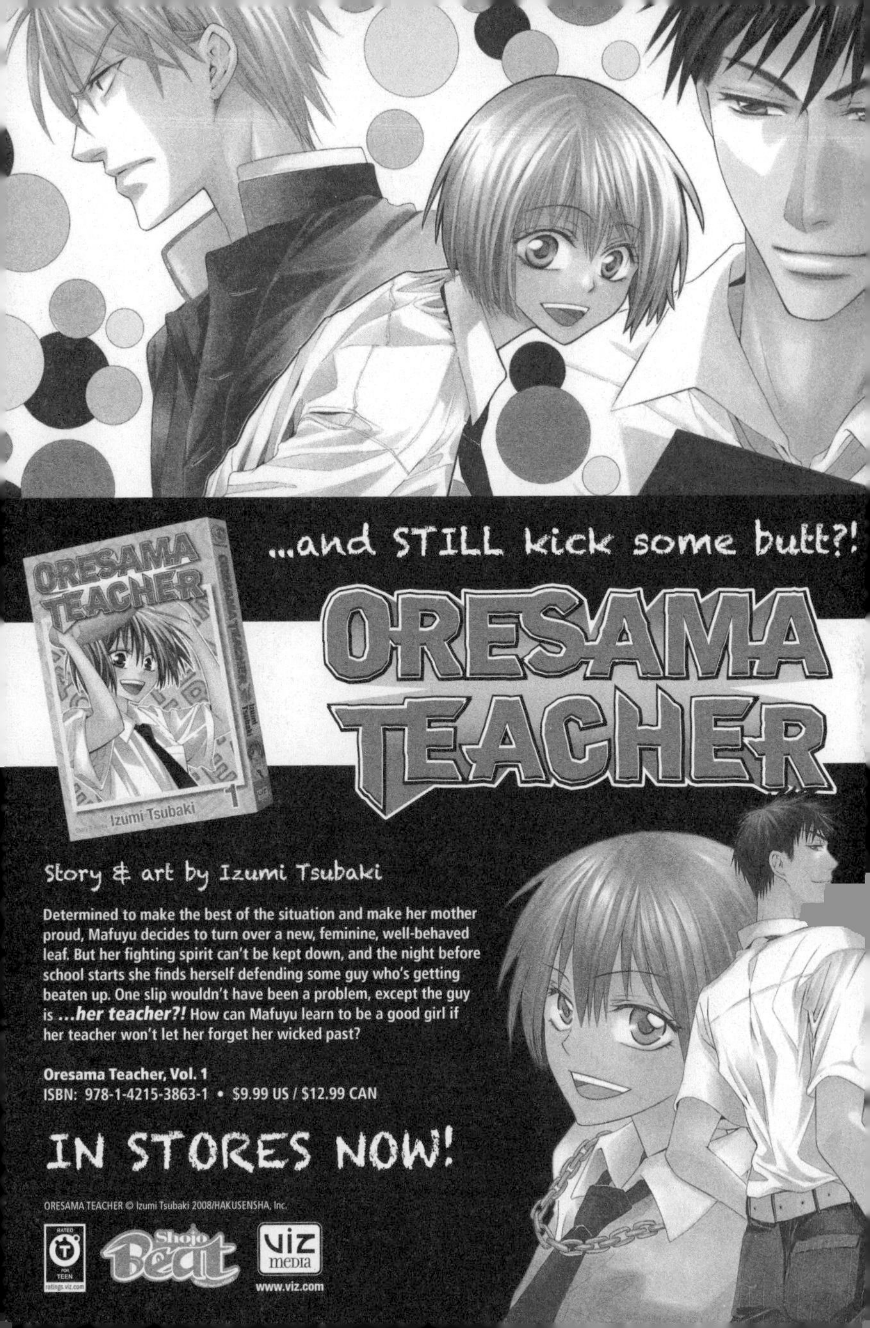

...and STILL kick some butt?!
ORESAMA TEACHER
Story & art by Izumi Tsubaki
Determined to make the best of the situation and make her mother proud, Mafuyu decides to turn over a new, feminine, well-behaved leaf. But her fighting spirit can't be kept down, and the night before school starts she finds herself defending some guy who's getting beaten up. One slip wouldn't have been a problem, except the guy is ***...her teacher?!*** How can Mafuyu learn to be a good girl if her teacher won't let her forget her wicked past?
Oresama Teacher, Vol. 1
ISBN: 978-1-4215-3863-1 • $9.99 US / $12.99 CAN
IN STORES NOW!
ORESAMA TEACHER © Izumi Tsubaki 2008/HAKUSENSHA, Inc.
RATED T FOR TEEN
ratings.viz.com
Shojo Beat
VIZ media
www.viz.com

Don't Hide What's *Inside*

OTOMEN
by AYA KANNO

Despite his tough jock exterior, Asuka Masamune harbors a secret love for sewing, shojo manga, and all things girly. But when he finds himself drawn to his domestically inept classmate Ryo, his carefully crafted persona is put to the test. Can Asuka ever show his true self to anyone, much less to the girl he's falling for?

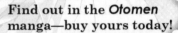

Find out in the *Otomen* manga—buy yours today!

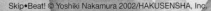

You may be reading the wrong way!

In keeping with the original Japanese comic format, this book reads from right to left, so action, sound effects and word balloons are reversed. This preserves the orientation of the original artwork. Check out the diagram below to get the order of things, and then turn to the other side of the book to get started!

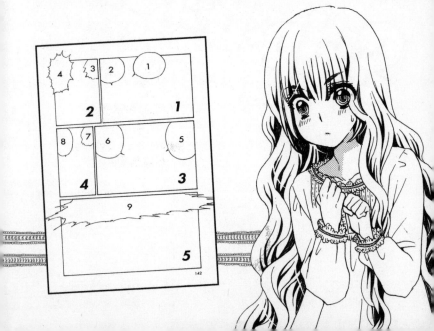